A Solution to the Ecological Inference Problem

A Solution to the Ecological Inference Problem

RECONSTRUCTING INDIVIDUAL BEHAVIOR FROM AGGREGATE DATA

Gary King

PRINCETON UNIVERSITY PRESS
PRINCETON, NEW JERSEY

Published by Princeton University Press, 41 William Street,
Princeton, New Jersey 08540
In the United Kingdom: Princeton University Press,
Chichester, West Sussex

Library of Congress Cataloging-in-Publication Data

King, Gary.
A solution to the ecological inference problem: reconstructing individual behavior from aggregate data / Gary King.
p. cm.
Includes bibliographical references and index.
ISBN 0-691-01241-5 (alk. paper). — ISBN 0-691-01240-7 (pbk.: alk. paper)
1. Political science—Statistical methods. 2. Inference.
I. Title.
JA71.7.K55 1997
320'.072—dc20 9632986
CIP

This book has been composed in Palatino

Princeton University Press books are printed on
acid-free paper and meet the guidelines
for permanence and durability of the Committee
on Production Guidelines for Book Longevity
of the Council on Library Resources

Printed in the United States of America
by Princeton Academic Press

1 3 5 7 9 10 8 6 4 2
1 3 5 7 9 10 8 6 4 2
(Pbk.)

For Ella Michelle King

Contents

Figures

Tables

Preface

IN THIS BOOK, I present a solution to the ecological inference problem: a method of inferring individual behavior from aggregate data that works in practice. *Ecological inference* is the process of using aggregate (i.e., "ecological") data to infer discrete individual-level relationships of interest when individual-level data are not available. Existing methods of ecological inference generate very inaccurate conclusions about the empirical world—which thus gives rise to the ecological inference *problem*. Most scholars who analyze aggregate data routinely encounter some form of the this problem.

The ecological inference problem has been among the longest standing, hitherto unsolved problems in quantitative social science. It was originally raised over seventy-five years ago as the first statistical problem in the nascent discipline of political science, and it has held back research agendas in most of its empirical subfields. Ecological inferences are required in political science research when individual-level surveys are unavailable (for example, local or comparative electoral politics), unreliable (racial politics), insufficient (political geography), or infeasible (political history). They are also required in numerous areas of major significance in public policy (for example, for applying the Voting Rights Act) and other academic disciplines, ranging from epidemiology and marketing to sociology and quantitative history.[1]

Because the ecological inference problem is caused by the lack of individual-level information, no method of ecological inference, including that introduced in this book, will produce precisely accurate results in every instance. However, potential difficulties are minimized here by models that include more available information, diagnostics to evaluate when assumptions need to be modified, and realistic uncertainty estimates for all quantities of interest. For political methodologists, many opportunities remain, and I hope the

[1] What is "ecological" about the aggregate data from which individual behavior is to be inferred? The name has been used at least since the late 1800s and stems from the word ecology, the science of the interrelationship of living things and their environments. Statistical measures taken at the level of the environment, such as summaries of geographic areas or other aggregate units, are widely known as ecological data. Ecological inference is the process of using ecological data to learn about the behavior of individuals within these aggregates.

results reported here lead to continued research into and further improvements in the methods of ecological inference. But most importantly, the solution to the ecological inference problem presented here is designed so that empirical researchers can investigate substantive questions that have heretofore proved intractable. Perhaps it will also lead to new theories and empirical research in areas where analysts have feared to tread due to the lack of reliable ecological methods or individual-level data.

Outline

This book is divided into five main parts. Part I contains two introductions. Chapter 1 is a qualitative introduction to the entire book and includes a summary of results, an overview of some of the uses to which the method can be put, and a brief outline of the statistical model; because it includes no technical details about the statistical method developed in the subsequent fifteen chapters, it should be accessible even to those without a background in statistics. Chapter 2 gives a formal statement of the ecological inference problem along with the mathematical notation used throughout the remainder of the book.

Part II is divided into aggregation problems (Chapter 3) and problems unrelated to aggregation (Chapter 4). In the first of these chapters, I prove that all of the diverse problems attributed to aggregation bias in the literature are mathematically equivalent, so that only one aggregation problem remains to be solved. The second of these chapters describes a series of basic statistical problems that, although unrelated to aggregation and mostly ignored in the literature, still affect ecological inferences. Any model intended to provide valid ecological inferences must resolve all non-aggregation problems as well.

Part III describes my proposed solution to the ecological inference problem. It reformulates the data by generalizing the method of bounds both algebraically and with easy-to-use graphical methods as well as providing narrower, more informative bounds for the aggregate-level quantities of interest than have been used in the literature (Chapter 5), and introduces a statistical approach to modeling the remaining uncertainty within the observation-level deterministic bounds (Chapter 6). Chapter 7 develops procedures for estimating the model; Chapter 8 shows how to compute quantities of interest at the aggregate level and for each individual observation. Chapter 9 explains how to verify model assumptions with only aggregate data, shows what can go wrong, and provides diagnostic tests, extensions of the basic model, and a fully nonparametric version to cope with any problems that may remain. Part III also explains how the ecological inference problem and the solution proposed are mathematically equivalent to aspects of the "tomography" problem, which involves reconstructing cross-sectional images of body parts using X-rays and CT scans rather than surgery, or images of the earth's interior via inferences from the detection of seismic waves, produced by earthquakes or nuclear explosions, instead of by digging.

Part IV validates the model by comparing myriad observation-level estimates from the model using aggregate data with their corresponding, known individual-level truths. These comparisons include a typical example of ecological inference, a study of registration by race in the 1960s Southern United States with all the intermediate results described (Chapter 10); an analysis of poverty status by sex in South Carolina which demonstrates that the model is highly robust to aggregation bias and restricted aggregate variances (Chapter 11); a study of black registration in Kentucky that shows how the model gives reasonable answers even in the face of ecological data with almost all relevant information aggregated away (Chapter 12); and two classic applications of ecological inference, the transitions of voters between elections and turn-of-the-century county data on literacy by race (Chapter 13). The method works in practice: it gives accurate answers and correct assessments of uncertainty even when existing methods lead to incorrect inferences or impossible results (such as −20% of African Americans voting).

Finally, Part V generalizes the basic model in several ways and then concludes. Chapter 14 analyzes three related non-ecological aggregation problems: solving the "modifiable areal unit problem" (a related problem in geography); combining survey and aggregate data to improve ecological inferences (as often studied in the discipline of statistics); and using aggregate-level data for inferences about relationships among continuous individual-level variables (a standard aggregation problem in econometrics). Chapter 15 generalizes the basic model to larger and multidimensional tables.

Chapter 16 concludes with a checklist of items to consider in applying the methods developed here. Technical appendices and a Glossary of Symbols follow.

Roadmaps

This book is intended to be read sequentially, as each chapter builds on the material that comes before. For example, Part I should be read by all, since it includes an overview, a formal statement of the ecological inference problem, and the notation used throughout the book. Nevertheless, for a first reading, some readers may wish to skip certain passages by following one of the roadmaps provided here.

Although Part II introduces several new results and provides motivation for many features of the solution offered in this book, readers uninterested in prior approaches to ecological inference may wish to skim this part by reading only pages 37–43 and Section 3.5 (on pages 54–55) in Chapter 3, along with the indented, italicized remarks in Chapter 4.

Those readers who wish a quicker introduction to the proposed methods should read Part I, and skim Part II as described above. Then, a brief summary of the most basic form of the statistical model requires the information about the data and bounds in Chapter 5 (especially the explanation of Figure 5.1), and the introduction to the model and interpretation on pages 91–96 in Chapter 6. See also Chapter 10 for an application.

All readers should be aware that the solution to the ecological inference problem put forth and verified in this book is more than the basic statistical model that lies at its core. It also includes various extensions to avoid specific problems, a variety of new diagnostic procedures, graphical techniques, and methods of interpretation. Each of these, discussed in the rest of the book, is an integral part of making valid inferences about relationships among individual variables using only aggregate data. Many of these features of the methodology are demonstrated during the verification of the method in Part IV. Especially important is Chapter 16, which provides a checklist for those who intend to use these methods.

Background

Although I hope the results reported here are useful to technically sophisticated political methodologists in building better models of ecological inference, my primary intended audience for this book is political scientists and others who need to make ecological inferences in real academic research, scholars for whom the substantive answer matters. Thus, the qualitative overview in Chapter 1 assumes no statistical knowledge. Parts I, II, and IV assume familiarity with linear regression. Although Parts III and V introduce a variety of tools to solve the ecological inference problem, most of the exposition assumes knowledge of only basic maximum likelihood methods (such as Cramer, 1986 or King, 1989a).

Software and Data

Two versions of an easy-to-use, public-domain computer program that implement all the statistical and graphical methods proposed herein are available from my homepage on the World Wide Web at `http://GKing.Harvard.Edu`. One version, *EI: A Program for Ecological Inference*, works under the Gauss software package and is also distributed with Gauss, as part of its Constrained Maximum Likelihood module.[2] The other version, *E_zI: A(n easy) Program for Ecological Inference*, by Ken Benoit and me, is a stand-alone, menu-based system that is less flexible but does not require any other software. The methods introduced here are also being incorporated in several general-purpose statistical packages; when these are complete, I will list this information at my homepage.

In order to meet the replication standard (King, 1995), I have deposited all data used in this manuscript, all computer software written for it, and all additional information necessary to replicate the empirical results herein with Inter-University Consortium for Political and Social Research (ICPSR) in their Publication-Related Archive.

Acknowledgments

Like many political methodologists, I have been interested in the ecological inference problem for a long time and have benefited from innumerable conversations with many colleagues. I wrote several papers on the subject while an undergraduate, and my first paper in graduate school and my first paper after graduate school attempted to make inferences from aggregate data to individuals. My thanks to Leon Epstein, Bert Kritzer, and Jerry Benjamin for teaching me about the problems in the literature and the more serious ones in my papers. For most of the years since, I followed the literature while working on other projects, but my interest was heightened by a grant I received at the end of the 1990 redistricting process from a now-defunct nonpartisan foundation. This grant included a donation of the largest set of U.S. precinct-level electoral data ever assembled in one place (originally collected to aid minorities during redistricting). The U.S. National Science Foundation provided another key grant (SBR-9321212) to enable me over the next several years to clean these data, merge them with U.S. Census data, and develop ecological inference methods for their analysis. My thanks goes to officials at the

[2] Gauss is available from Aptech Systems, Inc.; 23804 S.E. Kent-Kangley Road; Maple Valley, Washington 98038; (206) 432-7855; `sales@aptech.com`.

NSF Programs in Political Science (Frank Scioli, John McIver), Geography (J. W. Harrington, David Hodge), and Methods, Models, and Measurement (Cheryl Eavey) for arranging the grant, and for a creative conspiracy to introduce me to geographers working on related problems. I find that new methods are best developed while analyzing real data, and these data have proved invaluable. Thanks to my colleague Brad Palmquist, who joined with me in leading the data project soon after he arrived at Harvard, and to the extraordinarily talented crew of graduate students—Greg Adams, Ken Benoit, Grant Emison, Debbie Javeline, Claudine Gay, Jeff Lewis, Eric Reinhardt, and Steve Voss—and undergraduate students—Sarah Dix, Jim Goldman, Paul Hatch, and Robert Hutter—for their research assistance and many creative contributions.

Nuffield College at Oxford University provided a visiting fellowship and a wonderful place to think about these issues during the summer of 1994; my appreciation goes to Clive Payne for hosting my visit and for many interesting discussions. The John Simon Guggenheim Memorial Foundation deserves special thanks for a fellowship that enabled me to spend an exciting year (1994–1995) devoted full time, almost without interruption, to this project. The departments of Political Science and Geography at the University of Colorado provided a forum in September 1994, so that I could discuss my initial results. I presented the final version of the statistical model at the March 1995 meetings of the Association of American Geographers, and in May I presented this model along with most of the empirical evidence offered here in the political science and statistics seminar sponsored by the Institute for Governmental Studies at the University of California, Berkeley. My sincere thanks to Luc Anselin for very insightful comments at the geography meetings, and to Andrew Gelman for going beyond the call of duty in helping me correct several proofs and work out some computational problems following my Berkeley presentation. My first exposure to tomographic research came from Andrew's dissertation work at Harvard, and my understanding of its use as a heuristic device for portraying the model and developing diagnostic procedures came during our conversations and Andrew's many insightful suggestions, some of which are also acknowledged in the text of the book. Without what I learned from Andrew during our collaborations on other projects over the last decade, this book would probably look very different.

I am indebted to the exceptionally talented scholars who attend the always lively summer meetings of the Political Methodology Group. They have provided many years of encouragement, perceptive feedback, and numerous new ideas. The meeting in July 1995 was no exception: Chris Achen was my formally designated discussant, and numerous others were very helpful at the meetings and almost continuously thereafter. Mike Alvarez, Neal Beck, and John Freeman provided written suggestions and answered numerous questions about many topics. John also gave me some especially helpful comments as my discussant at the American Political Science Association meetings in August 1995. Neal Beck's remarkable ability to read my manuscript and simultaneously to write trenchant e-mail comments and respond to relentless further inquiries about it kept me very busy and improved the final product immeasurably; I have learned a great deal over the years from our frequent electronic communications. Thanks also to Henry Brady, Nancy Burns, Gary Chamberlain, Charles Franklin, Dave Grether, Jerry Hausman, Ken McCue, Doug Rivers, Jim Stock, Wendy Tam, Søren Thomsen, Waldo Tobler and Chris Winship for helpful conversations, to Larry Bartels, Gary Cox, Dudley Duncan, Mitchell Duneier, David Epstein, Sharon O'Halloran, and Bert Kritzer for insightful written comments, to Sander Greenland for helping me learn about epidemiological research, and to Danny Goldhagen for help with the literature on the Nazi vote.

My colleagues Jim Alt, Mo Fiorina, Brad Palmquist, and Sid Verba were very helpful throughout the process, providing many comments, numerous insightful discussions, and much encouragement. Nothing beats the off-hand comments at the mailboxes in the Department of Government. Brad Palmquist's careful readings of the manuscript, many useful suggestions, and deep knowledge of ecological inference saved me from several blunders and improved the final product substantially. Alex Schuessler and Jonathan Katz provided very insightful comments on painfully early versions of the manuscript. Curt Signorino was far more than my lead research assistant; he provided important, perceptive reactions to many of my ideas in their earliest forms, helped me reason through numerous difficult statistical and mathematical issues, corrected several proofs, and helped me work through a variety of computational issues. My appreciation goes to Chuck D'Antonio, Yi Wang, and William Yi Wei for their computer wizardry.

Alison Alter, Ken Scheve (Harvard); Barry Burden, David Kimball, Chris Zorn (OSU); Jeff Lewis, Jason Wittenberg (MIT); Fang Wang (Cal Tech); and other faculty and students deserve special thanks for letting me experiment on them with alternative drafts and computer programs and for their continual inspiration and suggestions. Most of these political scientists participated with me in a "virtual seminar" held over the 1995–1996 academic year: they helped me improve the manuscript by identifying passages that were unclear, unhelpful, or untrue, and I tried to return the favor with immediate explanations via e-mail of anything that was holding them up. No doubt I got the better end of this bargain!

When the project was farther along still, I had the great fortune to receive comments on this work from presentations I gave at Michigan State University's Political Institutions and Public Choice Program (February 16, 1996), the University of Iowa (February 29, 1996), the Harvard-MIT Econometrics Workshop (April 4, 1996), Columbia University's Center for Social Science (April 5, 1996), the University of California, Santa Barbara (April 10, 1996), the California Institute of Technology (April 11, 1996), the University of California, Los Angeles (April 12, 1996) and the ICPSR program at the University of Michigan (17 July 1996). I am also grateful to Jim Alt, Steve Voss, and Michael Giles and Kaenan Hertz for graciously providing access to their valuable (separate) data sets on race and registration. I especially appreciate the talented staff at Princeton University Press, including Malcolm Litchfield and Peter Dougherty (editors), Jane Low (production manager), and Margaret Case (copy editor), for their professionalism and dedication.

Elizabeth has my deepest appreciation for everything from love and companionship to help with logic and calculus. The dedication is to our daughter, who learned how to laugh just as I was finishing this book. I am reasonably confident that the two events are unrelated, although I will let you know after she learns to talk!

PART I

Introduction

Chapter 1 provides a qualitative overview of the entire book. It should be accessible even to readers without statistical background. Chapter 2 gives a formal algebraic statement of the ecological inference problem and sets out the basic notation used throughout the book.

CHAPTER 1

Qualitative Overview

POLITICAL SCIENTISTS have understood the ecological inference problem at least since William Ogburn and Inez Goltra (1919) introduced it in the very first multivariate statistical analysis of politics published in a political science journal (see Gow, 1985; Bulmer, 1984). In a study of the voting behavior of newly enfranchised women in Oregon, they wrote that "even though the method of voting makes it impossible to count women's votes, one wonders if there is not some indirect method of solving the problem. The height of a waterfall is not measured by dropping a line from the top to the bottom, nor is the distance from the earth to the sun measured by a rod and chain" (p. 414).[1]

Ogburn and Goltra's "indirect" method of estimating women's votes was to correlate the percent of women voting in each precinct in Portland, Oregon, with the percent of people voting "no" in selected referenda in the same precincts. They reasoned that individual women were probably casting ballots against the referenda questions at a higher rate than men "if precincts with large percentages of women voting, vote in larger percentages against a measure than the precincts with small percentages of women voting." But they (correctly) worried that what has come to be known as the ecological inference problem might invalidate their analysis: "It is also theoretically possible to gerrymander the precincts in such a way that there may be a negative correlative even though men and women each distribute their votes 50 to 50 on a given measure" (p. 415). The essence of the ecological inference problem is that the true individual-level relationship could even be the reverse of the observed aggregate correlation if it were the *men* in the heavily female precincts who voted disproportionately against the referenda.

Ogburn and Goltra's data no longer appear to be available, but the problem they raised can be illustrated by this simple hypothetical example reconstructed in part from their verbal descriptions. Consider

[1] In 1919, the possibility of what has since come to be known as the "gender gap" was a central issue for academics and a nontrivial concern for political leaders seeking reelection: Not only were women about to have the vote for the first time nationwide; because women made up slightly over fifty percent of the population, they were about to have *most* of the votes.

two equal-sized precincts voting on Proposition 22, an initiative by the radical "People's Power League" to institute proportional representation in Oregon's Legislative Assembly elections: 40% of voters in precinct 1 are women and 40% of all voters in this precinct oppose the referenda. In precinct 2, 60% of voters are women and 60% of the precinct opposes the referenda. Precinct 2 has more women and is more opposed to the referenda than precinct 1, and so it certainly *seems* that women are opposing the proportional representation reform. Indeed, it could be the case that all women were opposed and all men voted in favor in both precincts, as might have occured if the reform were uniformly seen as a way of ensuring men a place in the legislature even though they formed a (slight) minority in every legislative district. But however intuitive this inference may appear, simple arithmetic indicates that it would be equally consistent with the observed aggregate data for men to have opposed proportional representation at a rate four times higher than that of women.[2] These higher relative rates of individual male opposition would occur, given the same aggregate percentages, if a larger fraction of men in the female-dominated precinct 2 opposed the reform than men in precinct 1, as might happen if precinct 2 was a generally more radical area independent of, or even because of, its gender composition.

But if Ogburn and Goltra were Leif Ericson, William Robinson was Christopher Columbus: for not until Robinson's (1950) article was the problem widely recognized and the quest for a valid method of making ecological inferences begun in earnest.[3] Robinson's article remains one of the most influential works in social science methodology. His (correct) view was that, with the methods available at the time, valid ecological inference was impossible. He warned analysts never to use aggregate data to infer individual relationships, and thus to avoid what has since come to be known as "the ecological fallacy." His work

[2] That is, given these aggregate numbers, a minimum of 0% of females in precinct 1 and 20% in precinct 2 (for an average of 10%) could have opposed the referenda, whereas a maximum of 40% of males in each precinct could have opposed it. Chapter 5 provides easy graphical methods of making calculations like these.

[3] Other early works that recognized the ecological inference problem include Allport (1924), Bernstein (1932), Gehlke and Biehl (1934), Thorndike (1939), Deming and Stephan (1940), and Yule and Kendall (1950). Robinson (1950) cited several of these studies as well as Ogburn and Goltra. Scholars writing even earlier than Ogburn and Goltra (1919) made ecological inferences, even though they did not recognize the problems with doing so. In fact, even the works usually cited as the first statistical works of any kind, which incidentally concerned political topics, included ecological inferences (see Graunt, 1662, and Petty, 1690, 1691). See Achen and Shively (1995) for other details of the history of ecological inference research.

sent two shock waves through the social sciences that are still being felt, causing some scholarly pursuits to end and another to begin.

First, the use of aggregate data by political scientists, quantitative historians, sociologists, and others declined relative to use of other forms of data; scholars began to avoid using aggregate data to address whole classes of important research questions (King, 1990). In many countries and fields of study, this "collapse of aggregate data analysis ... and its replacement by individual survey analysis as the dominant method of quantitative social research" (Achen and Shively, 1995: 5) meant that numerous, often historical and geographical, issues were put aside, and many still remain unanswered. What might have become vibrant fields of scholarship withered. The scholars who continue to work in these fields—such as those in comparative politics attempting to explain who voted for the Nazi party, or political historians studying working-class support for political parties in the antebellum Southern U.S.—do so because of the lack of an alternative to ecological data, but they toil under a cloud of great suspicion. The ecological inference problem hinders substantive work in almost every empirical field of political science, as well as numerous areas of sociology, education, marketing, economics, history, geography, epidemiology, and statistics. For example, historical election statistics have fallen into disuse and studies based on them into at least some disrepute. Classic studies, such as V. O. Key's (1949) *Southern Politics,* have been succeeded by scholarship based mostly on survey research, often to great advantage, but necessarily ignoring much of history, focused as it is on the few recent, mostly national, elections for which surveys are available.

The literature's nearly exclusive focus on national surveys with random interviews of isolated individuals means that the geographic component to social science data is often neglected. Commercial state-level surveys are available, but their quality varies considerably and the results are widely suspect in the academic community. Even if the address of each survey respondent were available, the usual 1,000–2,000 respondents to national surveys are insufficient for learning much about spatial variation except for the grossest geographic patterns, in which a country would be divided into no more than perhaps a dozen broad regions. For example, some National Election Study polls locate respondents within congressional districts, but only about a dozen interviews are conducted in any district, and no sample is taken from most of the congressional districts for any one survey. The General Social Survey makes available no geographic information to researchers unless they sign a separate confidentiality agreement, and even then only the respondent's state of residence is released. Survey organizations in other countries are even more reticent about releasing local geographic information.

Creative combinations of quantitative and qualitative research are much more difficult when the identity and rich qualitative information about individual communities or respondents cannot be revealed to readers. Indeed, in most cases, respondents' identities are not even known to the data analyst. If "all politics is local," political science is missing much of politics. In contrast, aggregate data are saturated with precise spatial information. For example, the United States can be divided into approximately 190,000 electoral precincts, and detailed aggregate political data are available for each. Only the ecological inference problem stands between the scientific community and this rich source of information.

Whereas the first shock wave from Robinson's article stifled research in many substantive fields, the second energized the social science statistics community to try to solve the problem. One partial measure of the level of effort devoted to solving the ecological inference problem is that Robinson's article has been cited more than eight hundred times.[4] Many other scholars have written on the topic as well, citing those who originally cited Robinson or approaching the problem from different perspectives. At one extreme, the literature includes authors such as Bogue and Bogue (1982), who try, unsuccessfully, to "refute" the ecological fallacy altogether; at the other extreme are fatalists who liken the seventy-five year search for a solution to the ecological inference problem to seeking "alchemists' gold" (Flanigan and Zingale, 1985) or to "a fruitless quest" (Achen and Shively, 1995). These scholars, and numerous others between these extreme positions, have written extensively, and often very fruitfully, on the topic. Successive generations of young scholars and methodologists in the making, having been warned off aggregate data analysis with their teachers' mantra "thou shalt not draw conclusions about individual behavior from aggregate data," come away with the conviction that the ecological inference problem presents an enormous barrier to social science research. This belief has drawn a steady stream of social science methodologists into the search for a solution over the years, myself included.

Numerous important advances have been made in the ecological inference literature, but even the best current methods give incorrect answers a large fraction of the time, and nonsensical answers very

[4] This is a vast underestimate, as it depends on data from the *Social Science Citation Index*, which did not even begin publishing (or counting) until six years after Robinson's article appeared.

frequently (such as 115% of blacks voting for the Democrats or −4% of foreign-born Americans being illiterate). No proposed method has been scientifically validated. Any that have been tried on data sets for which the individual-level relationship of interest is known generally fail to give the right answer. It is a testimony to the difficulty of the problem that no serious attempts have even been made to address a variety of basic statistical issues related to the problem. For example, currently available measures of uncertainty, such as confidence intervals, standard errors, and others, have never been validated and appear to be hopelessly inaccurate. Indeed, for some important approaches, no uncertainty measures have even been proposed.

Unlike the rest of this book, this chapter contains no technical details and should be readable even by those with little or no statistical background. In the remainder of this chapter, I summarize some other applications of ecological inference (Section 1.1), define the problem more precisely by way of a leading example of the failures of the most popular current method (Section 1.2), summarize the nature of the solution offered (Section 1.3), provide some brief empirical evidence that the method works in practice (Section 1.4), and outline the statistical method offered (Section 1.5).

1.1 The Necessity of Ecological Inferences

Contrary to the pessimistic claims in the ecological inference literature (since Robinson, 1950), aggregate data are sometimes useful even without inferences about individuals. Studies of incumbency advantage, the political effects of redistricting plans, forecasts of macro-economic conditions, and comparisons of infant mortality rates across nations are just a few of the cases where both questions and data coincide at the aggregate level.[5] Nevertheless, even studies such as these that ask questions about aggregates can usually be improved with valid inferences about the individuals who make up the aggregates. And more importantly, numerous other questions exist for which only valid ecological inferences will do.

Fundamental questions in most empirical subfields of political science require ecological inferences. Researchers in many other fields

[5] There are even several largely independent lines of research that give conditions under which aggregate data is not worse than individual-level data for certain purposes. In political science, see Kramer (1983); in epidemiology, see Morgenstern (1982); in psychology, see Epstein (1986); in economics, see Grunfeld and Griliches (1960), Fromm and Schink (1973), Aigner and Goldfeld (1974), and Shin (1987); and in input-output analysis, a field within economics, see Malinvaud (1955) and Venezia (1978).

of academic inquiry, as well as the real world of public policy, also routinely try to make inferences about the attributes of individual behavior from aggregate data. If a valid method of making such inferences were available, scholars could provide accurate answers to these questions with ecological data, and policymakers could base their decisions on reliable scientific techniques. Many of the ecological inferences pursued in these other fields are also of interest to political scientists, which reemphasizes the close historical connection between the ecological inference problem and political science research. The following list represents a small sample of ecological inferences that have been attempted in a variety of fields.

- In American public policy, ecological inferences are required to implement key features of federal law. For example, the U.S. Voting Rights Act of 1965 (and its extensions in 1970, 1975, and 1982) prohibited voting discrimination on the basis of race, color, or language. If discrimination is found, the courts or the U.S. Justice Department can order a state or local jurisdiction to redistrict its political boundaries, or to impose or prevent various other changes in electoral laws. Under present law, legally significant discrimination only exists when plaintiffs (or the Justice Department) can first demonstrate that members of a minority group (usually African American or Hispanic) vote both cohesively and differently from other voters.[6] Sometimes they must also prove that majority voters consistently prevent minorities from electing a candidate of their choice. Since survey data are rarely available in these cases, and because they are not often trustworthy in racially polarized contests, an application of the Voting Rights Act requires a valid ecological inference from electoral data and U.S. Census data.

  Voting Rights Act assessments of minority and majority voting begins with electoral returns from precincts, the smallest geographic unit for which electoral data are available. In addition to the numbers of votes received by each candidate in a precinct, census data also gives the fraction of voters in the same precinct who are African American (or other minority) or white.[7] With these two sets of aggregate data, plaintiffs must make an ecological inference about how each racial group casts its ballots. That is, since the secret ballot prevents analysts from following voters into the voting booth and peering over their shoulders as they

[6] In this book, I use "African American" and "black" interchangeably and, when appropriate or for expository simplicity, often define "white" as non-black or occasionally as a residual category such as non-black and non-Hispanic.

[7] In some states, precincts must be aggregated to a somewhat higher geographical level to match electoral and census data.

cast their ballots, the voting behavior of each racial group must be inferred using only aggregate electoral and census data. Because of the inadequacy of current methods, in some situations the wrong policies are being implemented: the wrong districts are being redrawn, and the wrong electoral laws are being changed. (Given the great importance and practicality of this problem, I will use it as a running example.)[8]

- In one election to the German Reichstag in September 1930, Adolf Hitler's previously obscure and electorally insignificant National Socialist German Worker's party became the Weimar Republic's second largest political party. The National Socialists continued their stunning electoral successes in subsequent state, local, and presidential elections, and ultimately reached 37.3% of the vote in the last election prior to their taking power. As so many have asked, how could this have happened? Who voted for the Nazis (and the other extreme groups)? Was the Nazi constituency dominated by the downwardly mobile lower middle class or was support much more widespread? Which religious groups and worker categories supported the National Socialists? Which sectors of which political parties lost votes to the Nazis? The data available to answer these questions directly include aggregate data from some of the 1,200 Kreise (districts) for which both electoral data and various census data are available. Because survey data are not available, accurate answers to these critical questions will only be possible with a valid method of ecological inference (see Hamilton, 1982; Childers, 1983; and Falter, 1991).
- Epidemiologists and public policy makers need to know whether and to what extent residential levels of radioactive radon are a risk factor for lung cancer (Stidley and Samet, 1993; Greenland and Robins, 1994a). Radon leaks through basement floors and may pose a significant health risk. Legislators in many states are considering bills that would require homeowners to test for radon and, if high levels are found, to install one of several mechanical means of reducing future exposure.

  Policymakers' decisions about such legislation obviously depend in part on the demonstrated health effects of radon. Unfortunately, collecting random samples of individual-level data would be impractical, as it would require measures of radon exposure over many years for each subject. Moreover, because only a small fraction of people with or without radon exposure get lung cancer, and because other variables like smoking are powerful covariates, reliably estimating the differences in lung cancer rates for those with different levels of radon exposure in an individual-level study would require measurements for tens of thou-

[8] The litigation based on the Voting Rights Act is vast; see Grofman, Handley, and Niemi (1992) for a review.

sands of individuals. This would be both prohibitively expensive and ethically unacceptable without altering the radon levels for individuals in a way that would probably also ruin the study. Researchers have tried case-control studies, which avoid the necessity of large samples but risk sample selection bias, and extreme-case analyses of coal miners, where the effects are larger but their high levels of radon exposure makes the results difficult to extrapolate back to residential settings. The most extensive data that remain include information such as county-level counts of lung cancer deaths from the federal Centers for Disease Control, and samples of radon concentration from each county. Ecological inferences are therefore the only hope of ascertaining the dose-response effect of radon exposure from these data. Unfortunately, without a better method of making ecological inferences, the evidence from these data will likely remain inconclusive (Lubin, 1994).[9]

- In the academic field of marketing (and its real-world counterpart), researchers try to ascertain who has bought specific products, and where advertising is most likely to be effective in influencing consumers to buy more. In many situations, researchers do not have data on the demographic and socio-economic characteristics of individuals who buy particular products, data that would effectively answer many of the research questions directly. Instead, they have extensive indirect data on the average characteristics of people in a geographic area, such as at the level of the zip code (or sometimes 9-digit zip code) in the United States. Researchers generally also have information from the company about how much of a product was sold in each of these areas. The question is, given the number of new products sold in each geographic area and, for example, the fraction of households in each area that have children, are in the upper quartile of income, are in single-parent families, or have other characteristics, how does demand for the product vary by these characteristics within each community? Only with a valid ecological inference in each geographic area can researchers learn the answers they seek. With this information, scholars will be able to study how product demand depends on these family and individual characteristics, and companies will be able to decide how to target advertising to consumers likely to be interested in their products.
- Since voter surveys are neither always possible nor necessarily reliable, candidates for political office study aggregate election returns in order

[9] Most epidemiological questions require relatively certain answers and thus, in most cases, large-scale, randomized experiments on individuals. Because each such experiment can cost hundreds of millions of dollars, a valid method of ecological inference would probably be of primary use in this field for helping scholars (and funding agencies) choose which experiments to conduct.

to decide what policies to favor, and also to tailor campaign appeals. Understanding how the support for policies varies among demographic and political groups is critical to the connections between elected officials and their constituents, and for the smooth operation of representative democracy.

- Historians are also interested in the political preferences of demographic groups, and usually for time periods for which modern survey research had not even been invented. For example, only valid ecological inferences will enable these scholars to ascertain the extent to which working-class voters supported the Socialist party in depression-era America.
- An important sociological question is the relationship between unemployment and crime, especially as affected by race and as mediated by divorce and single parenthood. Unfortunately, the best available data are usually aggregated at the level of cities or counties (Blau and Blau, 1982; Messner, 1982; Byrne and Sampson, 1986). Official U.S. government data on race-specific crime rates (in the form of the Uniform Crime Report) are usually insufficient, and individual-level survey data are in very short supply and, because they are based on self-reports, are often of dubious quality (Sampson, 1987). Only better data or a valid method of ecological inference will enable scholars to determine the critical linkages between unemployment, family disruption, race, and crime.
- The ecological inference problem, and other related aggregation problems, are central to the discipline of economics, as explained by Theil in his classic study (1954: 1): "A serious gap exists between the greater part of rigorous economic theory and the pragmatic way in which economic systems are empirically analyzed. Axiomatically founded theories refer mostly to individuals, for instance the consumer or the entrepreneur. Empirical descriptions of economic actions in large communities, on the other hand, are nearly always extremely global: they are confined to the behavior of groups of individuals. The necessity of such a procedure can scarcely be questioned.... But the introduction of relations pretending to describe the reactions of groups of individuals instead of single individuals raises questions of fundamental importance, which are not very well understood." Economists have made much progress in clarifying the links between microeconomic and macroeconomic behavior in the more than forty years since these words were written (see Stoker, 1993). They also have some good survey data, and much more impressive formal theories, but a method of ecological inference would enable economists to evaluate some of their sophisticated individual-level theoretical models more directly. This would be especially important in a field where there is much reason to value individual responses to surveys less than revealed preference measures that are best gathered at the aggregate level. Economists are also interested in developing models of

aggregate economic indicators that are built from and consistent with individual-level economic theories and data, even when the individual level is not of direct interest (see Section 14.3).

- A controversial issue in education policy is the effects of school choice voucher programs, where states or municipalities provide vouchers to students who cannot afford to attend private schools. Private schools are then composed of students from wealthy families and from those who pay with state vouchers. One of the many substantive and methodological issues in this field is determining the differential performance of students who take advantage of the voucher system to attend private schools, compared to those who would be there even without the program. Thus, data exist on aggregate school-level variables such as the dropout rate or the percent who attend college, as well as on the proportion of each private school's students who paid with a voucher. Because of privacy concerns, researchers must make ecological inferences in order to learn about the fraction of voucher students who attend college, or the fraction of non-voucher students who drop out.

The point of this list is to provide a general sense of the diversity of questions that have been addressed by (necessarily) inadequate methods of ecological inference. No tiny sample of ecological inferences such as this could do justice to the vast array of important scholarly and practical questions about individual attributes for which only aggregate data are available.

1.2 The Problem

On 16 and 17 November 1994, a special three-judge federal court met in Cleveland to hear arguments concerning the legality of Ohio's State House districts. A key part of the trial turned on whether African Americans vote differently from whites. Although the required facts are only knowable for individual voters, and survey data were unavailable (and are unreliable in the context of racial politics), the only relevant information available to study this question was political and demographic data at the aggregate level.[10]

Table 1.1 portrays the issue in this case as an example of the more general ecological inference problem. This table depicts what is known

[10] I had a small role in this case as a consultant to the state of Ohio and therefore witnessed the following story firsthand. My primary task in the case was to evaluate the relative fairness of the state's redistricting plan to the political parties, using methods developed in King and Browning (1987), King (1989b), and Gelman and King (1990, 1994a, b).

Race of Voting-Age Person	Voting Decision			
	Democrat	Republican	No Vote	
black	?	?	?	55,054
white	?	?	?	25,706
	19,896	10,936	49,928	80,760

Table 1.1 The Ecological Inference Problem at the District Level: The 1990 Election to the Ohio State House, District 42. The goal is to infer from the marginal entries (each of which is the sum of the corresponding row or column) to the cell entries.

for the election to the Ohio State House that occurred in District 42 in 1990. The black Democratic candidate received 19,896 votes (65% of votes cast) in a race against a white Republican opponent. African Americans constituted 55,054 of the 80,760 people of voting age in this district (68%). Because this known information appears in the margins of the cross-tabulation, it is usually referred to as the *marginals*. The ecological inference problem involves replacing the question marks in the body of this table with inferences based on information from the marginals. (Ecological inference is traditionally defined in terms of a table like this and thus in terms of discrete individual-level variables. Most political scientists, sociologists, and geographers, and some statisticians, have retained this original definition. Epidemiologists and some others generalize the term to include any aggregation problem, including continuous individual-level variables. I use the traditional definition in this book in order to emphasize the distinctive characteristics of aggregated discrete data, and discuss aggregation problems involving continuous individual-level variables in Chapter 14.)

For example, the question mark in the upper left corner of the table represents the (unknown) number of blacks who voted for the Democratic candidate. Obviously, a wide range of different numbers could be put in this cell of the table without contradicting its row and column marginals, in this case any number between 0 and 19,896, a logic referred to in the literature as *the method of bounds*.[11] As a result, some other information or method must be used to further narrow the range of results.

[11] That is, although the row total is 55,054, the total number of people in the upper left cell of Table 1.1 cannot exceed 19,896, or it would contradict its column marginal.

Race of Voting-Age Person	Voting Decision			
	Democrat	Republican	No Vote	
black	?	?	?	221
white	?	?	?	484
	130	92	483	705

Table 1.2 The Ecological Inference Problem at the Precinct Level: Precinct P in District 42 (1 of 131 in the district described in Table 1.1). The goal is to infer from the margins of a set of tables like this one to the cell entries in each.

Fortunately, somewhat more information is available in this example, since the parties in the Ohio case had data at the level of precincts (or sometimes slightly higher levels of aggregation instead, which I also will refer to as precincts). Ohio State House District 42 is composed of 131 precincts, for which information analogous to Table 1.1 is available. For example, Table 1.2 displays the information from Precinct P, which in District 42 falls between Cascade Valley Park and North High School in the First Ward in the city of Akron. The sum of any item in the precinct tables, across all precincts, would equal the number in the same position in the district table. For example, if the number of blacks voting for the Democratic candidate in Precinct P were added to the same number from each of the other 130 precincts, we would arrive at the total number of blacks casting ballots for the Democratic candidate represented as the first cell in Table 1.1.

The ecological inference problem does not vanish by having access to the precinct-level data, such as that in Table 1.2, because we ultimately require individual-level information. Each of the cells in this table is still unknown. Thus, knowing the parts would tell us about the whole, but disaggregation to precincts does not appear to reveal much more about the parts.

With a few minor exceptions, no method has even been proposed to fill in the unknown quantities at the precinct level in Table 1.2. What scholars have done is to develop methods to use the observed variation in the marginals over precincts to help narrow the range of results at the district level in Table 1.1. For example, if the Democratic candidate receives the most votes in precincts with the largest fractions of African Americans, then it seems intuitively reasonable to suppose that blacks are voting disproportionately for the Democrats (and thus the upper left cell in Table 1.1 is probably large). This assumption is often reasonable, but Robinson showed that it can be dead wrong: the individual-level relationship is often the opposite sign of this aggregate correlation, as will occur if, for example, whites in heavily black areas tend to vote more Democratic than whites living in predominately white neighborhoods.

Unfortunately, even the best available current methods of ecological inference are often wildly inaccurate. For example, at the federal trial in Ohio (and in formal sworn deposition and in a prepared report), the expert witness testifying for the plaintiffs reported that 109.63% of blacks voted for the Democratic candidate in District 42 in 1990! He also reported in a separate, but obviously related, statement that a negative number of blacks voted for the Republican candidate. Lest this seem like one wayward result chosen selectively from a sea of valid inferences, consider a list of the results from all districts reported by this witness (every white Republican who faced a black Democrat since 1986), which I present in Table 1.3. A majority of these results are over 100%, and thus impossible. No one was accusing the Democratic candidates of stuffing the ballot box; dead voters were not suspected of turning out to vote more than they usually do. Rather, these results point out the failure of the general methodological approach. For those familiar with existing ecological inference methods, these results may be disheartening, but they will not be surprising: impossible results occur with regularity.

What of the analyses in Table 1.3 that produced results that were not impossible? For example, in District 25, the application of this standard method of ecological inference indicated that 99% of blacks voted for the Democratic candidate in 1990. Is this correct? Since no external information is available, we have no idea. However, we do know, from other situations where data do exist with which to verify the results of ecological analyses, that the methods usually do not work. The problem, of course, is that when they give results that are technically possible we might be lulled into believing them. As Robinson so clearly stated, even technically possible results from these standard methods are usually wrong.

When ridiculous results appear in academic work, as they sometimes do, there are few practical ramifications. In contrast, inaccurate results used in making public policy can have far-reaching consequences. Thus, in order to attempt to avoid this situation, the witness in this case used the best available methods at the time and had at his disposal far more resources and time than one would have for almost any academic project. The partisan control of a state legislature was at stake, and research resources were the last things that would be

Year	District	Estimated Percent of Blacks Voting for the Democratic Candidate
1986	12	95.65%
	23	100.06
	29	103.47
	31	98.92
	42	108.41
	45	93.58
1988	12	95.67
	23	102.64
	29	105.00
	31	100.20
	42	111.05
	45	97.49
1990	12	94.79
	14	97.83
	16	94.36
	23	101.09
	25	98.83
	29	103.42
	31	102.17
	36	101.35
	37	101.39
	42	109.63
	45	97.62

Table 1.3 Sample Ecological Inferences: All Ohio State House Districts Where an African American Democrat Ran Against a White Republican, 1986–1990. *Source*: "Statement of Gordon G. Henderson," presented as part of an exhibit in federal court. Figures above 100% are logically impossible.

spared if the case could be won. (The witness also had extensive experience testifying in similar cases.) Moreover, he was using a method (a version of Goodman's "ecological regression") that the U.S. Supreme Court had previously declared to be appropriate in applications such as this (*Thornburg v. Gingles*, 1986). If there was any way of avoiding these silly conclusions, he certainly would have done so. Yet, even with all this going for him he was effectively forced by the lack of better methods to present results that indicated, in over half the districts he studied, that more African Americans voted for the Democratic candidate than there were African Americans who voted.

Two types of statistical difficulties cause inaccurate results such as these in ecological inferences. The first is *aggregation bias*. This is the effect of the information loss that occurs when individual-level data are aggregated into the observed marginals. The problem is that in some aggregate data collections, the type of information loss may be selective, so that inferences that do not take this into account will be biased.

The second cause of inaccurate results in ecological inferences is a variety of *basic statistical problems,* unrelated to aggregation bias, that have not been incorporated into existing methods. These are the kinds of issues that would be resolved first in any other methodological area, although most have not yet been addressed. For example, much data used for ecological inferences have massive levels of "heteroskedasticity" (a basic problem in regression analysis), but this has never been noted in the literature—and sometimes explicitly denied—even though it is obviously present even in most published scatter plots (about which more in Chapter 4).

1.3 The Solution

This section sets forth seven characteristics of the proposed solution to the ecological inference problem not met by previous methods. However, unlike the proof of a mathematical theorem, statistical solutions can usually be improved continually—hence the phrase *a* solution, rather than *the* solution, in the title of this book. Modern statistical theory does not date back even as far as the ecological inference problem, so as we learn more we should be able to improve on this solution further. Similarly, as computers continue to get faster, we can posit more sophisticated models that incorporate more information. The method offered here is the first that consistently works in practice, but it is also intended to put the ecological inference literature on a firmer theoretical and empirical foundation, helping to lead to further improvements.

First, *the solution is scientifically validated with real data.* Several extensive collections of real aggregate data, for which the inner cells of the cross-tabulation are known from public records, are used to help validate the method. For example, estimates of the levels of black and white voter registration are compared to the known answer in public records. (These are real issues, not contrived for the purpose of a methodological treatise; they are the subject of considerable academic inquiry, and even much litigation in many states.) Data from the U.S. Census aggregated to precinct-sized aggregates in South Carolina are used to study the relative frequency with which males and females are in poverty. Also useful for this purpose are data from Atlanta, Georgia, that include information about voter loyalty and defection rates in the transitions between elections, and from turn-of-the-century U.S. county-level data on black and white literacy rates, in order to validate the model in those contexts. Finally, I have been able to study the properties of aggregate data extensively with a large collection of merged U.S. Census data and precinct-level aggregate election data for most electoral offices and the entire nation. The method works in practice. In contrast, if the only goal were to develop a method that worked merely in theory, then the problem might already have been considered "solved" long ago, as the literature includes many methods that work only if a list of unverifiable assumptions are met.

Using data to evaluate methodological approaches is, of course, good scientific practice, but it has been rare in this field that has focused so exclusively on hypothetical data, and on theoretical arguments without economic, political, sociological, psychological, or other foundations. Indeed, the entire ecological inference literature contains only forty-nine comparisons between estimates from aggregate data and the known true individual-level answer.[12] (Because this work includes a variety of new data sets, and a method that gives

[12] This estimate of the number of times authors in the ecological inference literature have made themselves vulnerable to being wrong is based on counting data sets original to this literature. Individual cross-tabulations that were used to study the method of bounds are excluded since no uncertainty, and thus no vulnerability, exists. I obviously also exclude studies that use data sets previously introduced to this literature. A list of data sets and the studies in which they were first used are as follows: Race and illiteracy from the 1930 U.S. Census (Robinson, 1950); race by domestic service from community area data (Goodman, 1959; used originally to study bounds by Duncan and Davis, 1953); infant mortality by race and by urbanicity in U.S. states (Duncan et al., 1961: 71–72); 1964–1966 voter transitions in British constituencies (Hawkes, 1969); a voter transition between Democratic primaries in Florida (Irwin and Meeter, 1969); a 1961 German survey (Stokes, 1969); voter transition in England from Butler and Stokes (1969) data (Miller, 1972); survey of first-year university students (Hannan and Burstein, 1974); vote for Labour by worker category (Crewe and Payne, 1976); voter transition in England compared to a poll (McCarthy and Ryan, 1977); voter transition February to October 1974 in England compared to a poll (Upton, 1978); voter transition from a general election in 1983 to an election to the European parliament in 1984 compared to an ITN poll (Brown and Payne, 1986); one comparison based on twenty-four observations from Lee County, South Carolina, comparing registration and turnout by race (Loewen and Grofman, 1989); two comparisons of a survey to Swedish election data (Ersson and Wörlund, 1990); twenty comparisons of aggregate electoral data in California and nationally compared to exit polls, comparisons using census data, and official data on registration and voter turnout (Freedman et al., 1991); eight voter transition studies in Denmark compared to survey data (Thomsen et al., 1991); race and registration data from Matthews and Prothro (1966) (Alt, 1993); race and literacy from the 1910 U.S. Census (Palmquist, 1994); housing tenure transitions from 1971 to 1981 in England from census data (Cleave, Brown, and Payne, 1995). If you know of any work that belongs on this list that I missed, I would appreciate hearing from you.

district- and precinct-level estimates, the book presents over sixteen thousand such comparisons between estimates and the truth.) Many of these forty-nine ecological inferences are compared to estimates from sample surveys, but scholars rarely correct for known survey biases with post-stratification or other methods.[13] Others use "data" that are made up by the investigator, such as those created with computerized random number generators. All these data sets have their place (and some will have their place here too), but their artificial nature, exclusive use, and especially limited number and diversity fail to present the methodologist with the kinds of problems that arise in using real aggregate data and studying authentic social science problems. Scholars are therefore unable to adapt the methods to the opportunities in the data and will not know how to avoid the likely pitfalls that commonly arise in practice.

Second, *the method described here offers realistic assessments of the uncertainty of ecological estimates.* Reporting the uncertainty of one's conclusions is one of the hallmarks of modern statistics, but it is an especially important problem here. The reason is that ecological inference is an unusual statistical problem in which, under normal circumstances, we never observe realizations of our quantity of interest. For example, since most German citizens who voted for the Nazi party are no longer around to answer hypothetical survey questions, and could hardly be expected to answer them sincerely even if they were, no method will ever be able to fill in the cross-tabulation with certainty. Thus a key component of any solution to this problem is that correct uncertainty estimates be an integral part of all inferences.

Many methods proposed in the literature provide no uncertainty estimates. Others give uncertainty estimates that are usually incorrect (as for example when 95% confidence intervals do not capture the correct answer about 95% of the time). The method proposed here provides reasonably accurate (and empirically verified) uncertainty estimates. Moreover, these estimates are useful since the intervals turn out to be narrower than one might think.

Third, *the basic model is robust to aggregation bias.* Although this book also includes modifications of this basic model to compensate for aggregation bias explicitly, these modifications are often unnecessary. That is, even when the process of aggregation causes existing methods to give answers that bear no relationship to the truth, the method proposed here still usually gives accurate answers.

[13] Surveys are also very underused in this literature, perhaps in part since many scholars came to this field because of their skepticism of public opinion polls.

In order to develop an explicit approach to avoiding aggregation bias, I prove that the numerous and apparently conflicting explanations for aggregation bias are mathematically equivalent, even though they each appear to offer very different substantive insights. This theoretical result eliminates the basis for existing scholarly disagreements over which approach is better, or how many problems we need to deal with. All problems identified with aggregation bias are identical; only one problem needs to be solved. In the cases where an explicit treatment of aggregation bias is necessary under the proposed model, this result makes possible the model generalization required to accomplish the task.

Fourth, *all components of the proposed model are in large part verifiable in aggregate data.* That is, although information is lost in the process of aggregation, and thus ecological inferences will always involve risk, some observable implications of all model assumptions remain in aggregate data. These implications are used to develop diagnostic tests to evaluate the appropriateness of the model to each application, and to develop generalizations for the times when the assumptions of the basic model are contradicted by the data. Thus, the assumptions on which this model is based can usually be verified in sufficient detail in aggregate data in order to avoid problems that cause other methods to lose their bearing.

Fifth, *the solution offered here corrects for a variety of serious statistical problems, unrelated to aggregation bias, that also affect ecological inferences.* It explicitly models the main source of heteroskedasticity in aggregate data, allows precinct-level parameters to vary, and otherwise includes far more known information in the model about the problem.

The sometimes fierce debates between proponents of the deterministic "method of bounds" and supporters of various statistical approaches are resolved by combining their (largely noncontradictory) insights into a single model. Including the precinct-level bounds in the statistical model substantially increases the amount of information used in making ecological inferences. For example, imagine that every time you run a regression, you could take some feature of the model (such as a predicted value), hold it outside a window and, if it is wrong—completely wrong with no uncertainty—the clouds would part and a thunderbolt would turn your computer printout into a fiery crisp. Remarkably, although they have not been exploited in previous statistical models, the bounds provide exactly this kind of certain information in all ecological inference problems for each and every observation in a data set (albeit perhaps with a bit less fanfare). In any other field of statistical analysis, this valuable information, and the other more ordinary statistical problems, would be addressed first, and yet most have been ignored. Correcting these basic statistical problems is also what makes this model robust to aggregation bias.

Sixth, *the method provides accurate estimates not only of the cells of the cross-tabulation at the level of the district-wide or state-wide aggregates but also at the precinct level*. For example, the method enables one to fill in not only Table 1.1 with figures such as the fraction of blacks voting for the Democrats in the entire district, but also the precinct-level fractions for each of the 131 tables corresponding to Table 1.2. This has the obvious advantage of providing far more information to the analyst, information that can be studied, plotted on geographic maps, or used as dependent variables in subsequent analyses. It is also quite advantageous for verifying the method, since 131 tests of the model for each data set are considerably more informative than one.

Finally, *the solution to the ecological inference problem turns out to be a solution to what geographers' call the "modifiable areal unit problem."* The modifiable areal unit problem occurs if widely varying estimates result when most methods are applied to alternate reaggregations of the same geographic (or "areal") units. This is a major concern in geography and related fields, where numerous articles have been written that rearrange geographic boundaries only to find that correlation coefficients and other statistics totally change substantive interpretations (see Openshaw, 1979, 1984; Fotheringham and Wong, 1991). In contrast, the method given here is almost invariant to the configuration of district lines. If precinct boundaries were redrawn, even in some random fashion, inferences about the cells of Table 1.1 would not drastically change in most cases.

Every methodologist dreams of inventing a statistical procedure that will work even if the researcher applying it does not understand the procedure or possess much "local knowledge" about the substance of the problem. This dream has never been fulfilled in statistics, and the same qualification holds for the method proposed here: The more contextual knowledge a researcher makes use of, the more likely the ecological inference is to be valid. The method gives the researcher with this local knowledge the tools to make a valid ecological inference. That is, with a fixed, even inadequate, amount of local knowledge about a problem, a researcher will almost always do far better by using this method than those previously proposed. But making valid ecological inferences is not usually possible without operator intervention. Valid inferences require that the diagnostic tests described be used to verify that the model fits the data and that the distributional assumptions apply. Because the basic problem is a lack of information, bringing diverse sources of knowledge to bear on ecological inferences can have an especially large payoff.

1.4 The Evidence

As a preview of Part IV, which reports extensive evaluations of the model from a variety of data sets, this section gives just two applications, one to demonstrate the accuracy of the method and the other to portray how much more information it reveals about the problem under study. The first application provides 3,262 evaluations of the ecological inference model presented in this book—67 times as many comparisons between estimates from an aggregate model and the truth as exist in the entire history of ecological inference research. The second is a brief geographic analysis in another application that serves to emphasize how much more information about individual behavior this method provides than even the (unrealized) goal of previous methods.

The data for the first application come from the state of Louisiana, which records by precinct the number of blacks who vote and the number of whites who vote (among those registered). These data make it possible to evaluate the ecological inference model described in this book as follows. For each of Louisiana's 3,262 precincts, the procedure uses only aggregate data: the fraction of those registered who are black and the fraction of registered people turning out to vote for the 1990 elections (as well as the number registered). These aggregate, precinct-level data are then used to estimate the fraction of blacks who vote in each precinct. Finally, I validate the model by comparing these estimates to the true fractions of blacks who turn out to vote. (That is, the true fractions of black and white turnout are not used in the estimation procedure.)[14]

One brief summary of the results of this analysis appears in Figure 1.1. This figure plots the estimated fraction of blacks turning out to vote in 1990 (horizontally) by the true fraction of blacks voting in that year (vertically). Each precinct is represented in the figure by a circle with area proportional to the number of blacks in the precinct. If the model estimates were exactly correct in every precinct, each

[14] The 3,262 evaluations of the model in this section are from the same data set and, as such, are obviously related. However, each comparison between the truth and an estimate provides a separate instance in which the model is vulnerable to being wrong. These model evaluations simulate the usual situation in which the ecological analyst has no definite prior knowledge about whether the parameters of interest are dependent, unrelated, or all identical.

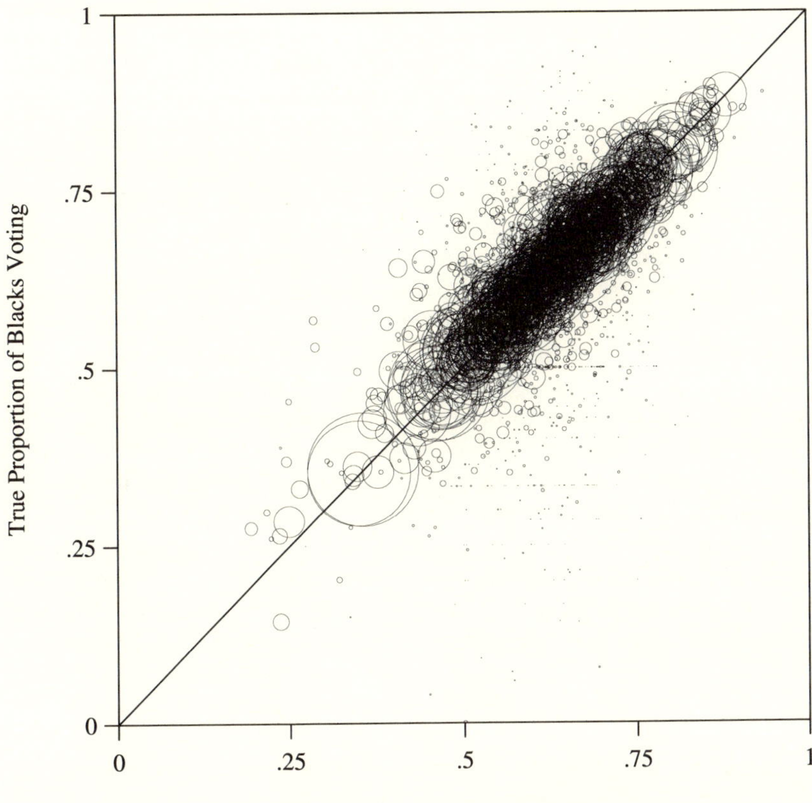

Figure 1.1 Model Verification: Voter Turnout among African Americans in Louisiana Precincts. This figure represents 3,262 precincts in 1990, with each circle size proportional to the number of voting-age African Americans in the precinct. That the vast majority of circles fall near the diagonal line, indicating that the estimated and true fractions of blacks voting are nearly identical, is strong confirmation of the model.

circle would be centered exactly on the 45° line. In fact, almost all of the 3,262 precincts fall on or near this diagonal line, demonstrating the success of this method of making inferences about individual behavior using only aggregate data. The few precincts that are farther from the line have tiny numbers of African Americans, so the vast majority of individual voters are correctly estimated.

The results are compelling. If Figure 1.1 were merely a plot of the observed values of a variable by the fitted values of the same variable used during the estimation procedure, any empirical researcher should be pleased: the fit is extremely good. If instead the figure were based on the harder problem of making out-of-sample predictions, where past realizations were used to calibrate the prediction, the result would be even better. But the result here is even more dramatic, since the estimates in the figure were computed from only aggregate data. The true fraction of blacks turning out to vote (the vertical dimension in the figure) was not part of the estimation procedure. Moreover, no past realizations of the truth being estimated were used.

Part IV provides many more model evaluations and of many types. These evaluations include data sets for which existing methods do reasonably well at estimating the statewide average, in which case the method offered here also gives reasonable statewide results and in addition much more information in the form of correct confidence intervals and accurate results for each precinct in the state. Part IV also gives examples of data sets where existing methods are hopelessly biased, but the method offered here gives highly accurate estimates. For example, the best existing method indicates that 20% fewer males in South Carolina fall below the poverty level than there are males in that state (see Table 11.2 on page 220). In contrast, the method offered here gives accurate answers for this statewide aggregate (see Figure 11.2 on page 222) as well as for the fraction of males in poverty in each of the 3,187 precinct-sized geographic units (see Figure 11.3 on page 223).

The book also includes situations in which almost all information was aggregated away and standard methods give even more ridiculous results; in those cases, the method described here gives reasonable results with wider confidence intervals, reflecting accurately the degree of uncertainty in the ecological inference (see Chapter 12). The method usually even gives accurate estimates when all the conditions for "aggregation bias" are met, when the process of aggregation eliminates most of the variation in one of the aggregate variables, and when extrapolations far from the range of observed data are necessary. In all these difficult examples, the method offered here gives accurate answers with correct confidence intervals. The method will not always work: since information is lost during aggregation, no method of ecological inference could work in all data sets. However, the procedures introduced here come with diagnostics that researchers can use to evaluate the risks and avoid the problems in most cases.

Finally, I give a brief report of an analysis of 1990 turnout by race in New Jersey's 567 minor civil divisions (mostly cities and towns). These data cannot be used to verify ecological inferences since the true individual-level answers are not known, but they can be used

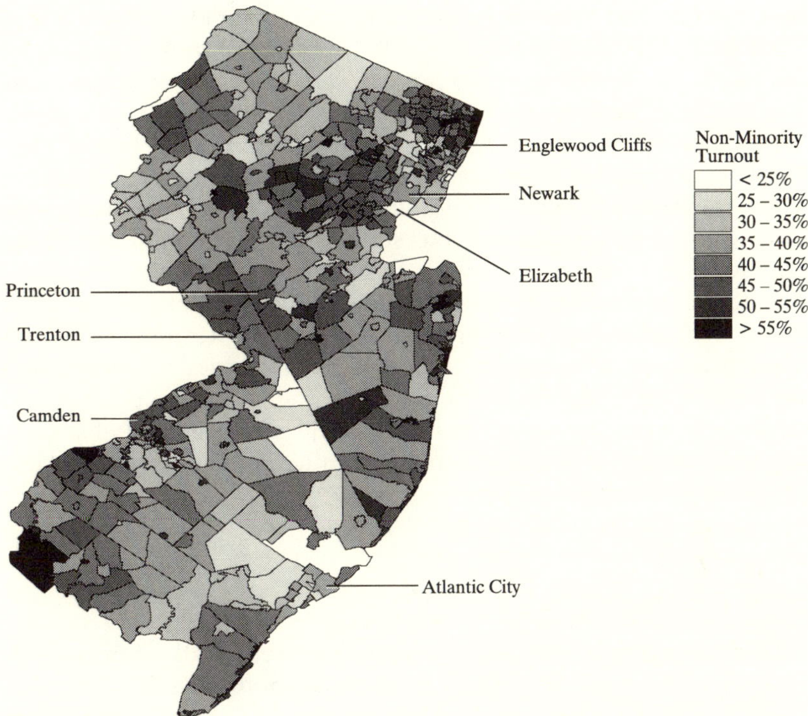

Figure 1.2 Non-Minority Turnout in New Jersey Cities and Towns. In contrast to the best existing methods, which provide *one* (incorrect) number for the entire state, the method offered here gives an accurate estimate of white turnout for all 567 minor civil divisions in the state, a few of which are labeled.

to demonstrate how much more information the method offered here provides to users. The most popular existing method (Goodman's regression) gives only two numbers of relevance, the state-wide fractions of blacks who vote and whites who vote (the latter estimate, incidentally, is five standard deviations above its maximum possible value given by the method of bounds). In contrast, the solution to the ecological inference problem offered here gives reliable estimates of these two numbers for the state-wide average as well as for each of the 567 cities and towns.

In order to emphasize the rich information this method unearths, Figure 1.2 maps the estimated degree of voter turnout among non-minorities. In this map, minor civil divisons in New Jersey are given darker shades when the estimated degree of non-minority voter turnout is higher. A few landmarks are labeled to give readers some bearing. The vast increase in information the method provides is represented by the interesting geographic variation in this map (and an *additional* complete map for minority turnout). For example, Figure 1.2 shows that non-minority turnout is substantially higher in the city of Newark than the neighboring city of Elizabeth. Is this because of a racial threat posed by Newark's larger minority population? Is the white mobilization in the wealthy towns of Bergen County near Englewood Cliffs a result of the state government's attempt to integrate schools by regionalizing its school districts? By providing reliable individual-level geographic-based information, the solution to the ecological inference problem can be used to raise numerous questions such as these. The method also provides opportunities for answering such questions by using the estimates provided as dependent variables in second-stage analyses (using, in this case, explanatory variables such as fraction minority population, or state attempts at integration).

1.5 The Method

This section gives a brief non-mathematical sketch of the nature of the basic model introduced. Although several approaches are discussed in the methodological literature, the only method of ecological inference widely used in practice is Goodman's model, which is based on a straightforward linear regression and effectively assumes that the quantities of interest (such as the proportion of blacks and whites who vote) are constant over all precincts (see Section 3.1). Allowing these quantities to vary over the precincts and estimating them all, as is done in this book, provides far more detailed information about the individual-level relationships, and moderately improves the overall results.

Applying the deterministic information from the method of bounds to each and every precinct-level quantity of interest provides very substantial improvements and makes inferences especially robust to aggregation bias. Goodman's regression does not restrict the quantities of interest (which are proportions) even to the [0,1] interval. Many have suggested modifying Goodman's regression by restricting these aggregate quantities of interest to this interval, but this results in implausible corner solutions and, more importantly, imposes no restrictions on any of the individual precinct quantities. In contrast, the method offered here uses the bounds on the quantities of interest in every precinct, most of which turn out in practice to be much narrower than [0,1]. Because, also, these bounds are known with certainty, this procedure adds a surprising amount of information to the statistical model.[15]

This combination of the precinct-level deterministic bounds with a statistical model unifies the two primary competing parts of the ecological inference literature. First, by treating each precinct in isolation, the method uses all available information to give a range of *possible* values for its precinct-level quantities of interest. Then, in order to close in further on the right answer, the statistical model "borrows strength" from all the other precincts in the data set to give the *probable* location of each true quantity of interest within its known deterministic bounds.

The method introduced also includes a model of variability that matches the patterns in real aggregate data and that is internally consistent even in the presence of areal units that are modified. This and other features provide another significant boost in the performance of the model. Extensions of the model allow for the model assumptions to be evaluated, modified, or dropped, and for several types of external information to be included. A fully nonparametric version is also provided.

Some features of the model are related in part to variable parameter models in econometrics (e.g., Swamy, 1971); empirical Bayesian models in statistics and biostatistics (Efron and Morris, 1973; Rubin, 1980; Breslow, 1990); Manski's (1995) approach to identification via parameter bounds; models of multiple imputation for missing values in surveys (Rubin, 1987) and for coarse data problems (Heitjan, 1989; Heitjan and Rubin, 1990); hierarchical linear models in education research (Bryk and Raudenbush, 1992); and "inverse problems" in tomographic imaging (Vardi et al., 1985; Johnstone and Silverman, 1990). The solution to the ecological inference problem offered here is also related to some statistical models for the aggregation of individual-level continuous variables developed in econometrics (Stoker, 1993), as described in Section 14.3.

[15] As an analogy, consider how much information could be added to the usual linear regression if we knew for certain a different narrow range within which each observation's $\hat{y}$ must fall.

CHAPTER 2

Formal Statement of the Problem

THIS CHAPTER formalizes the ecological inference problem as introduced in Chapter 1. It provides notation that will be used throughout the rest of the book and identifies the quantities of interest at each level of analysis (see also the Glossary of Symbols at page 313).

The ecological inference problem begins with a set of cross-tabulations for each of p aggregate units. Given the marginals from each of the p tables, the goal is to make inferences about the cells of each of the tables. The p cross-tabulations are usually from geographic units, such as precincts districts, or counties.[1] For electoral applications, choosing data in which all geographic units have the same candidates (such as precincts from the same district or counties from the same statewide election) is advisable so that election effects are controlled. The cross-tabulations could also be groups of survey respondents (such as the fractions of working-class and middle-class voters preferring the Labour party) in a series of independent cross-sections and for which we wish to estimate the transitions between groups.

All results and models in this book can be generalized to arbitrarily large contingency tables, as demonstrated in Section 8.4 and Chapter 15. The method of ecological inference introduced is also applicable to almost all types of aggregate data, and is not limited by substantive area. However, the method is capable of taking advantage of whatever additional substantive information is available about a specific ecological inference. In order to highlight the types of information to watch out for, I introduce the notation in this chapter and the model in the rest of the book in the context of a specific substantive example. This will also fix ideas and make it easier to follow the subsequent algebraic developments. The example causes no loss of generality, even though all applications have unique elements. The specific example is based on various aspects of race and voting, as introduced in Chapter 1. This example is real and has important practical, scholarly, legal, and public policy implications. Details about it appear throughout the book in order to give a better sense of how the arguments

[1] Wherever possible, I use notation that is mnemonic, and identify this in the text by underlying the relevant character in the corresponding word. Thus, in this case, p is mnemonic for precincts.

Race of Voting-Age Person	Voting Decision			
	Democrat	Republican	No Vote	
black	N_i^{bD}	N_i^{bR}	N_i^{bN}	N_i^b
white	N_i^{wD}	N_i^{wR}	N_i^{wN}	N_i^w
	N_i^D	N_i^R	N_i^N	N_i

Table 2.1 Basic Notation for Precinct i, $i = 1, \dots, p$. All items in this table are *counts* of the Number of people in each cell position. The two elements in each superscript refer to the row and column position, respectively, with mnemonics indicated by the underlined letter in the labels. The column and row marginals, which are sums of the elements in the corresponding row or column, are observed. The interior cell entries are the object of inference.

apply to similar problems in other empirical examples. Part IV analyzes real data from this particular example, and from a diverse variety of others.

Begin by delineating a formal version of Table 1.2 (page 14) for each of p individual precincts.[2] Table 2.1 provides some notation for observed data and unobserved quantities of interest.

This table describes a single precinct (or other geographic entity) labeled i from a data set of p precincts in a single electoral district (such as a state assembly seat). The table is based on a simple example with two variables, the race of the voting-age person (black or white, with "white" defined as non-black) and the voting decision (Democrat, Republican, or no vote).

Every symbol in Table 2.1 has a subscript i, referring to the ith precinct ($i = 1, \dots, p$). Each cell in Table 2.1 is a raw count of the number of people who fall in that cell. Superscripts refer to positions in the table (and thus values of the row and column variables, respectively). For example, N_i^{bD} is the Number of black persons of voting age casting a ballot for the Democratic candidate in precinct i. I denote

[2] In order to gather both race and electoral results, electoral precincts must be matched with census geography. This sometimes means that precincts must be aggregated to a slightly higher level. The Census Bureau calls these "voter tabulation districts" or VTDs, although it sometimes makes sense to use "places," "minor civil divisions," counties, school districts, or other census jurisdictions. I use the more familiar term "precincts" to refer to the lowest level of geography for which both variables can be collected within an electoral district.

Race of Voting-Age Person	Voting Decision: Democrat	Republican	*Subtotal* (*Turnout*)	No Vote	
black	λ_i^b	$1-\lambda_i^b$	β_i^b	$1-\beta_i^b$	X_i
white	λ_i^w	$1-\lambda_i^w$	β_i^w	$1-\beta_i^w$	$1-X_i$
	D_i		T_i	$1-T_i$	

Table 2.2 Alternative Notation for Precinct i. This table reexpresses the elements of Table 2.1 as *proportions*, and inserts an extra summary column for voter turnout. The goal is to estimate the quantities of interest, the fraction of blacks and whites who vote (β_i^b, β_i^w) and who vote for the Democratic candidate (λ_i^b, λ_i^w), from the aggregate variables, the fraction of voting-age people who are black (X_i), who vote (T_i), and who vote for the Democrat (D_i), along with the number of voting-age people (N_i).

aggregation by dropping the superscript or subscript corresponding to the dimension being summed. This includes column totals (such as the number of Republicans in precinct i, $N_i^R = N_i^{bR} + N_i^{wR}$), row totals (such as the number of blacks in precinct i, $N_i^b = N_i^{bD} + N_i^{bR} + N_i^{bN}$), and the number of voting-age people in the entire precinct (as indicated by the symbol in the bottom right corner of the table, N_i).

Although the basic ecological inference problem is described completely in Table 2.1, the following summaries of it will prove convenient for later analysis. First, denote the total number of blacks who Turn out to vote as $N_i^{bT} = N_i^{bD} + N_i^{bR}$, whites who Turn out as N_i^{wT}, and total Turnout as N_i^T. Then, Table 2.2 reexpresses all the counts as proportions, and also inserts a subtotal column between the "Republican" and "No vote" columns to refer to voter turnout proportions. The meaning of the proportion in the enclosed box in Table 2.2 corresponds to the count in the same position of each enclosed box in Table 2.1.

Table 2.3 is the final table of notation, and it is taken from the last three columns of Table 2.2. Whenever possible, this simpler 2×2 table serves as our running example, with variables black vs. white, and vote vs. no vote.

The key to the ecological inference problem is that researchers only observe the marginals in these tables—the final row (summarized by D_i and T_i) and final column (summarized by X_i), along with N_i:

- D_i Proportion of voting-age population choosing the Democratic candidate, N_i^D/N_i

Race of Voting-Age Person	Voting Decision		
	Vote	No Vote	
black	β_i^b	$1-\beta_i^b$	X_i
white	β_i^w	$1-\beta_i^w$	$1-X_i$
	T_i	$1-T_i$	

Table 2.3 Simplified Notation for Precinct i. This table was formed from the rightmost three columns of Table 2.2. The goal is to infer the quantities of interest, β_i^b (the fraction of blacks who vote) and β_i^w (the fraction of whites who vote), from the aggregate variables X_i (the fraction of voting-age people who are black) and T_i (the fraction of people who vote), along with N_i (the number of voting-age people).

T_i Proportion of voting-age population Turning out to vote, N_i^T/N_i
X_i Proportion of voting-age population who are black, N_i^b/N_i, an eXplanatory variable
N_i Number of people of voting age

The goal of ecological inference is to learn about the quantities within the body of the table on the basis of the information from the margins—to learn about the Greek letters, representing information at the individual level, from the information in the Roman letters, which stand for the aggregate data. The quantities of interest can be summarized by four parameters defined for each precinct i:

β_i^b Proportion of voting-age blacks who vote, N_i^{bT}/N_i^b
β_i^w Proportion of voting-age whites who vote, N_i^{wT}/N_i^w
λ_i^b Proportion of black voters choosing the Democratic candidate, N_i^{bD}/N_i^{bT}
λ_i^w Proportion of white voters choosing the Democratic candidate, N_i^{wD}/N_i^{wT}

When focusing on the pared-down Table 2.3, β_i^b and β_i^w are the only parameters of interest, and X_i, T_i, and N_i are the observed aggregate marginals.

Although the ultimate goal of ecological inference, and the problem solved in this book, is learning about these precinct-level parameters, virtually all previous scholars have limited their inquiry to learning about the quantities of interest averaged over all people in the voting-age population in the entire district. These aggregates may be obtained from the table either directly, by applying the precinct formulas to the district totals, or indirectly, by taking a *weighted* average of all p precinct parameters, where the weights are functions of the precincts' black or white voting-age populations. For example, the fraction of blacks voting in the entire district is computed either directly,

$$B^b = \frac{\sum_{i=1}^{p} N_i^{bT}}{N^b}$$

or indirectly,

$$= \frac{\sum_{i=1}^{p} N_i^b \beta_i^b}{N^b}$$

where the number of blacks of voting age in the entire district (that is, in all p precincts) is $N^b = \sum_{i=1}^{p} N_i^b$. The equivalence of these two expressions is obvious as expressed here (since $\beta_i^b = N_i^{bT}/N_i^b$), even though in the literature this weighted average is often confused with the unweighted average, which I denote as $\mathfrak{B}^b = \frac{1}{p}\sum_{i=1}^{p} \beta_i^b$. Since most analyses will be in terms of the precinct parameters, the appropriate weights are very important if interest shifts to the district-level parameters (about which more in Chapter 4).

The problem with ignoring the difference between the weighted B^b and unweighted $\mathfrak{B}^b$ is what we might call the *Manhattan Effect* due to this simple example: Suppose a researcher wishes to make an ecological inference about the fraction of blacks who support each candidate in a mayoral election in New York City. Because of the difficulties of matching electoral precincts and census geography in Manhattan (the largest of New York's five boroughs), it can not be broken down into smaller aggregate units, even though the rest of the city is broken into numerous precinct-sized units of about 700 people each. The problem is not only that that Manhattan's population is massive compared to any of the other units, but that it frequently votes differently from the rest of the city. Thus, weighting Manhattan's votes in making ecological inferences as equivalent to one 700-person precinct would discard an enormous amount of information and wreak havoc on any estimates of the city-wide proportion of blacks who vote for each candidate. The solution to the Manhattan Effect is to take into account the size of the population of each aggregate unit and to compute the weighted (B^b) rather than unweighted ($\mathfrak{B}^b$) average of the β_i^b's.

The four aggregate parameters of interest (using the corresponding upper case Greek letter in each case) include the district-wide fractions for blacks and whites who vote (B^b and B^w) and who vote for the Democrats (Λ^b and Λ^w). These are each expressed as weighted averages of the precinct-level parameters:

$$B^b = \sum_{i=1}^{p} \frac{N_i^b \beta_i^b}{N^b}, \qquad B^w = \sum_{i=1}^{p} \frac{N_i^w \beta_i^w}{N^w}$$

$$\Lambda^b = \sum_{i=1}^{p} \frac{N_i^{bT} \lambda_i^b}{N^{bT}}, \qquad \Lambda^w = \sum_{i=1}^{p} \frac{N_i^{wT} \lambda_i^w}{N^{wT}} \tag{2.1}$$

where the number of blacks and whites of voting age in the entire district (i.e., in all p precincts) are $N^b = \sum_{i=1}^{p} N_i^b$ and $N^w = \sum_{i=1}^{p} N_i^w$, respectively. These weighted averages do *not* equal the unweighted averages, except in the extremely unusual case where the black and white voting-age populations are identical within and across all precincts or, more generally, if the precinct parameters and the weights are independent. I also introduce notation for the unweighted average of β_i^w, in addition to that for β_i^b:

$$\mathfrak{B}^b = \frac{1}{p}\sum_{i=1}^{p} \beta_i^b, \qquad \mathfrak{B}^w = \frac{1}{p}\sum_{i=1}^{p} \beta_i^w \tag{2.2}$$

In general, we should be primarily interested in the precinct-level parameters (β_i^b, β_i^w, λ_i^b, and λ_i^w) in order to learn about geographic patterns in black and white turnout and voter support for each candidate and to extract the largest amount of information available from the ecological inference problem. These are the ultimate goals. However, it also makes sense to consider what district-wide summaries might be of interest. One possibility is the simple averages of the precinct-level parameters, $\mathfrak{B}^b$ and $\mathfrak{B}^w$ (and similarly for the λ_i's), but these are of little substantive interest (even though they will sometimes prove convenient in the following chapters as intermediate results). Precincts are usually of very different sizes and have boundaries that are convenient rather than politically relevant. Instead, the aggregate values of these parameters for all people in the district (B^b and B^w, as well as Λ^b, and Λ^w) are of considerable interest. In fact, the degree to which the average of the precinct parameters deviates from the population mean (that is, weighted average) is in part a result of the aggregation effects we would like to avoid.

Finally, I introduce θ_i^b (black vote for the Democratic candidate as proportion of the black voting-age population) and θ_i^w (white vote for the Democrat as a proportion of the white voting-age population).

$$\theta_i^b = \frac{N_i^{bD}}{N_i^b}, \qquad \theta_i^w = \frac{N_i^{wD}}{N_i^w} \tag{2.3}$$

These parameters are of no intrinsic interest, but they will prove useful in intermediate stages for calculating some parameters of interest (since $\lambda_i^b = \theta_i^b/\beta_i^b$ and $\lambda_i^w = \theta_i^w/\beta_i^w$). The weighted averages of these parameters will also prove useful:

$$\Theta^b = \sum_{i=1}^{p} \frac{N_i^b \theta_i^b}{N^b}, \qquad \Theta^w = \sum_{i=1}^{p} \frac{N_i^w \theta_i^w}{N^w} \tag{2.4}$$

PART II

Catalog of Problems to Fix

This part delineates the problems with current methods of ecological inference and provides motivation for features of the solution proposed in Part III. Chapter 3 demonstrates that the diverse list of problems identified in the literature as causes or consequences of aggregation bias are all mathematically equivalent, the result being that only one aggregation problem needs to be solved to make valid ecological inferences. Chapter 4 summarizes basic statistical problems unrelated to aggregation bias that must also be resolved to make valid ecological inferences.

CHAPTER 3

Aggregation Problems

THIS CHAPTER summarizes two sets of approaches to understanding the bias and information loss due to aggregation. Although much of the literature gives the impression that the problems discussed in each set are different, this chapter proves that they are mathematically equivalent (cf. Hannan and Burstein, 1974, and Smith, 1977). For those unfamiliar with the literature who may not have had this impression in the first place, the chapter also reviews some of the relevant prior work.

The most widely used statistical approach to ecological inference, *Goodman's regression,* is defined in Section 3.1. Most statistical approaches to ecological inference are based in some way on this model. Several versions of the *indeterminacy problem* are discussed and shown to be equivalent in Section 3.2, and similarly for the *grouping problem* in Section 3.3. The equivalence of the two is proven in Section 3.4. Having both approaches is useful for understanding the same problem from different perspectives, but knowing that they are the identical problem means that only one problem needs to be solved. These results also help to illuminate the problem and lead to its solution.

To foreshadow the results from Part III, even the encouraging evidence given in this chapter—that all aggregation problems reduce to a single problem—is far more pessimistic than necessary. For there exists considerable information in aggregate data ignored by existing statistical methods (such as the known bounds on the precinct-level parameters and dramatic levels of heteroskedasticity) to resolve what appears to be indeterminate or not identified under the Goodman framework discussed in this chapter. Part IV demonstrates that the solution proposed is robust even to high levels of aggregation bias, and even without introducing special techniques to cope with it. The result proven in this chapter also makes possible an extended ecological inference model (introduced in Chapter 9) that is useful in cases where an explicit approach to aggregation bias is necessary.

3.1 Goodman's Regression: A Definition

Leo Goodman introduced his approach in 1953, only three years after Robinson's article appeared. The dominance of this approach in academic analyses in the subsequent four decades is a testimony to the innovativeness of the approach and difficulty of improving on it (Goodman, 1953a, 1959). Indeed, along with double regression, which is discussed in Chapter 4, this procedure has been the most frequently used method of ecological inference by expert witnesses in voting rights cases since the U.S. Supreme Court endorsed the use of it in the case leading to *Thornburg v. Gingles* (1986). Goodman's (1959) article even anticipates many of the subsequent developments in the literature, and as a result essentially every method proposed since Goodman's incorporates or generalizes his approach.

Goodman avoided the empirical problems that can occur with his model by recommending that it not be used when his assumptions are not met. Unfortunately, despite these clear warnings in his original work, subsequent researchers chose to boldly go where Goodman had not gone before, or since. Lacking a satisfactory alternative for making ecological inferences, and because the empirical applicability of the assumptions were usually questionable, they frequently applied his model when the assumptions underlying it were inappropriate. Thus, although I follow the convention in the literature of referring to "Goodman's regression," it should probably be called "Goodman's regression when Goodman's assumptions are not met."

In terms of the notation in Table 2.3, Goodman's method involves a regression of T_i (proportion of the voting-age population turning out to vote) on X_i (proportion of the voting-age population who are black) and $(1 - X_i)$ (proportion who are white), with no constant term. The coefficients from this least squares regression, $\hat{B}^b$ and $\hat{B}^w$, are intended to be estimates of the district aggregates B^b (the fraction of blacks who vote) and B^w (the fraction of whites who vote) since the precinct-level parameters β_i^b and β_i^w are assumed constant over precincts.

If it seems confusing to have both X_i and $(1 - X_i)$ in the same regression equation, we can get the same estimates in a more familiar way. First run a regression of T_i on a constant term and X_i, and get coefficients $\hat{B}^w$ and $\hat{B}$. Then reparameterize to yield $\hat{B}^w$ and $\hat{B}^b = \hat{B} + \hat{B}^w$. Although the two approaches give identical results, I usually use the regression with X_i and $(1 - X_i)$ and no constant term because its coefficients $\hat{B}^b$ and $\hat{B}^w$ are somewhat more intuitive than $\hat{B}$ and $\hat{B}^w$.

Goodman's regression is based loosely on the following accounting identity:

$$T_i = \beta_i^b X_i + \beta_i^w (1 - X_i) \tag{3.1}$$

This expression is true by the definitions given in Table 2.3. The equation is linear, but no assumption of linearity is required, at least in the sense that the word "assumption" in common usage refers to not entirely verifiable restrictions on the model. In contrast, this equation is entirely verifiable, even without data.[1]

Goodman's regression does not produce estimates of β_i^b and β_i^w unless they really are constant for all i. Moreover, as demonstrated below, the regression coefficients are not even estimates of the correct district-level quantities of interest, B^b and B^w.[2] Goodman's model also does not include information from the method of bounds, or even the basic information that the parameters of interest are proportions and thus can only range between zero and one.

3.2 The Indeterminacy Problem

Because the basic accounting identity in Equation 3.1 has twice as many unknowns ($2p$) as observations (p), that is β_i^b and β_i^w for each of p precincts, computing unrestricted estimates of all unknowns seems hopeless. The Goodman model resolves the proliferation of parameters by making the extreme "constancy assumption": $\beta_i^b = B^b$ and $\beta_i^w = B^w$ for all i. If this assumption is appropriate, then Equation 3.1

[1] Proving that the equation holds requires substituting in raw counts in Table 2.1 for definitions of the right side variables in Equation 3.1 and showing that they equal the definition of the variable on the left side. Thus,

$$T_i = \beta_i^b X_i + \beta_i^w (1 - X_i) = \frac{N_i^{bT}}{N_i^b}\frac{N_i^b}{N_i} + \frac{N_i^{wT}}{N_i^w}\frac{N_i^w}{N_i} = \frac{N_i^T}{N_i}$$

The right side of this proof is the definition of T_i.

[2] Better than assuming constant parameters, as does Goodman's basic model and much of the subsequent literature, is his alternative suggestion that allows parameters to vary, but requires them to be independent of X_i, what Duncan et al. (1961: 70ff) call "practically constant." However, even if this assumption were true in an application, the heteroskedasticity that this specification implies, and the varying numbers of people per precinct (problems analyzed in Chapter 4), are still not taken into account. Thus, even with this alternative model justification, Goodman's regression does not estimate of the correct theoretical quantities of interest. In other words, Goodman's regression estimates are unbiased only if β_i^b and β_i^w are independent of X_i *and* N_i. Without independence of the quantities of interest and N_i, Goodman's regression is estimating $\mathfrak{B}^b$ and $\mathfrak{B}^w$ instead of the correct B^b and B^w. Moreover, even if these empirically demanding assumptions were met in an application, the estimates would still be inefficient and the standard errors inconsistent, except in lucky coincidences or if β_i^b and β_i^w were really constant over all precincts.

becomes manageable, since it has only two parameters:

$$T_i = B^b X_i + B^w(1 - X_i) \tag{3.2}$$

The problem is that if the assumption is wrong, as can be demonstrated with aggregate data alone in all known data sets (see Chapter 4), the answers this model produces will often be wrong.

The problem is that if the parameters do vary, and they turn out to be correlated with X_i, ordinary regression will not produce estimates of the average of these parameters (or any other relevant aggregate quantity). Figure 3.1 provides some intuition about this result through a simple example. Each graph in this figure has four data points. Each point corresponds to a particular precinct with actual values X_i and T_i (where $T_i = \beta_i^b X_i + \beta_i^w(1 - X_i)$). The line through each point shows the theoretical relationship between T_i and X_i that would arise were the parameters (β_i^b, β_i^w) held constant but the value of X_i were allowed to vary from zero to one. The lines from which the points are selected are identical in both graphs. In the left graph, the slope of the lines is uncorrelated with the value of X_i at each observed point, but in the right graph points with larger values of X_i have lines with steeper slopes. The goal is to estimate a regression line from the points alone that is the average of the individual lines (represented as the dark solid line in both graphs). Since the lines for the observations are the same in the two graphs, the average line we wish to estimate is the same in both. This same dark line on the left is also exactly the regression line fit to its four points, which is an example of unbiased regression estimates that result when the slopes and X_i are uncorrelated. On the right graph, the dashed line is the regression line fit to its points, but because X_i and the slopes are correlated, it is a biased estimate of the (dark solid) average line.

Another way to understand aggregation bias is in terms of our running example. Suppose we observe that turnout (T_i) is lower in heavily black areas (X_i). If aggregation bias were not an issue, we could conclude that black turnout (B^b) is lower than white turnout (B^w). However, we would be fooled by aggregation bias using this procedure if whites in heavily black precincts turn out at disproportionately higher levels than whites in other areas, as might occur if whites mobilize in response to a perceived black "threat." We would also be fooled by aggregation bias if whites in heavily black areas turn out at disproportionately lower levels, as might occur if whites in these areas have no serious chance of electing their candidates of choice. In the first case B^w would be overestimated and B^b underestimated; in

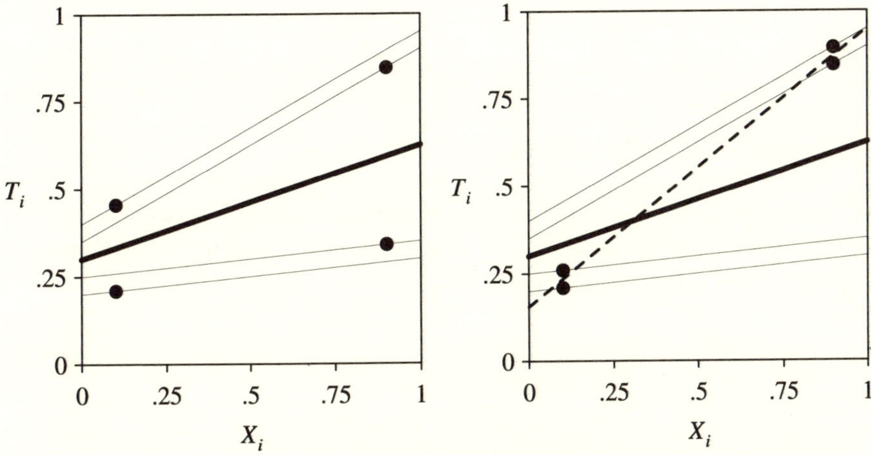

Figure 3.1 How a Correlation between the Parameters and X_i Induces Bias. Each observed point in these graphs appears with its (usually unobserved) line. The thin lines from which the points were drawn are identical in the two graphs, as is the average (dark solid) line, which is the goal of the estimation. In the left graph, the zero correlation between the slopes of the lines and the value of X_i for the corresponding points cause the regression line fit to the points to be coincident with the average line. However, because the lines are steeper for points with larger values of X_i in the right graph, the (dashed) regression line is a biased estimate of the (dark solid) average line.

the second case, B^w would be underestimated and B^b overestimated.[3] In both cases, a correlation between the fraction black (X_i) and the precinct-level parameters of interest (β_i^b and β_i^w) can confound naive analyses that ignore aggregation bias.

A possible solution to parameter variation being correlated with X_i might be to model the dependence directly (and hence control for it) by letting the parameters vary as linear functions of X_i, as has been considered by many scholars (e.g., Duncan et al., 1961: 77–79; Rosenthal, 1973; Iversen, 1973; Przeworski, 1974; Shively, 1985). The assumption (where the superscripts c and s stand for the constant and

[3] In the voting behavior literature, this relationship is sometimes labeled "contextual effects" or "breakage effects," as for example when the vote among Republicans in heavily Republican areas breaks for the Republican candidate even more strongly than the vote among Republicans does in more Democratic areas. See Berelson, Lazarsfeld, and McPhee (1954: Chapter 7), Putnam (1966), Sprague (1976, 1982), Huckfeldt and Sprague (1987), and Shively (1985).

slope, respectively) is then:

$$\beta_i^b = \alpha^c + \alpha^s X_i$$

$$\beta_i^w = \gamma^c + \gamma^s X_i. \tag{3.3}$$

Given this model, the aggregate quantities of interest (the district-wide fractions of blacks and whites who vote) are the weighted averages of Equations 3.3:

$$B^b = \frac{\sum_{i=1}^p N_i^b \beta_i^b}{N^b} = \alpha^c + \alpha^s \sum_{i=1}^p \frac{N_i^b X_i}{N^b}$$

$$B^w = \frac{\sum_{i=1}^p N_i^w \beta_i^w}{N^w} = \gamma^c + \gamma^s \sum_{i=1}^p \frac{N_i^w X_i}{N^w} \tag{3.4}$$

Thus, in order to estimate the aggregate parameters of interest from this model, one must estimate all four parameters in these equations (α^c, α^s, γ^c, and γ^s).

Substituting Equations 3.3 into Equation 3.1 reveals the model that these assumptions imply:

$$T_i = (\alpha^c + \alpha^s X_i)X_i + (\gamma^c + \gamma^s X_i)(1 - X_i)$$

$$= \gamma^c + (\alpha^c + \gamma^s - \gamma^c)X_i + (\alpha^s - \gamma^s)X_i^2$$

$$= (\alpha^c + \gamma^s)X_i + \gamma^c(1 - X_i) + (\alpha^s - \gamma^s)X_i^2 \tag{3.5}$$

This equation reveals the indeterminacy problem: four parameters must be estimated in order to learn about the quantities of interest, but only three are identified by this equation (which would be estimated by the three coefficients from a regression of T_i on a constant term, X_i, and X_i^2, or a regression of T_i on X_i, $1 - X_i$, and X_i^2 without a constant term). We can restrict the parameter space somewhat by noting that many data analyses find no evidence of nonlinearity. However, even if the quadratic term were dropped (the last term in the equation) or equivalently, if one assumed $\alpha^s - \gamma^s = 0$, the equation remains unidentified: the number of parameters is still one more than can be estimated.

Shively (1985) shows how to use non-sample information creatively to make assumptions about these parameters, thus restricting the parameter space and making the remaining parameters estimable. When such information exists, this approach can be valuable. In other cases, it may help to specify limits on the parameters of interest. Unfortunately, in most other cases, the indeterminacy remains. In fact, although external information may be available for a few precincts, or perhaps only for the district aggregate, most analysts will feel uncomfortable making untestable precinct-level assumptions for all p precincts. Indeed, the ecological inference literature does not offer a *single* such example of an assumption an analyst is willing to make about all observations in a real data set.

A second line of argument in the literature comes from Freedman et al. (1991). They develop a new model in order to critique the constancy assumption of Goodman's regression. However, their model turns out to be a special case of the quadratic model, and thus the problems they identify are equivalent to the indeterminacy problems identified above. Their "linear neighborhood model" assumes (1) the absence of racially polarized voting and (2) that voter preferences (of both blacks and whites) are a linear function of the racial composition of the precinct. This implies the following specialization of the quadratic model from Equation 3.5:

$$\beta_i^b = \beta_i^w = \alpha^c + \alpha^s X_i \tag{3.6}$$

It may seem odd that Freedman et al. are assuming the answer to their question. But their goal as expert witnesses in court (and in the article which resulted) was primarily to destroy confidence in Goodman's regression model. They were not interested in producing a useful model. In fact, this model can be ruled out on theoretical grounds alone, even without data, since the assumptions are not invariant to the districting plan. That is, although the assumption might hold for one set of precincts, it cannot simultaneously hold for any reaggregation of precincts, except in rare coincidences (cf. the analysis in Section 14.1). Moreover, the assumption that voting behavior is not racially polarized, despite the many differences within each racial group, contradicts solid empirical evidence from decades of survey and qualitative research.

Freedman et al. use their model to demonstrate the indeterminacy problem with Goodman's model by proving that these two very different models (assuming some degree of racially polarized voting, and assuming that none exists) lead to identical observable consequences, which I now describe.[4]

By substituting Equation 3.6 into Equation 3.1, the resulting model is:

$$\begin{aligned} T_i &= [\alpha^c + \alpha^s X_i]X_i + [\alpha^c + \alpha^s X_i](1 - X_i) \\ &= \alpha^c + \alpha^s X_i \\ &= (\alpha^s + \alpha^c)X_i + \alpha^c(1 - X_i) \end{aligned} \tag{3.7}$$

Freedman et al.'s point becomes clear by comparing the last line of this equation with Equation 3.2: the two models are observationally equivalent, but unfortunately the regression coefficients B^b and B^w from Goodman's model, and α^c and $\alpha^s + \alpha^c$ from this model, have very different meanings. For example, B^w is the districtwide fraction of whites who vote, but α^c (from Equation 3.6) is the fraction of only those whites living in all-white precincts who vote.

What Freedman et al. have shown is that changing the assumption produces a model with the same functional form, the same parameters, and a regression with numerically identical estimates. However, the meaning of the parameters is radically different. Yet, no information appears to exist in these data with which to decide which model one is using when regressing T_i on X_i and $(1 - X_i)$. *The answer depends entirely on the assumption, and the assumption is empirically unverifiable.* (In fact, as described in Chapter 9, information does exist in these data to resolve this indeterminacy problem if, unlike the Freedman et al. and Goodman approaches, the known precinct bounds and heteroskedasticity are also taken into account. Indeed, Sections 9.2.2–9.2.4, demonstrate how even the full quadratic model in Equation 3.5 can be estimated without indeterminacy.)

A third line of argument in the literature further illuminates this indeterminacy problem from a different perspective. Ansolabehere and Rivers (1994) creatively reformulate a known, but not widely under-

[4] Although under this model $\beta_i^b = \beta_i^w$ in every precinct, the weighted averages of these quantities across precincts are not necessarily equal. Thus, aggregate levels of racially polarized voting need not be zero in the neighborhood model (although the possible range of variation is less than 0%–100%; see Grofman, 1991b). Indeed Freedman et al. (1991) show that in some cases this model produces more accurate estimates than Goodman's regression model. Ansolabehere and Rivers (1994) provide some additional empirical evidence. In my experience, including most of the data analyzed in this book, Freedman et al.'s estimates are distant from the true values, even though they are sometimes closer than Goodman's.

stood, result (see Duncan, et al., 1961; Alker, 1969). For mathematical convenience, they use the the weighted least squares estimate of racially polarized voting from Goodman's regression, with weights based on population size (about which more in Chapter 4). This is the difference between the two coefficients, which I denote as $\check{B} = \check{B}^b - \check{B}^w$. (Thus, I use $\hat{B}$ for least squares estimates and $\check{B}$ for weighted least squares estimates.) This estimate is intended to correspond to the true level of racially polarized voting, $B = B^b - B^w$. Their paper is concerned with interpreting the Discrepancy between the estimate and true value:

$$\mathbf{D}(\check{B})_1 = \check{B} - B \tag{3.8}$$

Because this discrepancy is a simple function of the discrepancies for each individual coefficient, focusing on racially polarized voting does not sacrifice anything.[5]

Ansolabehere and Rivers show that the discrepancy in Equation 3.8 is a linear function of three unobserved slope coefficients from the regressions of β_i^b on X_i (which I denote as b_{bx}), β_i^w on X_i (denoted b_{wx}), and $\beta_i \equiv (\beta_i^b - \beta_i^w)$ on $h_i \equiv X_i(1 - X_i)$ (denoted b_{rh}). (Under the quadratic model, the difference is a function of only the first two slopes.) By rearranging the algebra somewhat, their result is equivalent to the following:

$$\mathbf{D}(\check{B})_1 = A_1 b_{bx} + A_2 b_{wx} - A_3 b_{rh} \tag{3.9}$$

The coefficients A_1, A_2, and A_3 are all calculable from aggregate data:

$$A_1 = \frac{F\sigma_x^2}{\bar{X}}, \quad A_2 = \frac{F\sigma_x^2}{1 - \bar{X}}, \quad A_3 = \frac{\sigma_h^2}{\sigma_x^2} \tag{3.10}$$

[5] That is, $\mathbf{D}(\check{B}^b)_1 = \check{B}^b - B^b = (1 - \bar{X})\mathbf{D}(\check{B})_1$ and $\mathbf{D}(\check{B}^w)_1 = \check{B}^w - B^w = -\bar{X}\mathbf{D}(\check{B})_1$, where the weighted mean of X_i is $\bar{X} = \frac{1}{N}\sum_{i=1}^p N_i X_i$, and N is the number of people in the entire district. Ansolabehere and Rivers use different notation. They also define what I call the discrepancy, $\mathbf{D}(\check{B}) = \check{B} - B$, to be the "bias" of $\check{B}$, although this is a nonstandard use of the term "bias." As they recognize, the problem is that the concept of bias requires an average over some type of random variability. Since ecological inferences do not involve sampling, we must be careful to identify the source of the random variability. Fortunately, in most applications of ecological regression—in academia, in court, and in public policy—the researcher has access to data from many districts and often from several offices and election years, and runs analyses on all the precincts within each district and race separately. Thus, one way to define the randomness in the data is the variation in parameters across these closely related data sets.

where the weighted mean and variance of any precinct-level variable a_i are $\bar{a} = \frac{1}{N}\sum_{i=1}^{p} N_i a_i$ and $\sigma_a^2 = \frac{1}{N}\sum_{i=1}^{p} N_i(a_i - \bar{a})^2$, respectively, and where $\eta^2 = \sigma_x^2/\bar{X}(1-\bar{X})$ is the ratio of aggregate variance to individual-level variance, and $F = \frac{1}{\eta^2} - 1$.

This result is entirely deterministic. After all, if we knew $\check{B} - B$, we would be able to calculate, and would not need to estimate, B. However, the expression helps to clarify the indeterminacy assumption since a method of ecological inference would be unbiased only if each of the unobserved slopes, b_{bx}, b_{wx}, and b_{rh}, were zero on average. That is, the Ansolabehere-Rivers result is another especially concise way of showing that the parameter variation must be unrelated to X_i in order to avoid bias, and it does so without any additional assumptions.[6] Put differently, any use of Goodman's regression must be accompanied by arguments, based on qualitative information or quantitative data other than X_i and T_i, that each of these slopes is zero (or the terms in Equation 3.9 cancel out). Since this type of information is rarely available, Goodman's regression is rarely applicable.

3.3 The Grouping Problem

In this section, I describe an alternative approach to the causes of aggregation bias that has been studied and gradually improved by many generations of scholars. This *grouping* or *clustering* approach formalizes the same parameters of interest in terms of unobserved variables at the level of individual voters. The basic estimation formulas would be correct at this individual level if data were available. The data and formulas are then aggregated into precincts, and a formal analysis demonstrates the types of aggregation that induce bias when using only aggregate data to make inferences.

To begin, define the individual-level variable $\mathbb{X}_{ij}$ (corresponding to the district-level variable X_i) as 1 if voting-age person j in precinct i is black and 0 if white ($i = 1, \ldots, p$; $j = 1, \ldots, N_i$). Let $\mathbb{T}_{ij}$ equal 1 if a person votes and 0 otherwise. Define ($N \times 1$) stacked vectors $\mathbb{X} = \{\mathbb{X}_{ij}\}$, $\mathbb{T} = \{\mathbb{T}_{ij}\}$, and $\dot{\mathbb{T}} = \mathbb{T} - \bar{T}$, where $\bar{T}$ is the weighted average

[6] Achen and Shively (1995: 105) also discuss this result. In addition, they (1995: 84, 90) give an expression for the discrepancy that is (essentially) a special case of Equation 3.9, where β_i^b and β_i^w are assumed to follow specific deterministic nonlinear functions of X_i. Unfortunately, their analyses are of theoretical but not practical interest because the unusual functions chosen do not fit the patterns in any known data sets.

of T_i (turnout in precinct i) or equivalently the simple average of $\mathbb{T}_{ij}$:

$$\bar{T} = \frac{1}{N}\sum_{i=1}^{p} N_i T_i$$
$$= \frac{1}{N}\sum_{i=1}^{p}\sum_{j=1}^{N_i}\mathbb{T}_{ij} \tag{3.11}$$

and similarly for $\dot{\mathbb{X}} = \mathbb{X} - \bar{X}$.

In order to aggregate, define the $(N \times p)$ Grouping matrix $\mathbb{G}$ as having an indicator variable in each column that codes in which precinct each voting age person lives (e.g., the fourth column has a 1 for each person in Precinct 4 and 0 for all other people). Then, if what is sometimes known as the Hat (or y-hat) matrix, $\mathbb{H} = \mathbb{G}(\mathbb{G}'\mathbb{G})^{-1}\mathbb{G}'$, is multiplied into a vector defined at the individual level, then each observation is replaced with its precinct mean. (This is equivalent to regressing the individual-level vector on the variables in $\mathbb{G}$ and computing the fitted values.)[7]

Focus now on $B = B^b - B^w$ as the parameter of interest, which is related to the data as follows:

$$\dot{\mathbb{T}} = \dot{\mathbb{X}}B + e \tag{3.12}$$

where $e = \dot{\mathbb{T}} - \dot{\mathbb{X}}B$. Then least squares applied to this individual-level equation gives exactly B, the parameter of interest, not merely an estimate thereof. That is, because the individual data are available, no uncertainty remains about the cells of the cross-tabulation and B is computed exactly via least squares. In fact, least squares is merely an algebraic convenience here, and is equivalent to doing a cross-tabulation and reading off the answer.

To aggregate, I follow the strategy first suggested in print by Prais and Aitchison (1954) and subsequently followed and improved by many other scholars (e.g., Hannan and Burstein, 1974; Smith, 1977; and Firebaugh, 1978). That is, first premultiply by $\mathbb{H}$, giving

$$\mathbb{H}\dot{\mathbb{T}} = \mathbb{H}\dot{\mathbb{X}}B + \mathbb{H}e.$$

[7] Readers who find "between and within" variance notation intuitive can generate the results in this section without matrices by modifying standard analysis of variance formulas (see Alker, 1969).

With this calculation, the data are aggregated, since each observation has been replaced by the precinct mean, but the unit of analysis is still the individual person. As a result, a *least squares* regression of the individual level variable $\mathbb{H}\dot{\mathbb{T}}$ on $\mathbb{H}\dot{\mathbb{X}}$, is equivalent to a *weighted least squares* regression of the precinct averages T_i on X_i. Either calculation gives the coefficient $\check{B}$. The key result of the grouping perspective can be seen by deriving a new expression for this coefficient:

$$\begin{aligned}\check{B} &= [(\mathbb{H}\dot{\mathbb{X}})'(\mathbb{H}\dot{\mathbb{X}})]^{-1}(\mathbb{H}\dot{\mathbb{X}})'(\mathbb{H}\dot{\mathbb{T}})\\ &= (\dot{\mathbb{X}}'\mathbb{H}\dot{\mathbb{X}})^{-1}\dot{\mathbb{X}}'\mathbb{H}(\dot{\mathbb{X}}B + e)\\ &= B + (\dot{\mathbb{X}}'\mathbb{H}\dot{\mathbb{X}})^{-1}\dot{\mathbb{X}}'\mathbb{H}e\\ &= B + \frac{\mathrm{C}(\mathbb{H}\dot{\mathbb{X}}, \mathbb{H}e)}{\mathrm{V}(\mathbb{H}\dot{\mathbb{X}})}\\ &= B + \frac{\mathbf{C}(X_i, e_i)}{\mathbf{V}(X_i)}\end{aligned}$$

since $\mathbb{H}'\mathbb{H} = \mathbb{H}\mathbb{H} = \mathbb{H}$ (the property of some matrices known as idempotency) and where $\mathbf{V}(a_i) = \mathbf{C}(a_i, a_i)$ is the weighted variance.[8]

Finally, express the discrepancy $\check{B} - B$ as

$$\mathbf{D}(\check{B})_2 = \frac{\mathbf{C}(X_i, e_i)}{\mathbf{V}(X_i)} \tag{3.13}$$

This discrepancy $\mathbf{D}(\check{B})_2$ is zero when at the individual level $\mathbb{H}\dot{\mathbb{X}}$ is uncorrelated with $\mathbb{H}e$: $\mathrm{C}(\mathbb{H}\dot{\mathbb{X}}, \mathbb{H}e) = 0$. This condition is equivalent to a zero value for the weighted covariance at the aggregate level, $\mathbf{C}(X_i, e_i) = 0$. Since at the individual level $\mathrm{C}(\dot{\mathbb{X}}, e) = 0$ by definition, only the aggregation (via $\mathbb{H}$) can induce the covariance between the aggregate variables $\mathbf{C}(X_i, e_i)$ to deviate from zero. That is, *the cause of the discrepancy is the aggregation induced by the precinct boundaries*, as formalized by $\mathbb{H}$.

[8] To be more specific, for precinct-level variables a_i and b_i, define their weighted covariance as $\mathbf{C}(a, b) = \frac{1}{N}\sum_{i=1}^{p} N_i(a_i - \bar{a})(b_i - \bar{b})$, where the weighted mean of any variable a_i is $\bar{a} = \frac{1}{N}\sum_{i=1}^{p} N_i a_i$. See also Appendix A.

At least since Hanushek, Jackson, and Kain (1974) (and in part since Ogburn and Goltra, 1919), the literature has included much discussion about whether the ecological inference problem can be solved by including extra variables in the aggregate equation so that the corresponding individual-level equation would be "correctly specified." For example, Achen and Shively (1995: 114) disagree that extra variables are of much help and conclude, on the basis of a version of Equation 3.13, that "proper specification of micro-regressions is a necessary but not sufficient step toward achieving unbiased estimation of the corresponding macroregression models." However, the concept of a "correctly specified" individual-level equation is not helpful in this context, since individual data contain the answer in ecological inference problems with certainty. That is, with individual data, we would not need to specify any equation; we would merely construct the cross-tabulation and read off the answer. Having extra variables around if individual-level data are available would provide no additional assistance. Thus, "proper specification of micro-regressions" is not a necessary condition for eliminating aggregation bias. That is, whatever is generating the individual-level data can be ignored, so long as the precinct boundaries do not induce a correlation between X_i and e_i. Because ecological inferences require no causal assumptions, even aggregate procedures that make use of causally incorrect "superpopulation models" for unobserved individual data (i.e., models from which we imagine the individual data being generated) can thus sometimes produce unbiased inferences. The point of these extra variables is not to match some hypothetical individual-level causal model, but rather to attempt to control for the correlation induced by the precinct boundaries—to reduce or eliminate the discrepancy caused by the correlation between X_i and e_i in Equation 3.13. For the purpose of reducing this correlation, extra variables can be of enormous assistance (about which more in Section 9.2.1).

Thus, asking for the cause of aggregation bias (i.e., a nonzero discrepancy) is equivalent to asking for the conditions under which precinct boundaries induce a correlation between X_i and e_i. Three logical possibilities are generally considered, the last two of which cause problems (see Blalock, 1964; Hammond, 1973).

First, if precincts are drawn in order to maximize racial segregation (i.e., based on $\mathbb{X}$), then grouping causes no bias. That is, the expectation of the discrepancy is zero, and even the discrepancy is usually close to zero. At the extreme, if all precincts are either homogeneously black or white, nothing is lost by the process of aggregation and the discrepancy is always zero. Even when this extreme case does not occur, grouping via racial segregation is the optimal method of grouping, if a choice is available.[9]

A second possibility is grouping based on a random variable, or one unrelated to $\mathbb{X}$ or e. In this case, X_i and e_i will be uncorrelated on average, but the discrepancy in any one analysis may often be far from zero. In other words, random grouping produces no bias but a huge level of relative inefficiency, which grows with the number of people per precinct (Cramer, 1964). This result helps to emphasize, in a way that was more difficult from the perspective of the indeterminacy problem, that aggregate units with fewer people per unit will usually have less risk of bias. At the extreme, with one person per precinct, there is no aggregation, there can be no aggregation bias, and the efficiency of the micro and macro regressions are identical.

A final possibility is grouping based on the dependent variable, $\dot{\mathbb{T}}$ in the present case. This form of grouping causes bias. By Equation 3.12, $\dot{\mathbb{T}}$ is a linear function of $\mathbb{X}$ and e. As such, grouping on $\dot{\mathbb{T}}$ is equivalent to grouping based on $\mathbb{X}$ and e simultaneously. This means that grouping based on $\dot{\mathbb{T}}$ will tend to produce precincts composed of people high on both $\mathbb{X}$ and e or low on both. Thus, grouping on the dependent variable induces a correlation between $\mathbb{X}$ and e and therefore generates aggregation bias. In fact, grouping on most other functions of $\mathbb{X}$ and e produces bias for similar reasons.[10]

To put it in the terms of our running example, bias is induced when the aggregates are drawn based on voter turnout. When making inferences about λ_i^b and λ_i^w, bias is induced by grouping based on voter preferences. Thus, this perspective suggests an important conclusion: scholars should be especially cautious in using available methods of ecological inference when the smallest aggregate units are districts drawn on the basis of partisan criteria such as the large number of state legislative and U.S. House of Representatives electoral systems

[9] This method of grouping is optimal from the perspective of minimizing aggregation bias, not necessarily from the perspective of precinct residents! Optimal grouping is an important concern to those collecting and summarizing government statistics for publication in a convenient manner that does not induce bias (David Cox, 1957; Orcutt, Watts, and Edwards, 1968), minimizes information loss (Marksjö, 1984), or best communicates its information content (Fisher, 1969; Leamer, 1990). The opposite problem, what might be called "minimally optimal grouping," is also an important area of research for those distributing data. The question is how to aggregate or suppress data in order to protect individuals from statistical disclosure while still providing useful information to researchers (e.g., Lawrence Cox, 1995).

[10] If $B < 0$, then grouping on $\dot{\mathbb{T}}$ means creating precincts based on high values of $\mathbb{X}$ and low values of e, or low values of $\mathbb{X}$ and high values of e. This technicality aside, the result is still the same: grouping on the dependent variable biases inferences in the same way as selecting observations on the dependent variable does.

that have been redistricted by partisans (Gelman and King, 1994a, b); these data should be avoided when possible for making electoral inferences with standard techniques. If such districts are the only data available, then the researchers should consider taking specific steps to correct for possible aggregation bias (see Chapter 9). Moreover, districts in other jurisdictions that were not drawn by partisans may still unfairly favor one party or the other (King, 1990). Fortunately, the equivalent of precincts in most countries are not often the subject of intentional gerrymandering and are smaller.[11] Ecological inferences based on precinct data or arbitrary units such as counties or other Census Bureau categories may therefore be somewhat more reliable.

I now complete this discussion of grouping-induced bias by presenting the newest, and exceptionally clear, statement of the grouping problem given by Palmquist (1993, 1994) who built upon results in this literature, especially Duncan et al. (1961:66) and most recently Erbring (1989).

Recalling that the individual-level regression gives exactly the parameter of interest, and defining $\mathbb{M} = I - \mathbb{H}$ and $C_1 = (\dot{\mathbb{X}}'\mathbb{H}\dot{\mathbb{X}})(\dot{\mathbb{X}}'\mathbb{H}\dot{\mathbb{X}})^{-1}$, we decompose the parameter of interest as follows:

$$\begin{aligned}
B &= (\dot{\mathbb{X}}'\dot{\mathbb{X}})^{-1}\dot{\mathbb{X}}'\dot{\mathbb{T}} \\
&= (\dot{\mathbb{X}}'\dot{\mathbb{X}})^{-1}\dot{\mathbb{X}}'(\mathbb{H} + \mathbb{M})\dot{\mathbb{T}} \\
&= (\dot{\mathbb{X}}'\dot{\mathbb{X}})^{-1}\dot{\mathbb{X}}'\mathbb{H}\dot{\mathbb{T}} + (\dot{\mathbb{X}}'\dot{\mathbb{X}})^{-1}\dot{\mathbb{X}}'\mathbb{M}\dot{\mathbb{T}} \\
&= (\dot{\mathbb{X}}'\dot{\mathbb{X}})^{-1}C_1\dot{\mathbb{X}}'\mathbb{H}\dot{\mathbb{T}} + (\dot{\mathbb{X}}'\dot{\mathbb{X}})^{-1}C_1\dot{\mathbb{X}}'\mathbb{M}\dot{\mathbb{T}} \\
&= (\dot{\mathbb{X}}'\dot{\mathbb{X}})^{-1}(\dot{\mathbb{X}}'\mathbb{H}\dot{\mathbb{X}})\check{B} + (\dot{\mathbb{X}}'\dot{\mathbb{X}})^{-1}\dot{\mathbb{X}}'\mathbb{M}\dot{\mathbb{X}}b_{tx\cdot z}
\end{aligned}$$

where $b_{tx\cdot z} = (\dot{\mathbb{X}}'\mathbb{M}\dot{\mathbb{X}})^{-1}\dot{\mathbb{X}}'\mathbb{M}\dot{\mathbb{T}}$, the coefficient on $\dot{\mathbb{X}}$ in an individual level regression of $\dot{\mathbb{T}}$ on $\dot{\mathbb{X}}$, controlling for $\mathbb{G}$.

Finally, if we let the scalar $F = (\dot{\mathbb{X}}'\mathbb{H}\dot{\mathbb{X}})^{-1}(\dot{\mathbb{X}}'\dot{\mathbb{X}}) - I$ (an equivalent expression for the same scalar F already defined in Section 3.2), and

[11] I know of only a few attempts to gerrymander precinct boundaries (all told to me in confidence). Most are in areas where precincts also serve as districts for electing local officials. I have also come across a few cases where selective placement of the polling place within the precinct was intended to reduce the odds of one group turning out to vote.

premultiply by $F + I$, we can solve for the discrepancy $\check{B} - B$:

$$\mathbf{D}(\check{B})_2 = F(B - b_{tx \cdot z}) \tag{3.14}$$

Since it was derived from the same individual-level equations, this expression is obviously equivalent to the discrepancy in Equation 3.13. However, it provides several new insights into the aggregation problem.

Palmquist labels F the *inflation factor* and $(B - b_{tx \cdot z})$ the *specification shift*. The specification shift is the source of bias and can be understood as the indirect effect of $\mathbb{X}$ on $\dot{\mathbb{T}}$ that passes through $\mathbb{G}$ (as compared to the quantity of interest which can be interpreted as the direct effect of $\mathbb{X}$ on $\mathbb{T}$). The size of the specification shift depends on the consequence of controlling for $\mathbb{G}$. Thus, the problem might be called *reverse omitted variable bias*. That is, with aggregate data, we are doing the equivalent of using individual data but being forced to include $\mathbb{G}$ in our regression. Logically, including $\mathbb{G}$ will have its largest effect when it causally intervenes between $\mathbb{X}$ and $\dot{\mathbb{T}}$, since this is exactly the situation in which we would want to omit $\mathbb{G}$ in estimating the causal effect of $\mathbb{X}$ (King, Keohane, and Verba, 1994: 173ff). Thus, if $\mathbb{G}$ were related to (i.e., if districts were drawn on the basis of) anything that is a consequence of race, bias would result. The leading example is grouping based on voter turnout (the dependent variable $\dot{\mathbb{T}}$), which is obviously a consequence of race and would thus cause bias. Other examples might include grouping based on income categories, which would also be a consequence of race.

Finally, if $\mathbb{G}$ and $\mathbb{X}$ are uncorrelated, the specification shift would be zero. No bias would occur because including $\mathbb{G}$ in the individual-level regression would have no effect or, in other words, the indirect effect through $\mathbb{G}$ would be eliminated because the chain from $\mathbb{G}$ to $\mathbb{X}$ would be broken. This is another way of saying that if the precincts were formed in a manner unrelated to $\mathbb{X}$ (a generalization of random grouping) there is no bias.

The inflation factor (F in Equation 3.14) multiplies the discrepancy induced by the specification shift to produce a larger actual bias since $F \geq 0$. F is based on the ratio of the aggregate to individual variance in the explanatory variable—the ratio of the variance of $\mathbb{X}_{ij}$ over individuals to the variance of X_i over precincts. These are equal only when voters are grouped in racially homogeneous precincts, in which case $F = 0$, no information is lost during aggregation, the discrepancy is zero, and no bias exists. This is an important point that can be expressed from some of the other perspectives on aggregation bias, but it is more transparent in Palmquist's setup.

As Palmquist's (1993) insightful analysis demonstrates, the inflation factor can be quite large, meaning that even small specification shifts can produce large discrepancies in making ecological inferences. Fortunately, F can always be calculated with observable aggregate data, so with this expression we can at least judge the potential problems that might be introduced by various-sized specification shifts, which are not observed.[12]

3.4 Equivalence of the Grouping and Indeterminacy Problems

The grouping approach discussed in Section 3.3 and the indeterminacy problem introduced in Section 3.2 are viewed as different problems in the literature and are usually discussed in separate articles by nonoverlapping sets of authors. When the approaches are mentioned in the same publications, they are typically either described as distinct problems that both need to be solved, or one approach is criticized as incorrect or inferior from the perspective of the other. In fact, the grouping and indeterminacy problems are mathematically equivalent. One cannot be right and the other wrong. Having two separate approaches to the same problem is useful for understanding the problem from different perspectives, but only one problem need be solved. Analysts can conceptualize the aggregation problem either as grouping or indeterminacy. The solution to one is exactly the solution to the other.

This result can be summarized by relating Equations 3.9 (page 45), 3.13 (page 48), and 3.14 (page 52), which were derived so that they would be in the same notation and have the same meanings.

$$\begin{aligned}
\mathbf{D}(\check{B}) &= \check{B} - B && (3.15)\\
&= A_1 b_{bx} + A_2 b_{wx} - A_3 b_{rh} && (3.16)\\
&= \frac{\mathbf{C}(X_i, e_i)}{\mathbf{V}(X_i)} && (3.17)\\
&= F(B - b_{tx\cdot z}) && (3.18)\\
&= f(N_i^{bT}, N_i^{wT}) && (3.19)
\end{aligned}$$

Appendix A proves the equality of these expressions. The novel per-

[12] When generalized to tables larger than 2 × 2, F cannot be computed from aggregate data alone, but it can be computed from the cross-tabulation of the explanatory variables. In some multicategory cases, such as when census data are available for the multivariate version of X_i, but not T_i, this can still be a useful result.

spectives each of these equations gives on the aggregation problem have already been presented. We now need to get used to the fact that they are all different perspectives on the identical problem, rather than different problems.

Equation 3.15 is the definition of the discrepancy, the difference between the estimated parameter from a single (weighted) Goodman's regression. It also emphasizes that we will not generally know the discrepancy for certain; otherwise, we would be able to calculate, rather than estimate, the quantity of interest.

Equation 3.16 represents one formalization of the indeterminacy problem discussed in Section 3.2. By using the insight about the inflation factor F from Palmquist (1993, 1994), we can further analyze this equation. Note that A_1, A_2, and A_3 (as defined in Equation 3.10) are directly calculable from aggregate data. They are also all nonnegative numbers. Their sizes inflate the discrepancy of each of the corresponding unobserved coefficients in this expression. Just as we can and should calculate F when making ecological inferences, we can also calculate (A_1, A_2, A_3) to help evaluate the likely biases from this alternative perspective.

Equation 3.17 is the traditional expression for grouping bias, which shows how precinct lines induce a correlation between X_i and the error term, even though there can be no such correlation at the individual level. Equation 3.18 is the latest version of the clustering or grouping perspective given by Palmquist. It can be interpreted as the product of the inflation factor and the specification shift. Both were discussed in Section 3.3.

Finally, Equation 3.19 emphasizes that the most basic unobserved quantities underlying each of these formulas are N_i^{bT} and N_i^{wT}, the number of blacks and whites voting. In this equation, $f(\cdot, \cdot)$ is a specific function, calculable (except for its arguments) from aggregate data. As these equations (and Appendix A) make clear, an infinite number of other expressions could also be derived for the discrepancy. In fact, new expressions will undoubtedly appear in the literature in future years and, although they may also literally add nothing new, they might help us to look at the same aggregation bias results from new angles, just as Equations 3.15–3.19 each make a different interpretive contribution. I hope as new perspectives are developed that they will be directly related to these existing results.

3.5 A Concluding Definition

One of the obvious implications of the results in this chapter is that Goodman's model gives biased inferences when applied to data with nonzero discrepancies. Since this problem can be entirely due to the process of aggregation, Goodman's estimator in these situations is said to have *aggregation bias*. That is, in applications with nonzero discrepancies, Goodman's model will not give the right answer even on average across many such applications. We could describe this aggregation bias as a grouping-induced correlation between X_i and e_i, or large specification shift and inflation factors, but for convenience I usually discuss it in terms of the indeterminacy problem as dependence between X_i and β_i^b or between X_i and β_i^w. In the remainder of this book, I continue to use the term "aggregation bias" to refer to those situations in which Goodman's model gives biased results (with or without weights) because of aggregation bias, even when discussing other models. This definition will generate a slight abuse of standard statistical terminology since, in the context of other models, aggregation bias will refer to a property of the data (or an ill-advised Goodman regression) rather than to the estimator being evaluated. In particular, the method introduced in this book can give unbiased answers even in the presence of aggregation bias in the data.

CHAPTER 4

Non-Aggregation Problems

THIS CHAPTER sets out the problems, unrelated to aggregation bias, in the two most widely used statistical approaches to the ecological inference problem—the *Goodman regression* and *double regression* models—as well as some problems with the methods of bounds. Valid ecological inferences require a solution to all of the issues discussed here. A few of the problems introduced in this chapter have been discussed before in the literature; others seem to be known by some methodologists but virtually unknown by those applying these methods; others are well known by applied researchers but unknown to most methodologists; and still others are original to this chapter. The solutions to all these problems, as well as those discussed in Chapter 3 on aggregation bias, appear in subsequent chapters.

The problems discussed in this chapter affect ecological inferences whether or not aggregation bias exists in a particular data set. In any more routine statistical analysis, the issues discussed here would be addressed as a matter of course, since ignoring them would cause empirical results to be severely biased or inefficient. Perhaps because of the apparently more difficult aggregation bias questions, methodologists have ignored these more basic statistical issues. However, they are not trivial. Indeed, these problems may account for some of the empirical problems previously, but incorrectly, attributed to problems with aggregation bias. They involve major concerns such as models that are not estimating the parameters of interest, massive levels of heteroskedasticity not incorporated into any model, and incorrect or missing measures of uncertainty such as standard errors and confidence intervals. Although these problems of modeling and estimation are serious, most are unrelated to the problems of information loss and bias due to aggregation.

4.1 Goodman Regression Model Problems

The most important problem, due only in part to aggregation bias, is that:

> *Empirical applications of Goodman's model frequently give wildly inaccurate and even impossible results.*

For example, Table 1.3 (page 16) gives examples in which Goodman's model estimates the fraction of the black population who voted for the Democrats to be over 100% even though B^b and B^w are proportions and thus cannot logically extend outside of the [0,1] interval.[1] Part IV includes examples in which Goodman's estimates are wrong even when falling inside these bounds.

Even when the estimate falls within the $[0, 1]$ interval, problems with this method are often still obvious because after taking into account the information in the marginals the maximum possible bounds on the unknown parameters are usually narrower than the entire $[0, 1]$ interval. For example, consider the extreme situation of a district with 100% African American population ($X_i = 1$ for all i). In this circumstance, B^b (the fraction of blacks in the district who vote) is equal to the the fraction turning out to vote in the district (or equivalently, the weighted average of T_i, that is $\sum_{i=1}^{p} N_i^b T_i / N^b$). The quantity of interest is thus known exactly. In other examples with districts that are heavily but not completely homogeneous in racial terms, narrow bounds on the parameters of interest can be easily calculated. Maximum possible intervals for the unknown parameters calculated with these procedures can be $[0, 0.1]$ or $[0.03, 1]$ or $[0.6, 0.65]$ or any other possibility. This is important—indeed deterministic—information, but Goodman's model ignores it. The method also ignores the analogous and more informative bounds on each of the precinct-level parameters. Thus,

> *Goodman's model does not take into account the information from the method of bounds and thus often gives estimates outside these known bounds.*

In fact, no existing statistical method of ecological inference explicitly takes into account the information from the method of bounds. Part of the reason for this difficulty is that the literature on this question works almost exclusively by means of simple numerical examples.

[1] Researchers have responded to nonsensical estimates by suggesting constraints (Telser, 1963), nonlinear transformations (Rosenthal, 1973), control variables (Hanushek, Jackson, and Kain, 1974; Stokes, 1969; Crewe and Payne, 1976), ignoring the problem unless the entire confidence interval falls outside the permissible range (Hawkes, 1969), ad hoc adjustment of the unrestricted estimates (Kalbfleisch and Lawless, 1984), ridge regression (Miller, 1972), and quadratic programming (Lee, Judge, and Zellner, 1970; McCarthy and Ryan, 1977). Unfortunately, none of these approaches has been proven in applications or won approval in the methodological literature. The problem, as recognized by many of these authors, is that estimates from Goodman's model of greater than one or less than zero suggest a problem with the model, not merely with its estimator.

Formal algebraic expressions have never been derived for most quantities of interest. For other parameters of interest, such as λ^b and λ^w in Table 2.2, even the simplest numerical examples of the bounds have not appeared in the literature.

As Chapter 5 shows, the precinct-level bounds are extremely informative about the district- and precinct-level quantities of interest, especially when combined with statistical information. To get a sense of how much information is being discarded by Goodman's model, consider this analogy. Imagine a regression model with an error term distributed as a uniform variable over the [0,1] interval. Now suppose someone gave you a different, narrower interval for each observation, such as for example [0.1,0.3] for the first observation and [0.6,1] for the second, with an average width covering about half the [0,1] space. You are told that the probability of the error term falling outside this narrower interval is zero. Ignoring the bounds is roughly as wasteful of information as not using the narrower intervals in deriving a model for this regression analogy. In addition, this deterministic information is even more valuable in the ecological inference context because Goodman's model is not even consistent with the wider [0,1] precinct-level bounds. That is, Goodman's model imposes no information from these deterministic bounds, giving estimates restricted only to the real number line, rather than roughly half the [0,1] interval for each observation in a data set. Moreover, as described in Part III, the precinct bounds can also be used as reliable guideposts in avoiding aggregation bias.

One of the most basic non-aggregation issues is that:

Goodman's procedure has been interpreted to assume that the parameters of interest are constant over observations.

The existence of this assumption is recognized in the model because the regressions are homoskedastic, whereas a heteroskedastic model would in most cases have been required to estimate the average (or weighted average) parameter values correctly in Equations 2.1.[2] Models that assume constant parameters do not generally produce unbi-

[2] For example, in the accounting identity, $T_i = \beta_i^b X_i + \beta_i^w(1 - X_i)$, from Equation 3.1, suppose $\beta_i^b = \mathfrak{B}^b + \epsilon_i^b$, where $\mathfrak{B}^b$ is the average over i of β_i^b and $\epsilon_i^b = \beta_i^b - \mathfrak{B}^b$ is a random error term with mean zero. Suppose also for simplicity that the other parameter is constant over precincts so that $\beta_i^w = \mathfrak{B}^w$. By substituting these expressions into Equation 3.1, we get $T_i = \mathfrak{B}^b X_i + \mathfrak{B}^w(1 - X_i) + [\epsilon_i^b X_i]$, where the term in square brackets is now an error term. But this equation should no longer be estimated by least squares because the variance of its error term, $V(\epsilon_i^b)X_i^2$, varies over the observations as a function of X_i even if $V(\epsilon_i^b)$ is constant (unless $V(\epsilon_i^b)$ happens to be proportional to exactly $1/X_i^2$).

ased or efficient estimates of average values of parameters that vary (see Figure 3.1, page 41). In addition, the model includes no features in the mean function whereby the parameters can vary as a function of X_i or any supplementary variables.[3]

Contrary to much discussion in the literature (see, most recently, Agnew, 1996), we know with absolute certainty that this "constant parameter" assumption is incorrect. In all nontrivial empirical applications, constant parameters are not mathematically possible, since constraints on the parameters calculated with the method of bounds and its generalizations rule this out (see Chapter 5). In fact, one can also rule out constant parameters more easily by looking at a scatter plot of the data, such as T_i by X_i in Figure 4.1. (This scatter plot includes all electoral precincts in Marion County, Indiana that could be matched with U.S. Census data from the 1990 U.S. Senate election. Marion County includes Indianapolis.) Since the only source of error in the basic accounting identity (Equation 3.1) is parameter variation, any deviation from the regression line is proof of parameter variation. The obvious scatter in this scatter plot proves the existence of parameter variation, and invalidates this key assumption of Goodman's model.

From a substantive perspective, constant parameters are also implausible in ecological inference applications. For example, even on average, we would not expect cosmopolitan, liberal whites to vote for a liberal black Democratic candidate at the same rate as would conservative, rural whites. In the best possible case, ignoring this parameter variation means that Goodman's regression procedure yields inefficient estimates and biased standard errors. In the vast majority

[3] Goodman's approach of building an aggregate model by imposing theoretical restrictions on the individual units is closely related to the more developed ideas in "exact aggregation theory" (See Stoker, 1993). This theory is powerful theoretically for ascertaining what individual-level assumptions are required to produce a meaningful aggregate model, but problematic empirically because the necessary assumptions (such as Goodman's constant parameter assumption) are not always empirically reasonable (see Lau, 1982; Jorgenson, Lau, and Stoker, 1982; Lewbel, 1989; Heineke and Sheffrin, 1990). A different way to interpret Goodman's constant parameter requirement is to assume that the aggregates behave as a "representative individual." This is analogous to the "representative agent" assumption widely used to justify macroeconomic analyses. However, as Kirman's (1992) survey demonstrates, by appealing to a mathematical theorem due to Sonnenschein (1972) and Debreu (1974), the representative agent assumption is highly questionable, if not logically impossible. Because there is also no reason to think that a district aggregate behaves as a "representative individual," however it might be defined, an analogous argument, along with the arguments in Chapter 3, provides sufficient reason to discard this interpretation.

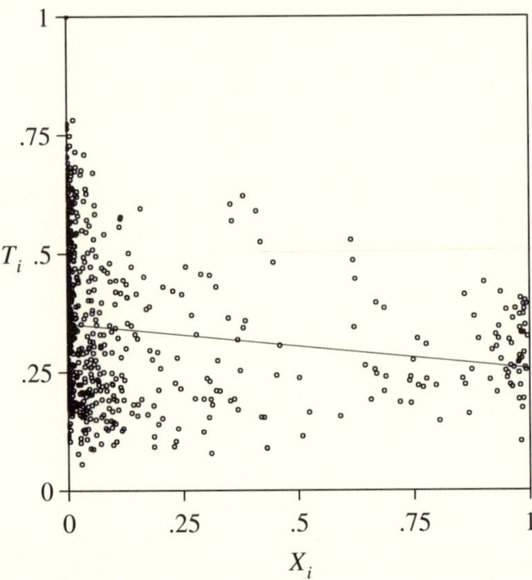

Figure 4.1 Scatter Plot of Precincts in Marion County, Indiana: Voter Turnout (T_i) for the U.S. Senate by Fraction Black (X_i), 1990. Scatter around the regression line, which can only be due to parameter variation, invalidates the key Goodman regression model assumption.

of cases, ignoring this parameter variation will also bias its parameter estimates.

Since Goodman's model does not weight the parameters from differently sized precincts any differently, the best-case scenario, given that the parameters vary, might be that this regression is estimating the averages of the precinct parameters ($\mathfrak{B}^b$ and $\mathfrak{B}^w$) instead of the more interesting fractions of blacks and whites who vote district-wide (B^b and B^w). Thus,

> *Goodman's regression is estimating parameters that are not the quantities of interest.*

The only situation in which Goodman's regression would seem to estimate the parameters of interest correctly is when all precincts have the same voting-age population and 50% of each precinct's voting-age population is black (and 50% white), in which case the regression variables would be perfectly collinear and the procedure would fail, or when the precinct population sizes are uncorrelated with the precinct parameters.

Some users of Goodman's model attempt to estimate the correct quantities of interest by running the regression with weighted least squares, but this does not generally solve the problem and, in some cases, creates new difficulties. The confusion may be due to different uses of the word "weighting." The *weighted averages* that are required to produce the parameters of interest are simply those in Equations 2.1 (page 33), with weights based on the size of the black or white voting-age population. In contrast, *regression weights* in weighted least squares primarily affects the efficiency of each regression's estimates and are based only on N_i (the total voting-age population). Unfortunately, the two forms of "weighting" have little to do with one another, except in one special case.

The special case where weighted least squares helps in computing the weighted average can be understood as follows. If X_i is not independent of β_i^b and β_i^w, we have aggregation bias, and Goodman's regression, with least squares or weighted least squares, is biased. Alternatively, if this independence assumption holds, unbiased estimates with Goodman's least squares regression occur only if N_i is independent of the β_is. (In Goodman's framework, these independence assumptions must be made on the basis of theoretical argument only in order to guarantee unbiased estimates, and even then the estimates will be inefficient and standard errors biased.) The one special case in which weighted least squares helps with the weighted average is that in which there is no aggregation bias but N_i is related in some way to β_i^b or β_i^w. In this case, if it is also true that N_i and X_i are independent, then least squares produces biased results and weighted least squares produces unbiased results. The problem is that this special case is very special: if X_i and N_i are not independent, then any relationship between N_i and β_i^b or β_i^w means that least squares and weighted least squares generate biased coefficients, whether or not there exists aggregation bias.

This leads us to the next problem with Goodman's model:

> *Using weighted least squares (with weights based on N_i) is often inappropriate even for the problem for which it was designed and can exacerbate other problems.*

The statistical logic of using weighted least squares in Goodman's regression more generally than the special case is based on a sound but inapplicable theoretical argument that has not been made explicit. In fact, the logic applies not just to ecological inference, but to almost any analysis based on geographic units.

First denote $\mathbb{T}_{ij}$ as the individual-level version of the variable T_i. That is, $\mathbb{T}_{ij}$ is 1 if voting-age person j ($j = 1, \ldots, N_i$) in district i ($i = 1, \ldots, p$) votes and 0 if he or she does not vote. Also denote π_{ij} as the ex ante probability that person j in district i votes; that is $\Pr(\mathbb{T}_{ij} =$

$1) = \pi_{ij}$. Then compute the observed precinct variance as follows:

$$\mathrm{V}(T_i) = \mathrm{V}\left(\frac{N_i^T}{N_i}\right) = \left(\frac{1}{N_i}\right)^2 \mathrm{V}(N_i^T) = \left(\frac{1}{N_i}\right)^2 \mathrm{V}\left(\sum_{j=1}^{N_i} \mathbb{T}_{ij}\right)$$

If $\mathrm{C}(\mathbb{T}_{ij}, \mathbb{T}_{ij'}) = 0$ for all $j \neq j'$,

$$= \left(\frac{1}{N_i}\right)^2 \left(\sum_{j=1}^{N_i} \pi_{ij}(1 - \pi_{ij})\right) \tag{4.1}$$

And if $\pi_{ij} = \pi_{ij'}$ for all $j \neq j'$,

$$\propto \frac{1}{N_i} \tag{4.2}$$

If all the lines (and corresponding assumptions) in this equation are correct, then the variance of the dependent variable is proportional to one over the number of voting-age people in the precinct, and thus weighted least squares based on the voting-age population is an appropriate response. However, the last two lines in this equation make dubious assumptions. Equation 4.1 holds only in the unlikely event that each person's vote in precinct i is independent of every other person's vote. So this assumption is violated if people influence each other to vote, such as would occur if they went together to cast their ballots, or car pools were available, or any form of civic culture encouraged voting among some groups, or if similar unobserved factors explained the decisions of different individuals to vote. The assumption would also be violated if some variable, such as campaign advertising, socio-economic status, or get-out-the-vote drives influences groups within the precinct to vote. Equation 4.2 holds only if, in addition, the ex ante probability of voting is identical for each person voting in the precinct. Obviously, neither the *independence* nor this *homogeneity* assumption holds in any real election, and thus the theoretical justification for population-based weights is unfounded.

Whether Equations 4.1 and 4.2 hold approximately in any application is an empirical question, as relevant empirical evidence generally dominates fact-free theorizing, at least when the theories are not based on anything other than reasonable arguments without some reliable foundation. Although they are unsure about its "theoretical status," Achen and Shively (1995: 59) claim that "as a practical matter, when district populations are highly variable, population weighting should ordinarily be used." In fact, the question is not whether populations (or voting-age populations) are variable, which is almost always the case, but whether the conditional variances change over geographic units in proportion to population size. The answer should depend on the empirical evidence. One way to assess this evidence is represented in Figure 4.2, which plots the squared residuals e_i^2 from an (unweighted) least squares regression of T_i on X_i and $(1 - X_i)$ (vertically), by weights computed based on precinct population, $1/N_i$ (horizontally). The squared residuals are an unbiased estimate of the variance of each observation. If these weights are correct, the points in Figure 4.2 should closely fit a positively sloping regression line. Obviously, no such clear relationship is evident. Since this same technique can be used in almost any aggregate data set, we need not leave empirical questions to unfounded speculation.[4]

Whenever the population-based variance assumption is not clearly supported by the data, as in this example, the weights should not be used, or a more flexible version of the assumption should be developed instead. In my experience, this assumption is occasionally appropriate but more often is not. This is because vote proportions (or other statistics) from precincts with 1,000 people are often nearly as variable as precincts with 500, and the difference in variability is different from what Equation 4.2 would indicate. Yet, there often is some relationship to population size, even if not the one generally assumed. For example, Figure 4.2 does not display the predicted linear pattern, but there does appear to be some relationship in the data:

[4] Achen and Shively (1995: 59) and others sidestep this issue by claiming that "many electoral data sets contain districts of roughly equal size, so that the problem evaporates." In fact, this is not true for almost any real legislative districts. Even the population of U.S. House districts, about which the Supreme Court is most obsessive, vary significantly across states: in 1992, the largest House district had 176% of the population of the smallest district. No legislature had remotely similar district sizes prior to the 1960s. Since then, the Supreme Court has allowed significant population variations for state legislatures based on the districting norm of not splitting local political subdivisions and maintaining communities of interest. U.S. Senate districts (i.e., states) vary in population by a factor of about sixty. District sizes in every other country are far more variable than in the United States. But much more important is the fact that the best ecological data sets, based on electoral precincts, voter tabulation districts, minor civil divisions, towns, or sometimes counties, vary enormously in population size (Manhattan is one county, for example). Moreover, population size is only relevant to Equations 4.1 and 4.2 if the dependent variable in ecological inference models is voter turnout, fraction registered, or other statistics based on population size. If the object of the ecological inference is voter choice, for example, then voter turnout would be substituted for population, and virtually all geographic units display large variations in turnout. Even U.S. House districts vary in turnout by a factor of more than seven.

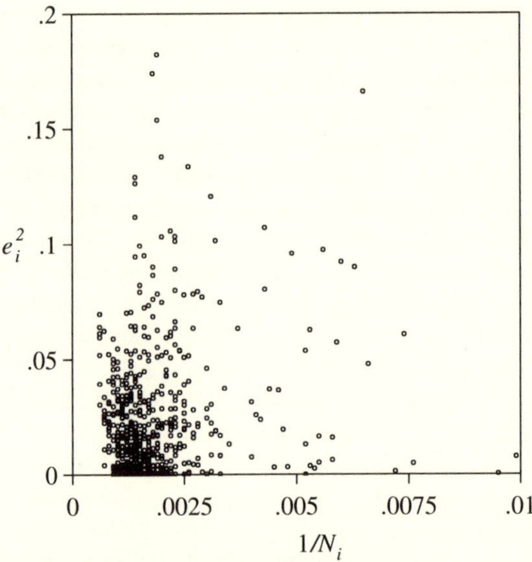

Figure 4.2 Evaluating Population-Based Weights, using the same data as in Figure 4.1. If population weights were appropriate, this scatter plot would closely fit a positively sloping regression line.

the largest cluster of points in the figure displays almost no pattern, but precincts with the smallest populations (to the right side of the graph) have larger variances on average than the largest precincts (to the left). (The smaller precincts also have a larger spread of estimated variances.)

If there exists evidence of conditional variance depending upon population, some empirical estimation rather than "theoretical" assumption would usually be preferable. For example, the log of the variance might be proportional to the population weights taken to a power, with the power estimated. A different nonlinear function could also be tried if, as in this figure, there appears to be some evidence for it, although it would be best to have multiple data sets available to confirm that a preliminary analysis is not modeling only idiosyncratic features of the data.[5]

[5] Scholars in agricultural statistics have wrestled with a nearly identical problem for many years. Using data from farms (or experimental plots) of different sizes, they regress the yield per acre of various crops on covariates such as fertilizer usage or soil moisture, and worry about the appropriate weights. The best model of heteroskedasticity in this field and some others (using notation from above) often turns out to be weights proportional to $(1/N_i)^\alpha$, where α is estimated to be something other than 1. In contrast, Equations 4.1 and 4.2 assume without evidence that $\alpha = 1$. See Fairfield Smith (1938), Whittle (1956), and Cressie (1993).

Using population-based weights when they are not appropriate will produce an incorrect variance function and lead to the same consequences as heteroskedasticity in least squares regressions. Population-based weights were used in theoretical analyses of aggregation bias in Chapter 3 in order to reduce the algebraic complexity of some arguments, but whether to use these weights in any specific empirical analysis remains an empirical question. Finally, even in the unusual case in which these weights are appropriate, Goodman's regression still does not estimate the quantities of interest. That is, weighting affects only the statistical properties of the estimates rather than what is being estimated. In the best case, Goodman's regression with or without population-based weights is estimating the unweighted averages of the precinct-level quantities of interest, not the district-wide fractions of blacks and whites who vote.[6]

A final problem also has to do with unequal variances. Demonstrating that population-based weights are usually inappropriate does not necessarily mean that the regression is homoskedastic. In fact,

Ecological data often exhibit strong heteroskedasticity (unrelated to N_i) that is not captured by the Goodman model.

No existing model is consistent with this pattern, but it is screamingly clear in almost all published scatter plots in the ecological inference literature. The heteroskedasticity is unambiguous in Figure 4.1 (page 60). It is even more obvious in voting-related analyses, where the heteroskedasticity is especially massive. For example, Figure 4.3 plots the Democratic fraction of the two-party vote (V_i) vertically and the black fraction of the voting age population (X_i) horizontally. These data are Philadelphia precinct returns from the 1990 Pennsylvania gubernatorial election, matched to U.S. Census data. The variability (measured vertically) at the left side of the figure is obviously much larger than at the right side, indicating that the predominately white precincts are much more variable in their voting preferences than mostly black precincts. (Moreover, as I show in Chapter 6, an ecological inference model that assumes homoskedasticity, or heteroskedasticity that is not a function of X_i, implies that the correlation between β_i^b and β_i^w is 1.0 and the variances of these parameters are exactly equal. This is as implausible as it is unnecessarily restrictive.)

From a substantive perspective, this result should not be surprising. Homogeneously black precincts are most often in poor, inner-city areas. Middle-class African Americans are more likely to live

[6] For earlier discussions of weighting in ecological inference, see Goodman (1959), Wildgen (1988), Krivo and Kaufman (1990), and Huston (1991).

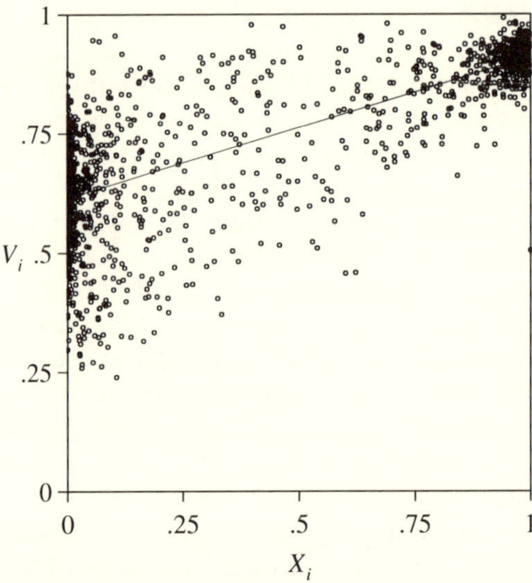

Figure 4.3 Typically Massive Heteroskedasticity in Voting Data. Philadelphia precinct results from the 1990 Pennsylvania gubernatorial election matched to U.S. Census data. Note how the variance, measured vertically around the regression line, is larger at the left than right side of the figure.

in nonsegregated communities. In comparison, homogeneously white precincts come in many varieties: some are inner-city segregated white neighborhoods or precincts in cities with few minorities; others are in wealthy suburbs; and still others are in conservative rural communities. Again, analogous substantive interpretations apply to ecological studies of class and voting and many others.

This massive level of heteroskedasticity exists even in data sets repeatedly used in the ecological inference literature. For example, in Robinson's (1950) original data, the range in the fraction illiterate for states with large foreign-born populations is five to seven times larger than that for states with very small foreign-born populations. Any efficient model of ecological data must take into account this wide diversity in types of heteroskedasticity.

Ignoring this high level of heteroskedasticity has the same consequences as in the worst cases analyzed in the textbooks and several more serious difficulties. For one, standard errors will be biased. In practice, standard errors from Goodman's regressions are implausibly small, often less than 0.01 (one percent). In contrast, the standard errors on precinct voter forecasts, which should provide something near to a lower bound on ecological inference standard errors, are at least six times larger.[7] Given the inaccuracy of the method in practice, Goodman's regression surely underestimates its standard error. The other consequence of this heteroskedasticity is that the coefficient estimates will be very inefficient, meaning that valuable information—especially valuable in the case of ecological inference where information is in such short supply—is being discarded.

Across statistical applications, it is not always obvious when to go to the extra effort to take heteroskedasticity into account. For example, regression coefficients are consistent in its presence, and standard errors can be fixed with procedures such as White's "heteroskedasticity-consistent standard errors." Thus, modeling heteroskedasticity will only improve the efficiency of coefficient estimates, in addition to generating a more realistic and verifiable model. Often, a little extra efficiency may not be worth the effort, especially if a more complicated model risks introducing bias.

The problem is that this intuition, developed in applications of the linear regression model, does not apply to ecological inference. Heteroskedasticity may not be enormously consequential in linear regression, but it is critical for inferences based on distributions that are bounded or functional forms that are anything other than unrestricted linear functions. As a simple analogy, the variance is very important for estimating the maximum of a variable or the probability that it is greater than some chosen value. Because aggregate data contains information on the bounds for all precinct-level parameters, modeling heteroskedasticity will prove essential to building an ecological inference model capable of providing accurate answers.

Modeling heteroskedasticity is especially important in the ecological inference problem if X_i varies over only a small region of its possible [0,1] range. For example, in many data sets the fraction of the population that is black might only range from zero to 0.3, yet to estimate the fraction of blacks who vote the analyst is forced to extrapolate all the way to $X_i = 1$. With an incorrect model of heteroskedasticity, uncertainty estimates at the end of the extrapolation can be very far off the mark.

Extrapolating out of the range of observable data is almost always a hazardous statistical procedure, and must be analyzed carefully. For example, the American politics literature indicates that higher levels of inflation reduce public support for the incumbent president. But what would happen if inflation increased to 200%? Obviously, pres-

[7] To put it differently, implausibly small standard errors are often indicative of heteroskedasticity in the first place. Of course, Goodman standard errors are also off due to aggregation bias and the other problems discussed in this chapter.

idential approval would not drop to −50%. In fact, we have no clue what would happen. Maybe the public would rally around the president in such a time of national crisis, or perhaps they would vote the president out in the next election, or not wait until then and storm the White House. Events this far from our range of experience cannot usually be predicted reliably. The ecological inference problem often requires some extrapolation (Freedman et al., 1991: 810–811). A reliable statistical approach must appropriately model the heteroskedasticity in the data in order to arrive at appropriately sized variances and uncertainty estimates.

Moreover, as demonstrated in Chapter 6, only the variance function contains information about several key features of the individual-level data being estimated. Thus, if heteroskedasticity is *ever* worth modeling well, it should be in making ecological inferences. As Chapter 6 demonstrates, the basic structure of the problem should lead us to expect heteroskedasticity of the type in evidence in Figure 4.3 and the numerous other data sets like it. In fact, any logically consistent model that allows for variable parameters will automatically imply that aggregate data can be heteroskedastic.

4.2 Applying Goodman's Regression in 2 × 3 Tables

This section shows the consequences of applying Goodman's single regression technique to estimate the parameters of a 2 × 3 table. Table 2.2 (page 30) is the running example for this section, and the goal is estimating the district aggregates Λ^b (fraction of blacks who vote for the Democratic candidate) and Λ^w (fraction of whites who vote for the Democrat).

In order to apply Goodman's model directly, we would need to regress V_i (the proportion of the vote for the Democratic candidate, $N_i^D/N_i^T = D_i/T_i$) on x_i (proportion of voters who are black, N_i^{bT}/N_i^T) and $(1 - x_i)$ (proportion of voters who are white) with no constant term. The coefficients from this least squares regression, $\hat{\Lambda}^b$ and $\hat{\Lambda}^w$, are intended to be estimates of Λ^b and Λ^w, since the precinct-level parameters λ_i^b and λ_i^w are assumed constant for all i.

The model underlying this regression is based loosely on the following accounting identity:

$$V_i = \lambda_i^b x_i + \lambda_i^w (1 - x_i) \tag{4.3}$$

Unfortunately, x_i is not generally observed in voting studies, and so X_i is used in its place. If the black proportion of voters x_i is the same as the black fraction of the voting-age population X_i, this substitution obviously changes nothing, and we are back to a standard Goodman regression equivalent to that considered earlier in this chapter. However, because turnout is often lower among African-Americans than other groups, this substitution can cause bias because of changes in the parameter meanings.

The consequences of using the observed, but incorrect, X_i instead of the correct, but unobserved, x_i is usually ignored in the methodological literature on ecological inference. Some (including Goodman) use a motivating example other than race and voting for which the equivalent of x_i is observed. Only about a half-dozen studies (discussed in Section 4.3) recognize the issue explicitly. No study has given the precise mathematical consequences of this substitution.

Begin by writing Equation 4.3 after substituting X_i for x_i.

$$V_i = \gamma_i^b X_i + \gamma_i^w (1 - X_i) \tag{4.4}$$

The γ's in this equation are not necessarily equal to the λ's in Equation 4.3, but we can derive their exact relationship. To do this, first decompose the unobserved variable x_i into a function of the observed X_i: $x_i = (\beta_i^b / T_i) X_i$, and for convenience, $(1 - x_i) = (\beta_i^w / T_i)(1 - X_i)$. Then substitute these expressions into Equation 4.3 in place of x_i:

$$\begin{aligned} V_i &= \lambda_i^b x_i + \lambda_i^w (1 - x_i) \\ &= \lambda_i^b \frac{\beta_i^b}{T_i} X_i + \lambda_i^w \frac{\beta_i^w}{T_i} (1 - X_i) \end{aligned}$$

By comparing the last line of this equation to Equation 4.4, we can see that instead of estimating λ_i^b and λ_i^w, Goodman's regression in the context of 2 × 3 tables is estimating:

$$\gamma_i^b = \lambda_i^b \frac{\beta_i^b}{T_i} \quad \text{and} \quad \gamma_i^w = \lambda_i^w \frac{\beta_i^w}{T_i} \tag{4.5}$$

These expressions demonstrate that:

The "accounting identity" on which Goodman's model is based does not hold for 2 × 3 *tables.*

This same point also applies to any other method that would use the incorrect expression in Equation 4.4 instead of the correct accounting identity (with an unobserved variable) in Equation 4.3.

		Then		
Case	If	*Blacks*	*Whites*	*Racial Bloc Voting*
1	$\beta_i^w = \beta_i^b$	$\lambda_i^b = \gamma_i^b$	$\lambda_i^w = \gamma_i^w$	$\lambda_i = \gamma_i$
2	$\beta_i^w > \beta_i^b$	$\lambda_i^b > \gamma_i^b$	$\lambda_i^w < \gamma_i^w$	$\lambda_i > \gamma_i$
3	$\beta_i^w < \beta_i^b$	$\lambda_i^b < \gamma_i^b$	$\lambda_i^w > \gamma_i^w$	$\lambda_i < \gamma_i$

Table 4.1 Comparing Goodman Model Parameters to the Parameters of Interest in the 2×3 Table. The table shows how the correct Democratic vote parameters (λ_i^b and λ_i^w) differ from the parameters of Goodman's model (γ_i^b and γ_i^w) in the 2×3 table context, as a function of the correct turnout parameters (β_i^b and β_i^w).

To interpret these results further, denote the degree of *racially polarized voting*—the fraction of voting-age blacks voting for the Democratic candidate minus the fraction of whites voting for the Democrat—thought to result from Goodman's regression model as $\gamma_i = \gamma_i^b - \gamma_i^w$. The actual degree of racially polarized voting is $\lambda_i = \lambda_i^b - \lambda_i^w$.

Table 4.1 summarizes three specific interpretations of these results (in precincts with at least one black and one white). The parameters being estimated equal the parameters of interest only when black and white turnout rates are equal, $\beta_i^w = \beta_i^b$ (Case 1 in the table), which is rarely true in practice. Indeed, it is assumed or found to be false in almost all studies in this literature. Case 2 portrays the more usual situation in which black turnout rates are lower than white turnout rates. In this situation, *using Goodman's model gives racially polarized voting numbers that are too small.* Case 3 shows that, in the relatively unusual case in which black turnout rates are higher than white turnout rates, Goodman's model gives results that are too high.

Equations 4.5 also prove that γ_i^b and γ_i^w vary over precincts, even in the extremely unusual case in which λ_i^b and λ_i^w do not. This has three main consequences. First, Goodman's least squares regression when applied in practice to voting data ignores this parameter variation during estimation, which is equivalent to ignoring heteroskedasticity which is present. Second, in most cases, the damage caused is a lot worse, since the parameters being estimated do not correspond to the parameters of interest. And finally, the results about what parameters Goodman's model is supposedly estimating in Table 4.1 are not a guide about what will happen in practice if this model is inappropriately run with data from a 2×3 table, since real applications will also be affected by aggregation bias and the other problems in this chapter. The relationship between the estimated parameters and the quantities of interest would be lost in this context.

4.3 Double Regression Problems

The "double regression" procedure was apparently invented by Kousser (1973) and reinvented independently in different disciplines by Loewen (1982), Kleppner (1985), and Grofman et al. (1985). It is not often used in academic work, and it is rarely discussed even in the course of the best methodological works on ecological inference. But as even the courts and most expert witnesses in voting rights cases recognize, double regression dominates Goodman's regression in studies with 2 × 3 contingency tables like Table 2.2 (page 30), for example in studies of race and voting. It will also prove useful for arbitrarily large contingency tables. Because double regression is a generalization of Goodman's regression for these larger tables, *all problems identified in Chapter 3 and Section 4.1 also apply to the double regression model.*

The purpose of the double regression method is to solve the problem posed in Section 4.2: that Goodman's model does not apply to tables larger than 2 × 2. Thus the goal is to estimate Λ^b (the proportion of blacks voting for the Democrats) and Λ^w (proportion of whites voting for the Democrats). Most methodological discussions of ecological inference avoid the issues that arise in this section by "assuming" that x_i (the proportion of those voting who are black) is known and used in place of X_i (the proportion of the voting-age population that is black). This is a decision made by methodologists, made in order to focus on other difficult issues. However, although data on x_i are available in a few data sets, these data are quite rare in real voting and most other applications. Thus, almost any practical use of aggregate data in race and voting studies to make inferences about individuals should include the insights from the double regression procedure.

Double regression is based on four accounting identities:

$$
\begin{aligned}
T_i &= \beta_i^b X_i + \beta_i^w (1 - X_i) \\
D_i &= \theta_i^b X_i + \theta_i^w (1 - X_i) \\
\lambda_i^b &= \frac{\theta_i^b}{\beta_i^b} \\
\lambda_i^w &= \frac{\theta_i^w}{\beta_i^w}
\end{aligned}
\tag{4.6}
$$

Proving these equalities requires substituting raw counts in Table 2.1 for definitions of the right side variables in Equations 4.6, and showing that they equal the definition of the variable on the left side.[8] The first accounting identity is easiest to see in Table 2.3. The second identity can be seen by collapsing Table 2.2 into vote Democrat (D_i) versus vote Republican or no vote ($1 - D_i$). (In other words, in Table 2.3, replace β_i^b, β_i^w, and T_i with θ_i^b, θ_i^w, and D_i, respectively.)

To implement the double regression method, the parameters in Equations 4.6 (all assumed to be constant over precincts) are estimated by least squares regressions of T_i (fraction of voting-age people turning out) and D_i (fraction voting for the Democrat of those in the voting-age population), one at a time, on X_i and $(1 - X_i)$ (without a constant term). These are merely two separate Goodman's regressions. Denote the estimates of the first equation as $\hat{B}^b$ and $\hat{B}^w$, as in Section 4.1. Estimates of the second equation are $\hat{\Theta}^b$ and $\hat{\Theta}^w$, although these are of indirect interest only.

To obtain estimates of Λ^b and Λ^w, use the last two lines of Equations 4.6. The calculation is therefore:

$$\hat{\Lambda}^b = \frac{\hat{\Theta}^b}{\hat{B}^b}$$

$$\hat{\Lambda}^w = \frac{\hat{\Theta}^w}{\hat{B}^w} \tag{4.7}$$

The double regression procedure is an intuitive approach to estimating the Λ's. It overcomes some problems with applying Goodman's model directly. Thus, unlike Goodman's model, the parameters of the double regression model do coincide with the parameters of interest at the precinct level (absent the problems discussed above).[9] Put differently, the model does not require the assumption that turnout rates are the same for blacks and whites ($\beta_i^b = \beta_i^w$). But although double regression solves this problem, all the problems of Section 4.1 still apply.

[8] For example,

$$D_i = \theta_i^b X_i + \theta_i^w(1 - X_i) = \frac{N_i^{bD}}{N_i^b}\frac{N_i^b}{N_i} + \frac{N_i^{wD}}{N_i^w}\frac{N_i^w}{N_i} = \frac{N_i^D}{N_i}$$

The right side of this expression is the definition of D_i in Table 2.2 (page 30).

[9] Due to Jensen's inequality, even if $\hat{\Theta}^b$ and $\hat{B}^b$ are unbiased estimates, their ratio is not necessarily an unbiased estimate of Λ^b, although it can be consistent. See Rao, 1989.

Finally, the double regression method adds another problem to the list:

No method of calculating uncertainty estimates, such as standard errors and confidence intervals, exists for the double regression model.

Although standard errors could be computed by such methods as bootstrapping, simulation, or analytical approximation, no method has been proposed. This is especially disturbing given how widely the method is used in state and federal courts to make real public policy decisions. Because the basic model is improved in subsequent chapters, I do not pursue these possibilities here.

4.4 Concluding Remarks

A valid method of inferring individual attributes from aggregate data requires a procedure for avoiding aggregation bias as well as a model that solves the non-aggregation problems discussed in this chapter. In particular, a working method of ecological inference should take into account the maximum information from the method of bounds. Rarely is deterministic information such as this available in a statistical context, and it can be very valuable in making ecological inferences. The method should be verified in data for which X_i varies over only a small portion of its possible [0,1] range. Implausible assumptions about the parameters of interest, such as constancy, should not be assumed; the parameters of interest are demonstrably not constant, and so modeling assumptions and empirical estimates should reflect this fact wherever possible. If the aggregate quantities are of interest, the weighted average of the precinct parameters (the district aggregate) should be the goal, not the average of the precinct quantities. Weighting should be used if it helps with the statistical properties of the estimates and in estimating the correct quantities of interest; care should be taken to avoid disrupting one goal while trying to achieve the other. Observable implications of the chosen model should include the possibility of massive heteroskedasticity, as seems common in at least some aggregate data sets. If a 2×3 table is the subject of inference, the insight from the double regression model could be used. Finally, any method should include accurate assessments of the uncertainty of all ecological inferences drawn.

PART III

The Proposed Solution

This part presents a solution to the ecological inference problem. Chapter 5 reexpresses the data in a more useful way by providing formal methods for computing the deterministic bounds on the observation-level parameters of interest, as well as easy-to-use visual methods. These formal expressions for the bounds are then integrated in Chapter 6 with a statistical approach to modeling the remaining uncertainty within the bounds. I explain how to summarize information about the model parameters in the data in Chapter 7, and how to compute the quantities of interest in Chapter 8. Finally, Chapter 9 evaluates the remaining risks of making ecological inferences, analyzes the consequences of violating each model assumption, and provides diagnostic procedures and extensions of the basic model to work around potential problems.

CHAPTER 5

The Data: Generalizing the Method of Bounds

THIS CHAPTER summarizes all deterministic information about each precinct-level quantity of interest from only the data in that precinct. This takes the form of formal algebraic expressions and an easy-to-use graphical method. As Duncan and Davis (1953) first noted, the [0,1] bounds required of any proportion can be narrowed further in making ecological inferences. Because these narrower bounds require no assumptions and involve no data reduction, the bounds are in this sense synonymous with the data. This chapter excludes all statistical information and other uncertain knowledge of the quantities of interest. In the chapters that follow, the bounds derived here provide valuable deterministic information, and statistical approaches give probabilistic information about the parameters of interest within these bounds.

Although in some cases these deterministic precinct-level bounds will be narrow enough to be useful alone, many examples in the literature are too wide for substantive purposes. Shively (1974, 1991) and Sigelman (1991) have developed creative ways to narrow these bounds further in the context of specific examples for small numbers of individual areal units by using external (nonstatistical) information or additional assumptions. Claggett and Van Wingen (1993) demonstrated how geometric interpretations of linear programming can be used to arrive at these bounds. However, despite this progress, the wide bounds and the unease scholars seem to have with the assumptions necessary to narrow them further has limited the application and usefulness of this method. In part as a result, the literature is now bifurcated between supporters of the method of bounds and those who prefer statistical approaches. Although progress has been made in each area, heated debates about which approach is better often substitute for efforts to join the two (see Flanigan and Zingale, 1985; Kousser, 1986b; Dykstra, 1986). This is unfortunate, since the insights from each literature are not logically contradictory and the contributions do not overlap. They provide separate, almost additive, information that can be used together to solve different aspects of the ecological inference problem.

Scholars have calculated the bounds on the β_i's (the fraction of blacks and whites who vote) and θ_i's (the intermediate parameters) for specific numerical examples but not for the λ's (the fraction of blacks and whites voting for the Democrats). However, in order to combine the insights of this literature with the various statistical approaches, we need formal algebraic expressions for each of the bounds, but these have not previously appeared in the literature. The general expressions for these bounds derived in this chapter make calculations much easier in general and in application to specific cases. Finally, scholars have often thought that the bounds on the precinct-level parameters imply even wider, and thus virtually useless, bounds on the aggregate quantities of interest (Equations 2.1). I demonstrate here that this belief is due to the use of incorrect procedures for computing these bounds.

Section 5.1 briefly analyzes homogeneously black or white precincts, and Section 5.2 discusses upper and lower bounds on the more common precincts composed of both blacks and whites. Section 5.3 provides a very easy graphical method of assessing how much deterministic information exists in a set of ecological data about the quantities of interest. Appendix B gives technical details.

5.1 Homogeneous Precincts: No Uncertainty

Homogeneous precincts are the best case from the perspective of recovering the underlying parameters. In this situation, the upper bound equals the lower bound, and no uncertainty remains about the location of the precinct-level parameter of interest. Because the ecological inference problem requires descriptive and not causal inferences, we can label either variable as explanatory or dependent. As such, homogeneity is helpful when it occurs either for X_i or T_i.

Consider first a precinct i composed of 100% African Americans, that is, $X_i = 1$. In this situation, the number of votes, which we observe, is the same as the number of blacks voting. In terms of the notation in Chapter 2, the absence of white people of voting age enables us to remove the second row of Table 2.3 (page 31). This means that the previously unknown values in the first row are equal to their corresponding values in the marginals from the last row and are thus known with certainty. This fact enables us to determine the precinct-level parameters without ambiguity. The same logic applies to the larger Table 2.2.

Thus, for homogeneously black precincts (i.e., for $X_i = 1$), $\beta_i^b = T_i$, $\theta_i^b = D_i$, and $\lambda_i^b = V_i$, and in the absence of white voters, β_i^w, θ_i^w, and λ_i^w are undefined. Similarly, in homogeneously white precincts (for which $X_i = 0$), $\beta_i^w = T_i$, $\theta_i^w = D_i$, and $\lambda_i^w = V_i$, and β_i^b, θ_i^b, and λ_i^b are undefined. Appendix B proves these results more formally.

Since T_i is usually a behavioral outcome variable, I will refer to homogeneity in T_i as *unanimity*. First consider a precinct for which all eligible voters cast ballots, $T_i = 1$. In this situation, all blacks and all whites are also unanimous, so that $\beta_i^b = 1$ and $\beta_i^w = 1$ (and if $T_i = 0$ then $\beta_i^b = 0$ and $\beta_i^w = 0$). Similarly, if the Democratic candidate wins unanimously in a precinct ($V_i = 1$), then $\lambda_i^b = \lambda_i^w = 1$ (and if $V_i = 0$ then $\lambda_i^b = \lambda_i^w = 0$).

5.2 Heterogeneous Precincts: Upper and Lower Bounds

Consider now the more difficult case of heterogeneous districts, where pinning down the exact position of the parameters of interest is impossible.

5.2.1 *Precinct-Level Quantities of Interest*

This section considers only precincts with at least one white and at least one black person of voting age, that is where $0 < X_i < 1$; at least one person votes and one does not, $0 < T_i < 1$; and, when computing bounds for the λ's, both the Democratic and Republican candidates receive at least one vote each, $0 < V_i < 1$.

As proven in Appendix B, the upper and lower bounds on the precinct-level quantities of interest are each functions of T_i and X_i (for β_i^b and β_i^w) and D_i and X_i (for θ_i^b and θ_i^w):

$$\max\left(0, \frac{T_i - (1 - X_i)}{X_i}\right) \leq \beta_i^b \leq \min\left(\frac{T_i}{X_i}, 1\right)$$

$$\max\left(0, \frac{T_i - X_i}{1 - X_i}\right) \leq \beta_i^w \leq \min\left(\frac{T_i}{1 - X_i}, 1\right)$$

$$\max\left(0, \frac{D_i - (1 - X_i)}{X_i}\right) \leq \theta_i^b \leq \min\left(\frac{D_i}{X_i}, 1\right)$$

$$\max\left(0, \frac{D_i - X_i}{1 - X_i}\right) \leq \theta_i^w \leq \min\left(\frac{D_i}{1 - X_i}, 1\right) \tag{5.1}$$

The β_i's and θ_i's corresponding to each precinct must fall within these deterministic bounds, and in practice they are almost always narrower than [0,1].

Moreover, the bounds in Equations 5.1 do *not* represent all existing deterministic information about the parameters. For example, we also know that β_i^b and β_i^w are linearly related, given knowledge of the aggregate data X_i and T_i. We can see this by rearranging the basic accounting identity (Equation 3.1, page 38) with one unknown expressed as a function of the other:

$$\beta_i^w = \left(\frac{T_i}{1 - X_i}\right) - \left(\frac{X_i}{1 - X_i}\right)\beta_i^b \tag{5.2}$$

Because the slope of this line, $-X_i/(1-X_i)$, is never positive, we know that *if β_i^b falls near its upper bound, β_i^w must fall near its lower bound.*

Since this formulation, and the graphics it implies, will provide an extremely useful summary of the data for the statistical model in Chapter 6, I now work through a simple numerical example and also give the corresponding visual representation. Thus, for example, in Precinct 52 in Pennsylvania's second state senate district in 1990, the Hispanic population was $X_{52} = 0.88$ and turnout was $T_{52} = 0.19$. By plugging these values into the first two lines of Equations 5.1, which give the bounds, we know that β_{52}^b must fall in the narrow interval from 0.07 to 0.21, whereas the bounds on β_{52}^w range all the way from zero to one. These calculations are useful, and the bounds on β_{52}^b are narrow enough to be informative substantively, but we can represent these facts along with other information in another way.

Thus, by substituting in the values for X_{52} and T_{52} into the equations for the intercept and slope in Equation 5.2, we know that whatever the quantities of interest are in this precinct, they are related by the following linear expression:

$$\begin{aligned} \beta_{52}^w &= \left(\frac{0.19}{1 - 0.88}\right) - \left(\frac{0.88}{1 - 0.88}\right)\beta_{52}^b \\ &= 1.58 - 7.33\beta_{52}^b \end{aligned} \tag{5.3}$$

The dark line in Figure 5.1 portrays the valid range of this linear equation visually, by where it intersects the unit square. To draw this line, note that β_{52}^b and β_{52}^w in Equation 5.3 are now the variables, whereas the intercept and slope are functions of the known quantities X_{52} and T_{52}. We can compute any point on this line by setting β_{52}^b to some number, plugging it into this equation, and computing β_{52}^w. For example, if $\beta_{52}^b = 0.1$, then $\beta_{52}^w = 1.58 - 7.33(0.1) = 0.85$. Similarly, if $\beta_{52}^b = 0.2$, then $\beta_{52}^w = 1.58 - 7.33(0.2) = 0.11$. This gives us two points on the line (at coordinates 0.1,0.85 and 0.2,0.11). To plot the entire dark line in Figure 5.1, draw a line through these two points and extend it to the edges of the unit square (cf. Achen and Shively, 1995: 207).

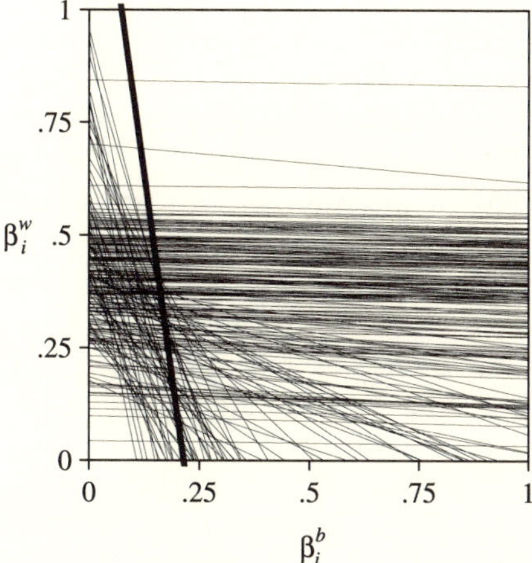

Figure 5.1 A Data Summary Convenient for Statistical Modeling. Each coordinate represents a unique possible value of β_i^b and β_i^w. Each line traces out, for a particular combination of T_i and X_i in a precinct, all possible values of the parameters (see Equation 5.2). The bounds for a precinct can be determined by projecting each line onto the horizontal (for β_i^b) and vertical (for β_i^w) axes. (The dark line is an example used in the text.) The data are the proportion Hispanic and proportion turnout from precincts in Pennsylvania's second state senate district in 1990.

Each coordinate in this square figure corresponds to a value of β_i^b (the fraction of Hispanics who vote) horizontally and β_i^w (the fraction of non-Hispanics who vote) vertically. This means that before X_i and T_i are observed, all we know is that the true β_i^b, β_i^w coordinate falls at some point in the unit square in the figure. Once we observe X_i and T_i for a precinct, we can compute the bounds for β_i^b and β_i^w from Equations 5.1 to narrow in on the true values. Alternatively, we could calculate the intercept $T_i/(1 - X_i)$ and slope $-X_i/(1 - X_i)$ from Equation 5.2, and then use these to draw a line on the figure. Thus, for Precinct 52, we know that the true $\beta_{52}^b, \beta_{52}^w$ coordinates must fall somewhere on the dark line in the figure. *Since this reduces the search from the entire unit square to a single line in the square, these computations substantially increase our knowledge about the parameters of interest.*

The bounds from each precinct can be determined from its line in Figure 5.1 by the maximum range it projects onto the horizontal and vertical axes. For example, the dark line projects downward onto the horizontal axis only in the range where $\beta_i^b \in [0.07, 0.21]$ and onto the left vertical axis where $\beta_i^w \in [0,1]$, the same bounds as computed above from Equations 5.1.

In addition to Precinct 52, Figure 5.1 plots 249 other lines based on Equation 5.2, using the proportions of the voting-age population who are Hispanic (X_i) and who vote (T_i) in the remaining 249 precincts in Pennsylvania's state senate District 2 in 1990. Each of these lines was computed by following the identical procedure as described for precinct 52, but for different values of X_i and T_i, and thus different intercepts and slopes, corresponding to the precinct from which they come.

This figure provides a view of the entire data set. Thus, for example, one feature of these data are the large number of nearly flat lines, which are from districts with small fractions of Hispanics (i.e., X_i is small and so the slope $-X_i/(1-X_i)$ is also small). These lines indicate very narrow bounds on β_i^w because points on each of the lines projects onto the left vertical axis in a very narrow range. These same lines imply wide bounds for β_i^b that cover the entire [0,1] interval, as can be seen by projecting them downwards. The lines that cut off the bottom left corner of the figure imply narrow bounds, and relatively small values, for both β_i^b and β_i^w.

Thus, Figure 5.1 reorganizes the basic X_i and T_i data so that they express the maximum deterministic information available about the quantities of interest β_i^b and β_i^w, but the figure adds no assumptions of any kind, and no information is lost. That is, it would be possible to reconstruct the original data set from the figure and vice versa, without any loss of information. Thus, either X_i and T_i or the lines in this plot could be thought of as "the data" for the ecological inference problem. After introducing a statistical model in Section 6.1, I return in Section 6.2.4 to this format and show how it also turns out to be a very convenient way of displaying all deterministic and statistical information about the quantities of interest. That is, the bounds and the lines in this figure give the available deterministic information about the quantities of interest, and the statistical model provides probabilistic information about the locations of β_i^b and β_i^w within its bounds, or, equivalently, somewhere along its line. Section 6.2.4 also shows how the concepts used in this figure are mathematically equivalent to an idealized version of the "tomography" problem, such as exists in X-rays and CT scans used to reconstruct images of the insides of objects without invasive techniques. Because of this connection, I will usually refer to this type of data display as a *tomography plot*.

The only remaining result required is the upper and lower bounds on λ_i^b (the proportion of blacks voters casting ballots for the Democrats) and λ_i^w (proportion of white voters casting ballots for the Democrats). Possibly because many of the most intuitive procedures lead to dead ends or especially difficult derivations, these bounds have not been computed. Fortunately, deriving bounds on the λ's, as shown in Appendix B, is straightforward.[1] The bounds are as follows:

$$\frac{\max[0, D_i - (1 - X_i)]}{\max[0, D_i - (1 - X_i)] + \min(T_i - D_i, X_i)} \leq \lambda_i^b \leq \frac{\min(D_i, X_i)}{\min(D_i, X_i) + \max[0, (T_i - D_i) - (1 - X_i)]}$$

$$\frac{\max(0, D_i - X_i)}{\max(0, D_i - X_i) + \min(T_i - D_i, 1 - X_i)} \leq \lambda_i^w \leq \frac{\min(D_i, 1 - X_i)}{\min(D_i, 1 - X_i) + \max[0, (T_i - D_i) - X_i]} \qquad (5.4)$$

As written, the specific algebraic forms in Equations 5.1 and 5.4 are not especially enlightening, but they will prove invaluable. They will also become very intuitive via the graphical techniques introduced in Section 5.3. (Recall that D_i is the fraction of voting-age people casting ballots for the Democratic candidate.)

5.2.2 District-Level Quantities of Interest

Although the literature provides no algebraic formulas for computing the bounds on the aggregate quantities of interest, the procedures used in the numerical examples given in the literature are, contrary to most subsequent claims, not maximally informative. Duncan and Davis (1953) use the correct procedure for the analogous bounds they calculate on correlation coefficients, but subsequent scholars have not used this insight in computing the correct bounds on the aggregate quantities of interest. In part because wider than necessary bounds are being used, the incorrect conclusion of the literature is that "the bounds usually turn out to be so wide as to be nearly useless" (Shively, 1991). In fact, the aggregate bounds can be quite informative. The key is that *the narrowest bounds on the aggregate quantities of interest can be computed by making use of precinct-level data.* That is, the

[1] The most obvious, but most difficult, method of derivation is to use the fact that $\lambda_i^b = \theta_i^b/\beta_i^b$ and to attempt to maximize λ_i^b by its component factors. This becomes difficult because the components are functions of the same quantities.

most informative aggregate lower bounds are weighted averages of the precinct-level lower bounds, and the most informative aggregate upper bounds are weighted averages of the precinct upper bounds. The impression in the literature may have been generated from scholars who used only district-level information, which generates wider bounds, rather than using all the precincts composing the district.

For example, the district-level quantity of interest,

$$B^b = \frac{1}{N^b}\sum_{i=1}^{p} N_i^b \beta_i^b$$

has an aggregate upper bound, if precinct-level information is appropriately used, that is the weighted average of the precinct upper bound:

$$\begin{aligned} \max(B^b|X_i, T_i \text{ for all } i) &= \frac{1}{N^b}\sum_{i=1}^{p} N_i^b \max(\beta_i^b) \\ &= \frac{1}{N^b}\sum_{i=1}^{p} N_i^b \min\left(\frac{T_i}{X_i}, 1\right) \end{aligned} \tag{5.5}$$

If, instead, only the district level information is used (i.e., $\bar{X}$ and $\bar{T}$, instead of X_i and T_i for all i), then the best we can do is to treat the district as a single precinct:

$$\max(B^b|\bar{X}, \bar{T}) = \min\left(\frac{\bar{T}}{\bar{X}}, 1\right) \tag{5.6}$$

The point is that the maximum aggregate bound based on the precinct level data in Equation 5.5 is smaller (more informative) than the bound based on only district-level information in Equation 5.6. That is,

$$\max(B^b|X_i, T_i \text{ for all } i) \leq \max(B^b|\bar{X}, \bar{T})$$

Similarly, the most informative lower bound for B^b, and upper and lower bounds for the remaining district-level parameters ($B^w, \Theta^b, \Theta^w, \Lambda^b, \Lambda^w$), are also computed via the weighted averages of their corresponding precinct-level parameters. This result provides more motivation to use the smallest aggregate units if available, even if the goal is knowledge of district- or state-level quantities. (A numerical example of this point appears at the end of this chapter.)

The results derived in this chapter represent the only certain information about the parameters of interest. Methods of ecological inference that ignore this information are inefficient, at a minimum an especially serious problem given the essential lack of information in the ecological inference problem. But, in fact, models that ignore the bounds, such as all existing statistical approaches, miss a valuable opportunity to calibrate many features of the model and hence avoid problems such as aggregation bias. Since these bounds can be easily combined with any statistical approach to produce better estimates, they are guaranteed to improve all methods of statistical estimation.

5.3 An Easy Visual Method for Computing Bounds

With the expressions given above, computing bounds is very easy: just feed in values of X_i, T_i, and D_i and out will come the bounds. In this section, I further simplify the process of computing bounds for β_i^b and β_i^w by providing a very easy visual method. This method requires no numerical calculations or computer runs, can be used with any data set, and updates with modern graphical techniques the venerable tradition in statistics of providing numerical tables to ease extensive arithmetic computations.[2]

The bounds are functions of X_i and T_i, which are easiest to represent graphically for all precincts in the usual X_i by T_i scatter plot (such as Figure 4.1, page 60). Because of this, I based the special graphs designed in this section on this form of presentation. For example, to determine the bounds on β_i^b for one precinct, locate its position in an X_i by T_i scatter plot and note the same position in each graph of Figure 5.2.

The interiors of these figures are white for combinations of T_i and X_i that imply a bound of zero and are solid black when the bound is one. As noted numerically on the figure, values in between are represented by various shades of gray, and labeled contour lines. (The darkness of the shading in the two graphs in this figure is determined by the left and right sides, respectively, of the first line in Equation 5.1, page 79.) Thus, for example, for a precinct with $X_i = 0.75$ and $T_i = 0.5$, the left panel of the figure indicates that the lower bound on β_i^b falls one-third of the way between the 0.25 and 0.5 contour lines. Thus, $\min(\beta_i^b) = 1/3$. Similarly, the graph on the right of Figure 5.2 gives an upper bound for $X_i = 0.75$ and $T_i = 0.5$ of $\max(\beta_i^b) = 2/3$. Thus, in

[2] The same methods (and figures) can be used to determine the bounds on θ_i^b and θ_i^w. Similar methods could be provided for λ_i^b and λ_i^w, but because these are functions of three variables, the algebraic methods are easier to apply.

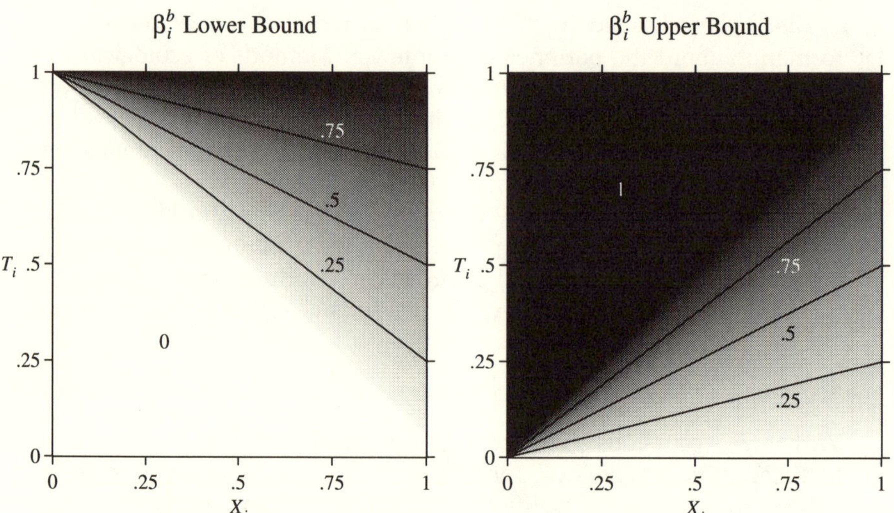

Figure 5.2 Image Plots of Upper and Lower Bounds on β_i^b. Locating a precinct on the left graph, according to its values on X_i and T_i, gives the lower bound on β_i^b, with darker areas representing higher values of the lower bound. The labeled contour lines show the numerical values of some of these bounds. The right graph gives analogous information for the upper bound. For example, if $X_i = 0.5$ and $T_i = 0.75$, then $\beta_i^b \in [0.5, 1]$.

this example, $\beta_i^b \in [1/3, 2/3]$. Figure 5.3 similarly gives the bounds for β_i^w (and is a mirror image of Figure 5.2).

By overlaying a scatter plot of X_i by T_i on Figures 5.2 and then 5.3 (or by visual comparison), a researcher can instantly ascertain the upper and lower bounds for a large set of precinct parameters.

An especially useful version of this visual method of bounds appears in Figure 5.4. Comparing a point, or scatter plot of points, to this figure instantly indicates how much deterministic information exists about a parameter. Shades of grey in this figure refer to the *width* of the bounds, with lighter areas indicating more information. Solid black maps the maximum possible width of 1.0 (which implies bounds on β_i^b or β_i^w respectively, covering the entire range from zero to one). All white areas (on the edges of three sides of each figure) indicate widths of zero, uniquely determining the position of the parameter; these are the homogeneous precincts discussed in Section 5.1. For help in interpreting, the figure also includes contours that trace out a few of the lines for which the shading, and thus the widths of the bounds, is the same. For example, any point from a scatter plot that falls on the β_i^b graph to the right of the 0.5 contour line has a

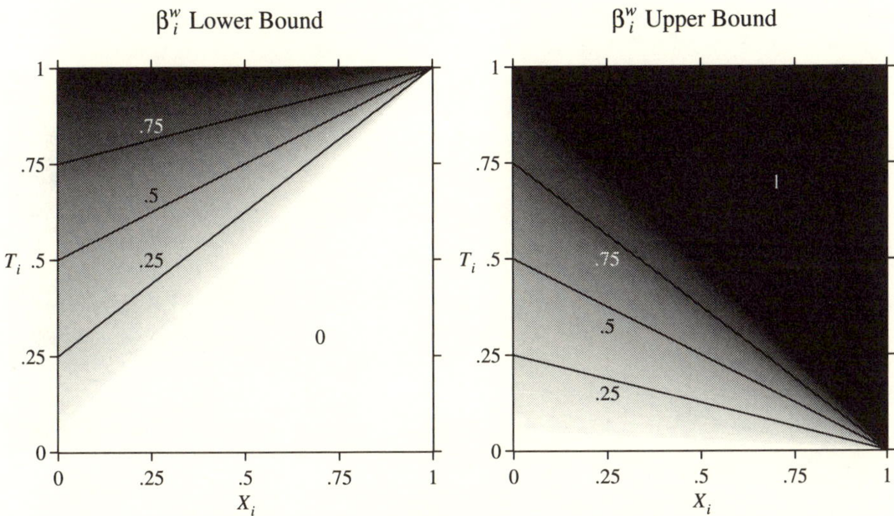

Figure 5.3 Image Plots of Upper and Lower Bounds on β_i^w. Locating a precinct on the left graph, according to its values on X_i and T_i, gives the lower bound on β_i^w, with darker areas representing higher values of the lower bounds. The labeled contour lines show the numerical values of some of these bounds. The right graph gives analogous information for the upper bound. For example, if $X_i = 0.5$ and $T_i = 0.75$, then $\beta_i^w \in [0.5, 1]$.

width that covers less than half of the [0,1] maximum bounds, effectively eliminating half of the ecological inference problem. This area, which includes more than half the area of the scatter plot, shows the large range of precinct-level outcomes that yield moderate to very informative bounds. Although reducing the [0,1] bounds to half that range may not be sufficient for some substantive purposes without additional information, it is extremely informative as part of a larger statistical model. Indeed, rarely are statistical analysts of any problem fortunate enough to have this degree of deterministic information about the parameters of interest at the level of the observation. Ignoring this certain knowledge in a problem where considerable content has been aggregated away from the start is a stunning waste of valuable information.

As an example of how to use these figures to determine the bounds on β_i^b for a set of p precincts, consider the scatter plot in Figure 5.5. This figure plots the Hispanic fraction of the voting age population (X_i) by voter turnout (T_i). The circles in the plot are coded from the same 250 precincts in Pennsylvania's state senate District 2, matched to U.S. Census data, as used in Figure 5.1. In fact, this graph reex-

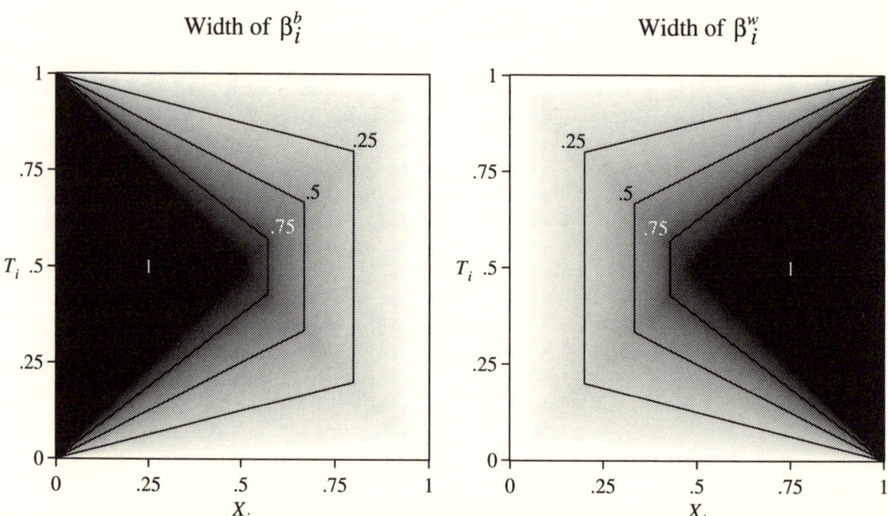

Figure 5.4 Image Plots of Width of Bounds for β_i^b and β_i^w. Locating a precinct on the left graph, according to its values on X_i and T_i, gives the width of the bounds on β_i^b, with darker areas representing wider (less informative) widths. The labeled contour lines show the numerical values of some of these widths. The right graph gives analogous information for β_i^w. For example, if $X_i = 0.5$ and $T_i = 0.25$, the upper bound minus the lower bound for both β_i^b and β_i^w is 0.5.

presses the identical data in a different way, with each circle corresponding to one of Figure 5.1's tomography lines. (For example, the circle at the right with the small box around it is the same precinct, number 52, as the dark line in Figure 5.1.) The bounds can be determined by studying Figure 5.1 or from this figure. To use this figure, we could superimpose the scatter plot on Figures 5.2 and 5.3, but a quicker procedure not requiring sophisticated graphics is to draw in the two diagonal lines on the graph, as in Figure 5.5. This figure, which I will refer to as a *scattercross* graph, is very easy to draw in almost every graphics program. If that is difficult, drawing in the ⊠ by hand over a scatter plot is also easy. Failing even that, it is also not difficult to imagine the cross superimposed on the scatter plot.

It is easy to use this scattercross graph to get a quick sense of how wide the bounds are for the precincts represented in Figure 5.5. The large group of points clustered in the triangle on the left contain no additional deterministic information about β_i^b (fraction of Hispanics who vote); that is, their bounds are all [0,1]. This is easy to see by comparing the position of the points in this graph to the position

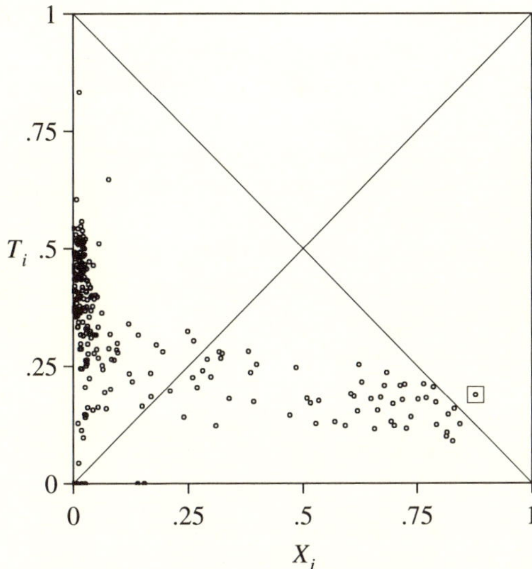

Figure 5.5 A Scattercross Graph of Voter Turnout by Fraction Hispanic: Precincts from Pennsylvania's 2nd State Senate District, 1990. Compare the position of the points in this figure to Figures 5.2–5.4 to determine the bounds for any precinct represented here. For example, the points in the left triangle have [0,1] bounds for β_i^b and very narrow bounds for β_i^w. (These are the same data used in the tomography plot in Figure 5.1. For example, the dark line in the tomography plot represents the same data point appearing with a small square around it in this figure.)

on the left graph in Figure 5.4. Fortunately, the points in the left triangle do provide very narrow bounds on β_i^w (the fraction of non-Hispanics who vote), in most cases narrower than a width of 0.1, and near a value of $\beta_i^w \approx 0.5$. That considerable information exists in these points can be seen quickly by consulting the right panel in Figure 5.4; the specific upper and lower bounds on β_i^w can be seen by locating the position of these points on Figure 5.3. Finally, the group of points spread across the bottom triangle have narrow bounds, and are therefore very informative, about both β_i^b and β_i^w.

Overall, as is often the case, the bounds on the precinct-level parameters implied by these points are very informative. As a consequence, the bounds on the aggregate quantities of interest, when properly computed, are also very narrow. For example, the proportion of Hispanics who voted in Philadelphia (B^b) must fall between 0.001 and 0.437. Even more informative are the bounds on the proportion of non-Hispanics who vote (B^w), which the aggregate bounds indicate must range between 0.295 and 0.365. (In contrast, the wider bounds on B^b, computed with the inferior procedure used in the literature formalized in Equation 5.6, page 84, range all the way from zero to one. Similarly, the incorrect wider bounds on B^w range from 0.20 to 0.37.)

The tools and results presented in this section should also make clear that the optimal scatter plot from the perspective of making ecological inferences is not necessarily one that closely approximates a steeply sloping regression line. Indeed, the conventional wisdom about optimal scatter plots is quite misleading. For example, the slope of the regression line is immaterial: even a flat line (zero slope) can be very informative in ecological inference problems. In fact, the best situation, at least from the perspective of available deterministic information, is instead one with points falling along the edges of the scatter plot. If the goal is to estimate β_i^b, then the best scatter plot looks like ⊐, that is, with points around all the edges except the left margin. If the goal is instead β_i^w, a ⊏-shaped graph is preferable, that is, one with points near all edges but the right margin. Of course, researchers do not usually get to choose the data to be analyzed based on the certainty of the results, but we should at least understand how much information different types of data are likely to contain.

CHAPTER 6

The Model

THIS CHAPTER sets forth a method of ecological inference that solves the problems identified in Part II using the aggregate data as reexpressed in Chapter 5. The statistical model has the following features:

1. The model combines the insights of the various statistical approaches and the deterministic method of bounds approach, using only those assumptions with at least some observable implications in aggregate data.
2. It allows parameters to vary over precincts in a manner consistent with and verifiable in observable data.
3. The model has a variance function that requires no assumptions, but fits an important feature of ecological data.
4. It takes advantage of available information in the data to avoid aggregation problems. External data may also be used if available.
5. The model is strongly robust to aggregation bias, even when not using the explicit procedures designed to ameliorate it.
6. The estimation method gives accurate estimates of district- and precinct-level quantities of interest and provides estimates of uncertainty such as confidence intervals and posterior distributions.

In addition, I follow a strategy that helps to satisfy two important but conflicting goals of good statistical models: fitting the data, and estimating the correct quantities of interest. The tension between these goals is at the heart of many problems in social science statistical applications. The tension is often caused by the understandable desire of analysts to trick existing canned statistical packages into printing out the quantities of interest directly, but they too often compromise on one of the goals in seeking to accomplish the other. The various failed attempts at "cookbook" statistical procedures, most of which do not contain sufficient recipes to cover what we have in our data-filled refrigerators, commonly result in highly parameterized model-dependent inferences (as in some structural equation models), or atheoretical data-fitting exercises (such as stepwise regression or "automatic interaction detectors"). Like trying to make a contraption that would serve the purposes of both a car and a peanut butter sandwich, the result may be fun to watch but you wouldn't want to drive it or take a bite.

The tension between these conflicting goals is resolved by using a two-stage, hierarchical approach. First fit the data with a model parameterized in a manner most convenient for this purpose. This makes fitting the data and estimation straightforward, even though the estimated parameters are not the quantities of interest. Then, in a separate computation, but with no new assumptions, use the first-stage results to compute the quantities of interest. With this procedure, each stage can be optimized to achieve its goal without the constraints from the other stage.

Although this tension affects most areas of statistical inquiry, consider one example of it from the ecological inference literature. Achen and Shively (1995: 45) are explicitly ambivalent about recommending nonlinear specifications in ecological inference models: "Bounding probabilities between zero and one means that a likelihood function straining to produce ... estimates of 150% or −20% will be forcibly prevented from doing so, and thus important clues to incorrect specification will be lost .... Nonetheless..., the gain in accuracy from nonlinearity may be worthwhile." Achen and Shively's conundrum would be easily resolved by the approach taken here. They could use a nonlinear specification if appropriate, and then also conduct separate diagnostic specification tests if desired. By not trying to create strained models that are also "self-diagnosing," researchers can produce better models and also better diagnostic procedures. Models that are self-diagnosing can be useful, but we do not usually need to sacrifice more fundamental goals to create such models.

This chapter is devoted to the simplest version of the theoretical model. Section 6.1 gives a brief statement of the model, and Section 6.2 interprets it from five different perspectives. Extensions of the model are given in Chapter 9.

6.1 The Basic Model

This section summarizes the most basic version of the model for inferences about β_i^b and β_i^w in Table 2.3 (page 31).[1] The model consists

[1] As described in Section 8.4, an analogous model applies to the intermediate parameters θ_i^b and θ_i^w. Estimating the parameters of interest from Table 2.2, λ_i^b and λ_i^w or larger $2 \times C$ tables require two separate applications of this basic model. Larger $R \times C$ tables will require a generalization of the model, which I put off until Chapter 15.

of three assumptions built on the basic accounting identity in which T_i and X_i are observed, and β_i^b and β_i^w are the quantities of interest, for $i = 1, \ldots, p$ precincts:

$$T_i = \beta_i^b X_i + \beta_i^w (1 - X_i) \tag{6.1}$$

Equation 6.1 is a statement of fact, not an assumption of linearity or anything else. The three model assumptions I add to this identity are all at least in part verifiable in aggregate data. That is, because observable implications of each do exist, the assumptions can be verified in sufficient depth to weed out many applications for which similar assumptions in other models might lead one astray. Chapter 9 discusses these observable implications, provides a variety of diagnostic tests, and introduces extensions of this basic model that allow each of these three assumptions to be modified, extended, or dropped.

First, model β_i^b and β_i^w as if they are generated by a truncated bivariate normal distribution, conditional on X_i. Thus, instead of assuming these parameters are constant over precincts, we only assume, roughly speaking, that they have something in common—that they vary but are at least partly dependent upon one another. (For help in visualizing this important but relatively simple assumption, look ahead to the three-dimensional surface plots of this distribution in Figure 6.2, page 105.) This distribution has a single mode, indicating where most values of β_i^b and β_i^w lie, and also allows any degree of variation in each around the mode. For example, most values of β_i^b could be narrowly dispersed around 0.7, while values of β_i^w might vary widely over the entire [0,1] interval. The distribution also allows β_i^b and β_i^w to have any degree of correlation from -1 to 1. Formally, the probability density of (β_i^b, β_i^w) is

$$\mathrm{P}(\beta_i^b, \beta_i^w) = \mathrm{TN}(\beta_i^b, \beta_i^w | \mathfrak{B}, \Sigma) \tag{6.2}$$

where TN stands for the truncated normal distribution with truncation limits $\beta_i^b \in [0, 1]$ and $\beta_i^w \in [0, 1]$ (As demonstrated below, after conditioning on T_i, this specification implies truncation according to the narrower precinct-level bounds in Chapter 5.) The mean vector and variance matrix of (β_i^b, β_i^w) are[2]

$$\mathfrak{B} = \begin{pmatrix} \mathfrak{B}^b \\ \mathfrak{B}^w \end{pmatrix} \quad \text{and} \quad \Sigma = \begin{pmatrix} \sigma_b^2 & \sigma_{bw} \\ \sigma_{bw} & \sigma_w^2 \end{pmatrix} \tag{6.3}$$

The purpose of the model is to estimate β_i^b and β_i^w for all p observations. Thus, the parameters $\mathfrak{B}$ and Σ are not of direct interest. In addition, $\mathfrak{B}^b = \mathrm{E}(\beta_i^b)$ and $\mathfrak{B}^w = \mathrm{E}(\beta_i^w)$ are based on simple averages of the precinct parameters rather than the more interesting aggregate quantities of interest, B^b and B^w, which are weighted averages (see Chapter 2). The only direct use $\mathfrak{B}$ and Σ have in the following analyses is to help understand intermediate results on the way to computing the parameters of interest.

Second, assume for the time being that β_i^b and β_i^w are "mean independent" of X_i, which is a weaker assumption than requiring β_i^b and β_i^w to be stochastically independent (that is, completely unrelated; see Goldberger, 1991: 61). This assumption, which is equivalent to assuming the absence of aggregation bias, is technically necessary to obtain consistent estimates of $\mathfrak{B}$ and Σ. However, and somewhat surprisingly, this assumption is not always necessary to obtain accurate estimates of the quantities of interest, about which more in Chapter 9.

Finally, assume, as in all previous ecological inference research, that values of T_i in different precincts are independent after conditioning on X_i. As explained in Section 9.1.3, violating this assumption does not have major consequences for most aspects of this model.

If there exists evidence that the bivariate distribution is not truncated normal, that there is aggregation bias to which the model is not robust, or that the observations are spatially dependent, this information can be detected and incorporated in the model via the procedures discussed in Chapter 9.

6.2 Model Interpretation

The remainder of this chapter provides interpretations of the model in Section 6.1 from different perspectives and with several graphical

[2] If there exists evidence that, conditional on this specification, model variances are proportional to, or in some other way related to, precinct size, the correct specification would be to *add* this "sampling" variance to the elements of Σ. This would change the definition of Σ, but since this is an *additional* source of variation, it makes little sense to allow it to reduce the total variance, as sometimes occurs when designing models based entirely on unsupported assumptions such as independence and identical probability of votes, as in Equations 4.1 and 4.2 (page 62).

and algebraic methods. No new assumptions are added. This section begins with a brief overview of the results to follow as well as a general sense of how the model will be estimated (as explained in detail in Chapter 7) and quantities of interest computed (as developed in Chapter 8). The ultimate goal is calculating the posterior (or sampling) distribution of β_i^b and β_i^w in each precinct (the mean and standard deviation of which could serve as point estimates and standard errors, respectively, for example). Accomplishing this goal requires four steps.

First, represent the precinct data on a β_i^b by β_i^w tomography plot (as in Figure 5.1, page 81). In this figure, each precinct observation of X_i and T_i appears as a line, just as was described originally in Equation 5.2, page 80. This presentation narrows the known possible coordinates of the true β_i^b, β_i^w point in each precinct from the entire unit square to one line in the square, and thus also incorporates the deterministic bounds on each parameter.

Second, estimate the means, standard deviations, and correlation of β_i^b and β_i^w across precincts. These five quantities are the parameters of the truncated bivariate normal distribution (from the statistical model's first assumption) and can be estimated from the information in a scatter plot of X_i by T_i like those in Figure 6.1 (page 100). As this figure explains, the means can be estimated from the expected value of T_i given X_i, which is linear and thus can be estimated by a regression (although this procedure will be substantially improved upon), and the standard deviations and correlation are estimated from the pattern of heteroskedasticity around the linear expected value.

The third step is to represent the particular truncated bivariate normal distribution, as indicated by its five estimated parameters, in the same β_i^b by β_i^w square as the data (see, for example, Figure 6.3 page 114). In the figure, this is done with contour ellipses, which are two-dimensional projections of the three-dimensional distributions looking down from above (the same idea as the contour lines used to represent mountain ranges on geographic maps). For example, the identical distribution represented in the contours in Figure 6.3 is represented as a three-dimensional surface plot in Figure 6.4 (page 116). The contour representation is more useful because the data, represented as lines, can more easily appear in the same figure.

Finally, in order to learn more about where on each line, and thus where within their bounds, the true β_i^b and β_i^w fall, the model *borrows strength* statistically from the truncated bivariate normal distribution of all the precincts. That is, the posterior distribution for one precinct is exactly the univariate distribution sliced out of the contours by its line in Figure 6.3 and projected onto the vertical or horizontal axis.

This tells us that the location of the true β_i^b, β_i^w point known for certain to fall on its line is most likely to lie on that portion of the line passing closest to the center of the truncated bivariate normal distribution contours estimated from all the lines.

Examples of the posterior (or sampling) distributions of the precinct parameters that result from these calculations appear in Figure 8.1 (page 148). Some comparisons of these estimates with the true values of the quantities of interest are given in Part IV (such as Figure 10.5, page 210). Posterior distributions of district-level quantities, and comparisons with the truth appear in, for example, Figure 10.4 (page 208).

I now explain these points in more depth and with all the necessary technical details. Thus, the remainder of this chapter discusses how the model's parameters affect observable features of aggregate data (Section 6.2.1), how an alternative parameterization can be useful (Section 6.2.2), and how to compute $2p$ quantities of interest from only p observations (Section 6.2.3). Section 6.2.4 gives a geometric interpretation of the model related to statistical analyses of "tomography" problems in medical and seismic imaging, and Section 6.2.5 shows why models based on individual-level (within-precinct) assumptions would not be helpful.

6.2.1 *Observable Implications of Model Parameters*

In order to understand the model, it is essential to see how its five parameters are revealed in aggregate data. Identifying these observable implications of the model will prove especially important for estimation (as described in Chapter 7).

To begin, write the model parameters as unconditional (unweighted) means and variances of the precinct-level parameters of interest:

$$E\begin{pmatrix}\beta_i^b\\ \beta_i^w\end{pmatrix} = \begin{pmatrix}\mathfrak{B}^b\\ \mathfrak{B}^w\end{pmatrix} = \mathfrak{B}$$

$$V\begin{pmatrix}\beta_i^b\\ \beta_i^w\end{pmatrix} = \begin{pmatrix}\sigma_b^2 & \sigma_{bw}\\ \sigma_{bw} & \sigma_w^2\end{pmatrix} = \Sigma \tag{6.4}$$

and the relationship between the precinct parameters and their means as

$$\beta_i^b = \mathfrak{B}^b + \epsilon_i^b$$

$$\beta_i^w = \mathfrak{B}^w + \epsilon_i^w \tag{6.5}$$

where the error terms ϵ_i^b and ϵ_i^w have zero means because they are defined as deviations from their corresponding conditional expected values.

Now, by following the procedures first suggested by Goodman (1959), substitute the right sides of Equations 6.5 into the accounting identity of Equation 6.1:

$$\begin{aligned} T_i &= \beta_i^b X_i + \beta_i^w (1 - X_i) \\ &= (\mathfrak{B}^b + \epsilon_i^b) X_i + (\mathfrak{B}^w + \epsilon_i^w)(1 - X_i) \\ &= \mathfrak{B}^b X_i + \mathfrak{B}^w (1 - X_i) + \epsilon_i \qquad (6.6) \end{aligned}$$

where

$$\epsilon_i = \epsilon_i^b X_i + \epsilon_i^w (1 - X_i) \qquad (6.7)$$

With these preliminaries aside, it is easy to see that $E(\epsilon_i|X_i) = 0$ and, as a result, the mean function of the outcome variable is

$$E(T_i|X_i) = \mathfrak{B}^b X_i + \mathfrak{B}^w (1 - X_i) \qquad (6.8)$$

This equation shows that $\mathfrak{B}^b$ and $\mathfrak{B}^w$ could be estimated by something like Goodman's regression (although this procedure will be substantially improved upon). Indeed, any estimate of the conditional expectation of T_i given X_i, based on these aggregate data alone, provides some useful information about $\mathfrak{B}^b$ and $\mathfrak{B}^w$, which are features of the precinct-level parameters of interest β_i^b and β_i^w. For a simple example, $E(T_i|X_i = 1) = \mathfrak{B}^b$ can be estimated by the average of T_i for homogeneously black districts, as $E(T_i|X_i = 0) = \mathfrak{B}^w$ can be estimated by the average of T_i in all-white districts. These simple examples are meant to provide intuition as to where in the data there exists information about $\mathfrak{B}^b$ and $\mathfrak{B}^w$. Chapter 7 uses this intuition but develops a more sophisticated model built on all useful information in the data.

Whereas $\mathfrak{B}^b$ and $\mathfrak{B}^w$ affect aggregate data through the conditional expectation function, the remaining three parameters of the truncated bivariate normal—the variances $V(\beta_i^b) = \sigma_b^2$ and $V(\beta_i^w) = \sigma_w^2$, and the covariance $C(\beta_i^b, \beta_i^w) = \sigma_{bw}$—affect aggregate data through the conditional variance function, which is heteroskedastic (that is, the variance changes over precincts). We can see this by applying the rules for the variance of linear functions:

$$\begin{aligned} V(T_i|X_i) &= V(\epsilon_i|X_i) \\ &= \sigma_b^2 X_i^2 + \sigma_w^2(1-X_i)^2 + \sigma_{bw} 2X_i(1-X_i) \qquad (6.9) \\ &= (\sigma_w^2) + (2\sigma_{bw} - 2\sigma_w^2)X_i + (\sigma_b^2 + \sigma_w^2 - 2\sigma_{bw})X_i^2 \qquad (6.10) \end{aligned}$$

Equation 6.10 indicates that the variance is a *quadratic* function of X_i, with the three factors in parentheses as coefficients. (Equation 6.9 is more useful for evaluating partial estimation results, since the σ's are more directly interpretable than the parenthetical terms of Equation 6.10.) In addition, I will usually refer to the correlation, $\rho = \sigma_{bw}/\sigma_b\sigma_w$ which ranges from -1 to 1, instead of the covariance σ_{bw}. Although expected value and variance calculations such as these have been suggested in theoretical discussions as early as Goodman (1959), previous researchers have confused the parameters $\mathfrak{B}$ (and Σ) with the aggregate quantities of interest B, and have not developed methods of computing the correct quantities of interest from either.

In order to interpret these variance function results, consider some special cases. With X_i at its extremes, indicating precincts with only blacks or only whites, the variances refer to parameter variation among only blacks or whites:

$$\begin{aligned} V(T_i|X_i = 1) &= V(\beta_i^b) = \sigma_b^2 \\ V(T_i|X_i = 0) &= V(\beta_i^w) = \sigma_w^2 \end{aligned}$$

In our running example, the variances of black voter preferences are often smaller than the variances of whites ($\sigma_b^2 < \sigma_w^2$), as for example in the scatter plots in Figures 4.1 (page 60) and 4.3 (page 66), although the pattern of heteroskedasticity will differ across applications. The basic model is thus a heteroskedastic linear regression model of T_i on X_i, where the parameters of interest are related to, but not coincident with, the parameters of the regression. The theoretical variance around the regression line is fairly wide to begin and gets narrower as X_i moves from zero (whites) to one (blacks) if $\sigma_b^2 < \sigma_w^2$. This suggests a clear pattern that we should, and in fact almost always do, see in real data of this kind. Many published scatter plots of percent black by percent voting for the Democratic candidate (or similarly for other ethnic groups) display this strong pattern.

The pattern by which the heteroskedasticity gets narrower as X_i increases is governed by the covariance term, σ_{bw}, which indicates the degree to which black and white support for Democrats covary. For example, at the mid-point, the variance around the expected value line is:

$$V(T_i|X_i = 0.5) = \frac{\sigma_w^2 + \sigma_b^2 + 2\sigma_{bw}}{4}$$

The heteroskedasticity in many voting data sets appears to get narrower quickly when X_i is between 0 and around 0.3 and then gradually thereafter. In other cases, the variance is a nearly linear function of X_i. The covariance indicates the degree to which the parameters vary together or independently over precincts. The covariance will equal zero when the two parameters (β_i^b and β_i^w) vary independently, conditional on X_i, and will reach its theoretical maximum (the product of the variances, so that the correlation is 1.0) when they are identical ($\beta_i^b = \beta_i^w$). They could also vary inversely if the covariance is negative.

Other data sets should be expected to display different types of heteroskedasticity, and fortunately most plausible types will fall within the possibilities that can be represented by this model. Figure 6.1 displays some of the types of heteroskedasticity which the model allows by setting the five parameters at various specific values and randomly generating data from the specified model. The straight, solid line in each graph of Figure 6.1 is the expected value of T_i from Equation 6.8, and the dashed lines are drawn at plus and minus one standard deviation (the square root of the variance in Equation 6.9). As the figure demonstrates, the model is quite flexible. The variance can grow or shrink as X_i increases. It can also shrink and then grow in the same graph, with the inflection point also varying over the range of X_i.

Figure 6.1 is also useful for understanding precisely what features of the data will be used (in Chapter 7) to estimate each of the five parameters. In summary, $\mathfrak{B}^b$, $\mathfrak{B}^w$, σ_b, and σ_w will prove relatively easy to estimate, as they are each related to gross, easy-to-identify features of the data. The correlation of β_i^b and β_i^w, ρ, is related to a more subtle feature of the data and will therefore prove more difficult to estimate precisely (although it is statistically identified and fortunately the parameters of interest will turn out not to depend heavily on ρ).

More specifically, $\mathfrak{B}^b$ is the point at which the solid line intersects the right vertical axis (that is, where $X_i = 1$, meaning that all voting-age people are African Americans). $\mathfrak{B}^w$ is the point where this expected value line intersects the left vertical axis. A rough estimate of $\mathfrak{B}^b$ and $\mathfrak{B}^w$ could be based on a least squares regression, or even the average of the points near their respective extreme. (These rough methods of estimation can obviously be improved upon, but consid-

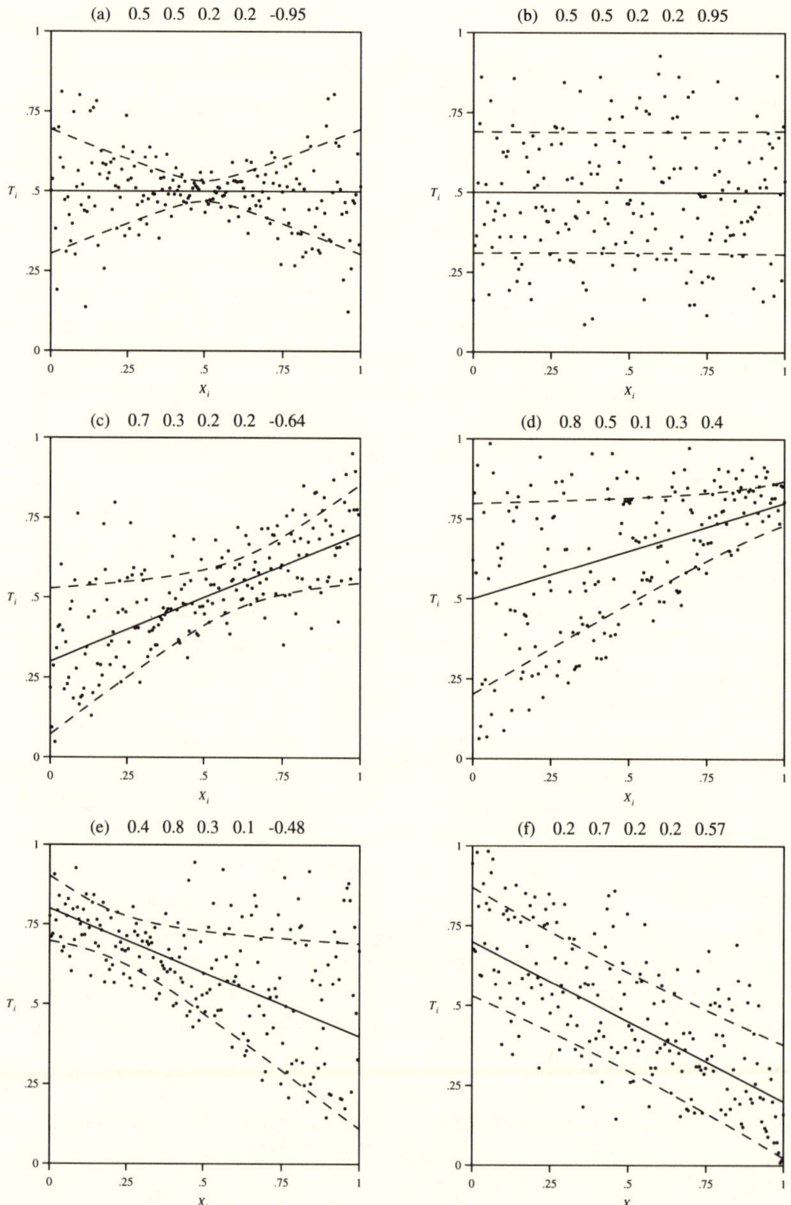

Figure 6.1 Features of the Data Generated by Each Parameter. Each graph is a plot of X_i by T_i with dots representing individual precincts. Data were randomly generated from the model with parameter values of $\mathfrak{B}^b$, $\mathfrak{B}^w$, σ_b, σ_w, and ρ, indicated at the top of each graph. $\mathfrak{B}^b$ and $\mathfrak{B}^w$ are the values at which the solid (expected value) line crosses the right and left axes, respectively. σ_b and σ_w are the standard deviations of points around the solid line at the right and left axes, as indicated by the dashed lines. ρ influences the degree of dip in the dashed standard deviation curves near the middle.

ering them helps to understand the kind of information in the data being relied upon during more sophisticated estimation procedures.) The primary difficulty with estimating these parameters occurs when extrapolating the regression to one extreme if most of the data points fall far from that end of the graph. For example, if most of the data have values of $X_i \in [0, 0.1]$, extrapolating to the right vertical axis to estimate $\mathfrak{B}^b$ should generate fairly uncertain inferences.

Only slightly less information exists in the data to estimate the variances. The parameter σ_b is the vertical distance between the solid line and either dashed line at the right side of the graph; σ_w is the same at the left side of the graph. These can be roughly estimated by calculating the standard deviation of the points near their respective sides of the graph (although a better procedure is to use all points with a full model). Estimating variances is usually somewhat more difficult than estimating means, and extrapolating them in the situation where no data are near the relevant extreme would be even more difficult.

In contrast to $\mathfrak{B}^b$, $\mathfrak{B}^w$, σ_b, and σ_w, the correlation $\rho = \sigma_{bw}/(\sigma_b\sigma_w)$ does not depend on such easy-to-recognize features of aggregate data. For example, compare panels (a) and (b) in Figure 6.1. All parameters are the same in the two graphs except for the correlation, which is set at two extreme values, $-.95$ and $.95$. The correlation between β_i^b and β_i^w is revealed in ecological data only in the degree of dip in the variance between the two ends. A large dip implies a negative correlation, as in panel (a), whereas no heteroskedasticity in the data (that is, only linear changes in the variance) is the aggregate information that indicates a strong positive correlation at the individual level, as in panel (b). Fortunately, ecological inferences depend on ρ to only a relatively minor degree.

To see how this pattern emerges, note that T_i is generated from a linear combination of β_i^b and β_i^w, due to the accounting identity in Equation 6.1. The closer β_i^b and β_i^w come to being identical, as is nearly the case in graph (b), the more the accounting identity approximates $T_i = \beta_i^b = \beta_i^w$, and thus the less the variability in T_i responds to changes in X_i. The result is that a large value of ρ produces the homoskedastic pattern in graph (b). In contrast, the reduced variance near $X_i = 0.5$ in graph (a) emerges from the natural consequence of averaging two negatively correlated parameters with equal weights (i.e., with $X_i = (1 - X_i) = 0.5$). Averaging negatively correlated variables reduces variance even more than with independent components.

Figure 6.1, panels (b) and (f), shows that the model also allows for very low or nonexistent levels of heteroskedasticity, which do occur in some data. Such data sets will thus pose no difficulties for this model. Indeed, it is a common misconception in some statistical literature that expanding a model by adding parameters (or having fewer constraints on existing parameters) will necessarily make inferences less certain. This concept is correct only if the data are analyzed improperly or if a larger number of dependent inferences are being made. In the present situation, almost no matter how complicated the model that fits the data, the quantities of interest do not lose precision if they are calculated by averaging over the estimated parameters. Thus, more complicated models will not necessarily cause inefficiencies in estimates of the parameters of interest. A more realistic model is certainly better than incorrectly assuming that the variance function is homoskedastic. Moreover, the complication induced by the heteroskedastic variance function is a natural feature of the problem, and it does not require more assumptions to derive.

6.2.2 *Parameterizing the Truncated Bivariate Normal*

The truncated bivariate normal distribution in Equation 6.2 has five parameters—two means, two standard deviations, and a correlation, all of β_i^b and β_i^w. These parameters can be represented in three ways:

$$\psi = \{\mathfrak{B}^b, \mathfrak{B}^w, \sigma_b, \sigma_w, \rho\} = \{\mathfrak{B}, \Sigma\} \tag{6.11}$$

Although these are not the parameters of interest, they have direct interpretations as unweighted functions of β_i^b and β_i^w. Unfortunately, ψ turns out to be very difficult to use directly in the necessary mathematical derivations to follow. The problem is that although ψ can serve as the parameters of the truncated bivariate normal, it cannot do so algebraically in the usual manner that probability distributions are represented. Indeed, the model in Equation 6.2 (page 93), using the parameters ψ, can only be defined implicitly, whereas we need an explicit algebraic expression. In order to develop this explicit expression, an alternative parameterization will prove useful.[3] That is, instead of ψ, denote $\breve{\psi}$ as a vector of five new parameters of the truncated bivariate normal distribution. With this new parameterization we now provide an explicit algebraic expression that can be translated back into the original, and more interpretable, ψ.

In order to explain this problem and how the new parameterization serves as its solution, I show how to derive the truncated bivariate normal distribution from the corresponding *untruncated* bivariate

[3] I thank Andrew Gelman for helpful suggestions regarding this alternative parameterization.

normal. This procedure reveals the direct, algebraic form of the parameters $\breve{\psi}$ that will prove immensely useful for subsequent computations. Thus, begin by (temporarily) writing β_i^b and β_i^w *as if they were* generated by an untruncated bivariate normal probability density:

$$\begin{aligned} N(\beta_i^b, \beta_i^w | \breve{\mathfrak{B}}, \breve{\Sigma}) \\ = (2\pi)^{-1} |\breve{\Sigma}|^{-1/2} \exp\left[-\frac{1}{2}(\beta_i - \breve{\mathfrak{B}})' \breve{\Sigma}^{-1} (\beta_i - \breve{\mathfrak{B}}) \right] \end{aligned} \tag{6.12}$$

where β_i is a vector containing β_i^b and β_i^w. This is the usual formula for the bivariate normal distribution, and it is readily interpretable. The only unknowns are its five parameters—two means ($\breve{\mathfrak{B}}$), two standard deviations, and a correlation ($\breve{\Sigma}$). For given values of these parameters, this expression gives the probability density of the variables β_i^b and β_i^w; the volume under the surface of this distribution in different regions gives probabilistic statements about where β_i^b and β_i^w fall. Because these are parameters of the untruncated bivariate normal, we can reuse the same symbols as in Equation 6.11, but with the addition of ˘ on top of each:

$$\breve{\psi} = \{\breve{\mathfrak{B}}^b, \breve{\mathfrak{B}}^w, \breve{\sigma}_b, \breve{\sigma}_w, \breve{\rho}\} = \{\breve{\mathfrak{B}}, \breve{\Sigma}\} \tag{6.13}$$

It is important to recognize that the untruncated parameters $\breve{\psi}$ are not restricted in the same way as are the truncated parameters ψ. Thus, for example, although the truncated means $\mathfrak{B}^b$ and $\mathfrak{B}^w$ must fall within the [0,1] interval, the untruncated parameters $\breve{\mathfrak{B}}^b$ and $\breve{\mathfrak{B}}^w$ can fall anywhere on the real number line.

In order to create the desired truncated bivariate normal distribution assumed for β_i^b and β_i^w, we must perform two operations on this untruncated normal: first, we must truncate it, so that the probability of β_i^b or β_i^w falling outside of the [0,1] interval is zero. This has the effect of cutting off pieces of the untruncated normal outside the unit square. Second, we must rescale the (remaining) volume under the distribution above the unit square so that it still integrates to one (indicating that β_i^b and β_i^w each always take on *some* value). The result is the same truncated bivariate normal distribution as in the model from Equation 6.2, but now written in terms of the untruncated bivariate normal with its untruncated parameters:

$$\mathrm{TN}(\beta_i^b, \beta_i^w | \breve{\mathfrak{B}}, \breve{\Sigma}) = N(\beta_i^b, \beta_i^w | \breve{\mathfrak{B}}, \breve{\Sigma}) \frac{\mathbf{1}(\beta_i^b, \beta_i^w)}{R(\breve{\mathfrak{B}}, \breve{\Sigma})} \tag{6.14}$$

This truncated normal differs from the untruncated normal in Equation 6.12 due to the extra factor on the right side of Equation 6.14. The numerator of this factor performs the truncation, guaranteeing that β_i^b and β_i^w (each proportions) have a zero probability of varying outside the unit interval: $\mathbf{1}(\beta_i^b, \beta_i^w)$ is an indicator function that equals one if $\beta_i^b \in [0,1]$ and $\beta_i^w \in [0,1]$ and zero otherwise. The normalizing factor in the denominator, $R(\breve{\mathfrak{B}}, \breve{\Sigma})$, is the volume under the untruncated normal distribution above the unit square:

$$R(\breve{\mathfrak{B}}, \breve{\Sigma}) = \int_0^1 \int_0^1 \mathrm{N}(\beta^b, \beta^w | \breve{\mathfrak{B}}, \breve{\Sigma}) d\beta^b d\beta^w \tag{6.15}$$

When divided into the untruncated normal, this factor keeps the volume under the truncated distribution equal to one.

The vectors ψ and $\breve{\psi}$ are alternative representations of the same parameters of the *truncated* bivariate normal distribution. The advantage of ψ is that it is relatively easy to interpret, which can be useful for understanding the model (as used in Section 6.2.1), and evaluating intermediate results during estimation. The advantage of $\breve{\psi}$ is that the algebraic form of the probability distribution can be written down explicitly and thus easily used in subsequent calculations. The same is not true of ψ. The disadvantage of using $\breve{\psi}$ is that it does not have as direct an interpretation. For example, unlike $\mathfrak{B}^b$ and $\mathfrak{B}^w$, $\breve{\mathfrak{B}}^b$ and $\breve{\mathfrak{B}}^w$ are not unweighted averages of β_i^b and β_i^w, respectively; indeed, they are not even proportions. Although the output of the procedure discussed in this book includes estimates of the quantities of interest in exactly the scale and with precisely the interpretation desired, it is helpful to have a full understanding of $\breve{\psi}$ and ψ in order to understand the inner workings of the model.

Fortunately $\breve{\psi}$ does have some interpretative value in one particular circumstance. That is, the core of the truncated normal is the corresponding (untruncated) normal distribution, $\mathrm{N}(\beta^b, \beta^w | \breve{\mathfrak{B}}, \breve{\Sigma})$. When $R(\breve{\mathfrak{B}}, \Sigma)$ is nearly one, the truncation has little effect on the distribution, in which case ψ is numerically close to $\breve{\psi}$. This occurs when the means of β_i^b and β_i^w, on the untruncated or truncated scale fall well within their bounds (such as $\breve{\mathfrak{B}}^b = 0.5$ and $\breve{\mathfrak{B}}^w = 0.5$) and the variances are small (such as $\sigma_b = 0.01$ and $\sigma_w = 0.01$). In this situation, only a very small amount of the area under the untruncated bivariate normal distribution falls outside of the $[0,1] \times [0,1]$ square, and so the truncation has very little effect. This relationship is useful for interpreting $\breve{\psi}$, although using $\breve{\psi}$ does not involve any approximation.

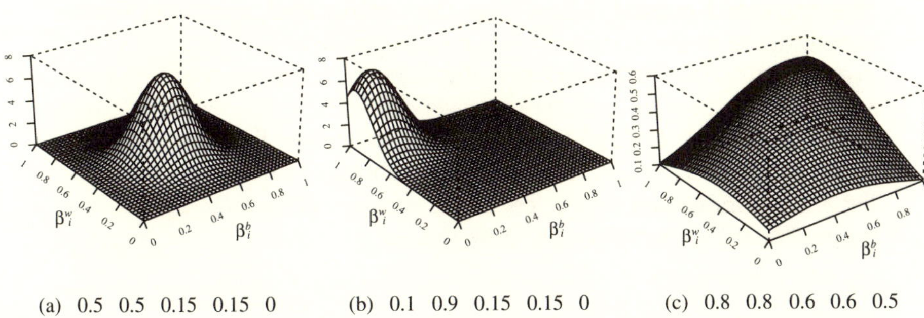

(a) 0.5 0.5 0.15 0.15 0 (b) 0.1 0.9 0.15 0.15 0 (c) 0.8 0.8 0.6 0.6 0.5

Figure 6.2 Truncated Bivariate Normal Distributions, $\text{TN}(\beta_i^b, \beta_i^w | \breve{\mathfrak{B}}, \breve{\Sigma})$. Graph (a) is a distribution relatively unaffected by the truncation bounds. The graphs (b) and (c) are strongly truncated. Parameter values $\breve{\mathfrak{B}}$, $\breve{\mathfrak{B}}$, $\breve{\sigma}_b$, $\breve{\sigma}_w$, and $\breve{\rho}$ are indicated beneath each graph.

These concepts are portrayed in the three-dimensional surface plots of the truncated bivariate normal distributions in Figure 6.2. Note how the distribution in graph (a) is very nearly flat as it approaches the edges of the square (i.e., near the [0,1] extremes of β_i^b and β_i^w). This special case is useful to keep in mind as a leading example when trying to understand the role of $\breve{\psi}$. But one must also remember that $\breve{\psi} \neq \psi$ in general. For example, although $\mathfrak{B}^b$ and $\mathfrak{B}^w$ always fall within the [0,1] interval, $\breve{\mathfrak{B}}^b$ and $\breve{\mathfrak{B}}^w$ have no such restrictions. The graphs (b) and (c) in Figure 6.2 give examples of truncated bivariate normal distributions where the truncation limits have a clear effect, and thus ψ is not close to $\breve{\psi}$.

The precise functional relationship between ψ and $\breve{\psi}$ cannot be solved analytically, but translating numerically (with any desired degree of precision) is straightforward. Doing this requires an increasingly popular technique from statistics called "simulation" that is described in detail in Section 8.1. For example, to go from $\breve{\psi}$ to ψ, draw a large number of random samples of β_i^b and β_i^w from the truncated normal distribution $\text{TN}(\beta_i^b, \beta_i^w | \breve{\mathfrak{B}}, \breve{\Sigma})$, that is, with mean vector $\breve{\mathfrak{B}}$ and variance matrix $\breve{\Sigma}$. To compute $\mathfrak{B}$, take the means of the random samples. The sample variance matrix of the random draws gives Σ. This procedure is an approximation, but *any* degree of accuracy may be achieved by merely increasing the number of random draws, and so nothing is lost.

In order to make continued analogies to the special case where $\breve{\psi}$ can be interpreted as ψ, denote the "expected value" as $\breve{\text{E}}(a)$ and "variance" as $\breve{\text{V}}(a)$, regardless of the degree to which the variable a is affected by truncation. Thus, $\breve{E}(\beta_i^b) = \breve{\mathfrak{B}}^b$ and $\breve{V}(\beta_i^b) = \breve{\sigma}_b^2$. In situations with little or no truncation, $\breve{E}(a) = E(a)$ and $\breve{V}(a) = V(a)$, in which case $\breve{\mathfrak{B}}^b$ and $\breve{\sigma}_b^2$ have direct interpretations as the mean and variance of β_i^b.

A logic parallel to that for the conditional expected values and variances in Section 6.2.1 applies for this alternative parameterization. Thus, the conditional "expected value" is:

$$\breve{E}(T_i|X_i) = \mu_i = \breve{\mathfrak{B}}^b X_i + \breve{\mathfrak{B}}^w(1 - X_i) \tag{6.16}$$

and the conditional "variance" is

$$\begin{aligned}\breve{V}(T_i|X_i) &= \sigma_i^2 \\ &= \breve{\sigma}_b^2 X_i^2 + \breve{\sigma}_w^2(1 - X_i)^2 + \breve{\sigma}_{bw} 2X_i(1 - X_i) &(6.17)\\ &= (\breve{\sigma}_w^2) + (2\breve{\sigma}_{bw} - 2\breve{\sigma}_w^2)X_i + (\breve{\sigma}_b^2 + \breve{\sigma}_w^2 - 2\breve{\sigma}_{bw})X_i^2 &(6.18)\end{aligned}$$

Obviously, these expressions directly parallel the original truncated versions in Equations 6.8 to 6.10. This means that we can understand μ_i and σ_i^2 to be the conditional expected value and variance when truncation is relatively minor. In addition to their interpretive value, these expressions will also prove useful in the next section for deriving further implications of this model. In that section, μ_i and σ_i^2, which are exact in all cases (and thus no approximation is involved), are used even if the truncation has a large effect. The only consequence is that these parameters can no longer be interpreted as the expected value and variance. They are, however, still equivalent to the right sides of Equations 6.16 and 6.18.

6.2.3 Computing 2p Parameters from Only p Observations

The model given in Section 6.1 contains very useful implications about the precinct-level quantities of interest. Working out these implications in detail is one of the most important differences of the approach taken here from that in previous research. For, even though the precinct-level parameters may at first seem impossible to estimate, they are the parameters of interest relevant for aggregate data. Statistical modeling is often improved by beginning with micro-foundations at the lowest level for which observations are available (for example, Dunn et al., 1976). This is often the level at which assumptions are best made and their observable implications most easily verified. In this case, attention to these basic parameters has substantial additional payoff since not only does it enable one to include the very informative precinct-level bounds in estimating the district aggregates, and take into account differing numbers of people per precinct, it also (surprisingly) enables one to derive informative estimates of all $2p$ precinct-level quantities of interest from only p precinct observations. Indeed, we will even be able to fit p lines to p points without indeterminacy (Figure 10.8, on page 214, gives one such example). This may seem counterintuitive, but most commonly used statistical models have similar properties, even though they are not usually exploited in this fashion. Even the simple linear regression model can provide estimates of numerous quantities if, for example, fitted values are of interest. These implications are derived here, but issues of estimation are saved for Chapters 7 and 8.

The distribution derived in this section is *conditional* on the parameters of the truncated bivariate normal distribution, parameterized as in Section 6.2.2 according to the corresponding untruncated normal, $\breve{\psi} = (\breve{\mathfrak{B}}^b, \breve{\mathfrak{B}}^w, \breve{\sigma}_b^2, \breve{\sigma}_w^2, \breve{\rho})$. The parameters $\breve{\psi}$ are not known, and therefore a model which conditions on knowledge of them cannot be used directly for making empirical inferences.[4]

After deriving the distribution conditional on the $\breve{\psi}$ parameters here, I show how to estimate the parameters and average over our information about, and uncertainty in, them to yield the goal of this derivation—the *unconditional* posterior distribution of β_i^b and β_i^w. This should be a familiar strategy. For example, most textbook presentations of regression analysis first derive the variance of the coefficient vector conditional on the regression variance. In the usual notation, $V(b|\sigma^2) = (X'X)^{-1}\sigma^2$. Only after this calculation do we average over the uncertainty in σ^2 to yield the unconditional variance $V(b) = (X'X)^{-1}\hat{\sigma}^2 = (X'X)^{-1}e'e/(n-k)$.

The other feature of this distribution is that it is conditional on T_i. However, unlike $\breve{\psi}$, T_i is observed. Thus, conditioning on it is essential, as it includes valuable information about β_i^b and β_i^w. For

[4] In other words, the probability statement we would like is Pr(`unknown|known`) or, in our case, Pr(`quantity of interest|aggregate data`). That is, since we do not know our quantity of interest, we do the next best thing and try to describe its *likely* value with a probability distribution. This distribution should be based on (i.e., conditional upon) as much (known) information as we have available. A distribution that conditions on quantities that are unknown is not useful until the unknown is removed by "averaging over the uncertainty" we have in this unknown.

example, since the bounds on these parameters are functions of X_i and T_i, conditioning on T_i automatically narrows the bounds from [0,1] to those given in Chapter 5. In the description below, the conditional distribution of the precinct-level parameter β_i^b, $P(\beta_i^b|T_i, \breve{\psi})$ is derived first. Once β_i^b is known (or drawn from this distribution), β_i^w, and thus $P(\beta_i^w|T_i, \breve{\psi})$, is calculated via the basic accounting identity (Equation 6.1). This is explained below.[5]

A detailed derivation appears in Appendix C, the key feature of which is conditioning on T_i, which in precinct i is now observed. The result of this derivation appears complicated at first, and it has a surprising substantive interpretation, but once understood it is quite intuitive. The technical form is a univariate truncated normal distribution (for $X_i > 0$):

$$P(\beta_i^b|T_i, \breve{\psi}) = \mathrm{TN}\left(\beta_i^b|\breve{\mathfrak{B}}^b + \frac{\omega_i}{\sigma_i^2}\epsilon_i,\ \breve{\sigma}_b^2 - \frac{\omega_i^2}{\sigma_i^2}\right)$$

$$= \mathrm{N}\left(\beta_i^b|\breve{\mathfrak{B}}^b + \frac{\omega_i}{\sigma_i^2}\epsilon_i,\ \breve{\sigma}_b^2 - \frac{\omega_i^2}{\sigma_i^2}\right)\frac{\mathbf{1}(\beta_i^b)}{S(\breve{\mathfrak{B}}, \breve{\Sigma})} \tag{6.19}$$

where

$$\omega_i = \breve{\sigma}_b^2 X_i + \breve{\sigma}_{bw}(1 - X_i), \tag{6.20}$$

$$\epsilon_i = T_i - \breve{\mathfrak{B}}^b X_i - \breve{\mathfrak{B}}^w(1 - X_i), \tag{6.21}$$

and σ_i^2 is from Equation 6.17. Because this distribution conditions on T_i (as well as X_i), the bounds on β_i^b are now narrowed to those derived in Chapter 5. This univariate truncation is accomplished algebraically in Equation 6.19 via the same two steps as for the truncated bivariate normal distribution analyzed in Section 6.2.2 (Equation 6.14, page 103). First truncate the (untruncated) normal distribution: $\mathbf{1}(\beta_i^b)$ equals one if β_i^b falls within the permissible bounds

$$\beta_i^b \in \left[\max\left(0, \frac{T_i - (1 - X_i)}{X_i}\right),\ \min\left(1, \frac{T_i}{X_i}\right)\right] \tag{6.22}$$

[5] Parallel procedures can be used to model θ_i^b, and θ_i^w if desired. From these results, we will also be able to compute the posterior distributions of λ_i^b and λ_i^w, posteriors for the aggregate parameters, and any other quantities that may be of interest. See Section 8.4.

and zero otherwise. Second, the remaining area of the distribution within the bounds must be renormalized so that it integrates to one (indicating that β_i^b always takes on some permissible value); this is accomplished in Equation 6.19 by dividing the untruncated normal by the area under this distribution within the permissible bounds:

$$S(\breve{\mathfrak{B}}, \breve{\Sigma}) = \int_{\max\left(0, \frac{T-(1-X_i)}{X_i}\right)}^{\min\left(1, \frac{T_i}{X_i}\right)} \mathrm{N}\left(\beta^b | \breve{\mathfrak{B}}^b + \frac{\omega_i}{\sigma_i}\epsilon_i, \ \breve{\sigma}_b^2 - \frac{\omega_i^2}{\sigma_i^2}\right) d\beta^b \qquad (6.23)$$

I now interpret this result and then proceed to average over the uncertainty in $\breve{\psi}$ (which will have the effect of replacing the parameters in $\breve{\psi}$ by their estimates). Consider first the "expected value" from Equation 6.19, the first parameter of the truncated normal:

$$\breve{\mathrm{E}}(\beta_i^b | T_i, \breve{\psi}) = \breve{\mathfrak{B}}^b + \frac{\omega_i}{\sigma_i^2}\epsilon_i \qquad (6.24)$$

This is the real expected value of the parameter of interest β_i^b when the truncation limits have little effect. Otherwise it merely represents a parameter of the truncated distribution. (That is, to help with interpretation, refer to graph (a) of Figure 6.2.)

Why the first term is there should be obvious: $\breve{\mathrm{E}}(\beta_i^b) = \breve{\mathfrak{B}}^b$ is the unconditional average of the precinct parameters. What might be less obvious is why the second term is present. After all, in ordinary regression analysis we routinely make predictions at the level of the observation with just the fitted value (which is just the constant term in a regression model without covariates). If the parameters are known, as they are, and $\breve{\mathfrak{B}}^b$ is constant, as it is, then the analogous regression predicted value would be based on $\breve{\mathfrak{B}}^b$. So why is the second term included?

The difference here is the random coefficient terms (Equation 6.5, page 96), and the result is that more information exists in the model about β_i^b than exists in $\breve{\mathfrak{B}}^b$. This counterintuitive result can be interpreted in several ways. First, under the model, ω_i is the covariance of β_i^b and ϵ_i, and σ_i^2 is the variance of ϵ_i. Thus, the ratio ω_i/σ_i^2 is the theoretical regression coefficient of β_i^b on ϵ_i, which can be interpreted as the fraction of ϵ_i that makes up β_i^b. Thus, adding $(\omega_i/\sigma_i^2)\epsilon_i$, which varies over i, to $\mathfrak{B}^b$ improves the calculation of the expected value.

For a second interpretation of Equation 6.24, note that if there is not much of a truncation effect, $\beta_i^b = \breve{\mathfrak{B}}^b + \epsilon_i^b$, and so we can add to the information in $\breve{\mathfrak{B}}^b$ an estimate of ϵ_i^b. To compute ϵ_i^b, begin with ϵ_i from Equation 6.7, which is reproduced here:

$$\epsilon_i = \epsilon_i^b X_i + \epsilon_i^w (1 - X_i) \tag{6.25}$$

Conditional on $\breve{\psi}$, we know ϵ_i, since $\epsilon_i = T_i - \breve{\mathfrak{B}}^b X_i - \breve{\mathfrak{B}}^w (1 - X_i)$ (and later, unconditional on $\breve{\psi}$, we will be able to estimate ϵ_i). The logic of the second term of Equation 6.24 is that ϵ_i in Equation 6.25 is multiplied by a factor, ω_i/σ_i^2, that pulls ϵ_i^b out of ϵ_i. To see that this is the case, we reformulate this factor:

$$\frac{\omega_i}{\sigma_i^2} = \left(\frac{\breve{\sigma}_b^2 X_i^2 + \breve{\sigma}_{bw} X_i (1 - X_i)}{\breve{\sigma}_b^2 X_i^2 + 2\breve{\sigma}_{bw} X_i (1 - X_i) + \breve{\sigma}_w^2 (1 - X_i)^2} \right) \left(\frac{1}{X_i} \right)$$

The denominator of the first factor on the right side of this equation is the total variance in ϵ_i, $\breve{V}(\epsilon_i|X_i)$, and the numerator of this factor is equal to the first term and half the second term of the denominator. Thus the entire first factor is the fraction of variation in the first term of Equation 6.25, $\epsilon_i^b X_i$, with the covariance split equally between the two terms. Thus, the first factor times ϵ_i is a good approximation to $\epsilon_i^b X_i$ and the entire fraction $(\omega_i/\sigma_i^2)\epsilon_i$, that is after dividing by X_i, is a good approximation to ϵ_i^b. (Because the covariance term is split between the two terms, the quantities of interest are not very sensitive to the value of $\breve{\rho} = \breve{\sigma}_{bw}/(\breve{\sigma}_b \breve{\sigma}_w)$. This is fortunate, since less information exists in the aggregate data about $\breve{\rho}$ than the other parameters; see Figure 6.1.)

Put one final way, $\omega_i X_i$ is the amount of variation in $\epsilon_i^b X_i$, and $(\omega_i X_i/\sigma_i^2)$ is the fraction of variation in the known (or estimable) ϵ_i attributable to $\epsilon_i^b X_i$. And, thus, $(\omega_i/\sigma_i^2)\epsilon_i$ is a good approximation to ϵ_i^b. As a result, adding $(\omega_i/\sigma_i^2)\epsilon_i$ to $\mathfrak{B}^b$ is like computing $\mathfrak{B}^b + \epsilon_i^b$, which gives a better approximation to β_i^b than $\mathfrak{B}^b$ alone.

The variance from Equation 6.19 has a similarly substantive interpretation:

$$\breve{V}(\beta_i^b | T_i, \breve{\psi}) = \breve{\sigma}_b^2 - \frac{\omega_i^2}{\sigma_i^2}$$

The first term is the variance without conditioning on T_i: $\breve{V}(\beta_i^b|\breve{\psi}) = \breve{\sigma}_b^2$. The second term, which is always between 0 and 1, is the amount the variance is shrunk by conditioning on the additional information from the dependent variable T_i. Thus, ω_i^2/σ_i^2 is a direct measure of how much benefit we receive in each precinct by conditioning on T_i. Furthermore, since ω_i^2/σ_i^2 depends inversely on X_i, the model's estimate of β_i^b is more variable when a smaller fraction of the voting-age population is black. That is, not surprisingly, when relatively few blacks are submerged in an overwhelming white precinct, ascertaining black voter behavior from only aggregate data is considerably more difficult. At the other extreme, when $X_i = 1$, the variance is zero because β_i^b is known with certainty.

Once β_i^b is known, computed, simulated, or estimated, β_i^w may be calculated directly by solving the accounting identity in Equation 6.1:

$$\beta_i^w = \frac{T_i - \beta_i^b X_i}{1 - X_i} \tag{6.26}$$

This procedure is self-consistent, so that the distribution for β_i^w could be computed, and from that β_i^b calculated. The results would be identical. Then, of course, means and variances of the parameters of interest, β_i^b and β_i^w, can easily be computed from these results.

Although this model contains only five parameters to be estimated (the elements of $\breve{\psi}$), it provides (non-independent) information about all $2p$ parameters of interest, β_i^b and β_i^w (for $i = 1, \ldots, p$). The quantities of interest are dependent parameters, of course, which explains the apparent paradox. As discussed in Chapter 7, another way to think about this model is that knowledge of $\breve{\psi}$ is summarized in an *estimation* stage from which β_i^b and β_i^w will be calculated in a *prediction* stage.

The distribution reported in Equation 6.19 is conditional on $\breve{\psi}$, which is unknown. Averaging over the uncertainty in $\breve{\psi}$ to produce the unconditional result is explained in Chapter 8, but this conditional distribution is useful for one final interpretive purpose.

Imagine we knew $\breve{\psi}$ or, equivalently, we were fortunate enough to have an extremely large number of aggregate units so that uncertainty in $\breve{\psi}$ were small or nonexistent. In this situation, the distributions of the precinct-level parameters in Equations 6.19 and 6.26 do not collapse to spikes. That is, *perfect knowledge of* $\breve{\psi}$ *does not imply perfect knowledge of the precinct-level parameters of interest* β_i^b *and* β_i^w. Although this feature is not common among models of ecological inference, it is a required part of making honest inferences in this always uncertain problem. After all, larger numbers of precincts do not eliminate the ecological inference problem. In more standard regression problems, in which one observes realizations of the quantity being estimated, more data will usually enable one to make more and more error-free evaluations. In contrast, the fundamental uncertainty of making ecological inferences must be a part of any reasonable model of ecological inference and, fortunately, is well represented in the distributions in the model given here.

6.2.4 *Connections to the Statistics of Medical and Seismic Imaging*

It turns out that the ecological inference problem is mathematically equivalent to an idealized version of an aspect of the statistical problem underlying medical imaging with X-rays or CT scans and some aspects of seismic imaging.[6] The problem of *tomography* (from the Greek word τόμος meaning slice) involves reconstructing an image of the inside of an object from information gathered outside the object. The information outside comes from passing beams, such as X-rays, through the object and observing the pattern of shadows formed on photographic plates (the pattern resulting from the differential absorption of X-rays by tumors, bones, or normal tissue). The goal of tomography is to reconstruct a full two-dimensional image of a thin slice of an object, such as of a human head, from millions of individual X-rays passed through the object from many different angles. Versions of tomography are used in many fields, including seismology, where the beams are often generated by earthquakes or devices placed in drill-holes; the field of nondestructive testing, where X-rays are used to identify flaws in manufactured parts; astronomy, where images of the sun have been generated; and oceanography, where it has been used to map ocean currents and temperatures.

Because the logic behind the ecological inference problem parallels a specific idealized version of one imaging technique, the concept of tomography will prove to be a useful heuristic in understanding the model proposed in this book. However, due to the numerous special features of medical and seismic imaging equipment and feasible data

[6] My special thanks goes to Andrew Gelman for helping me make this connection and for related suggestions, and to Paul Martin for help in understanding the physics of PET scans. See Beran et al. (1996) for a similar connection between tomography problems and random effects models; Webb (1990) for a detailed history of tomography; Vardi et al. (1985), Johnstone and Silverman (1990), and Worsley et al. (1991) for related statistical models of PET-generated data; and Natterer (1986) and Gardner (1995a, b) for details of the mathematics of tomographic analysis.

collection techniques, the statistical and mathematical models used in real tomography problems differ substantially from the ecological inference problem and the model proposed here (see note 7, page 119). Thus, like any heuristic, this one is not essential to the presentation that follows, and readers who do not care for analogies to the physical and natural sciences may wish to skip the relevant paragraphs in this section.

In general terms, the model first imposes the known bounds. Within these bounds all knowledge of the quantities of interest is uncertain. The statistical model then estimates a probability distribution to represent this uncertainty within the bounds.

To be specific, the goal for each precinct is knowledge of β_i^b and β_i^w. These two quantities of interest are represented, from this perspective, as a single point in Figure 6.3 with the parameters as coordinates. The unit square in this figure corresponds to a cross-section of a body part in some medical imaging experiments. The true values of β_i^b, β_i^w correspond to coordinates within the cross-section of the object being imaged. The data for this figure were randomly generated from the model with the parameter values indicated at the top of the figure.

Consider now the available information in the ecological inference problem as it arrives according to the model, in order, one piece at a time, using Figure 6.3 as a guide. Before any data are known from a precinct, we know that β_i^b and β_i^w are each between zero and one, which are the limits of each axis in the figure. In this geometric interpretation, the goal is to narrow the plane (or square) represented in the figure to a single point. Still before any data arrive, slightly more information does exist. That is, from Chapter 5 (Figure 5.1, page 81), we know that the true answer lies on a line that expresses β_i^w as a linear function of β_i^b. The algebraic expression underlying this is a reformulation of the basic accounting identity (Equation 5.2, page 80), which is reproduced here:

$$\beta_i^w = \left(\frac{T_i}{1 - X_i}\right) - \left(\frac{X_i}{1 - X_i}\right)\beta_i^b \tag{6.27}$$

Because the slope and intercept of this line are still unknown (i.e., T_i and X_i are unknown presently), the line is also unknown. However, we do know that except for homogeneous precincts, the true (β_i^b, β_i^w) point lies on a line with a negative slope, since $-X_i/(1 - X_i)$ is never positive. This is equivalent to a medical imaging experiment without positively sloping camera angles, which makes inferences more

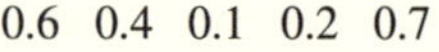

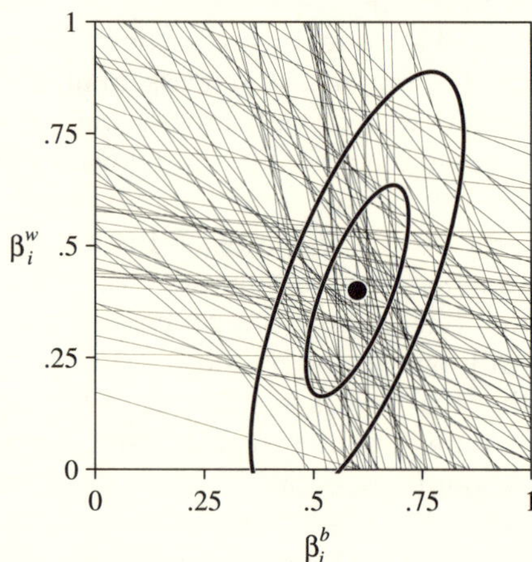

Figure 6.3 A Tomography Plot. Each coordinate represents a unique value of β_i^b and β_i^w. Each line traces out, for a particular combination of T_i and X_i, the algebraic expression in Equation 6.27. The contour lines on the figure represent the truncated bivariate normal distribution of β_i^b and β_i^w, with parameters $\breve{\mathfrak{B}}^b$, $\breve{\mathfrak{B}}^w$, $\breve{\sigma}_b$, $\breve{\sigma}_w$, and $\breve{\rho}$ indicated at the top of the graph. (See Figure 6.4 for a surface plot representation of these contours, which may be more familiar.)

difficult. Of course, only knowing that the slopes are negative is not sufficiently helpful.

For a single precinct, the first piece of relevant information available is the value of X_i. If we retain the assumption of mean independence (which will not change until Chapter 9), then by definition the value of X_i in precinct i provides *no* information about the point (β_i^b, β_i^w). In terms of Figure 6.3, knowledge of X_i enables an analyst to narrow the plane to a line with known slope but still with unknown position (or intercept). Thus, knowing X_i uniquely determines the slope of this line, $-X_i/(1 - X_i)$. But because T_i is still unknown at this point, the position of the line is not known and no helpful information is provided. (And, of course, the unique point on the line, wherever the line is, is also unknown.) Because the model is conditional on X_i, the figure should be treated as conditional on the slopes (or camera angles) that happen to be available in any application. The observable uncertainty in the problem is due to T_i, the intercepts in the figure.

The next piece of information that arrives according to the model is T_i. That is, according to the model, first X_i is observed; then β_i^b and β_i^w

are generated but not observed; and finally, T_i is formed and observed as $\beta_i^b X_i + \beta_i^w(1 - X_i)$. Once T_i is observed, the slope $-X_i/(1 - X_i)$ and now the position $T_i/(1 - X_i)$ of the line are uniquely determined. T_i is also the point at which the line crosses the 45° line in Figure 6.3, so that for example if $T_i = 0.6$, the line passes through the ($\beta_i^b = 0.6, \beta_i^w = 0.6$) point. We can now therefore narrow the (β_i^b, β_i^w) plane to a specific line represented by Equation 6.27. Some examples of these lines are given in Figure 6.3 for specific values of T_i and X_i for each precinct.

As described in Chapter 5, each line in the figure determines the bounds on β_i^b by the projection downward of its endpoints onto the horizontal axis. Thus, a line that cuts across the entire graph horizontally, without reaching the ceiling or floor, implies bounds on β_i^b covering the entire range, zero to one; in contrast, a line that only intersects the top right corner of the graph implies bounds on β_i^b that are much narrower, say [0.95,1]. Similarly, projecting the same line onto the left vertical axis determines the bounds on β_i^w. Thus, for example, relatively flat lines give very narrow bounds on β_i^w and wide bounds on β_i^b. The line representing each precinct provides more useful information than the separate bounds on each parameter, because of the deterministic information in Equation 6.27. For example, this equation implies that if β_i^b falls near its upper bound, β_i^w must fall near its lower bound.

Knowing that the desired (β_i^b, β_i^w) point lies on a specific line is helpful but not sufficient in many empirical analyses. That is, the parameter bounds are often fairly wide. Since no additional information can be extracted from the data in precinct i alone to learn about β_i^b and β_i^w, a key feature of the model is that it *borrows strength* from data in other precincts via the statistical portion of the model. The statistical information appears via an estimate of $\breve{\psi}$, the parameters of the truncated bivariate normal distribution (as described in Chapter 7).

This distribution with parameters $\breve{\psi}$ is represented in Figure 6.3 by two contour lines, which trace out the shape of the distribution of β_i^b and β_i^w from Equation 6.14. Contour plots are one way to represent a three-dimensional image, and have a venerable history for representing bivariate normal distributions (see Yule, 1911: 320). (They are also used to represent mountain ranges on geographic maps, for example.) Contours give an alternative perspective of a distribution to the three-dimensional surface plot in Figure 6.2 (page 105), from the top looking down. Thus, the center of the contours is the mode of the truncated bivariate normal distribution, and the farther from the the mode, the larger the fall-off. The con-

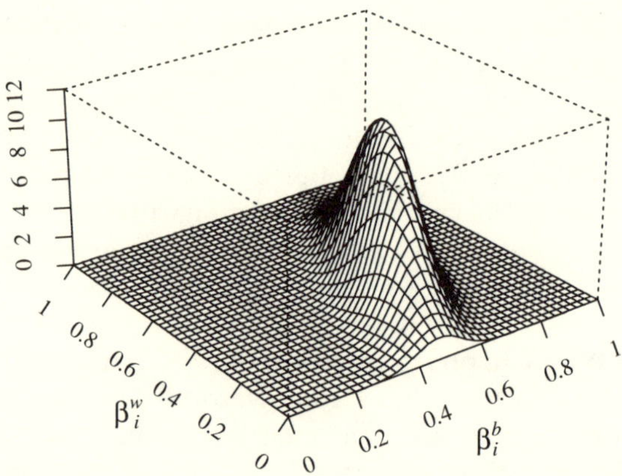

Figure 6.4 Truncated Bivariate Normal Surface Plot. This distribution is identical to the one represented with contours in Figure 6.3. Figure 6.3 appears as the floor of this three-dimensional surface looking down from the top. The purpose of this figure is to understand better the corresponding contour plot representation.

tour ellipses trace out lines of equal height. Thus, the mode is the coordinates near the place where most of the β_i^b and β_i^w values fall.

In order to become accustomed to contour lines, it may help at first to see the more familiar surface plot representation of the same distribution. Figure 6.4 thus gives such a surface plot for the identical truncated bivariate normal distribution from Figure 6.3. The contour lines in Figure 6.3 provide a perspective on the distribution looking down from the top of Figure 6.4, and are more convenient for tomography graphs, where it is important that the lines are also visible.

To combine the information available only in precinct i, and represented by a single line in the tomography graph in Figure 6.3, with this statistical information from the set of precincts, focus on the slice of the bivariate distribution cut out by this line. This slice is a univariate distribution over the line that represents the borrowed probabilistic information about the location of β_i^b and β_i^w in precinct i. Note that the height of the univariate distribution is indicated in the figure by the intersection of the line with the contour curves. This univariate distribution is the posterior distribution of the quantities of interest in precinct i, conditional on information shared from the other precincts. This concept will prove very useful for additional interpretation and specific calculations in Chapter 8. Figure 8.1 (page 148) gives an example of posterior distributions for the precinct-level parameters sliced out of the bivariate normal and projected onto the β_i^b axis.

The truncated bivariate normal distribution corresponds to a brain tumor in a medical imaging experiment. Each line represents one X-ray taken at a specific camera angle. The exact angle is given by the slope in Equation 6.27, which is solely a function of X_i. Thus, just as a larger range of camera angles would make locating a tumor in a cross-section of a brain easier, a set of precincts with a larger range of X_i values would help in locating the position of the truncated bivariate normal distribution and ultimately generate more reliable ecological inferences. This problem is more difficult than medical imaging in part because "camera angles" in ecological inference problems cannot be positively sloped. It will therefore pay to search for data with a large range of X_i values, if possible, so we will at least have a large range of negatively sloping angles. Combining precincts from different areas and ranges of X_i (such as from adjacent congressional districts, one largely white and the other mostly black) may therefore substantially improve inferences. Of course, we must weigh this known benefit from combining data sets with the possible costs of misspecification if more than one mode appears. (The procedures described in Chapter 9 can be used to evaluate this possibility and, if necessary, to generate a combined specification.)

Although this figure is best for understanding the precise role of the distribution assumed for β_i^b and β_i^w, for most purposes separate univariate posterior distributions for each parameter are easier to interpret. These are direct functions of the posterior distribution of (β_i^b, β_i^w) sliced out of the truncated bivariate normal by the line for each precinct. $\breve{\psi}$ are also the parameters of the distribution of the precinct-level quantities of interest (see Equation 6.19).

The analogy to X-rays and CT scans is also useful for emphasizing that the model is conditional on X_i, since the camera angle is determined by the medical researcher. This fact becomes especially important for evaluating distributional assumptions with tomography plots, as described in Section 7.1. In particular, the slope of the lines, $-X_i/(1 - X_i)$, are determined prior to, and are thus not relevant for judging, the fit of the model. However, although X_i is exogenous in the ecological inference model, the researcher still has no effect over X_i except by selecting data and merging additional precincts with different values of X_i. In order to understand how X_i can be exogenous even though the analyst of ecological data cannot experimentally manipulate it, I introduce the analogy of the field of "emission tomography" (as in positron emission tomography, or PET), where the same situation holds. The mathematical structure of ecological inference is also closer to PET than the more familiar CT scans or X-rays.

In both PET and ecological inference problems, the analyst has little control over where each tomography line is drawn. PET requires administering, via inhalation or intravenous injection, a radiopharmaceutical—a drug that is radioactive so that it can be detected, but with a sufficiently short half-life so it does not kill the patient. (Fortunately, the odds of dying in a failed ecological inference experiment are somewhat lower than in an incorrect application of medical imaging technology.) The radiopharmaceutical concentrates in areas of the body with high metabolism, such as the blood vessels that form in and around tumors. At random times, an electron in the body and positron (anti-electron) from the radiopharmaceutical meet and decay. The particles vanish and their masses are turned into radiation. Most often, this radiation takes the form of two X-rays which, by the conservation of momentum, must shoot out in precisely opposite directions. When X-ray detectors outside the body register two hits on opposite sides at exactly the same instant, one line in the tomography plot can be drawn. That is, we only know that the emission came from somewhere on the line, but not precisely where. With more emissions and thus more lines, the analyst has a better chance of reconstructing where the major points of X-ray emissions, and thus tumors, are located. The key to this analogy is that, in PET, the laws of physics guarantee that the angle of the line is independent of the position of the emission, thus ensuring unbiased inferences; in ecological inference, only knowledge of the substantive problem (along with the bounds, the truncation, and observable implications described in Chapter 9) can help rule out the equivalent relationship between the (β_i^b, β_i^w) point and X_i.

Thus, in the ecological inference model developed here, each observation can be understood as providing one tomography line and thus deterministic bounds on each of the coordinates being estimated, but no information about where within the bounds the true point lies. Then the collection of all observations, and thus all tomography lines, is used to identify the location and five parameters of the truncated bivariate normal distribution. The posterior distribution of each of the precinct parameters within the bounds indicated by its tomography line is derived by the slice it cuts out of the bivariate distribution of all the lines; in this way, we borrow strength from all the observations to provide maximal information about each one.[7]

6.2.5 *Would a Model of Individual-Level Choices Help?*

A key feature of the model offered in Section 6.1 of this chapter is that the *precinct-level* quantities of interest, β_i^b and β_i^w, follow a truncated bivariate normal distribution. Each of these quantities is a function of *individual-level* dichotomous variables (race $\mathbb{X}_{ij}$ and turnout $\mathbb{T}_{ij}$). Thus, it might seem reasonable to suppose that the well-developed rational choice and statistical literatures on individual choice processes (Manski and Mcfadden, 1981) might provide insights for constructing an ecological inference model. Building such a model based on assumptions about individuals would be straightforward, and it is possible that some version of it could result in an improved ecological inference model. Unfortunately, unless the information in these models increases substantially, beyond what is available about individuals, the value added is likely to be relatively small. I explain this conclusion in three ways and then briefly illustrate the resulting problems with two previous attempts at building such a model.

First, a key problem is that individual-level models do not have any necessary connection with the process of aggregation from indi-

[7] Tomography plots like Figure 6.3 are not used in medical research because the immense amount of data generally available (usually well over a million observations) would make such a figure an undifferentiated block of ink. Thus, although the concepts from tomography are analogous, analysts making ecological inferences will not be able to draw on the wisdom of those in a better-developed field of inquiry to guide them in interpreting these graphs. A few analogous graphs have appeared in the seismology literature, where data are harder to come by (e.g., Ivansson, 1987: 172–176).

Statistical models for image reconstruction with PET technology differ from ecological inference models in many specific ways. For example, many emissions and thus tomography lines are missed entirely by the relatively small number of detectors that can be placed around an object being imaged. Positrons can move 2–4mm in random directions prior to annihilation; the X-rays are often a few degrees short of 180°; and body tissues can attenuate the X-ray photons. Each detector is really a three-dimensional tube, and so measured lines can only be located within a specific cylindrical volume. These types of measurement error do not occur in ecological inference models. Conditioning the model on one coordinate is not reasonable in PET as it is in ecological inference. In ecological inference, but not imaging, tomography lines cannot be upwardly sloping. Many other measurement issues arise from the technical issues in engineering PET machines, designing radiopharmaceuticals, and coping with the large individual variability in live biological systems.

viduals to precincts, and thus they do not address this essential component of the ecological inference problem. We could aggregate an individual-level model, such as a logit or probit, to the precinct level but this would still require additional, mostly unrelated, assumptions about how the individuals sort into precincts—assumptions analogous to the truncated bivariate normal. Additional assumptions at the individual level provide little or no information about how to construct these precinct-level aggregation assumptions. Thus, no matter how much more comfortable we may be with making assumptions about individuals, the assumptions required for making ecological inferences are aggregation assumptions, at the precinct level. Individual-level assumptions may not hurt, but they will not help in this regard either.

To put it a second way, we can begin with a set of individuals living in a district and divide them up into precincts in a variety of ways. No matter what the underlying model of individuals is, a sufficiently careful division of people into areal units can produce almost any distribution of the precinct-level quantities. However, the key to solving the ecological inference problem is the distribution of β_i^b and β_i^w across precincts; it is the division of people into precincts, not the processes that generated the individual-level choices within each. We might think about developing models that explain how precinct lines are drawn, but precincts are for the most part arbitrary administrative units that are not based on individual motivations. Even restricting cases to partisan gerrymanders would not be especially helpful (see Gelman and King, 1994a).

A final, and perhaps clearest, way of understanding why individual-level, within-precinct assumptions are not very helpful is to focus on the sources of variability at each level of analysis. Choice-based models assume that individual decisions are probabilistic and are modeled either directly, via an unobserved threshold (of say the propensity to turn out), or random utility maximization (whether turning out has a higher expected utility than staying home) (see King, 1989a: Section 5.3). The problem is that whatever model is used for the individual-level decision, the number of individuals aggregated into each precinct is large, and so individual-level variability is obliterated in the aggregation process. As Achen and Shively (1995) emphasize, individual-level random error in $\mathbb{T}_{ij}$ and $\mathbb{X}_{ij}$ contributes little or no variability to the precinct-level averages, $T_i = \frac{1}{N_i}\sum_{j=1}^{N_i}\mathbb{T}_{ij}$ and $X_i = \frac{1}{N_i}\sum_{j=1}^{N_i}\mathbb{X}_{ij}$. To put it another way, all the hard work a researcher might put in to develop a model of individual-level variability would be lost once the data are aggregated and observed. This means that most within-precinct features of an ecological inference model will have almost no observable implications, will be nearly unverifiable, and will have little or no weight in the ultimate ecological inferences drawn from the aggregate data.

These problems can be seen in the two leading models of ecological inference that were built by making assumptions about individuals. These are among the most creative contributions to the literature since Goodman's original model, and both have been studied in real ecological data, but each runs into some severe difficulties in both theory and practice, in large part because of the problems identified above. Both models are also closely related to Goodman's.

Brown and Payne's (1986) "aggregated compound multinomial" model is the most complete approach to modeling $\mathbb{T}_{ij}$ conditional on $\mathbb{X}_{ij}$. They begin by modeling individual decisions and logically aggregating all the way to the ecological level. Unfortunately, the model requires covariates with substantial amounts of information and is computationally infeasible even without the covariates. For empirical analyses, Brown and Payne introduce normal approximations that turn their model in practice into a heteroskedastic version of Goodman's regression that is still very computationally burdensome (Cleave, Brown, and Payne, 1995).[8]

Thomsen's (1987) "logit approach" (or "ecological factor analysis") models $\mathbb{T}_{ij}$ and $\mathbb{X}_{ij}$ as joint outcome variables without conditioning. An unusual feature of Thomsen's model is the multiple unobserved variables that generate the observed ones but, in my view, its key insight is that the absence of conditioning would seem to have the potential to avoid the aggregation bias that occurs when X_i is treated as fixed but is correlated with the parameters. The logic is analogous to modeling endogenous explanatory variables in simultaneous equations systems, except that Thomsen's estimator requires no instruments. Unfortunately, like simultaneous equation models, the benefits of stochastically modeling $\mathbb{X}_{ij}$ are counterbalanced by the extensive and largely untestable, and in some cases impossible, assumptions required. The leading special case of the model turns out to be equivalent to Goodman's (1959) at the aggregate level. Perhaps most

[8] Brown and Payne's (1986; see also Forcina and Marchetti, 1989; Lupia and McCue, 1990; King, 1990) model includes no information from the precinct-level bounds, allows no inferences about the precinct parameters, estimates the wrong aggregate parameters due to not including precinct size, and requires covariates to get the probability structure correct; moreover, and running it is "an awesome computational task" (Brown and Payne, 1986: 454), that would take over 100 years to compute a single observation from one iteration of the likelihood function (Cleave, 1992).

troubling is that even if the individual-level data were observed so that the ecological inference problem would normally be resolved by a mere cross tabulation, this model would still be unidentified; plausible individual-level models cannot result even from arbitrary parameter restrictions. As a result, this is a model of aggregate data but not one that enables scholars even in theory to make inferences across the levels of analysis.[9]

Although modeling within-precinct variation does not seem especially useful for making ecological inferences, we can use intuition from empirical analyses of survey (or other individual-level) data to help inform the types of models we choose in making ecological inferences. That is, the intuition learned from numerous applications of discrete choice models to available individual-level data can be useful in judging whether the assumptions of the ecological inference model proposed here are appropriate or should be modified (as discussed in Chapter 9). In addition, if even limited survey data are available and are combined with aggregate data, ecological inferences can be made much more certain (see Section 14.2).

[9] Thomsen's model also includes built-in biases due to the approximations used (unless every precinct is a microcosm of the entire district), makes no use of information from the precinct-level bounds, does not allow covariates, does not estimate precinct-level quantities or the correct aggregate-level quantities of interest (although this can be corrected), provides no standard errors or other measures of uncertainty, and requires numerous crucial untestable assumptions. It is possible to write down a logically consistent model that implies Thomsen's estimator, but there is little reason or available evidence to believe the required assumptions. Much of the complication of this method arises from its multiple unobservable factors, but, even though all but two of the factors are superfluous, simplifying to one factor (such as in Achen and Shively, 1995: 183ff) does not work: it requires that the aggregate correlation between X_i and T_i be exactly 1.0, an assumption rejected in all (nontrivial) real aggregate data.

CHAPTER 7

Preliminary Estimation

THE MODEL described in Chapter 6 is fixed except for the five unknown parameters of the truncated bivariate normal distribution, symbolized by the vector $\breve{\psi}$. The sole purpose of this chapter is to develop a method for estimating these parameters using only aggregate data. Since $\breve{\psi}$ are not the parameters of interest, the results I derive here are of intermediate use only. The ultimate goal is reached in Chapter 8, which shows how to calculate the quantities of interest and their uncertainties from these results.[1]

The procedures described in this chapter can be thought of from a "classical" or "Bayesian" perspective. From a classical perspective, the likelihood model in Section 7.2 serves the purposes of *estimation*. Maximizing the likelihood function yields point estimates of $\breve{\psi}$ and the curvature of the function at the maximum (the negative of the inverse of the matrix of second derivatives) gives the variance-covariance matrix. All knowledge of $\breve{\psi}$ is then summarized by the approximately multivariate normal sampling distribution $P(\breve{\psi}|T)$, with mean and variance set to these point and variance-covariance matrix estimates (see King, 1989a). In Chapter 8, then, these estimates are used for *prediction* of the $2p$ precinct-level quantities of interest, which includes their point estimates and uncertainty estimates such as confidence intervals or hypothesis tests. These results can also be summarized with a complete "sampling distribution," the mean (or mode) and standard deviation of which are the point estimates and standard errors, respectively.

From a Bayesian perspective, information about $\breve{\psi}$ is summarized by its posterior distribution (which serves nearly the same practical

[1] Many features of this chapter were substantially improved with the assistance of Andrew Gelman, Martin van der Ende, and Ron Schoenberg. Andrew helped me correct the proof of the likelihood function, was an expert sounding board for my attempts at using importance sampling and choosing reparameterizations and priors, and made many helpful suggestions. Martin wrote a far more accurate but still fast version of a cumulative bivariate normal distribution function that is especially useful for computing the area above the unit square, a part of the likelihood function. Ron made some changes in, and gave me advice about, his constrained maximum likelihood algorithm, and helped with some related computational problems. I very much appreciate the generosity of these scholars in providing their time and suggestions. However, I am solely responsible for any errors that may remain.

role as the sampling distribution in classical inference):

$$\mathrm{P}(\breve{\psi}|T) \propto \mathrm{P}(\breve{\psi})\mathrm{P}(T|\breve{\psi})$$

where $\mathrm{P}(T|\breve{\psi}) = \mathrm{L}(\breve{\psi}|T)$ is the likelihood function described in Section 7.2, and $\mathrm{P}(\breve{\psi})$ is the optional prior distribution given in Section 7.4. Like the sampling distribution, the mean and standard deviation of the posterior can serve as a set of point estimates and standard errors. Fortunately, to derive the posterior, point estimates are not needed, as some approximation of the entire distribution is required. (Indeed, the existence of a unique maximum is not even necessary.) One way to approximate the distribution is with its limiting asymptotic form, the multivariate normal, using the same mean and variance matrix that came from maximizing the likelihood function viewed from a classical perspective. This posterior distribution can then serve as a (data based) prior distribution for $\breve{\psi}$ in computing the goal of the analysis—the posterior distribution of the precinct-level parameters. However, instead of using the multivariate normal as an asymptotic approximation to the posterior distribution of $\breve{\psi}$, I use the actual, "finite sample" posterior distribution.

Section 7.1 begins by extending the tomography heuristic provided in Section 6.2.4. This heuristic is not required for the model or its estimates, but it does help in providing a more understandable, qualitative perspective on the workings of the proposed solution to the ecological inference problem. The likelihood function is then derived in Section 7.2; an alternative parameterization more useful for estimation is given in Section 7.3; optional priors appear in Section 7.4; and Section 7.5 shows how to summarize information in the data with (classical) sampling distributions or (Bayesian) posterior distributions.

7.1 A Visual Introduction

This section provides a qualitative overview of the entire chapter, as well as demonstrating one way to check the distributional assumptions about individuals with only the available aggregate data. A more complete approach to verifying assumptions is given in Chapter 9.

A key assumption of the model is that β_i^b and β_i^w are distributed as a truncated bivariate normal distribution with parameters $\breve{\psi}$ (or ψ, depending on parameterization).[2] If β_i^b and β_i^w were observed, we would

[2] See Section 8.4 for how to use these results to estimate the parameters of $2 \times C$ tables, and Chapter 15 for $R \times C$ tables.

be able to estimate $\breve{\psi}$ directly. That is, if β_i^b and β_i^w were observed, the likelihood function would be exactly a truncated bivariate normal (that is, based on Equation 6.14 instead of the function derived below in Equation 7.1). ψ could be estimated by taking the means, standard deviations, and correlation of β_i^b and β_i^w. Unfortunately, the aggregation problem eliminates the possibility of using this *direct* estimation method.

Instead, the likelihood derived below, based only on aggregate data from the marginals of cross-tabulations, is *indirect*. The exact procedure for finding evidence of individual-level effects in these aggregate data comes from the fact that expected values of β_i^b and β_i^w ($\mathfrak{B}$) appear in the mean function of the aggregate variable T_i and the variances and covariance (Σ) turn up in the variance function of T_i (see Section 6.2.1). The fact that these parameters reveal themselves by affecting specific features of aggregate data is what makes ecological inference possible. The indirect nature of this estimation problem is also critical to understanding the likelihood portion of the model. The difference between it and the direct approach that would be available if β_i^b and β_i^w were observed is also a precise measure of some of the information lost due to aggregation.

One disadvantage of indirect estimation is that checking whether the distributional assumptions are correct is more difficult than statistical problems for which direct estimation methods are possible. Fortunately, information does exist in ecological data with which to verify distributional assumptions at least partially such as the one in this model. This fact is critically important, as unverified assumptions can easily lead to fallacious conclusions.

A simple example of how the distributional assumption can be partially verified in this model appears in Figure 7.1, which displays a tomography plot like that in Figure 6.3 (page 114). This figure differs from Figure 6.3 in several ways. First, the parameter values of the model that generated this graph are different (for variety). In addition, I have added a small dot to each solid line to indicate where the true values of β_i^b and β_i^w lie. If, in a real application, these points were known, the truncated bivariate normal, and the corresponding contour lines, could be fit to them directly. Instead, the information aggregated away means that the corresponding distribution (the likelihood function derived below) can only be fit based on the lines, with no direct knowledge of where the points fall on each line. As described in Section 6.2.4, these lines show what information is still available in each precinct after aggregation, and it is obviously less certain data than if we knew where on the line the (β_i^b, β_i^w) point fell.

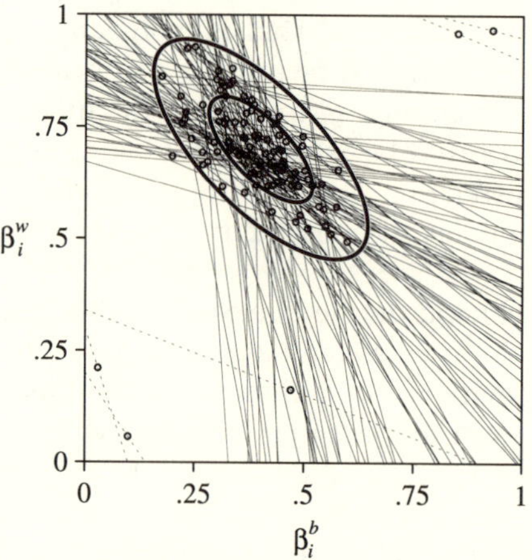

Figure 7.1 Verifying Individual-Level Distributional Assumptions with Aggregate Data. Each coordinate in this tomography plot represents a unique possible value of β_i^b and β_i^w, with small circles indicating (usually unobserved) true values. Each line traces out Equation 6.27 for one precinct, summarizing knowledge of where the true value can lie if only X_i and T_i are observed. The contour lines represent the estimated truncated bivariate normal distribution of β_i^b and β_i^w. All data were randomly drawn from the model except for the dashed lines, which represent outliers.

The dashed lines in the corners of the figure are examples of precinct results that would seem to violate the model assumption, as they imply that, wherever the (β_i^b, β_i^w) point is on each of these lines, it would fall 4–5 standard deviations away from the mode of the distribution. (The inner and outer contour ellipses were drawn so that the distribution above the areas they encircle includes 50% and 95% of the volume of the entire distribution, respectively.) Although these results are technically possible, they are so improbable they should cause an analyst to question the modeling assumption. Thus, verifying the distributional assumption is not as easy in ecological inference models as in some other statistical problems, but observable implications of individual-level distributional assumptions do exist. Remedies to problems such as this and more extensive methods of verification, are developed in Chapter 9.

Finally, although the model presented in Chapter 6 and the methods of inference discussed in this chapter require no concepts from tomography, these concepts are often useful. Thus, in order to help interpret the plots, which take some getting use to, Figure 7.2 provides a set of these graphs for several different possible parameter values and ranges of X_i. To construct these graphs, I drew 100 random val-

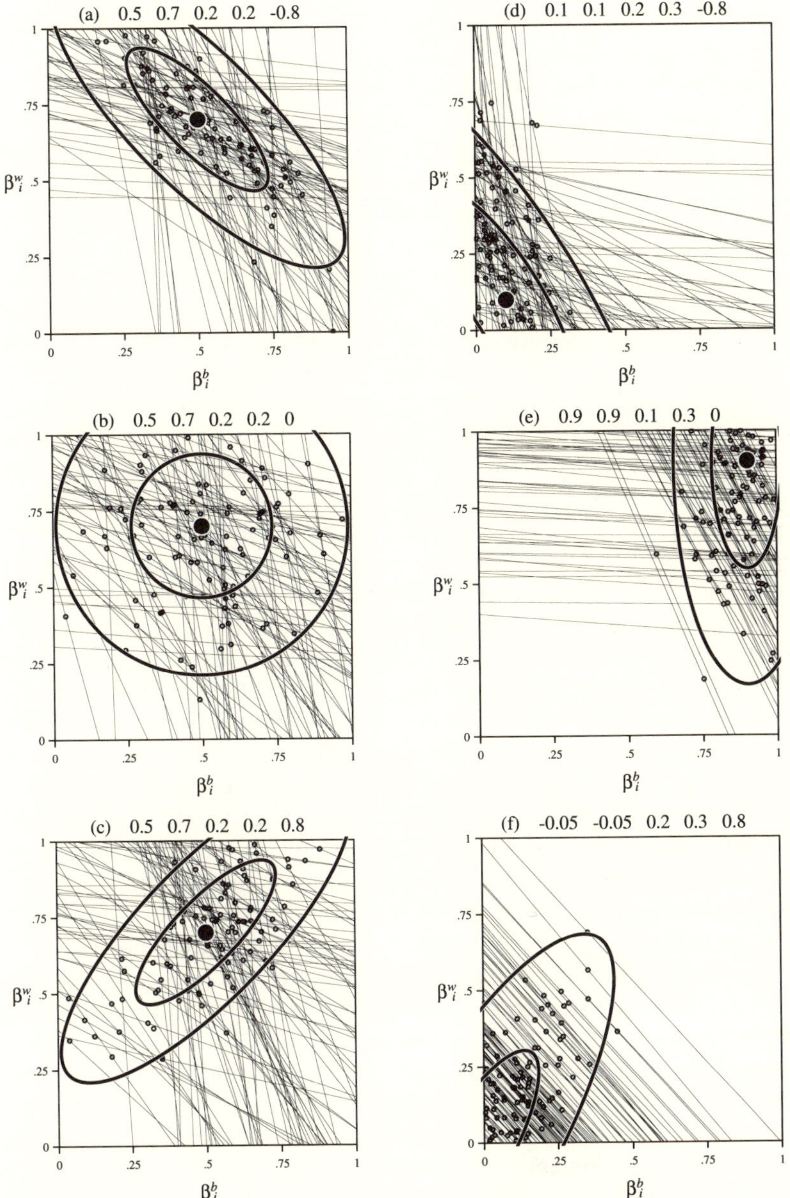

Figure 7.2 Observable Implications for Sample Parameter Values. The numbers at the top of each tomography plot are the parameter values for the distribution from which data were randomly generated: $\breve{\mathfrak{B}}^b$, $\breve{\mathfrak{B}}^w$, $\breve{\sigma}_b$, $\breve{\sigma}_w$, and $\breve{\rho}$.

ues of β_i^b and β_i^w from a bivariate truncated normal distribution with parameters $\breve{\psi}$ indicated at the top of each graph (that is, on the untruncated scale). These "true" values are plotted as small circles. For graphs (a)–(d), I fixed X_i to 100 numbers evenly spaced between zero and one and then calculated T_i via the accounting identity. Values of X_i for Graph (e) were generated evenly spaced on the intervals (0,0.1) and (0.6,0.7), and graph (f) on the interval (0.5,0.55). All lines were drawn using Equation 6.27 (page 113).

Figure 7.2 can be studied as a reference. It is useful to compare graphs based on real data to these prototypical graphs in order to see whether the estimated parameter values, and corresponding estimated contour lines, fit the data. Several features are apparent from these graphs. For example, distinguishing graphs in the first column (with $\breve{\mathfrak{B}}^b = 0.5$ and $\breve{\mathfrak{B}}^w = 0.7$) and the second column (with different means) on the basis of the lines alone is quite easy. That means that aggregate data reveal a lot of information about the means (and, to a slightly lesser extent, the variances).

In addition, just as was seen in the implications of these parameters for lines fit to scatter plots of X_i by T_i (as in Figure 6.1, page 100), values of $\breve{\rho}$ affect the data in relatively minor ways. This same feature arises again when the problem is viewed from the tomography perspective given in Figure 7.2. For example, graphs (a), (b), and (c) share the same means and standard deviations, but different values for $\breve{\rho}$. The differences among the pattern of lines in these graphs are fairly subtle. For example, clearer evidence exists for negative than positive correlations. This is apparent by noting that graph (a) ($\breve{\rho} = -0.8$) is easier to distinguish from graph (b) ($\breve{\rho} = 0$) than (b) is from (c) (with $\breve{\rho} = 0.8$) on the basis of the lines alone. This difference is similar to the problem in medical imaging where tumors in some places and at certain angles are easier to detect than at others, and it relates to the ecological inference problem where all "camera angles" always have a negative slope (due to the slope of Equation 6.27). A good way to distinguish these three graphs is to check the minimum value that the width of the contours could be in the direction of the 45° diagonal line (not shown). For example, in graph (c), focus on the lines that cut off the top right or bottom left corners. Since one true point must fall on each of these lines, the contours should be roughly that wide. The correlation is revealed from the lines by noting how much wider graph (c) should be, based on these lines, than graph (a), and how graph (b) falls in the middle.

Graphs (e) and (f) in Figure 7.2 have a distinct pattern because the range of X_i is highly restricted, making inferences more difficult. Since the model is conditional on X_i, these patterns do *not* indicate that the fit is poor. Indeed, all data in Figure 7.2 were randomly generated from the model, so fit is not an issue. However, a restricted variance of X_i will generate more uncertain inferences. The nearly parallel lines of graph (f) correspond to a medical imaging problem with X-rays taken from approximately one camera angle, which makes reconstructing the full two-dimensional cross-section difficult. For example, suppose an X-ray of your head were taken from the front, with the photographic plate placed behind your head to catch the image. The shadows of the X-rays on the photographic plate might indicate that a tumor exists on the right side, but the X-ray provides no information about whether the tumor is immediately behind your right eye or all the way near the back of your head. (To see this, note that the one X-ray taken from the front would yield identical information to an X-ray taken from the back, with the photographic plate placed in the front.) The only way to determine the depth of the tumor would be to take another X-ray from a different camera angle, such as from the side. This second image would also not be sufficient by itself, but the two images, taken together, would be quite informative. Note how the second "camera angle" in graph (e) helps to locate the mode of this distribution.

The same problem occurs in ecological inference: Locating the truncated bivariate normal distribution becomes very difficult when the range of X_i (and thus the diversity of slopes $-X_i/(1-X_i)$) is restricted. Thus, in graph (f) of Figure 7.2, we know that the bulk of the distribution falls on the lines somewhere, but there exists little evidence to ascertain whether it belongs where it is pictured or instead should be slid up or down the lines somewhat. This uncertainty in locating the distribution will translate into uncertainty in our ultimate inferences about β_i^b and β_i^w. Finally, note that the mode in graph (f) falls outside the unit square; this is not a problem because the parameters are from the untruncated normal which indeed allows for additional flexibility in fitting the data.

The problem portrayed by these graphs is described in the tomography literature as an *ill-posed inverse problem*. To understand this perspective, let $f(\cdot)$ represent a function that maps the truth onto the observed data:

$$f(\text{truth}) = \text{data}$$

In the ecological inference problem, the "truth" refers to values of β_i^b and β_i^w; in medical imaging the "truth" is often the locations of tumors or other internal features of the human body; in seismology, "truth" might refer to an ore deposit or chemical spill. The "data" are what is observed on the outside, either the ends of the lines outside the square in figures like 7.2 or outside the head in imaging problems. This is an "inverse problem" since the function $f(\cdot)$ needs to be inverted to reason from the data to the truth. That is, a solution requires $f^{-1}(\cdot)$. As described, this "inverse" problem is of course identical to recovering parameters in a likelihood or Bayesian framework (see King, 1989a: Chapter 2). However, this problem is different because of its indeterminacies. In recognition of this problem, tomography is referred to as "ill-posed," which more formally means that the data do not depend approximately continuously upon the truth, and so $f^{-1}(\cdot)$ may not necessarily even have a unique solution. Similarly, the ecological inference problem would also have no unique solution without some distributional assumption.[3]

Thus, from only the lines, we need to identify where the contours should be drawn. Maximizing the likelihood function is obviously the best way to determine their placement, but to understand where they should be (on the basis of the lines alone), the best procedure is usually to begin by locating the likely mode of the underlying distribution. Thus, first look for the area with the greatest density of lines, from which "emissions" might be coming. This is sometimes near the middle of the graph, as is clear in Figure 7.2, graph (a) (or even more clearly in Figure 7.1), although it can also be at an extreme, such as in graph (d). In graphs (a) and (d), the area with the greatest line density is where all the lines are crossing. Crossing lines are consistent with the presence of a mode, but they do not prove that a mode exists at that point, since if the true points fell on the same lines along the borders of the figure, the graph would look identical (this being another way to express the loss of information due to aggregation). Of course, there exists no information in ecological data to distinguish between the situations in which the true points fall near the center and those in which they fall along the borders. However, there does exist more information, even if not in X_i and T_i.

That is, in virtually all cases, analysts generally know at least that the precincts (or other areal units) in the data set have something in common. At a minimum, the precincts are all from the same state and are near one another. The same elections are generally held in all the precincts; all the people in these precincts are governed by the same state and federal governments. In most situations, many other reasons

[3] Computerized tomography, as used in most imaging applications, requires distributional assumptions also. The related field of geometric tomography has as its aim the reconstruction of fixed geometric objects, and so unique solutions are sometimes possible. See Gardner (1995a).

could also be found. A reasonable inference in these common situations is that β_i^b and β_i^w, while not constant over precincts as in the Goodman model, may cluster around a single mode, although perhaps with a wide variance. This is one possible motivation for the modeling assumption of a single truncated bivariate normal distribution. But the extra information from this knowledge is sufficient to identify features of the distribution from which the lines were generated. This is also equivalent to the assumption in medical imaging that a single tumor or cluster of tumors exists rather than a large number of small tumors randomly spread round the subject's brain. In both problem areas, assuming the existence of a single mode is a reasonable assumption that is in part verifiable in the tomography plot. (If multiple modes are suspected, or if evidence is found for them, one can either run separate analyses on the data from each mode, or follow other procedures described in Chapter 9.)

Note that the mode of the distribution is not necessarily located at the visual average of the lines in the graph, as if we were looking at a scatter plot. Instead, the mode is at the average of where the true β_i^b and β_i^w points lie, which in turn give rise to the lines. In judging where the points (and thus the mode of the distribution) might be, from the lines only, we need to think of the problem as inverted and ask: where is the clump of points that give rise to the "emissions" represented as lines? Each point could fall anywhere along its corresponding line, but the assumption that they are truncated bivariate normal enables us to use all the precincts together to locate the mode of the points common to all the lines. For example, panel (d) of Figure 7.2 has a mode all the way in the corner. This mode is easiest to recognize from the lines alone by noting that the highest density of lines, and line crosses, is in the lower left corner of the graph. It is also important that the density of lines drops in all directions as we move away from that corner, which is a property of a unimodal distribution.

Another useful procedure for parsing the information in the tomography plots is to begin with the recognition that the model is conditional on X_i. This means that the slope of any line alone should not be used to evaluate the fit of the model. Thus, one could consider sets of lines with roughly the same slope and use their positions to evaluate the fit of the model. For example, graph (d) contains lines with approximately two distinct slopes. That lines from each group pass through the same small area on the graph helps to confirm the existence of a mode near the bottom left of the figure.

As should be apparent, an infinite variety of other patterns can occur in tomography graphs. In all cases, the basic non-identification problem must be kept foremost in mind and weighed against available qualitative information about the areal units being analyzed. A tomography plot for data that meet Goodman's unrealistic assumption of constant parameters have lines that all pass through a single point (and look something like $*$, except that all lines must be negatively sloped). Under Freedman et al.'s (1991) "nonlinear neighborhood model," where the similarly unrealistic assumption that $\beta_i^b = \beta_i^w$ is imposed, the precinct estimates are taken from the intersection of each tomography line with the 45° diagonal with no random error of any kind. Tomography plots based on real, nontrivial data sets never resemble a star pattern supporting Goodman's model assumption, and only in rare applications is Freedman et al.'s assumption substantively or empirically plausible. In practice, each model is correct on occasion, but largely by coincidence. In the examples in Part IV, Goodman's and Freedman et al.'s estimates are, with a few unpredictable exceptions, usually far from the true values.

7.2 The Likelihood Function

If the truncation limits have relatively little effect, the parameter vector $\breve{\psi}$ can be estimated through a modification of the generalized least squares or iterative estimators developed for random coefficient models (following Hildreth and Houck, 1968, and the subsequent literature). Unfortunately, these procedures have not worked as well in practice as their developers had hoped. The most common problem is that the variances are not always estimated as positive numbers. In addition, the condition $\breve{\sigma}_b^2\breve{\sigma}_w^2 - \breve{\sigma}_{bw}^2 \geq 0$, required to ensure that the implied variance matrix $\breve{\Sigma}$ is positive definite (or, in other words, so that the correlation lies between -1 and 1), does not always hold for the estimates.[4]

Various suggestions have appeared in the literature to fix these problems, such as changing negative variance estimates to zero, using restricted least squares, reparameterizations, approximate Bayesian estimation, mixed estimation, or minimum norm quadratic estimators (see Griffiths, Drynan, and Prakash, 1979; Srivastava, Mishra, and Chaturvedi, 1981; Swamy and Mehta, 1975; Schwallie, 1982). In my experience, none of these fixes is sufficiently satisfactory when applied to ecological inference problems (an experience similar to those reporting other applications in the statistics and econometrics literatures). Moreover, these generalized least squares estimators

[4] Many methodological descriptions of random effects models do not mention these problems, but virtually all authors in this literature who have had experience with these models in real data analyses usually run into and report these problems immediately.

are not appropriate for most cases when truncation does have an effect.

Fortunately, we can use some of the insights from these attempts to solve the problem with a more straightforward simultaneous maximum likelihood approach. According to the model, T_i is a linear function of truncated bivariate normal variates, β_i^b and β_i^w, since $T_i = \beta_i^b X_i + \beta_i^w(1 - X_i)$, and X_i is fixed. However, this does not mean that T_i follows a truncated univariate normal distribution. The formal mathematical derivation of the correct distribution is given in Appendix D. This section derives the likelihood function more qualitatively (and perhaps more intuitively) by close reference to the concept of a tomography plot and the truncated bivariate normal distribution positioned over it. The total volume *above* the unit square and *beneath* the truncated bivariate normal probability density equals 1.0 (as for all proper distributions). Portions of this volume above regions of the square (such as $\beta_i^b > 0.9$ and $\beta_i^w < 0.2$) indicate the probabilities of these events occurring under the model. The key to understanding this derivation is keeping straight the pieces of the corresponding untruncated joint normal distribution above (1) one line segment and (2) the entire unit square, both truncated at the edges of the tomography square, and the corresponding portions of the untruncated normal distributions above (3) the line and (4) the plane.

The likelihood function is based on the observable information in aggregate data about the parameters of interest in combination with the modeling assumptions. The only observable information for a precinct is represented by the area above its tomography line segment. We also know that the entire unit square represents all the places this line might have appeared. The corresponding area above the untruncated line and the volume above the untruncated plane are introduced for mathematical convenience only, just as we previously introduced untruncated parameterizations. The following proof connects the most substantive interpretation, at the start, with the formal mathematical notation, at the end. (If the math were sufficiently easy, the third line of this equation would be sufficient.)

Thus, for heterogeneous precincts (i.e., for X_i not equal to one or zero), the likelihood function is proportional to a probability density that can be decomposed as follows:

$$\begin{aligned} L(\breve{\psi}|T) &\propto \prod_{X_i \in (0,1)} P(T_i|\breve{\psi}) \\ &= \prod_{X_i \in (0,1)} \left(\frac{\text{What we observe}}{\text{What we could have observed}} \right) \end{aligned}$$

$$= \prod_{X_i \in (0,1)} \left(\frac{\text{Area above line segment}}{\text{Volume above square}} \right)$$

$$= \prod_{X_i \in (0,1)} \left(\frac{\text{Area above line}}{\text{Volume above plane}} \right) \frac{\left(\frac{\text{Area above line segment}}{\text{Area above line}} \right)}{\left(\frac{\text{Volume above square}}{\text{Volume above plane}} \right)}$$

$$= \prod_{X_i \in (0,1)} \mathrm{N}(T_i | \mu_i, \sigma_i^2) \frac{S(\breve{\mathfrak{B}}, \breve{\Sigma})}{R(\breve{\mathfrak{B}}, \breve{\Sigma})} \tag{7.1}$$

The core of the likelihood function, $\mathrm{N}(T_i|\mu_i, \sigma_i^2)$, is an untruncated normal distribution with mean $\breve{\mathrm{E}}(T_i|X_i) = \mu_i$ defined as linear in X_i in Equation 6.16 (page 106):

$$\mu_i = \breve{\mathfrak{B}}^b X_i + \breve{\mathfrak{B}}^w (1 - X_i)$$

and variance $\breve{\mathrm{V}}(T_i|X_i) = \sigma_i^2$ defined as quadratic in X_i in Equation 6.18:

$$\sigma_i^2 = (\breve{\sigma}_w^2) + (2\breve{\sigma}_{bw} - 2\breve{\sigma}_w^2)X_i + (\breve{\sigma}_b^2 + \breve{\sigma}_w^2 - 2\breve{\sigma}_{bw})X_i^2,$$

The remaining factor in the likelihood function in Equation 7.1, which allows this function to deviate from a normal distribution, is composed of two scale factors. The first, $R(\breve{\mathfrak{B}}, \breve{\Sigma})$, is the normalizing constant for the truncated bivariate normal of β_i^b and β_i^w (defined in Equation 6.15, page 104), which indicates how much of the corresponding untruncated bivariate normal distribution covers the unit square:

$$R(\breve{\mathfrak{B}}, \breve{\Sigma}) = \int_0^1 \int_0^1 \mathrm{N}(\beta^b, \beta^w | \breve{\mathfrak{B}}, \breve{\Sigma}) d\beta^b d\beta^w \tag{7.2}$$

Procedures for computing this function are described in Appendix F.

The final piece of the likelihood function, $S(\breve{\mathfrak{B}}, \breve{\Sigma})$, is the fraction of an untruncated normal distribution falling above the line segment for one precinct in a tomography plot. It turns out that $S(\breve{\mathfrak{B}}, \breve{\Sigma})$ also happens to be the normalizing constant from the truncated normal posterior distribution of β_i^b given T_i and $\breve{\psi}_i$ (defined in Equation 6.23, page 109):

$$S(\breve{\mathfrak{B}}, \breve{\Sigma}) = \int_{\max\left(0, \frac{T-(1-X_i)}{X_i}\right)}^{\min\left(1, \frac{T_i}{X_i}\right)} \mathrm{N}\left(\beta^b \,\middle|\, \breve{\mathfrak{B}}^b + \frac{\omega_i}{\sigma_i}\epsilon_i,\ \breve{\sigma}_b^2 - \frac{\omega_i^2}{\sigma_i^2}\right) d\beta^b \qquad (7.3)$$

and which is easily calculated as the difference between two cumulative normal distribution functions.

The factor $S(\breve{\mathfrak{B}}, \breve{\Sigma})/R(\breve{\mathfrak{B}}, \breve{\Sigma})$ is the difference between this likelihood and a normal distribution. The factor is roughly one, and can thus be ignored, only when the corresponding truncated bivariate normal distribution on β_i^b and β_i^w is not heavily influenced by the bounds, as in graph (a) of Figure 6.2 (page 105). In this situation, the likelihood function would then reduce to a normal distribution with a mean that is a linear function of X_i, just as in an ordinary regression but with a variance function that is quadratic in X_i. Since likelihoods are functions of the parameters, ignoring this factor is only appropriate when it is approximately one for all combinations of parameters with reasonably high likelihood values. Since this will not happen in general, this factor should not normally be ignored.

Because homogeneous precincts reveal the true value of the quantity of interest without uncertainty, they need no distribution. However, they are very useful in helping to locate the truncated bivariate normal distribution, which can then be used to improve estimation of the distribution of precinct parameters from heterogeneous districts. Recall that if β_i^b and β_i^w were observed, the distribution could be fit to them directly, and that it is only the aggregation process that forces us into an indirect estimation procedure. In homogeneous precincts, these parameters are observed and so they can be used directly in the estimation procedure. That is, although this estimation provides no help for these precincts, it does help by sharing their considerable strength in estimating the quantities of interest for the other precincts.

The algebraic form of the likelihood function for homogeneous precincts is fairly simple because T_i reduces to β_i^b (for $X_i = 1$) or β_i^w (for $X_i = 0$). The likelihood function is also easy for unanimous precincts since if $T_i = 0$ or $T_i = 1$, then $\beta_i^b = \beta_i^w = T_i$. These cases are covered in Appendix D.

7.3 Parameterizations

In order to maximize the likelihood function more easily, and then later to summarize the information about it, choosing a parameterization close to the normal distribution is best. (That is, the parameterization should be close to the normal in the parameters, not necessarily in T_i.) This procedure also helps to avoid numerical difficulties that sometimes occur when computing the double integral in Equation 7.2. Since maximum likelihood is invariant to reparameterization, this reformulation does not affect where the maximum is located on the scale of $\breve{\psi}$.

For example, as is very common in the statistical literature, I estimate $\ln(\breve{\sigma}_b)$ instead of $\breve{\sigma}_b$. This parameterization has the advantage of being unbounded and more nearly symmetric, as a normal variate must. To compensate for the correlation that often appears between $\breve{\mathfrak{B}}$ and σ_b^2, I use a modified ratio of the two for estimation. The full set of parameterizations is as follows:

$$\phi_1 = \frac{\breve{\mathfrak{B}}^b - 0.5}{\breve{\sigma}_b^2 + 0.25}$$

$$\phi_2 = \frac{\breve{\mathfrak{B}}^w - 0.5}{\ddot{\sigma}_w^2 + 0.25}$$

$$\phi_3 = \ln(\breve{\sigma}_b)$$

$$\phi_4 = \ln(\breve{\sigma}_w)$$

$$\phi_5 = 0.5 \ln\left(\frac{1+\breve{\rho}}{1-\breve{\rho}}\right) \tag{7.4}$$

where ϕ_5 is Fisher's (1915) "Z transformation."

An example of the advantages of these parameterizations appears in Figure 7.3. The left panel of this figure gives a sample contour plot of $\breve{\mathfrak{B}}^b$ by $\breve{\sigma}^b$ (using the data set described in Chapter 10, and with the other values set at their maximum likelihood estimates). Each contour line traces out all places on the corresponding three-dimensional image that have a certain height, labeled as the fraction drop-off from the mode. Thus, the concentric lines on the left graph portray a long thin hill that peaks at the center of the 0.9 loop. The fact that the contour plot is long and thin is indicative of highly correlated parameters.

In contrast, the right panel in Figure 7.3 plots the contours of the corresponding reparameterized version, ϕ_1 by ϕ_3. The parameters in this distribution are nearly uncorrelated, making numerical maximization much easier. For other data sets, the original distribution is more skewed or "banana-shaped", whereas the reparameterized version is much closer to the elliptically shaped normal distribution. Thus, a normal distribution will much more closely approximate the variabil-

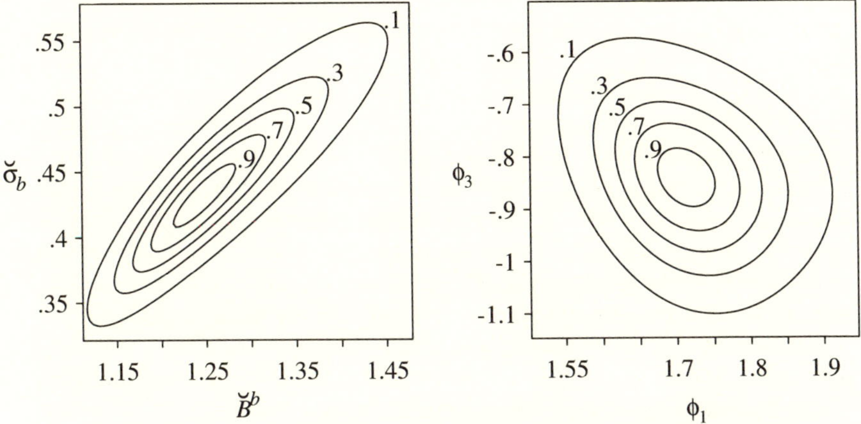

Figure 7.3 Likelihood Contour Plots. The left panel shows the contour plots with highly correlated parameters under the original $\breve{\psi}$ parameterization. The right panel gives the more nearly uncorrelated normal contours for the reparameterized version, ϕ.

ity in the likelihood function under this new parameterization. This is not an essential step from a theoretical perspective, and has no effect on the ultimate estimates, but it vastly reduces computational burdens in maximizing the likelihood function, in drawing samples from the exact posterior distribution, and in understanding and evaluating intermediate results. A smaller correlation is also useful since when the maximization routine tests parameter values far from the mode, standard numerical calculations of $R(\breve{\mathfrak{B}}, \breve{\Sigma})$ become imprecise. Reducing the correlation lessens the chance of running into these numerical difficulties.

This is the third parameterization used for the parameters of the truncated bivariate normal distribution in Equation 6.14. We began with the (unweighted) moments of β_i^b and β_i^w,

$$\psi = \{\mathfrak{B}^b, \mathfrak{B}^w, \sigma_b^2, \sigma_w^2, \rho\}$$

and then transformed to the corresponding untruncated scale to ease the mathematical derivations,

$$\breve{\psi} = \{\breve{\mathfrak{B}}^b, \breve{\mathfrak{B}}^w, \breve{\sigma}_b^2, \breve{\sigma}_w^2, \breve{\rho}\}$$

and now transform to the most convenient scale for the purposes of estimation,

$$\phi = \{\phi_1, \phi_2, \phi_3, \phi_4, \phi_5\}$$

Neither ψ nor $\breve{\psi}$ nor ϕ are the parameters of interest, even at the aggregate level, but keeping the parameterization flexible and changing it to suit different needs in different parts of the analysis like this is easier mathematically and computationally. It makes estimation faster, and it is more straightforward to understand (at least as compared to the algebraic mess that would result if only one parameterization were used). Moreover, the flexibility facilitates making inferences about exactly the desired quantities of interest because they are computed in a separate step, described below. The only disadvantage is that more steps are required to switch between the parameters.

In practice, ϕ is estimated first and then translated into $\breve{\psi}$ (by inverting Equations 7.4). From $\breve{\psi}$, the quantities of interest can be computed directly (as described in Chapter 8) or, to interpret the results of this preliminary estimation stage of the analysis, ψ can be calculated (using the methods of simulation indicated in Section 6.2.2).

7.4 Optional Priors

The likelihood function can be maximized fairly easily as given. However, to facilitate computation in difficult cases, priors can be useful for ϕ_3, ϕ_4, and ϕ_5, the parameters about which the least information exists in the data but some prior information does exist. Because of the extensive information available in the data, priors for ϕ_1 and ϕ_2 are usually best omitted unless substantial precise external information is available.

Since β_i^b and β_i^w are each truncated, the variances cannot logically get huge. In particular, $\breve{\sigma}_b$ and $\breve{\sigma}_w$ should be greater than about 0.5 only very infrequently. I therefore use a half-normal prior for each (or equivalently for e^{ϕ_3} and e^{ϕ_4}) with variance 0.5.[5]

The least information in the data exists for estimating ρ. Fortunately, the empirical results are not very sensitive to estimated values of ρ. Substantively, ρ can range from -1 to 1 but in real applications it should not be too large or small. For example, the correlation between the fraction of blacks and whites voting for the Democrats

[5] A half-normal distribution is the right half of a normal distribution with mean zero, normalized to have an area of one. The resulting distribution has a mean equal to $\sqrt{2/\pi}$ times the variance of the original untruncated normal.

should rarely get above 0.95 (or below −0.95) and in most applications will normally range between roughly −0.7 and 0.7. I therefore usually use a normal prior on ϕ_5 with hyper-parameters of mean zero and standard deviation 0.5. Although the priors on σ_b and σ_w rarely have any significant effect, this prior on ρ sometimes does. The effect is almost entirely on the uncertainty of the ultimate inferences, as the values of ρ very close to 1 or −1 imply unrealistically narrow confidence intervals on the parameters of interest. (The ellipse in Figure 6.3 becomes very thin and the conditional distribution cut across it by the tomography lines have very small variances.) The prior compensates for the lack of information in some data sets and keeps the variances realistically sized (see Section 9.3).

Since ecological data sets generally contain numerous observations, the prior (which is equivalent to adding one strategically selected extra observation to the data set) is usually overwhelmed by the likelihood function. The priors help for small data sets, and for the start of the maximization process, but so would collecting data for smaller areal units or merging data from adjacent geographic areas.

7.5 Summarizing Information about Estimated Parameters

The likelihood function (which is proportional to the sampling distribution), or from a Bayesian viewpoint the posterior distribution, is used to summarize all information in the data about the parameters ϕ. To do this, first maximize the log-likelihood function yielding estimates of the mode $\hat{\phi}$ and corresponding variance matrix $\hat{\mathrm{V}}(\hat{\phi})$. (If the number of observations p were to increase, the estimation variance would tend toward zero, but elements of $\hat{\phi}$ including the variance terms would tend toward fixed numbers. This is evidence that the model does not ignore the fundamental uncertainty inherent in the ecological inference problem.)

One easy summary of knowledge of ϕ is via a normal approximation. Because of the reparameterization developed for estimation purposes, the normal is not far off. Thus, we could use the multivariate normal as an approximation to the posterior distribution:

$$\phi \sim \mathrm{N}\left(\phi|\hat{\phi}, \hat{\mathrm{V}}(\hat{\phi})\right) \tag{7.5}$$

Since the correct posterior distribution is asymptotically normal, and aggregate data are rarely in short supply in ecological inference problems, this approximation should work reasonably well for many data sets.[6] But, since it will not work for every data set, I go the extra step of using the actual, rather than approximate, posterior distribution. This is done via *importance sampling*. The idea is to use the normal distribution in Equation 7.5 as a first approximation to the correct posterior, $P(\phi|T) = P(\phi)P(T|\phi)$, and then to improve the approximation to reach $P(\phi|T)$. To be specific, first draw a random value of ϕ from the normal distribution $N(\phi|\hat{\phi}, \hat{V}(\phi))$ in Equation 7.5, which is easily done. Then accept this randomly drawn value with probability proportional to its importance ratio, $P(\phi|T)/N(\phi|\hat{\phi}, \hat{V}(\hat{\phi}))$. If rejected, draw a second value from $N(\phi|\hat{\phi}, \hat{V}(\hat{\phi}))$ and repeat the procedure. See Chapter 8 for details of this procedure. Using the exact posterior has the additional advantage of working correctly even if the maximization routine were to fail. Indeed, even if the posterior has no unique maximum, multiple modes, or a plateau at the maximum, importance sampling will take longer but it will still yield random draws from the correct posterior, $P(\phi|T)$. Although these problems do not seem to occur in this model, a diagnostic for it occurring would be the importance sampling taking an inordinately long time.

[6] The normal in Equation 7.5 is, by the central limit theorem, a possible distribution for the *parameters*. The distribution for the outcome *variable* T_i is still the original posterior, which is the likelihood times the prior.

CHAPTER 8

Calculating Quantities of Interest

THIS CHAPTER shows how to use the model in Chapter 6 and preliminary estimates in Chapter 7 to make inferences about the various quantities of interest. These quantities of interest include the precinct-level parameters β_i^b and β_i^w from Table 2.3 and λ_i^b and λ_i^w from Table 2.2, as well as the corresponding district-wide aggregates B^b, B^w, Λ^b, and Λ^w. Other more specialized quantities of interest are also described. The inferences include point estimates, and uncertainty estimates such as confidence intervals, or complete posterior distributions.

The technique of *simulation* is the easiest way to compute the quantities of interest. Simulation requires no additional assumptions and is a lot easier, faster, and more intuitive than the corresponding mathematical derivations, which are not even solvable in many cases. Section 8.1 gives a brief review of this technique. Section 8.2 then describes how to simulate the precinct-level parameters, and Section 8.3 describes district-level parameters. Simulation of quantities of interest in 2×3 and larger $2 \times C$ tables are described in Section 8.4. A variety of other quantities of interest are given in Section 8.5.

8.1 Simulation Is Easier than Analytical Derivation

"Simulation" (also called "stochastic simulation," "Monte Carlo simulation," "random simulation," or "Bayesian simulation") substitutes computer effort for human effort and is used to compute features of probability distributions, such as means, variances, covariances, and the like. It involves mathematical approximation rather than statistical estimation, and is not used for estimating these features from data. Simulation can approximate the numerical value of the quantity of interest to any degree of precision. The basic idea involves taking random samples of the parameters of interest from the given probability distribution and averaging to approximate the mean, taking the standard deviation for the standard error, etc. In some ways simulation, as compared to mathematical derivation, can be thought of as the canonical approach, since it so closely mirrors statistical procedures for mathematical purposes. Its computational advantage is that the integrals required for analytical solutions are often difficult or impossible to compute. In contrast, we can get equivalent results via simulation if we can only figure out how to draw repeated independent random samples from the distributions. Simulation is becoming increasingly popular in statistical modeling because drawing random samples from a distribution is frequently easier than integrating. As such, nothing is lost by this approach, and much is gained in terms of time and resources. Because simulation is probably not very familiar to most readers, and since it has not before been used in the ecological inference literature, I briefly describe it here. See Ripley (1987), Tanner (1996), Gelman et al. (1995), and Jackman (1996) for more detailed expositions.

8.1.1 Definitions and Examples

As a simple example, suppose we wish to compute the expected value of a variable from a complicated probability distribution $P(y)$. (For simplicity, assume that the distribution has no parameters or that they are fixed and need not be estimated.) The goal, then, requires a solution to a straightforward mathematical problem. The analytical solution calls for computing this integral:

$$E(y) = \int_{-\infty}^{\infty} yP(y)dy$$

Unfortunately, integrals such as this are often very difficult or impossible to solve.

Alternatively, to compute the same expected value via simulation, follow these much simpler steps:

1. Draw 1,000 random numbers from $P(y)$
2. Compute the arithmetic mean of these random draws

The mean of the random draws serves as the approximation to the expected value. The precision of this approximation can be computed easily via the same sampling theory used to decide how many observations to draw in conducting public opinion polls when using simple random sampling. But in practice an easier alternative is to repeat the procedure and observe how much the approximation changes. If only three places after the decimal point will be used in reporting the expected value, and the approximations change only after the fourth decimal point in repeated applications, then the approximation is sufficiently precise and nothing is lost. If there is any doubt about whether a sufficient degree of precision has been reached, just increase the number of random draws from 1,000 to some larger number. The number of draws required depends on the nature of the distribution being sampled from, the quantity of interest, and the desired degree of precision. For most problems in this book, 100 draws is sufficient; for a few as many as 10,000 are required.

Using simulation to *approximate* the mean of a probability distribution is logically almost the same as using sampling theory to *estimate* the mean of a real population. To estimate a mean, average a large number of independent random draws from some real population. To approximate the mean of given probability distribution, average a large number of independent random draws from that distribution. For the model described in this book, and for many complicated statistical models, simulation is conceptually very natural because of the parallels between these two important activities.

Other features of the probability distribution besides the mean can also be computed by simulation. For example, to compute the variance of y, take the sample variance of a large number of random draws. To approximate $\Pr(y > 7)$ under this distribution, compute the proportion of random draws of y that are larger than 7. To approximate the entire distribution, plot a histogram of all the random draws.

The only difficulty in applying simulation is figuring out how to draw random numbers from specialized distributions. Most computer programs include random number generators for the uniform distribution on the interval [0,1], and for the standard normal distribution. Some programs include other useful distributions, too. For more unusual or new distributions, special procedures need to be followed, and a large statistical literature seeking to provide useful methods has developed to meet this need.

For one simple example relevant to the problem in this book, suppose we desire random numbers from the truncated standard univariate normal distribution with bounds at 0 and 1. The easiest approach is called *rejection sampling*: draw many random numbers from the (untruncated) standard normal available in most computer packages, and discard those draws that fall outside the [0,1] interval. The remaining random draws can then be used to compute the mean or other features of the probability distribution, just as before. The slight complication here is that a larger number of draws would need to be taken initially if many are rejected for falling outside the truncation bounds. Fortunately, if too few are accepted, we can redraw additional values until we have a sufficient number, and the precision of the ultimate approximations can be checked by repeating the procedure. (See Appendix F for further refinements.)

8.1.2 Simulation for Ecological Inference

The specific goal of this chapter is to compute the posterior distribution (or sampling distribution from a classical perspective) of each quantity of interest, and to draw random samples from it. For example, once we are able to draw random numbers from the posterior distribution $\mathrm{P}(\beta_i^b|T)$, we will be able to make any desired statement about β_i^b, given the information in the aggregate data. If we wish to know our best guess (point estimate) about the value of β_i^b, we could take the mean of a large number of random draws. Its standard error could be computed by calculating the standard deviation of the random draws. The full posterior distribution of β_i^b could be approximated by plotting a histogram of these random numbers.

The complication here is that the exact form of $\mathrm{P}(\beta_i^b|T)$ has not yet been calculated. If the five parameters of the truncated bivariate normal distribution, ϕ (or in its alternative parameterizations, ψ or $\breve{\psi}$), were known, the posterior distribution of the precinct-level parameter β_i^b would be $\mathrm{P}(\beta_i^b|T, \phi)$ which was given in Section 6.2.3 (see Equation 6.19 on page 108, and the derivation in Appendix C). Of course, ϕ is not known, and so $\mathrm{P}(\beta_i^b|T, \phi)$ is only the *conditional* posterior distribution. To produce the desired *unconditional* posterior distribution, $\mathrm{P}(\beta_i^b|T)$, we need to average over the uncertainty in the posterior of ϕ given the data (see Section 7.5). With this information, we will be able to compute any quantity of interest, such as racially polarized voting estimates or the district aggregates.

For example, the unconditional posterior distribution of β_i^b requires solving this formidable expression:

$$
\left.
\begin{aligned}
\mathrm{P}(\beta_i^b|T) &\propto \int \mathrm{P}(\beta_i^b, \phi|T)\, d\phi \\
&\propto \int \mathrm{P}(\phi|T)\mathrm{P}(\beta_i^b|T, \phi)\, d\phi \\
&\propto \int \mathrm{P}(\phi) \prod_{i=1}^{p} \mathrm{N}(T_i|\mu_i, \sigma_i^2) \frac{S(\breve{\mathfrak{B}}, \breve{\Sigma})}{R(\breve{\mathfrak{B}}, \breve{\Sigma})} \\
&\quad \times \mathrm{TN}\left[T_i \,\middle|\, \breve{\mathfrak{B}}_i^b + \frac{\omega_i}{\sigma_i^2}\epsilon_i,\ \breve{\sigma}_b^2 - \frac{\omega_i^2}{\sigma_i^2} \right] d\phi
\end{aligned}
\right\}
$$

This is too hard!

These five-dimensional integrals appear to have no closed form solution. Fortunately, as the following sections demonstrate, simulation will solve these problems quite easily.

8.2 Precinct-Level Quantities

This section first describes how to simulate values of β_i^b and β_i^w, and then what to do with these values to learn what the data and model say about the fraction of blacks who turnout in precinct i. (Section 8.4 shows how to simulate values of λ_i^b and λ_i^w, and how simulating θ_i^b and θ_i^w require procedures parallel to this section.)

Consider first the general logic, saving the practical details until afterward. In homogeneous precincts, β_i^b and β_i^w are known and need not be simulated. Simulating from the posterior distribution in heterogeneous precincts depends on its structure:

$$P(\beta_i^b|T) = \int_{-\infty}^{\infty} P(\phi|T)P(\beta_i^b|T, \breve{\psi})\, d\breve{\psi}$$

(Recall that ϕ is a deterministic function of $\breve{\psi}$.) Instead of carrying out the integration, we draw a single β_i^b from $P(\beta_i^b|T)$ by following these steps:

1. Draw one value of ϕ from its posterior $P(\phi|T)$ (derived in Section 7.5) and label it $\tilde{\phi}$,
2. Reparameterize $\tilde{\phi}$ (which is on the scale of estimation) into the untruncated scale, producing $\tilde{\breve{\psi}}$ (which is a simulated value of $\breve{\psi}$).
3. Insert $\tilde{\breve{\psi}}$ into the conditional posterior distribution of β_i^b (derived in Section 6.2.3), which is now $P(\beta_i^b|T, \tilde{\breve{\psi}})$, and draw a value of β_i^b randomly from it.

Following these steps is equivalent to drawing β_i^b directly from its posterior $P(\beta_i^b|T)$. The specific details of how to carry out each of these operations is somewhat more technical, but the underlying logic is no more complicated than these three steps.

I now proceed to explain these steps with a slightly different organization, and in more detail. Thus, in order to take a single random draw of $\tilde{\beta}_i^b$ from its posterior distribution $P(\beta_i^b|T_i)$, for precinct i, follow these steps:

1. Draw one random sample of the parameter vector ϕ using the normal approximation, and label it $\tilde{\phi}$. This requires two steps:
   a. Find the values of ϕ that maximize the log of the likelihood function in Equation 7.1 (page 134), plus the log of the prior if used,

and summarize the results with the vector of point estimates $\hat{\phi}$ and a variance-covariance matrix, $\hat{V}(\hat{\phi})$. Any standard maximum likelihood program can produce these estimates (see Appendix F).

b. Draw one value of ϕ from a normal distribution with mean $\hat{\phi}$ and variance $\hat{V}(\hat{\phi})$ (Equation 7.5, page 139).

2. Reparameterize the simulated elements of $\tilde{\phi}$ into the untruncated version, $\tilde{\breve{\psi}}$, by substituting the elements of $\tilde{\phi}$ into the left sides of Equations 7.4 (page 136) and solving (see for example, Equation 10.1, page 202).[1]

3. Improve the normal approximation by using "importance sampling" (see Tanner, 1996). The result is a single random draw of $\breve{\psi}$ from its posterior distribution, which is also labeled $\tilde{\breve{\psi}}$. To do this, follow these steps:

   a. Compute the "importance ratio," which is the the ratio of the value of the likelihood function $L\left(\tilde{\breve{\psi}}|T\right)$, to this the normal approximation, $N\left(\tilde{\phi}|\hat{\phi}, \hat{V}(\hat{\phi})\right)$, each evaluated at the simulated parameter vector, and normalized across repeated draws to a scale of zero to one.

   b. Accept the sampled value $\tilde{\breve{\psi}}$ with probability equal to the importance ratio. That is, keep the sampled value if it is larger than a number drawn randomly from a uniform distribution on the interval [0,1]. If the sampled value is rejected (because it is less than the randomly drawn uniform number), go to step 1.b. and draw another.

4. Insert $\tilde{\breve{\psi}}$, which is the result of the importance sampling, into the conditional posterior distribution of β_i^b, $P(\beta_i^b|T_i, \tilde{\breve{\psi}})$, and draw a value of β_i^b randomly from it. To do this, follow these steps:

   a. Compute $\tilde{\sigma}_i^2$ from Equation 6.17 (page 106), $\tilde{\omega}_i$ by using Equation 6.20, and $\tilde{\epsilon}_i$ by Equation 6.21 (page 108).

   b. Substitute these values into the truncated conditional normal posterior distribution in Equation 6.19 (page 108), and draw one value of $\tilde{\beta}_i^b$.[2]

A summary of what the model and the data have to say about β_i^b can be displayed by taking a large number of random draws of $\tilde{\beta}_i^b$

[1] The notation $\tilde{\breve{\psi}}$ refers to a simulated value of $\breve{\psi}$, the untruncated parameterization of the truncated bivariate normal distribution parameter vector.

[2] To draw from this truncated normal, sample rejection, as described in Section 8.1.1, is often fastest. For hard cases, where the [0,1] region is distant from the mean of the untruncated normal and the variance is small, the inverse CDF method can be used. In addition, if the precinct is racially homogeneous (i.e., X_i =1 or 0), then the value of the parameter is given in Equation B.1. Since it is known exactly, its standard error is zero, and no simulation is necessary.

(by repeating this algorithm) and plotting a histogram. This histogram represents the posterior density of β_i^b, which is a representation of all knowledge we have about the parameter. If enough simulations are taken, the histogram becomes smooth; alternatively, a "kernel density estimate" can be used instead, which is a smooth version of a histogram (see Silverman, 1986; and King, Alt, Burns, and Laver, 1990, for a political science application).

For example, I collected data from the 1990 election held in Pennsylvania's 8th state senate district. This district has 244 precincts that could be matched to demographic data from the U.S. Census. The algorithm described in this section was then applied in order to estimate the fraction of blacks who turned out to vote in each precinct. Figure 8.1 plots four kernel density estimates of β_i^b, the fraction of blacks who voted in 1990, from four precincts in Pennsylvania's 8th state senate district. These four were selected to show the diversity of empirical results. For example, the top two posterior distributions appear symmetric, unaffected by truncation, and imply reasonably narrow confidence intervals, but with very different means for β_i^b. The third distribution gives an even more confident prediction; it is also skewed and heavily influenced by its upper bound. The final distribution is much flatter, spreading out its information over a larger interval, meaning that inferences from it are much less certain. This fourth posterior is also skewed even though it is not influenced by the bounds, and it is slightly multi-modal.

The mean of each of these distributions can be used as a point estimate and the standard deviation could summarize the degree of variation, and hence uncertainty, around the mean, although the full distribution as in Figure 8.1 contains all relevant information and should always be presented if there is sufficient room. Posterior distributions like these also make possible specific probabilistic statements about each value of β_i^b. For example, we could easily compute the probability that $\beta_{238}^b > 0.4$ by adding up the area under precinct 238's curve to the right of 0.4 on the horizontal axis (this can also be done directly from the simulated values by counting the proportion of simulated values greater than 0.4).

We can arrive at a point estimate of a precinct-level parameter by repeating these steps to yield a large number (K) of simulated values and averaging them ($K = 100$ will usually be sufficient, although any degree of precision can be achieved by drawing a sufficiently large number). For example, a point estimate of the proportion of blacks

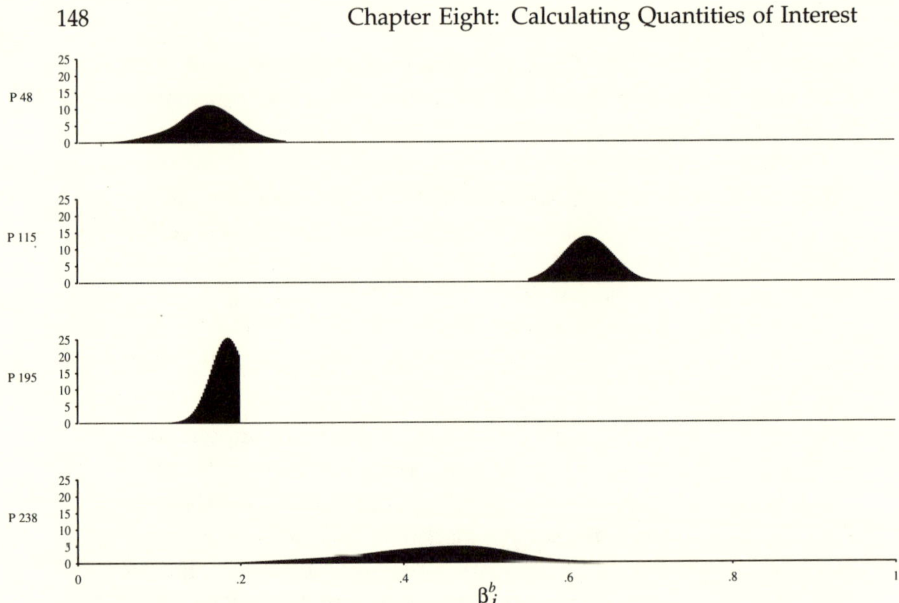

Figure 8.1 Posterior Distributions of Precinct Parameters β_i^b. Proportion of blacks voting in selected precincts from Pennsylvania's 8th senatorial district in 1990. The first two posteriors are symmetric; the third is strongly affected by its upper bound; and the last has a wide variance and is thus less informative. These figures are "density estimates" (smooth versions of histograms) drawn using the simulations $\tilde{\beta}_i^b$.

voting in precinct i is:

$$\hat{\beta}_i^b = \frac{1}{K}\sum_{k=1}^{K}\tilde{\beta}_i^{b(k)} \tag{8.1}$$

where $\tilde{\beta}_i^{b(k)}$ is simulation k. If the posterior is skewed as is often the case, the median value might serve as a better point estimate summary. However, because the posterior distribution is always truncated, the median is not often far from the mean.

It would be possible to calculate a standard error of this proportion by taking the standard deviation across these K simulations:

$$\mathrm{SE}(\beta_i^b) = \sqrt{\frac{1}{K}\sum_{k=1}^{K}(\tilde{\beta}_i^{b(k)} - \hat{\beta}_i^b)^2}$$

However, because the posterior distribution is truncated, the standard error is not always the best measure of uncertainty for estimates from this model, even though it will often prove to be a useful summary. In general, standard errors are approximations for use with a normal posterior (or sampling) distribution. Although standard errors can always be computed, they do not always correspond to the usual t-statistics and confidence intervals unless the underlying posterior is normal. One would still want to compute hypothesis tests and confidence intervals, but the familiar rules of thumb no longer apply. For example, without a normal posterior, ± 2 standard errors would no longer be approximately the 95% confidence interval.

So the question is how best to represent the uncertainty about our point estimates. By far the best summary of our knowledge of the parameter, with or without knowledge that the distribution is normal, is the entire posterior distribution. With simulation, this is easy to compute: merely plot a histogram of all the simulated values from a precinct, such as in Figure 8.1. The problem is that this is unwieldy if the problem includes many precincts (such as in Part IV, which includes thousands of estimates.)

As a convenient summary of the model's uncertainty, confidence intervals are very useful. These are also easy to compute from simulations. For example, to compute the 80% confidence interval for β_i^b, use the values at the 10th and 90th percentiles of the simulated values. That is, sort the K simulated values of this parameter. Then take the value which is $0.1K$ from the smallest for the lower end of the confidence interval and $0.1K$ from the largest (or equivalently $0.9K$ from the smallest) for the upper end. Thus, if we used 100 simulations, the 10th and 90th smallest values form the confidence interval.

To draw random values of β_i^w, follow the steps for drawing random values of β_i^b and then compute $\tilde{\beta}_i^w$ deterministically using Equation 5.2 (page 80). We would follow parallel procedures for $\tilde{\theta}_i^b$, and $\tilde{\theta}_i^w$ from Equation 2.3 (page 34). The parameters from larger tables require similar, but slightly more complicated, procedures described in Chapter 15.

8.3 District-Level Quantities

The district aggregates are also of obvious interest, as they were the original, more limited, goal of previous studies of ecological inference. They can also serve as convenient summaries of detailed precinct-level results.

One set of district-level parameters are those explicitly represented in the likelihood model, ψ (or $\breve{\psi}$ or ϕ, depending on parameterization). However, because these parameters are based on the simple unweighted averages and do not include the full information from the precinct-level bounds, they are not the district-level parameters of interest. The correct district-level parameters of interest are the weighted averages of the precinct parameters computed in Section 8.2.

To draw a single random value of a district aggregate, draw one value for the corresponding parameter in each precinct and then take their weighted average. To compute one simulation of the district aggregate, $\hat{B}^b$, follow these steps:

1. Apply the steps described in Section 8.2 once for each of the p precincts, producing $\tilde{\beta}_i^b$ (for $i = 1, \ldots, p$).
2. Take the average weighted by the numbers of blacks in each precinct by following Equation 2.1 (page 33):

$$\tilde{B}^b = \sum_{i=1}^{p} \frac{N_i^b \tilde{\beta}_i^b}{N^b}$$

(These will automatically fall within the correct bounds for the district aggregate.)

To produce a set of K simulated values of the district aggregate, repeat this procedure K times. The resulting simulations can then be used in the same way the precinct-level simulations were used in Section 8.2. For example, the best summary of our knowledge about the district aggregate is the posterior distribution, which can be approximated by plotting a histogram of the district simulations (for an example, see Figure 10.4, page 208).

We could similarly compute a point estimate for the district aggregate quantity of interest by taking the mean of the simulated values:

$$\hat{B}^b = \frac{1}{K} \sum_{k=1}^{K} \tilde{B}^{b(k)}$$

where $\tilde{B}^{b(k)}$ is simulation k of the district aggregate.

As with the precinct-level quantities of interest, we could compute the standard error of this quantity, based on the standard deviation of the simulations,

$$\mathrm{SE}(\hat{B}^b) = \sqrt{\frac{1}{K} \sum_{k=1}^{K} (\tilde{B}^{b(k)} - \hat{B}^b)^2}$$

Although the standard error is not always a good summary of the posterior for the aggregate quantities of interest, the definition of these quantities as weighted averages over all p observations makes standard errors much more appropriate than at the precinct level. Of course, in all cases, histograms or density estimates of the entire posterior is preferred if space allows.

8.4 Quantities of Interest from Larger Tables

This section provides two methods of simulation for making inferences about λ_i^b and λ_i^w from 2×3 tables (such as Table 2.2, page 30), as well as the analogous quantities of interest from arbitrarily large $2 \times C$ tables, for $C > 2$. (General $R \times C$ tables are discussed in Chapter 15). The unknown quantities in the 2×3 table include β_i^b and β_i^w, which can be estimated via the procedures introduced in Section 8.2. They also include λ_i^b (the fraction of blacks voting for the Democratic candidate) and λ_i^w (the fraction of whites voting for the Democratic candidate).

The first method introduced here is easier to apply because it requires two applications of the procedures used for 2×2 tables, and because the variable codings used are more natural. It is also easier to apply to larger $2 \times C$ tables. The second method maintains closer connections with the literature, as it builds on insights from the double regression model.

8.4.1 A Multiple Imputation Approach

The first method of simulating the λ's begins with the fact that if x_i (the fraction of voters who are black, N_i^{bT}/N_i) were observed, we would have a 2×2 table of Democratic/Republican vote by black/white race with both marginals observed (V_i, the Democratic fraction of the vote, and x_i). This means that if x_i were observed, we would be able to substitute the accounting identity $V_i = \lambda_i^b x_i + \lambda_i^w(1 - x_i)$ (from Equation 4.3, page 68) for the one used in our running example, $T_i = \beta_i^b X_i + \beta_i^w(1 - X_i)$, and no generalization would be necessary. All the same methods, graphics, and models could be applied without modification. To make use of this result, I use the decomposition $x_i = \beta_i^b X_i / T_i$ (originally introduced in Section 4.2) and estimate x_i by using an estimate of the only part of x_i that is unknown, β_i^b. Fortunately, we already have a good method of estimating β_i^b by applying the basic model.

Thus, to estimate the λ's, we could use the following procedure. First estimate β_i^b with its mean posterior point estimate in the turnout by race 2×2 case with marginals T_i and X_i. Then substitute this estimate, for each i, into $\beta_i^b X_i/T_i$ to generate an estimate of x_i. Finally, draw simulations of the λ's by analyzing a second 2×2 table with marginals V_i and x_i.

This is a reasonable approach and I find that it works well in practice and in Monte Carlo simulations. But there are at least two opportunities for improving this procedure (short of using the methods in Chapter 15). First, the second-stage 2×2 analysis conditions on x_i, as if it were known without error. This conditioning is obviously incorrect since we are estimating x_i. The result of ignoring this source of variability is that confidence intervals will be too short, although in my experience the shortfall is relatively minor in many, although not all, cases. Fortunately, this extra variability can easily be included in the model by appealing to the ideas of multiple imputation (Rubin, 1987) and treating x_i as a variable containing (all) missing values. To apply this method, impute m values of x_i (for each i) by drawing m values of β_i^b from its posterior distribution (by following the steps in Section 8.2) and computing $\tilde{x}_i = \tilde{\beta}_i^b X_i/T_i$ for each. Then λ_i^b, λ_i^w, or any other quantity of interest is computed in each of the m imputed data sets, and the results are combined. For example, if a point estimate is desired, we use the average of the point estimates computed in each of the m completed data sets. To compute the squared standard error of this point estimate, we average the variances computed *within* each of the m data sets and add to this the sample variance *across* the m point estimates times $(1+1/m)$. The last term corrects for bias given that $m < \infty$; in fact, in most cases, $m = 4$ is sufficient. A slightly easier alternative way to combine the separate runs is to draw K/m simulations of λ_i^b and λ_i^w from each of the m completed data sets, and to use the resulting K simulations as draws from their posterior distribution.

A second opportunity for improving this procedure occurs because the λ's are treated as if they are independent of V_i (and β_i^b and β_i^w). If they are instead related, we can improve on this approach by allowing dependence in the model. (This is a somewhat related argument to concerns about making the "independence of irrelevant alternatives" assumption in individual-level models for multinomial choice.) The simplest way to include this information is by using V_i as a covariate in the first-stage analysis for estimating β_i^b or possibly using an estimate (or imputations from the posterior distribution) of β_i^b as a covariate for estimating λ_i^b and λ_i^w in the second stage. (Including covariates is described in Sections 9.2.1–9.2.3).

This procedure (with or without these two improvements) can be used to estimate quantities of interest in larger $2 \times C$ tables, that is with any number of outcome categories C. The procedure is first to divide the categories into a series of sequential, dichotomous outcomes. In the present case, we have taken a three-category outcome and treated it as (1) vote/no vote and (2) Democratic/Republican, given vote. If we had four catgories, say also a minor party candidate, we could use (1) vote/no vote; (2) major party/minor party, among those who vote; and (3) Democratic/Republican, among those who vote for major party candidates. It is most convenient if the dichotomization parallels some substantive organization of the problem at hand or even a model for the individual's decision process. This will make it easier to interpret the diagnostic procedures and graphics. However, the ordering of the dichotomies is not necessarily material to the method: so long as one is careful to get good estimates of the early stages, the later stages will be properly estimated.

The deterministic bounds on the λ's should always be computed using the original derivations in Equation 5.4 (page 83) rather than using formulas for the bounds from 2×2 tables in Equation 5.1 (page 79) with V_i and the estimated x_i as marginals. The latter procedure incorrectly treats x_i, and thus β_i^b, as if they are known. The differences between these correct and incorrect procedures for computing the bounds also helps quantify precisely why ecological inferences in larger tables are necessarily more uncertain: the farther down the sequential list of dichotomies a quantity of interest appears (and thus the deeper it is buried within a large table), the wider and thus less informative the bounds become. Or, to put it in reverse, if β_i^b and thus x_i were really known, the bounds on the λ's given this information would become narrower.

8.4.2 An Approach Related to Double Regression

The second method of simulating the λ's requires simulations of the β's and the θ's separately. The former were described in Section 8.2. The latter can be simulated using the same procedures applied to a different 2×2 table also collapsed from the 2×3 Table 2.2. Thus, instead of collapsing the Democratic-Republican-no vote choice into turnout (T_i) versus no vote ($1 - T_i$), as in Table 2.3 (page 31), we now collapse this table into vote Democratic (D_i) versus vote Republican or no vote ($1-D_i$). This is equivalent to Table 2.3 with D_i replacing T_i and θ_i^b and θ_i^w replacing β_i^b and β_i^w, respectively. Thus, to estimate the θ's requires applying exactly the same model and estimation procedures as already described, only to this different 2×2.

A single random draw of $\tilde{\lambda}_i^b$ can be simulated by drawing one value each of $\tilde{\beta}_i^b$ and $\tilde{\theta}_i^b$ (by following the procedures described in Section

8.2), and completing the division implied in the definition Equation 4.6 (page 71):

$$\tilde{\lambda}_i^b = \frac{\tilde{\theta}_i^b}{\tilde{\beta}_i^b}$$

and verifying that the result falls within the bounds specified by Equation 5.4 (page 83). If a random draw of λ_i^b falls outside of its bounds, discard it and draw another. This is equivalent to drawing directly from the truncated normal.

The difference here is that drawing permissible values for the bounds on β_i^b and θ_i^b does not guarantee admissible values for λ_i^b. The bounds on λ_i^b, in terms of the bounds on θ_i^b and β_i^b can be seen in Figure 8.2. The unit square in this figure is made up of coordinates of β_i^b, θ_i^b. From this figure, we can determine how the value of λ_i^b is constrained by the various bounds. Thus, β_i^b must fall within its upper and lower bounds, which appear as vertical dotted lines. Similarly, the bounds on θ_i^b are given as horizontal dotted lines. Each of these lines can move, as a function of X_i, T_i, and D_i, as the formulas for these bounds indicate (Equation 5.1, page 79).

Thus, so far, λ_i^b must fall within the inner rectangle defined by the dotted lines. In addition, the upper and lower bounds on λ_i^b further constrain the permissible area, as determined by their bounds (Equation 5.4, page 83). These diagonal lines can also move as a function of X_i, T_i, and D_i, although they must remain below the 45° line so that λ_i^b is always less than one. The result of all these restrictions is an irregular pentagon, which appears in the figure as a shaded area. Depending on where the lines move, the shaded area will also move to any space beneath the lower diagonal. The permissible area will not always have five sides. Depending on its position, it can have three, four, five, or six sides.

Figure 8.2 can be used to improve the procedure for drawing random values. Instead of the sample rejection method, it would be possible to draw directly from this area via some procedure such as Gibbs sampling. For difficult cases, this should be much faster computationally.

One possible problem is that this procedure implies that β_i^b and θ_i^b are independent after conditioning on X_i, which may not be accurate. The independence can be seen since separate likelihood functions and separate posterior distributions are used for each parameter. Especially after conditioning, independence is a reasonable assumption for our running example since voter turnout and voter choice are

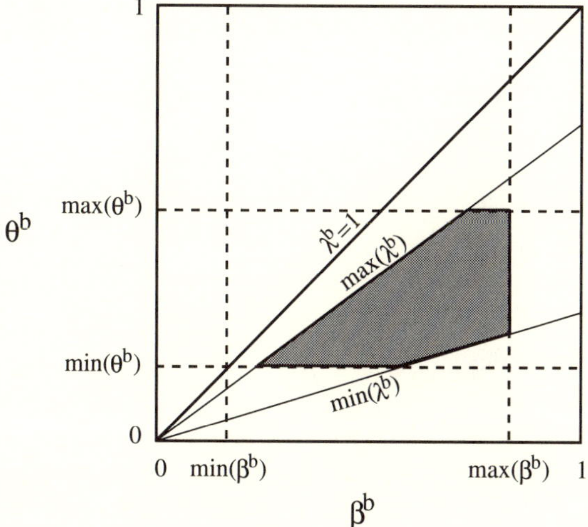

Figure 8.2 Support of the Joint Distribution of θ_i^b and β_i^b with Bounds Specified for Drawing λ_i^b. The shaded area indicates permissible values for λ_i^b, which can move as a function of X_i, T_i, and D_i to anywhere beneath the 45° line. The minimum and maximum values of each parameter in this figure refer to the upper and lower bounds computed in the text.

not closely related empirically (even though there are some theoretical reasons to suspect otherwise). A generalization of the model to include dependence is introduced in Chapter 15.

The other precinct-level parameter of interest, $\tilde{\lambda}_i^w$, can be drawn deterministically by using $\tilde{\theta}_i^b$ and $\tilde{\beta}_i^b$, which were used in the process of drawing simulations of $\tilde{\lambda}_i^b$. The procedure is to use the first, second, and last accounting identities in Equations 4.6 (page 71). That is, we compute:

$$\tilde{\lambda}_i^w = \frac{\tilde{\theta}_i^w}{\tilde{\beta}_i^w} = \frac{\dfrac{D_i}{1-X_i} - \dfrac{X_i}{1-X_i}\tilde{\theta}_i^b}{\dfrac{T_i}{1-X_i} - \dfrac{X_i}{1-X_i}\tilde{\beta}_i^b}$$

Each of the parameters of interest can then be drawn for all precincts, $i = 1, \ldots, p$, by repeating these procedures. With repeated simulations for each precinct parameter one can calculate any quantity of interest.

To draw a single random value of a district aggregate, using either method, draw one value for the corresponding parameter in each precinct and then take their weighted average. That is,

$$\tilde{\Lambda}^b = \sum_{i=1}^{p} \frac{\tilde{N}_i^{bT} \tilde{\lambda}_i^b}{\tilde{N}^{bT}}$$

$$\tilde{\Lambda}^w = \sum_{i=1}^{p} \frac{\tilde{N}_i^{wT} \tilde{\lambda}_i^w}{\tilde{N}^{wT}}$$

where $\tilde{N}_i^{bT} = \tilde{\beta}_i^b N_i^b$ and $\tilde{N}_i^{wT} = \tilde{\beta}_i^w N_i^w$. Simulations of these quantities of interest will automatically fall within their proper aggregate bounds so long as the constituent precinct parameters are properly drawn. As before, the posterior distribution of these parameters can be approximated via the histogram of many simulated values. Confidence intervals can be calculated as before via percentiles of the sorted simulations.

8.5 Other Quantities of Interest

Other quantities can also be computed in a similar fashion. For example, the difference $\beta_i \equiv (\beta_i^b - \beta_i^w)$ is the degree of racially polarized voting in district i. To compute the posterior distribution of this quantity of interest, draw one simulated value of β_i^b and β_i^w, and compute their difference. Then repeat this procedure K times and plot the histogram of these simulated values.

To compute a posterior distribution for the degree of racially polarized voting for the district aggregate, $B \equiv (B^b - B^w)$, draw simulated values of B^b and B^w and take their difference; then plot a histogram of the simulated values of $\tilde{B}$. The histogram of any quantity of interest that is a function of the parameters discussed here can be similarly computed. The key is to do computations at the level of individual simulations, and to avoid doing computations after averaging.

Finally, for displaying the fit of the model to the aggregate data points, it is often helpful to display the expected value $E(T_i|X_i)$ and confidence intervals around this expected value. As an easier alternative, Figure 6.1 (page 100) plotted the expected value and plus and minus one standard deviation. The expected value was easily computed because estimates of $\mathfrak{B}^b$ and $\mathfrak{B}^w$ provided the end points at $X_i = 1$ and $X_i = 0$, respectively (see Equation 6.8, page 97). The standard deviations were also easy to compute, from the estimates of σ_b, σ_w, and ρ (see Equation 6.9), and it was especially useful for that figure in displaying the theoretical properties of the model. However, in applications, the standard deviations will not be as useful, since adding them to the mean is only appropriate if the underlying distribution is normal, which is not the case here. Confidence intervals are thus an appropriate alternative, and used frequently in applications in succeeding chapters.

For example, to compute the 80% confidence intervals around $E(T_i|X_i)$, we need to draw samples from the conditional distribution, $P(T_i|X_i)$. To draw one value, take random samples of β_i^b and β_i^w using the procedures described in Section 8.2. Then set X_i at (say) 0.5, and compute

$$\tilde{T}_i = \tilde{\beta}_i^b X_i + \tilde{\beta}_i^w (1 - X_i) \tag{8.2}$$

Then repeat this procedure a large number of times to draw many values of $\tilde{T}_i$, all for $X_i = 0.5$. To compute the expected value $E(T_i|X_i = 0.5)$ via simulation, take the mean of these random draws. To compute the 80% confidence intervals around this point, sort the values and take the 10th and 90th percentile values of $\tilde{T}_i$. To draw the complete 80% confidence intervals, repeat this procedure for all the values of X_i (say all the values between 0 and 1 in increments of 0.01), and connect the dots either directly or with some minor smoothing to eliminate variation in the lines due to approximation variability (cf. Keane, 1994: 100). Figure 10.3 (page 206) gives an example of 80% confidence intervals of $T_i|X_i$ from a real data set.

CHAPTER 9

Model Extensions

THE BASIC ecological inference model presented thus far relies on three assumptions that are inappropriate for some data sets. Fortunately, because many basic statistical problems unrelated to aggregation have already been solved and incorporated in the model (such as those discussed in Chapter 4), inferences even without model extensions to deal with aggregation issues explicitly are far more robust than with other techniques. As demonstrated in Part IV, in many real data sets the problems of inaccurate estimates that occur with Goodman's model vanish without any special attention to the model extensions discussed in this chapter. Of course, reliably generalizing to all empirical examples likely to arise in the future is impossible, and, as demonstrated here, generating data that will send the basic model off track is possible and thus may occur in practice if the analyst has insufficient contextual knowledge about the desired inference. In other words, because the essence of aggregation is the loss of some individual-level information, ecological inferences will always entail some risk. The purpose of this chapter is to evaluate these risks, to highlight the precise consequences of violating each model assumption, and to provide a set of tools for modifying or dropping the assumptions and avoiding the problems that can result.

Section 9.1 outlines what can go wrong with the basic model and reviews the observable implications of its three assumptions (originally introduced in Section 6.1). The specific diagnostic tools and model extensions designed to cope with these problems are then provided in the succeeding two sections. Monte Carlo evidence, and a fully nonparametric version of the model are also provided. Section 9.2 discusses aggregation bias, and Section 9.3 considers possible problems with the distributional assumption.

9.1 WHAT CAN GO WRONG?

In this section, I generate artificial data sets that represent worst-case scenarios for making ecological inferences. These data sets are not intended to be realistic, only to show what we would be up against in a world where nature is maximally malevolent and social scientists are unusually naive. These problems are most likely to happen to empirical researchers who make inferences without taking the time to learn about local context, and even then only sometimes. Succeeding sections show what to do to avoid these problems.

The precise role of each assumption in the estimation process is gauged by isolating the effects of violating each while satisfying the remaining two. But it pays to remember that most real applications that deviate from the basic ecological inference model do not violate one assumption while neatly meeting the requirements of the others. This makes diagnosis somewhat more difficult because more than one problem is often occurring simultaneously. However, although each extension of the basic model may represent only one small step for diagnosis, it is often a giant leap for amelioration. That is, because the logically distinct problems are empirically identical, fewer modifications of the basic model are necessary to produce valid inferences.

9.1.1 Aggregation Bias

I first create a reference data set by randomly generating observations that meet all model assumptions. Define X_i as 75 points equally spaced between zero and one. Then randomly generate β_i^b and β_i^w from a truncated bivariate normal distribution with means (on the untruncated scale) $\breve{\mathfrak{B}}^b = 0.5$ and $\breve{\mathfrak{B}}^w = 0.5$, standard deviations $\breve{\sigma}_b = 0.4$ and $\breve{\sigma}_w = 0.1$, and correlation $\breve{\rho} = 0.2$. Graph (A) in Figure 9.1 presents the tomography plot with estimated maximum likelihood contours for these data; the true points appear as black dots.

The location and shape of the contours and true points correspond to the parameters from which the data were drawn: For example, the mode is near dead center, which is 0.5 on both axes. In addition, most of the distribution is far from the edges of the square, except the ends, which are clipped horizontally. Another representation of the same data appear in graph (B) of Figure 9.1. This graph plots X_i by T_i with one circle for each precinct. By extending the logic of Figure 3.1 (page 41), one line is drawn through each point from the true β_i^w at the left vertical axis to the true β_i^b at the right vertical axis. The variation in the lines highlights the nature of parameter variation over the precincts.

Thus, each precinct is represented in graph (A) by one line where the true β_i^b, β_i^w coordinate *could* fall when observing only aggregate data, and one black dot where it *does* fall. In graph (B) the same precincts are each represented by one circle where the observed coordinates for X_i and T_i are, and one line for the true slope of that precinct's line. The lines in graph (A) and the points in graph (B) are observable in aggregate data, whereas the points in the tomography

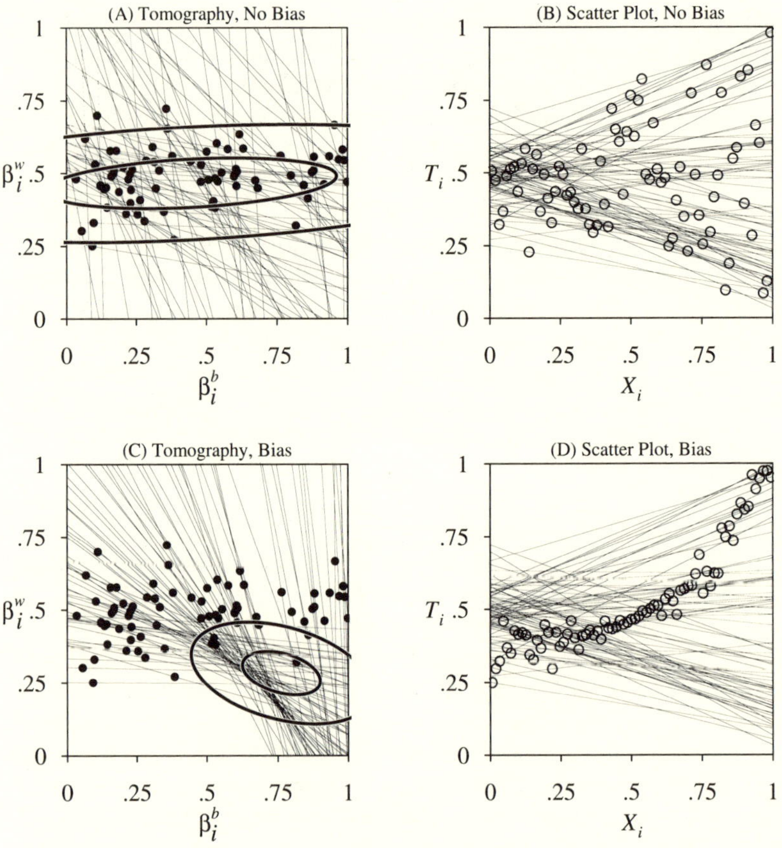

Figure 9.1 The Worst of Aggregation Bias: Same Truth, Different Observable Implications. Graphs (A) and (B) represent data randomly generated from the model with parameters $\breve{\mathfrak{B}}^b = \breve{\mathfrak{B}}^w = 0.5$, $\breve{\sigma}_b = 0.4$, $\breve{\sigma}_w = 0.1$, and $\breve{\rho} = 0.2$. Graphs (C) and (D) represent data with the same values of β_i^b and β_i^w but different aggregate data, created to maximize the degree of aggregation bias while still leaving the generating distribution unchanged. Graphs (A) and (C) are tomography plots with true coordinates appearing as black dots, and with contour ellipses estimated from aggregate data only. Graphs (B) and (D) are scatter plots of X_i by T_i with lines representing the true precinct parameters.

plot and the lines in the scatter plot are usually unobserved. The expected value line from graph (B) is omitted to reduce visual clutter, but it is easy to see that it would lie flat at about $T_i = 0.5$ for all values of X_i.

The model fits the data represented in these graphs well. For example, the (inner) 50% contour line (estimated from only the aggregate data) captures about 50% of the true points. This is no surprise, of course, since the data were generated to meet the model's assumptions. In addition, the slope of the lines in the scatter plot appears to be uncorrelated with the value of X_i at each point, which is one way of indicating the absence of aggregation bias (as per the definition in Section 3.5).

To create the first type of worst case scenario, the β_i^b, β_i^w points are exactly as in graphs (A) and (B), but the aggregate data that are generated by (but still consistent with) these points have been changed. To create these new aggregate data, sort the two precinct parameters according to their sum and match them to sorted values of X_i. This procedure induces an especially large aggregation bias, as indicated by the relationship between β_i^b and X_i, and between β_i^w and X_i, while still not altering the truncated bivariate normal distribution of the parameters.

These data are analyzed in graphs (C) and (D) of Figure 9.1 in precisely parallel fashion to the original data set. The true β_i^b, β_i^w points in the tomography plots, and the true lines in the scatter plots have not changed, but the aggregate data have changed so the tomography lines and X_i, T_i points differ from graphs (A) and (B) to graphs (C) and (D). The high level of aggregation bias can be seen in these figures in several ways. For example, the points in graph (D) have sharply increasing slopes for points with larger values of X_i. Or, to put it another way, the steeper the slope of a tomography line in graph (C) (which implies larger values of X_i), the larger are β_i^b and, to a lesser extent, β_i^w.

Unless one has some sense that different assumptions are appropriate for these two data sets, no method of ecological inference could ever distinguish between the two. The problem created for the unwitting researcher can be seen in Figure (C), where the the contour ellipses, estimated from the aggregate data alone, exclude most of the true β_i^b, β_i^w points. This can also be seen in graph (D), since the expected value line would be sharply increasing to fit the circles whereas the average line in that graph, which is the goal of the estimation, is flat at $T_i \approx 0.5$ for all X_i.

9.1.2 Incorrect Distributional Assumptions

Section 9.1.1 analyzed data sets for which the truth remained the same but the observable implications differed, in order to demonstrate the effects of aggregation bias. I now create two new data sets with the opposite problem in order to demonstrate the consequences of the wrong distributional assumptions. That is, these data sets have different true parameter values with identical observable implications—that is, the same values of X_i and T_i but different values of β_i^b and β_i^w.

For comparison, first generate a data set that meets all of the model's assumptions. Graphs (A) and (B) in Figure 9.2 analyze this new data set in parallel fashion to Graphs (A) and (B) in Figure 9.1. These data were randomly generated from the model with means $\breve{\mathfrak{B}}^b = \breve{\mathfrak{B}}^w = 0.5$, standard deviations $\sigma_b = \sigma_w = 0.07$, and correlation $\rho = 0$. The contour ellipses computed from aggregate data in graph (A) fit the true points (represented as black dots) very well. The inference from the lines to the contours are also especially clear in this example: with the assumption that there exists a single mode (that is, that the precincts have something in common), a researcher can look at the lines in the tomography plot and clearly see that the middle of the graph is where all the lines are crossing, and is likely to be where the "emissions" are mostly likely to be coming from (and thus is the probable location of most of the true points). The maximum likelihood procedure picks up on this same information and correctly locates the contours at the center of the graph. The scatter plot in graph (B) gives the observed aggregate data points, X_i and T_i, as circles and true β_i^b, β_i^w parameters as lines. As can be seen from this graph, these data have no aggregation bias because the slopes and intercepts of the lines are unrelated to the value of X_i at each point on the lines.

Now consider a new data set that maximizes distributional problems, without inducing aggregation bias, created by keeping X_i and T_i the same and moving the β_i^b and β_i^w points to different locations. This can be seen by the tomography plots in graphs (A) and (C) in Figure 9.2, where the lines remain unchanged and the points are moved to near the edges of the graph. In order to avoid creating a correlation between X_i and the precinct parameters, move precincts with an even-numbered first digit after the decimal point for X_i toward the upper left of the graph, and those with an odd-numbered first digit down to the right. This is an extremely artificial procedure that will probably never occur in a real application, but it does serve the purposes of demonstrating one type of ecological inference problem without having to consider others simultaneously.

The problem created by this data set is severe but different from that in Figure 9.1. Since aggregate data are the same in the two data sets in this figure, the estimated contour lines are identical. These contours fit fine in graph (A) of Figure 9.2, where the data generation process is a good model of precincts that have something in common. Not surprisingly, if this assumption is incorrect, the results are far off: in

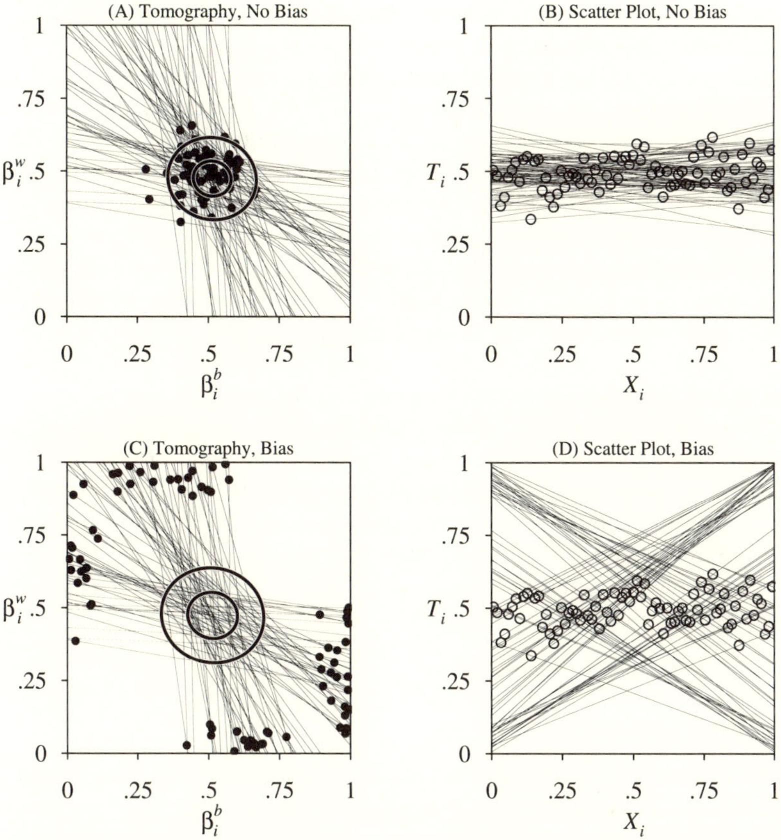

Figure 9.2 The Worst of Distributional Violations: Different True Parameters, Same Observable Implications. Graphs (A) and (B) represent data randomly generated from the model with parameters $\breve{\mathfrak{B}}^b = \breve{\mathfrak{B}}^w = 0.5$, $\breve{\sigma}_b = \breve{\sigma}_w = 0.1$, and $\breve{\rho} = 0$. Graphs (C) and (D) represent data with the same values of X_i and T_i but different values of β_i^b and β_i^w, created to minimize the fit of the truncated bivariate normal distribution while not introducing aggregation bias. Graphs (A) and (C) are tomography plots with true coordinates appearing as black dots, and with contour ellipses estimated from aggregate data only. Graphs (B) and (D) are scatter plots of X_i by T_i with lines representing the true precinct parameters.

graph (C), even the 95% contours miss all the points. Note that these problems occur in data without aggregation bias.

To see the absence of aggregation bias, note that the average of the lines in either graph (B) or graph (D) would still be flat at $T_i = 0.5$. Since this expected value line could be estimated well from the X_i, T_i points, this absence of aggregation bias will create no difficulty in estimating averages of the precinct parameters. That is, $\breve{\mathfrak{B}}^b$ and $\breve{\mathfrak{B}}^w$ will be estimated correctly. If the number of people per precinct is constant (as it is in this artificial data set) or independent of β_i^b and β_i^w, then the district aggregates, B^b and B^w, will be accurately estimated even when the distributional assumption is wrong.

The precinct-level estimates will be far off in all cases except when the bounds narrowly constrain the answer. For example, the relatively flat lines in the tomography plot give highly accurate estimates for β_i^w because of highly constrained bounds. The tomography lines with the steepest slopes will give similarly accurate estimates for β_i^b. Because none of the lines cut off the top right or bottom left corners, no precincts have narrow bounds on both β_i^b and β_i^w. In addition to these point estimates, the data represented in Figure 9.2, graphs (C) and (D), will also have incorrect uncertainty estimates. For example, although the expected value would be estimated well in graph (D), the variance around this expected value would be much too small. That is, confidence intervals around the expected value line would be fairly narrow because the circles have a small variance, whereas the true lines being estimated have much wider dispersion that would not be captured by the basic model.

9.1.3 *Spatial Dependence*

The third and final assumption of the basic model is that, conditional on X, T_i and T_j are (spatially) independent for all $i \neq j$. Fortunately, because spatial dependence only affects the variance of ϕ (instead of biasing estimates of Σ, which is a function of ϕ), the consequences of violating this last assumption are usually not very serious. That is, the inefficiencies created by ignoring spatial dependence only affect how precisely placed the contours are when estimated from aggregate data, and is equivalent to inadvertently dropping some fraction of the observations. In contrast, most of the estimated uncertainty in the parameters of interest arises from the width of the contours where they are intersected by each tomography line, but this width is reasonably well estimated even in spatially dependent data.

Put differently, spatial dependence (just like time series autocorrelation) makes estimates of parameters like ϕ inefficient, but not inconsistent. This means that if observations are plentiful, as is the case in most aggregate data sets, then this source of inefficiency is a minor issue and the point estimates will be more than adequate. The only major issue, as in most statistical models with dependence, is that the estimated standard errors will be wrong unless some special procedures are used. A similar story holds here, although the problem is not particularly severe. The reason is that *both* the point estimates and confidence intervals of these quantities of interest are computed primarily from the point estimates of ϕ. The estimated variance of ϕ does come into the calculation, but it does not have as major a role. This means that even if spatial dependence is very strong and powerfully biases estimates of the estimated variance matrix of ϕ, our inferences about β_i^b and β_i^w will not always be greatly affected.

The basic model assumes that the truncated bivariate normal distribution is independent over precincts. This assumption is used in the model to compute the full likelihood function by taking the product of the probability distributions over all of the observations (see Equation 7.1, page 134). Deviations from independence assumptions like this are generally divided into two categories, *spatial variation* and *spatial autocorrelation*.

For the ecological inference model, spatial variation refers to situations in which β_i^b, β_i^w vary over the observations in a geographically interesting way. A significant degree of spatial variation is already included in the basic model since these quantities are allowed to vary over precincts. Additional levels of spatial variation can be included via the extended model in Section 9.2.1, which allows $\breve{\mathfrak{B}}^b$ and $\breve{\mathfrak{B}}^w$ (and thus the entire contours) to vary over the observations as a function of measured covariates.

Spatial autocorrelation is defined as the deviations from independence after conditioning on X_i. Although spatial variation can obviously be modeled with covariates, spatial autocorrelation can also often be modeled in the same way. This is best done by trying to include, among the covariates, the reasons for the dependence among the observations. For example, measures of residential mobility, frequency of commuting, and extent of interconnected transportation systems provide some explicit measures of the dependence for some applications. Spatial autocorrelation can also be modeled more indirectly in the stochastic component of most models.

Studying spatial variation and spatial autocorrelation provide important opportunities for extracting new interesting information from ecological data. Given that the essential character of the aggregation problem is the loss of information, it behooves us to search for this type of information in aggregate data. An important minimum step should be to take the results of the model, such as point estimates of the precinct-level quantities of interest, and to portray them in geographic form such as with a colored or shaded map (as in Figure 1.2, page 25). In addition, researchers could take advantage of econometric models of spatial autocorrelation and variation to make further studies. See Anselin (1988) for an extensive presentation of econometric models that incorporate spatial information (see also King, 1991).

The only issue that remains is the precise consequences for the basic model of ignoring spatial variation and spatial autocorrelation. First, if the spatial variation is independent of X_i, there is no problem, and the basic model works without a hitch. If, instead, spatial variation exists and is related to X_i, then we have aggregation bias by definition, and the techniques introduced in Section 9.2 can be used if necessary.[1]

I analyze the consequences of spatial autocorrelation here by way of some Monte Carlo experiments. For simplicity, consider a special case of spatial autocorrelation where all the precincts are arranged in a line, and influence is unidirectional—exactly as would occur if the precincts were from time series data (that is, I take advantage of the fact that time series models are formally special cases of spatial processes). There are many ways to modify the basic model so that the parameters follow some non-independent time series process, while still avoiding aggregation bias and distributional problems.

One way to generate data that meet the necessary conditions is as follows. First define U^b and U^w as truncated bivariate normal random draws for β_i^b and β_i^w, respectively, given a fixed parameter vector $\breve{\psi}$. In this case, set the elements of $\breve{\psi}$ so that $\mathfrak{B}^b = \mathfrak{B}^w = 0.5$, $\sigma_b = \sigma_w = 0.2$ and $\rho = 0.3$. These parameter values imply relatively low levels of truncation. Other parameter values I tried gave similar results, although when truncation levels are much higher, it is not possible for any statistical problems to have much effect on the ultimate estimates. Finally, randomly generate the first values for β_1^b and β_1^w from this random number generator, and define the remaining values $i = 2, \ldots, p$

[1] If $\breve{\mathfrak{B}}$ varies randomly over the observations, but is unrelated to X_i, then inferences will be right on average, but in some cases confidence intervals will be too small. However, because the variable parameter model offered here is already a generalization over the basic Goodman setup in exactly the same direction as this, most problems likely to arise in practice are already taken into account in the model. Trying to generalize further in this direction leads to infinite regress. That is, the Goodman model assumes that the bivariate distribution of β_i^b, β_i^w is a single spike. The basic model proposed here generalizes this to allow a non-degenerate distribution with five fixed parameters. The extended model in Section 9.2.1 allows the means to vary according to fixed covariates. One could generalize further by trying to estimate the parameters of the prior distributions given for these five parameters. Of course, by this logic, there is also no reason to leave the parameters of the prior fixed, and so we could add yet another level of variation, for which we could then add more variation, etc. Obviously, when the generalizations do not improve estimates in practice, it is time to devote one's energies to something more productive.

via these recursive definitions:

$$\beta_i^b = \delta\beta_{i-1}^b + (1-\delta)U^b$$

$$\beta_i^w = \delta\beta_{i-1}^w + (1-\delta)U^w \tag{9.1}$$

where δ indicates the degree of autocorrelation by the fraction of the previous observation's random draw used to form the current value. Thus, if $\delta = 0$, there is no autocorrelation, and we are back to the basic model. If $\delta = 1$, every observation's value is equivalent. I generated X_i with values equally spaced between zero and one, and T_i from the accounting identity given the fixed X_i and the randomly generated β_i^b and β_i^w.

Table 9.1 presents the Monte Carlo evidence. Each row in the table represents the average of results from separate runs on 250 data sets, each with p observations, randomly drawn from the model and as modified by the autocorrelation parameter δ. As a baseline, the first pair of rows gives results for data with no autocorrelation ($\delta = 0$). As expected, these rows reveal no problems. For both 100 and 1,000 observations, the average absolute error of the district-level quantity of interest is approximately zero. The true standard deviation across the 250 simulations (given in parentheses) equals the average of the estimated standard errors from each simulation, indicating that the aggregate uncertainty estimates are accurate. In addition, the average error in covering the true precinct values for the 80% confidence intervals is very close to zero for both $p = 100$ and $p = 1,000$.

The remaining two pairs of rows in Table 9.1 analyze the same types of results for moderate ($\delta = 0.3$) and high ($\delta = 0.7$) levels of autocorrelation. For all four rows, the average error in estimating the district-level quantities of interest is approximately zero, indicating that spatial autocorrelation induces no bias in model estimates. For moderate levels of spatial autocorrelation and $p = 100$, the true standard deviation across the 250 estimates (0.020) looks like it might be slightly underestimated by the average standard error (0.016), although the confidence interval coverage of the precinct-level parameters is accurate. In addition, this minor problem is substantially reduced with the larger sample size ($p = 1,000$). A more interesting problem occurs with the highest levels of spatial autocorrelation examined ($\delta = 0.7$) and few observations. In this case, the estimates are still empirically unbiased but the uncertainty measures are underestimated, both at the aggregate and precinct levels. This problem is much reduced with the larger sample size, but still remains to a degree.

		Aggregate Level			*Precinct Level*	
δ	p	*Error*	*(S.D.)*	*Avg.S.E.*	*Error*	*(S.D.)*
0	100	.001	(.020)	.020	.02	(.07)
0	1000	.000	(.007)	.007	−.02	(.06)
.3	100	.001	(.020)	.016	−.01	(.07)
.3	1000	.000	(.006)	.005	−.02	(.06)
.7	100	.001	(.022)	.009	−.09	(.13)
.7	1000	.001	(.006)	.003	−.03	(.08)

Table 9.1 Consequences of Spatial Autocorrelation: Monte Carlo Evidence. Each row summarizes 250 simulations drawn from the model with the degree of spatial autocorrelation δ and number of observations p. The aggregate-level columns report the average absolute difference between the truth and estimates from the model. The precinct-level columns give the deviation from 80% in coverage of the 80% confidence intervals (in both cases with standard deviations across simulations in parentheses).

It may pay for future researchers to follow up these studies to try to identify other portions of the parameter space, or other types of spatial dependence, that produce more serious consequences for this model, and to develop more general models to avoid any problems identified. Although spatial autocorrelation does not appear to have major consequences for the validity of inferences from the basic model, we should not overlook the common and valuable opportunities in spatially arranged information to extract more information from aggregate data.

9.2 Avoiding Aggregation Bias

The generalizations of the model described in this section enable researchers to detect aggregation bias, to evaluate whether the bounds will help avoid it, and to understand several procedures for extending the model that allow β_i^b and β_i^w to be correlated with X_i.

The ecological researcher can rely on four types of information to assess and avoid aggregation bias. The first is nonquantifiable knowledge of the problem. From a qualitative understanding of the literature, or the politics or other features of the region under analysis, a researcher may be comfortable concluding that β_i^b and β_i^w do not increase or decrease with X_i. Some knowledge of these precinct parameters is often readily available, for instance by interviewing a few citizens, reading newspaper accounts, visiting the precincts, or observing regional differences in politicians' appeals. Even if only limited information is available about a few of these parameters from precincts with widely ranging values of X_i, it will often provide sufficient information to make aggregation bias unlikely, or to narrow in on the type of relationship likely to exist between β_i^b and X_i and between β_i^w and X_i. Although this is the least precise type of information that can be brought to bear on the problem, it is often the most valuable. Because the ecological inference problem is due to a lack of information, bringing new information, especially from diverse sources, to bear on the same inference can be extremely valuable (see King, Keohane, and Verba, 1994).

Second, if detailed survey data are available, and they are trustworthy, then no ecological inference problem exists. However, even when surveys have been conducted there are rarely sufficient survey respondents polled so that each precinct-level parameter can be reliably estimated. Usually at best only the aggregate quantities can be reliably estimated. Fortunately, as Section 14.2 demonstrates, even a few survey observations per precinct can be used in a slight extension of the present model to avoid ecological inference problems such as aggregation bias.

A third type of information that can be used to evaluate and remedy aggregation bias is variables measured at the same level of analysis as the original aggregate data in use. As Section 9.2.1 describes, these external covariates are more widely available and useful than has been recognized.

Finally, and perhaps most distinctively, the model offered here highlights observable implications of aggregation bias in the original aggregate data—that is, with X_i and T_i, but with or without additional external information. This information in aggregate data about aggregation bias is not available to other methods because they do not incorporate the information in the deterministic bounds. Sections 9.2.2, 9.2.3, and 9.2.4 provide tools for understanding this information and using it to avoid aggregation bias problems.

9.2.1 *Using External Information*

The idea of using additional explanatory variables to avoid aggregation bias dates to the first research on the ecological inference problem (Ogburn and Goltra, 1919) and has been suggested repeatedly since (e.g., Rosenthal, 1973; Hanushek, Jackson, and Kain, 1974). However, it is a strategy that has not often been used in applications. In part, this may be because scholars have underestimated the degree to which these external data are available.

In this section, the assumption of no aggregation bias is dropped and substituted with the more benign assumption that β_i^b and β_i^w are mean independent of X_i after conditioning on two (different, overlapping, or identical) sets of external variables Z_i^b and Z_i^w.

The variables $Z_i = \{Z_i^b, Z_i^w\}$ are used in the model to allow the previously constant means of the truncated bivariate normal, $\breve{\mathfrak{B}}^b$ and $\breve{\mathfrak{B}}^w$, to vary over the observations. If chosen correctly, these variables will control for the portions of β_i^b and β_i^w that are correlated with X_i. These additional covariates are to be included for the purpose of ameliorating aggregation bias. If instead a researcher is interested in explaining the variation in β_i^b or β_i^w over precincts as a function of measured explanatory variables, then it is usually best to perform a separate second-stage analysis with the point estimates of these parameters as dependent variables in regressions, geographical analyses, or other statistical procedures.[2]

Since $\breve{\mathfrak{B}}_i^b$ and $\breve{\mathfrak{B}}_i^w$ are on the untruncated scale, restricting the functions of Z_i to the unit interval, such as with logit or probit transformations, is unnecessary. To implement this, solve the first two lines of Equations 7.4 (page 136) for the means, and add the new covariates linearly:

$$\breve{\mathfrak{B}}_i^b = \left[\phi_1(\breve{\sigma}_b^2 + 0.25) + 0.5\right] + (Z_i^b - \bar{Z}^b)\alpha^b$$

$$\breve{\mathfrak{B}}_i^w = \left[\phi_2(\breve{\sigma}_w^2 + 0.25) + 0.5\right] + (Z_i^w - \bar{Z}^w)\alpha^w \tag{9.2}$$

where α^b and α^w are parameter vectors to be estimated along with the original model parameters and that have as many elements as Z_i^b and Z_i^w have columns. The covariates Z_i^b and Z_i^w are entered as deviations from their mean vectors $\bar{Z}^b$ and $\bar{Z}^w$ so as not to change the interpretation of the original parameters and so that Z_i need not include a constant term. If Z_i^b or Z_i^w contain no variables, they are set to zero and α^b and α^w are not estimated so that Equations 9.2 reduce to the equivalent of the first two lines of the original Equations 7.4.

In this extended model, the assumptions $E(\beta_i^b|X_i) = E(\beta_i^b)$ and $E(\beta_i^w|X_i) = E(\beta_i^w)$ are not required to estimate $\breve{\psi}$ well. (In the basic model, these assumptions are required in theory, but not always in practice because biased estimates of $\breve{\psi}$ still often give excellent estimates of the quantities of interest.) Instead, the researcher only needs

[2] A second-stage procedure such as this should also make use of the estimated variability of each of the point estimates. This could be done by using the standard error of each in a weighted least squares analysis. Or a model analogous to that in Section 9.2.4 could be used. See Chapter 16 for further details.

to assume mean independence, conditional on Z_i:

$$E(\beta_i^b|X_i, Z_i) = E(\beta_i^b|Z_i)$$

$$E(\beta_i^w|X_i, Z_i) = E(\beta_i^w|Z_i)$$

For example, as before, the model allows the proportion of blacks β_i^b and whites β_i^w voting to vary over districts randomly or according to the wealth of the community, development of the mass transit systems, degree of residential mobility, education levels, or other factors. But in addition, the model now also allows for the possibility that blacks vote at higher (or lower) rates according to the degree of racial homogeneity of their neighborhood. The only element that must be provided is some measures of the causes of these differences, which is often easier than it seems.

Put differently, if X_i and β_i^b are unrelated, there is no problem, and we can set $\alpha^b = \alpha^w = 0$ for all i and use the original model in Section 6.1. If they are related, then it can be helpful to control for some of the consequences of X_i. Anything that intervenes between the racial composition of precincts and β_i^b can be used. For example, Freedman et al. (1991: 686–687) justify their neighborhood model by making continual reference to the causes of this parameter variation (for Hispanics and non-Hispanics, in their example), which all are measurable: "Hispanic registrants in highly Hispanic precincts differ in many ways from Hispanics in other precincts. The same is true for non-Hispanics.... In the heavily Hispanic precincts, both Hispanics and non-Hispanics have lower incomes and educational levels and are more likely to be renters than owners." Thus, the readily available measures like education, income, and rates of home ownership could be used in Z_i to solve the aggregation problem in these data.

The U.S. Supreme Court in *Thornburg v. Gingles* rejected measures of ecological inference that control for the consequences of race. They wanted a measure of the total effect of race, not the effect of race after controlling for all the consequences of race—which was obviously smaller than its total causal effect. The court's statistical reasoning was sound in this instance. They also agree with Achen (1986) and Flanigan and Zingale (1985: 78–79), who criticize models that include control variables, such as Hanushek, Jackson, and Kain (1974), because they change the question being asked. In contrast, using external variables in this model need not change the question being asked since the procedure averages over these external variables in computing the quantities of interest (as suggested by Palmquist, 1993: 107). This uses essentially the court's logic to solve a problem in ecological inference, while still estimating the total effect of race.

Although it is not widely recognized, researchers are fortunate that the required additional information, and a lot more, is already part of most ecological data collections, even though it has often been discarded or ignored. In most cases, ecological data are based on geographic units, which may be the most common organizational scheme for data collection in the social sciences. Because so many data sets are keyed to geography, additional information is almost always available. To demonstrate this assertion in general seems impossible, but in any specific example additional data are usually available.

For example, whenever researchers collect precinct-level political data for (say) the U.S. House of Representatives, electoral results from statewide or nationwide offices are almost always available. In almost all U.S. counties, all precinct-level data are collected on the same paper or electronic media. So even if the goal is to collect only votes for the House, the data analyst is forced to stare at a rich variety of other information. We now have an important use for it. In addition to votes for other offices, such as president, governor, and numerous minor posts, and votes for the same office in earlier elections as well as party registration are often available, as is the relative fraction of people voting in Democratic versus Republican primaries.[3]

In most other aggregate data collections, similar valuable external data are usually available. Aggregate data at the electoral district level in any country include at least information about the candidates, such as incumbency, and usually many more variables. Occasionally, researchers may have to merge information from related geographic

[3] In order to gather information on black and white voting age populations, a researcher must use data files from the U.S. Census, which include a lot more than just race. To be specific, most people matching political and census data use the Census Bureau's PL94-171 data files. These were created to study redistricting and include only a small subset of census variables, including race, ethnicity, and various types of population counts. This information is available at the "voter tabulation district" level, which is usually the precinct or a level slightly higher than the precinct. However, almost identical information is also available as part of the bureau's more complete STF3A data files, the advantage of which is considerably more information, most of which is disaggregated to only slightly higher levels than the PL94-171 data. This information includes income, education, home ownership vs. renting, household type, spoken languages, degree of linguistic isolation, family types, place of work, means of transportation to work, poverty status, urban vs. rural, type of housing stock, residential mobility, and detailed precinct-level cross-tabulations of these and numerous other variables. For the 1990 census, data are also available by school district, which corresponds with precincts in some jurisdictions. School district data includes all the variables from both the PL94-171 and STF3A data.

data sets, but the necessary variables will often be available to solve this feature of the aggregation bias problem.

Direct evidence of the degree to which the information in Z_i is adequate is not available since β_i^b is unobserved (and similarly for β_i^w or other parameters). However, getting a sense of the problem by using observable data is possible. For example, a reasonable surrogate for β_i^b in thinking about Z_i in many cases is T_i (the fraction of people voting). That is, it is reasonable to suppose that β_i^b and T_i are highly correlated.[4] In particular, the relationship between T_i and X_i may often be at least as strong as between β_i^b and X_i. More importantly, most of the variables Z_i that seem likely to affect β_i^b probably also affect T_i. Thus, the variables Z_i which would be necessary to cause the coefficient on X_i, in a regression of T_i on X_i and Z_i, to go to zero are probably the same ones that cause the coefficient on X_i, in a regression of β_i^b on X_i and Z_i, to also go to zero. (This task should be even easier when making ecological inferences about voter preferences.) Fortunately, when regressing T_i on X_i, it is not difficult to find control variables Z_i which make the coefficient on X_i go to zero. This can be accomplished with the right combination of census variables. But even easier is using almost any political variable—party registration, presidential vote, or the vote for a minor statewide office. Even the precinct population size should be helpful in some cases.

Although we cannot be certain of relationships between X_i and unobserved variables, it seems likely that the variables which do exist and are straightforward to collect are sufficient in some cases to solve this aspect of the aggregation problem in ecological voting studies. This analogy is not exact, but it is probably close in many situations. For it to be useful, one needs to assume that the loss from thinking about the wrong variables is more than compensated for by substituting observable for unobserved variables.

The variables Z_i can include X_i, although I save discussion of the issues that arise in this specification until Section 9.2.2, where they are treated explicitly. Researchers should also use caution in including variables in Z_i. Additional variables put more demands on the data; including the wrong variables does not help with aggregation bias and, as demonstrated on Section 9.2.3, can reduce statistical efficiency (and mean square error). As with any model specification, the specific content of Z_i should be justified with specific reference to prior substantive knowledge about a problem. Researchers should also be wary of the additional linearity assumption involved in in-

[4] Indeed, if it were not for β_i^w, β_i^b and T_i would be deterministically related, since $T_i = \beta_i^b X_i + \beta_i^w(1 - X_i)$.

cluding continuous variables in Z_i. With continuous covariates, there is more chance of having to extrapolate to portions of the parameter space for which few observations exist. Researchers thus might consider a more flexible functional form, such as by dichotomizing some of the covariates. Whatever the form of the external variables, analysts can avoid the dichotomous choice between the extremes of including or excluding variables by adding a prior distribution on α^b and α^w, with mean zero and positive standard deviation; this is discussed in Section 9.2.3.

Achen (1986, 1993) has noted that past efforts to avoid bias in ecological inference by using external variables have failed, and he concludes that external variables will not be helpful. However, the few studies he cites (such as Upton, 1978 and MacRae, 1977) use a very small quantity of only one specialized type of data that does not generalize to the vast array of ecological analyses. These data are from voter transitions, where the goal is to make inferences about the degree to which voters remain loyal to a party or defect to the opposition between two elections. Unfortunately, obtaining appropriate variables Z_i in these cases is more difficult than in most other types of data. Following the logic above, we can use the vote at time 2 as a surrogate for the unobserved transition rate in thinking about the composition of Z_i. Thus, what control variables Z_i would cause the coefficient on time 1 vote, in a regression of time 2 vote on time 1 vote and Z, to go to zero? Including incumbency advantage, campaign spending, candidate quality, etc., would not have much of an effect on the time 1 vote coefficient (which in a regression usually retains a coefficient of approximately 0.6–0.8 no matter what is included). The optimal variable would be something like voting intentions a month before time 2 or an exhaustive list of campaign events, weather forecasts for election day, detailed regional polls, etc., but these and other possible influential intervening variables are often unavailable for voter transition studies for each individual areal unit. This makes using external variables to remove aggregation bias in voter transition studies more likely to be impractical. Fortunately, finding appropriate variables in ecological studies of race and voting and numerous others applications is considerably easier. And, moreover, the method given here can work well in voter transition data even without covariates (see Section 13.1).

9.2.2 *Unconditional Estimation: X_i as a Covariate*

This section relaxes the assumption that the model is conditional on X_i (that is, that there is no aggregation bias) by extending the procedure in Section 9.2.1 and allowing X_i to be included among the covariates in Z_i^b, Z_i^w, or both. The logic here follows the first instinct of most scholars new to the ecological inference field who, upon learning that the parameters may be correlated with X_i, propose modeling the relationship explicitly by letting both of Goodman's parameters be linear functions of X_i. Unfortunately, as Section 3.2 (especially Equation 3.5, page 42ff) details, this procedure leads to indeterminacy under Goodman's model. That is, under the Goodman framework, *no* information exists with which to estimate the model controlling for X_i in the equations for both $\breve{\mathfrak{B}}_i^b$ and $\breve{\mathfrak{B}}_i^w$. Only three of the necessary four parameters are identified in aggregate data, and thus the likelihood function is flat over the entire real number line.

In fact, contrary to widely held conclusions (e.g., Rosenthal, 1973; Iversen, 1973; Przeworski, 1974; Shively, 1985; Achen and Shively, 1995), there does exist sufficient information in aggregate data with which to generate a meaningful likelihood function and informative estimates of all model parameters and quantities of interest even when controlling for X_i. Because this additional information is incorporated in the model developed here, its likelihood function is not flat, and thus information does exist in the data, even without external variables, with which to avoid some of the problems of aggregation bias. Put differently, the analysis of indeterminacy in Section 3.2 would be correct only if the precinct-level parameters were unbounded, as previous statistical approaches effectively assume. However, β_i^b and β_i^w are bounded at their widest at [0,1], and usually much more narrowly in each and every precinct. In addition, β_i^b and β_i^w are constrained to vary inversely within their bounds by Equation 6.27 (page 113). Thus, once the model includes this and other valuable additional information, the likelihood function is quite informative, and all parameters can be estimated even when $Z_i^b = X_i$ and $Z_i^w = X_i$.

The remainder of this section first demonstrates exactly how the bounds provide this identifying information; second, contrasts the concave likelihood function under this approach with the flat one under the Goodman model; and third, shows how including X_i in Z_i^b and Z_i^w ameliorates aggregation bias problems even in the data from the worst case scenario developed in Section 9.1.1.

How do the bounds reveal information about aggregation bias from the aggregate data alone? Figure 9.3 provides an answer in as simple a form as possible. This is a tomography plot for a simple hypothetical data set. All the lines cut off the top right or lower left corners, indicating that only precincts with very tight bounds on both β_i^b and β_i^w are included. The values of β_i^b and β_i^w, represented by lines in the top right corner, are sure to be large regardless of where the true points

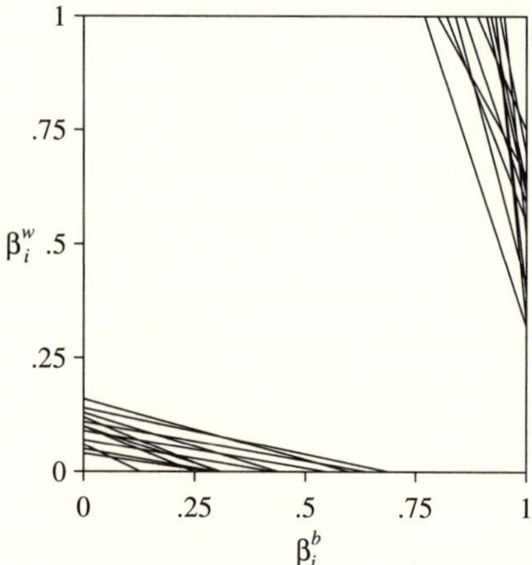

Figure 9.3 Conclusive Evidence of Aggregation Bias from Aggregate Data. In this hypothetical example, the tomography lines at the top right imply high values for both β_i^b and β_i^w and, as indicated by the steep lines, large values of X_i. In contrast, the lines near the bottom left have small values for both parameters and, as represented by the relatively flat lines, small values of X_i. This demonstrates that aggregation bias (a correlation between the precinct parameters and X_i) can be detected with aggregate data alone.

fall on the tomography lines. Similarly, the points in the bottom left have small values for these precinct parameters. Thus, these aggregate data are highly informative about the quantities of interest. In addition, they also reveal that X_i, which is represented in the figure by the slope of the corresponding tomography line, is highly correlated with these parameters: the small values of β_i^b and β_i^w have relatively flat slopes and correspondingly small values of X_i, whereas large values of these parameters have steep slopes and thus larger values of X_i. In this simple example aggregation bias can be conclusively detected in aggregate data.

Figure 9.3 also gives significant information about the nature of aggregation bias, information that we shall exploit to remedy problems that may arise. In this figure, the information available about aggregation bias in the ecological data is very substantial, revealing very clearly the degree and precise nature of aggregation bias. More typically, only some observations in a data set provide this very certain information about the relationship between β_i^b and X_i and between β_i^w and X_i. There does exist information even for observations without narrow bounds, but it comes primarily from the piece of the distribution that is truncated at the edges of the unit square. Since inferences based on parts of distributions like this tend to be more uncertain and model-dependent than other types of inferences, one must be cautious when using this information. Thus, the goal is to exploit all available information in aggregate data while still having a relatively robust ecological inference, one that does not depend too sensitively on arbitrary features of the model. As section 9.2.3 demonstrates, putting prior distributions on α^b and α^w can be an especially useful approach.[5]

Second, to help emphasize that the model is identified even in its fully extended form, consider a profile likelihood approach. Begin by defining $Z_i^w = X_i$ but leave Z_i^b empty, so that the model (now with parameters $\breve{\psi}$ and α^w) is estimable even without the bounds or other new information. One way to understand this specification is in the equivalent form, where we define $Z_i^b = Z_i^w = X_i$, estimate α^w, and fix $\alpha^b = 0$. Thinking about the model in this way also reveals that it is not the $\alpha^b = 0$ assumption that is necessary to estimate the model without the bounds, only the restriction of α^b to some fixed number.

The idea of the profile likelihood is to maximize the likelihood (or posterior distribution) *conditional* on α^b set to zero, and then to maximize it again given α^b set to some other number. This procedure is repeated for a wide range of values, and the results are plotted.[6] Figure 9.4 gives an example of the profile likelihood for the data generated in Figure 9.1, graphs C and D (page 160).

This figure plots the value of the maximum likelihood conditional on each of a range of values of α^b. Although for the Goodman model the corresponding profile likelihood plot would be a flat line for all possible values of α^b, indicating nonidentification, this plot indicates that the data are highly informative about the likely values of α^b. In particular, the results indicate that, conditional on the rest of the model and the data, α^b is most likely around the value 1.3. This is quite far from $\alpha^b = 0$, as the enormous likelihood ratio for these two values unambiguously indicates.

Finally, I now apply the full expanded model with $Z_i^b = Z_i^w = X_i$ to the first problematic data set represented in Figure 9.1 (page 160), the

[5] Incorporating the bounds in the basic model is part of what make it especially robust. When the bounds are very informative, the model is more robust and more likely to produce accurate inferences even in the face of massive aggregation bias. In other situations, when the bounds are not so informative, the method will still often give accurate results but it will be more dependent upon assumptions about aggregation bias and thus less robust.

[6] The procedure requires rerunning the maximization algorithm many times, but it is easy to cut down on how much time this takes. The trick is to use sequential values of α^b and to define as starting values for any one run the converged values from the previous run.

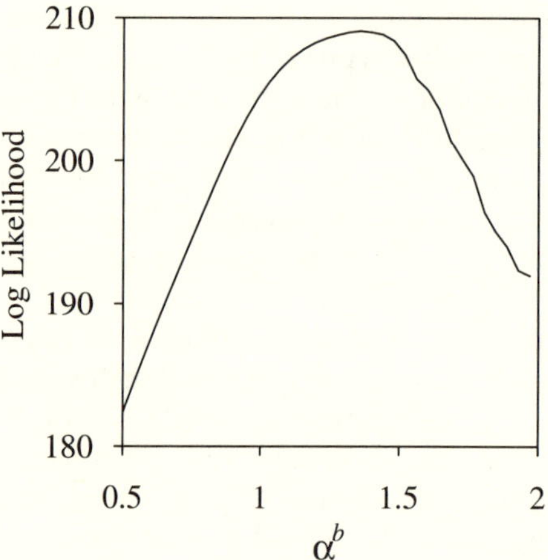

Figure 9.4 Profile Likelihood. Using the same data analyzed in graph C of Figure 9.1, this figure plots the value of the likelihood at the maximum for a specification where $Z_i^w = Z_i^b = X_i$, and where ϕ and α^w are estimated, but where α^b is set to a series of fixed values and not estimated. The results clearly indicate, conditional on the linear specification, that the correct value of α^b is far from zero. The same plot under the Goodman approach would be flat over the entire real number line.

one with a maximal level of aggregation bias. In order to understand the results from the reestimated model, Figure 9.5 redisplays the same tomography lines and true β_i^b, β_i^w points as graph (C) of Figure 9.1. Of course, in order to evaluate the results of this estimation, we also need to display the newly estimated contour lines. The problem is that, because $\breve{\mathfrak{B}}_i^b$ and $\breve{\mathfrak{B}}_i^w$ now vary over all the precincts, each observation is associated with a different set of estimated contours (with different means and, by assumption, the same variances and covariance). In order to avoid a graphical mess of 75 sets of contours, each contour ellipse is replaced with an 80% confidence interval for each precinct.[7]

The pattern of darkened tomography lines, indicating confidence intervals, corresponds very well to the pattern of true points. Indeed, nearly 80% of the points are covered by these 80% confidence intervals. The results are not perfect, as there seems to be some asymmetry

[7] These 80% confidence intervals were computed with the methods described in Section 8.2. That is, first draw 100 simulations of β_i^b and β_i^w for each precinct, sort them, and record the values at the 10th and 90th percentiles. Because β_i^b and β_i^w are negatively related by Equation 6.27, the darkened area of each tomography line is the line segment with coordinates starting at the lower confidence limit on β_i^b and upper limit on β_i^w and ending with the upper limit on β_i^b and lower limit for β_i^w.

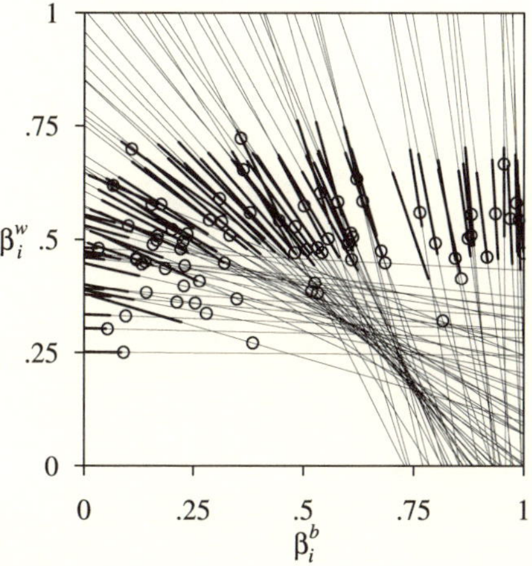

Figure 9.5 Controlling for Aggregation Bias. This tomography plot includes the same aggregate data (represented as lines) and true individual values of β_i^b, β_i^w (represented as circles) as the problematic data set introduced in graph (C) of Figure 9.1. The dark portion of each line represents the 80% confidence interval from the model estimated with only the aggregate data and with covariates defined as $Z_i^b = Z_i^w = X_i$. The success of this reestimation is indicated by the fact that nearly 80% of the true points fall within these confidence intervals.

in the errors, but this is obviously far better than the estimation from Figure 9.1, graph (C), which does not take into account the possibility of aggregation bias, and hence misses most of the true points.

9.2.3 *Tradeoffs and Priors for the Extended Model*

Although this model is estimable with X_i in both Z_i^b and Z_i^w, researchers should study the diagnostic evidence for aggregation bias, evaluate their own qualitative knowledge of the situation, and generally use caution before adopting any particular form of extended model. Most important is that the fully unrestricted version should not be used automatically whenever a researcher worries about the remote possibility of aggregation bias. As Figure 9.5 demonstrates, this extended model works well when the data are generated from this specification. However, there are risks to all specifications.

To demonstrate the costs and benefits here more precisely, Figure 9.6 provides some Monte Carlo evidence. The overall point of the analysis represented in the figure is to evaluate the consequences of misspecification—including a variable in Z_i when it does not belong

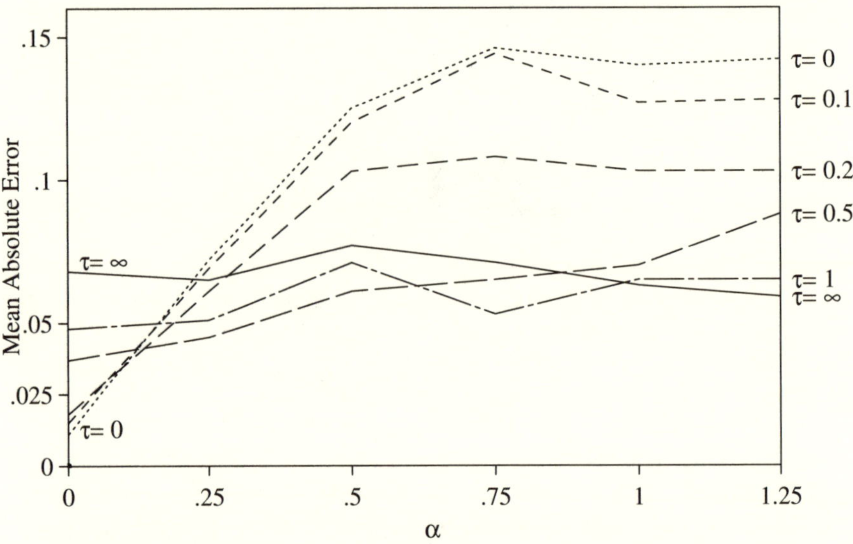

Figure 9.6 Extended Model Tradeoffs. This figure plots the mean absolute error of the district-level quantities of interest (averaged over 90 Monte Carlo simulations for each point) by the degree of aggregation bias ($\alpha = \alpha^b = \alpha^w$ set at points on the horizontal axis) for models with normal prior distributions on α with mean zero and standard deviation τ. Estimation with low levels of aggregation bias favors models with small values of τ; the existence of high levels of aggregation bias implies that the fully unrestricted model is best. The upper limit on risk, due to the effect of the bounds, has most of its effect at $\alpha > 0.75$.

or excluding it when it does belong. In practice, of course, researchers need not make a dichotomous choice between including and excluding variables, since a prior on α^b and α^w, with a mean of zero and an appropriately chosen variance, represents a compromise at any chosen point between the two extremes. Thus, the figure also evaluates some of these possible compromise model specifications.

Each point in Figure 9.6 represents the mean absolute error of the district-level quantities of interest averaged over 90 Monte Carlo simulations. Each simulation is composed of $p = 100$ observations drawn from the model with $\mathfrak{B}^b = \mathfrak{B}^w = 0.5$, $\sigma_b = \sigma_w = 0.2$ and $\rho = 0.3$, with $Z_i^b = Z_i^w = X_i$, and with $\alpha = \alpha^b = \alpha^w$ set to 0, 0.25, 0.75, 1, or 1.25. For each simulated data set, I estimated six models. All six models included X_i in both Z_i^b and Z_i^w, and added a normal prior distribution on α with mean zero and standard deviation τ, with τ taking on values 0, 0.1, 0.2, 0.5, 1, and ∞. Note that $\tau = 0$ is equivalent to excluding X_i from Z_i, whereas $\tau = \infty$ is equivalent to the fully unrestricted extended model, including X_i in Z_i without an informative prior. The other values of τ are a few of the possible compromises one could make between these two extremes. The points representing the mean absolute error for labeled values of α, where the estimation was conducted, are connected for visual clarity; thus, each line in the graph connects the mean absolute error levels at different values of α for a single statistical model (specified by τ). These parameter values, which produce wide bounds and minimal truncation, were chosen to make the differences among the models relatively large. Many other combinations of parameter values show the same patterns but within smaller ranges and levels of mean absolute error.

Figure 9.6 demonstrates the important tradeoffs in deciding what to include in Z_i, and how these tradeoffs depend on the levels of aggregation bias in the data (α). For example, at the right side of the figure, where α is large, the models with the lowest mean absolute error are those with the largest values of τ and thus the more unrestricted versions of the extended model. This extends the result from Figure 9.5: if the data have extremely high levels aggregation bias, then the unrestricted extended model is most useful. Suppose, however, the data contain little or no aggregation bias. The left side of the figure indicates that at this extreme, we would be best off running the models that most restrict α to be zero.[8]

The tradeoff arises because α is unobserved. Thus, the specific procedure chosen must depend on the researcher's prior beliefs about α. The goal is to choose a model (value of τ) that minimized the expected mean absolute error (or other loss function, such as mean square error). One way to do this, if the researcher can quantify his or her prior beliefs over α, is to compute, for each model, the sum of the prior probability of each α times the mean absolute error in this figure. This is the average mean absolute error weighted by the prior probability of α. Of course, a more optimal model could be chosen by adjusting τ more finely, or by allowing the mean of the prior to differ from zero. If a researcher cannot approximately quantify his or her priors (an unusual situation if all available information is being

[8] The figure reports the mean absolute error, which is a combination of bias and variance. Bias is small or nonexistent when α is small, regardless of which model is chosen, although variance in these situations is high when τ is large. Bias only becomes substantial, compared to variance, when α is very large and τ is small.

brought to bear on the problem), then it will be worthwhile to estimate the model for several values of τ and see the degree to which the ultimate quantities of interest differ. (Researchers could even extend the procedure farther and average over uncertainty in τ as well.)

For the particular parameter values chosen to compute this figure, and perhaps for others as well, the results seem to indicate that X_i could be included routinely in both Z_i^b and Z_i^w, so long as a sufficiently small value for τ is chosen. For example, when aggregation bias is small, $\tau = 0$ is better than $\tau = 0.1$ by a very small amount; yet, when aggregation bias is large, $\tau = 0.1$ has a substantially lower mean absolute error than $\tau = 0$. Thus, if choosing between these two models, we might almost always prefer $\tau = 0.1$ (unless one had very strong priors that $\alpha = 0$ and a loss function that was exquisitely sensitive to small errors). The question, which must depend on the prior on α, is whether to use an even larger value of τ, risking even higher mean absolute errors if aggregation bias is small in order to achieve a possible substantial reduction in error if aggregation bias in the data is large.

Finally, Figure 9.6 also demonstrates the beneficial effects of the bounds on the estimation problem. This can be seen by observing how the mean absolute error gets larger with the level of aggregation bias until α is between 0.5 and 0.75, at which point it levels off. This leveling off is the effect of the bounds, which provide a deterministic guarantee on the maximum risk a researcher will have to endure, no matter how massive aggregation bias is. The parameter values for this Monte Carlo experiment were chosen so that the bounds were not especially informative, and so for many problems, the maximum risk will be reached at much smaller values of α.

Perhaps the most important reason for the increased inefficiency with the unrestricted version of the extended model is the nonrobustness or inefficiency due to the additional linear function now being estimated (rather than restricted to zero). As demonstrated in Section 3.2, including X_i linearly as a covariate turns the accounting identity into a quadratic, and quadratics are notoriously sensitive to outliers in certain situations. In particular, researchers should be especially careful of this specification when values of X_i do not cover most of the unit interval. For example, if X_i never gets above 0.2, then estimating $\breve{\mathfrak{B}}^b$ will require extrapolating very far from the data (to $X_i = 1$). With a relatively small number of badly placed outliers, a quadratic specification can send this expected value far off the mark. Fortunately, these possibilities can be evaluated with a scatter plot of X_i by T_i, supplemented with the expected value line, $E(T_i|X_i)$, and confidence intervals around it. (Section 8.5 explains how to compute these quantities; see Figure 10.3, page 206, for an example.) By studying the fit of the model to the data through diagnostics such as this, researchers should be able to avoid most of the possible pitfalls of alternative specifications.

Many other alternatives, in addition to a prior on α, might also be considered. For example, if sufficient data are available, researchers could divide X_i into several intervals and use indicator variables to code these in place of X_i among the covariates. This alternative specification has the advantage of avoiding linearity assumptions, and the consequent quadratic specification. Researchers will need to judge whether this advantage is outweighed by the disadvantage of a cruder measurement of X_i as a control. Finally, some version of X_i is not always needed in both sets of covariates. For example, in modern U.S. county data, blacks are usually a small fraction of the population. As a result, β_i^w can be estimated very precisely, but inferences about β_i^b are more uncertain. In an example like this, researchers might consider putting X_i into Z_i^w and omitting it from Z_i^b.

9.2.4 *Ex Post Diagnostics*

In this section, several closely related tools for evaluating and remedying aggregation bias are introduced. These tools enable researchers to evaluate results after an estimation is complete.

To implement the method, first run the model offered here without taking any special action to deal with aggregation bias. Then compute point estimates for each precinct value of β_i^b and β_i^w (the means of their posterior distributions, calculated as described in Section 8.2). Although the model used made the assumption of no aggregation bias, incorporating the bounds as part of the computation means that these precinct-level estimates can nevertheless be correlated with X_i after conditioning on T_i.

Thus, the relationship between X_i and these estimated precinct parameters contains information about what α^b and α^w would be if we were to let $Z_i^b = Z_i^w = X_i$. The only issue is how to make use of this information to provide a diagnostic estimate of these parameters. The easiest and first diagnostic method is to plot the estimates of β_i^b by X_i and β_i^w by X_i. Any indication that the precinct-level parameters are predictable by X_i would be indicative of aggregation bias.

To get a somewhat more precise understanding of the information in the data, we can try to produce direct ex post estimates of α^b and α^w. If $\breve{\mathfrak{B}}^b$ and $\breve{\mathfrak{B}}^w$ were on the truncated instead of untruncated scale, we could simply regress the estimated values of β_i^b on X_i to estimate α^b, and similarly for α^w. This does provide a quick method of checking whether any aggregation bias exists, and it may often be worth doing, but the scale is wrong.

Thus, a more precise, if slightly more computationally intensive, method of ex post estimation would be to maximize the implied likelihood function. That is, define a model such that the estimates of β_i^b and β_i^w are truncated bivariate normal dependent variables with each mean being a linear function of X_i, and with constant variances and correlation. (Since the narrower bounds on the precinct-level parameters have already been taken into account in the original model, the truncation for this model is on the unit square.) The likelihood function is then maximized and the coefficient on X_i in the two means serve as diagnostic estimates of α^b and α^w. If these estimates are substantially different from zero, the main model can be rerun while restricting α^b and α^w to these estimates, and using its standard errors in the second simulation stage.

This procedure can be improved in several ways. However, because it is most useful as a diagnostic tool, most of the improvements seem to be unnecessary. Nevertheless, I briefly list two of the possibilities here, since they are likely to be useful in particular circumstances. First, the uncertainty in each estimate of β_i^b and β_i^w can be incorporated in the diagnostic estimate by repeating the procedure for 4 or 5 of the individual simulations of β_i^b and β_i^w, instead of the mean of all 100, and averaging the results according to the logic of "multiple imputation" for survey nonresponse (see Rubin, 1987, who also shows why 4 or 5 simulations is almost fully efficient). Second, the whole procedure could be iterated. That is, after estimating α^b and α^w from the model output, and restricting them to their estimates in rerunning the main model, the diagnostic procedure could be run again. This would produce another estimate with which to restrict α^b and α^w in the main model. The iterations would then proceed until convergence.

Finally, with this diagnostic tool, as with the procedures introduced in Sections 9.2.1 and 9.2.2, functional forms other than linearity should be considered, the most obvious possibility being indicator variables coding intervals of X_i.

9.3 Avoiding Distributional Problems

In the basic model, β_i^b and β_i^w follow a truncated bivariate normal distribution. The model is fairly robust to many deviations from this distributional assumption because only the univariate distributions cut out of the truncated bivariate normal by the tomography lines are used for computing the quantities of interest, and the tomography lines are known with certainty. Thus, although the full truncated *bivariate* normality assumption is made, only a set of p truncated conditional *univariate* normals are used, which is a considerably less demanding assumption once we condition on X_i since all uncertainty about each quantity of interest is restricted to a single known univariate distribution. The fact that the only distributional information needed is that over the known univariate tomography lines means that different bivariate distributions can lead to the same estimates. Often, this is an advantage because the same underlying truncated bivariate normal can accurately represent many different true bivariate distributions of β_i^b and β_i^w. Of course, in some cases, if the ultimate conditional distributions are not reasonably close approximations to the truth, incorrect inferences may result.

Section 9.3.1 discusses the robustness of the basic model, as well as several parametric generalizations. Section 9.3.2 begins at the other end of the continuum to consider what information can be learned about the underlying distribution without any assumptions and builds from there; this leads to useful diagnostics as well as a fully nonparametric approach, effectively dropping the assumption of truncated bivariate normality.

9.3.1 *Parametric Approaches*

In this section, I outline parametric approaches to four types of deviations from the truncated bivariate normality assumption.

One type of deviation from truncated bivariate normality is *outliers*, where a subset of the observations do not follow the same distribution as the rest. Figure 7.1 (page 126) gives a clear example of a tomography plot with several distinct outliers that are easily detectable with aggregate data. If evidence of outliers are found, either from examining a tomography plot, or the corresponding scatter plot of X_i by T_i with an expected value line and confidence intervals, or by studying the resulting quantities of interest, the best procedure is to look much closer at the observations in question and to see if they have some feature in common that could be controlled with meaningful covariates, as per the extended model described in Section 9.2.1 as corrections for aggregation bias. That is, letting the means of the truncated bivariate normal distribution vary over the observations is equivalent to assigning a different truncated bivariate normal distribution to each precinct, and with the resulting joint distribution having as many modes as observations. Indeed, the confidence intervals given in tomography plots like that in Figure 9.5 (page 179) are nonelliptical (non-normal) because of the covariates. This same non-normal distribution result could have been computed by using some new bivariate distribution to fit this unusual shape, even without covariates to cope with aggregation bias. This emphasizes that using covariates to cope with aggregation bias is one way of changing the distributional assumptions. Although the reverse procedure of changing distributional assumptions to solve aggregation bias problems is more difficult computationally, it is logically equivalent and may occasionally prove useful.

Fortunately, the fact that the precincts are real places means that there are many possibilities for locating covariates to deal with outliers. Drawing a map with the outlier precincts identified is often very helpful, but if the data are contemporary it might also pay to go to the precinct and look around. This is not common practice among quantitative analysts, but it is by far the best way to gain additional empirical information about the subject at hand. For example, one might learn that all of the outlier precincts are located in one part of the state with an especially strong local party organization, have an unusually high average income, are composed of a large fraction of transient residents, or are from a county government known for poor record keeping. If no relevant covariates are discovered, as a last resort the outliers might be dropped or brought under the model by including a dummy variable or set of dummy variables. If no substantive reason can be found for a set of outliers, and if the effect of leaving them in is to expand the area covered by the truncated bivariate normal contours, thus generating more conservative inferences, a researcher might opt not to modify the original model.

A second deviation from truncated normality consist of the cases where the data cannot plausibly be modeled as coming from a single distribution, even after making allowances for outliers. Put differently, when the number of outliers becomes a sufficiently large fraction of the sample, it may be worthwhile to model this other group of observations in an analogous fashion to the original group. For example, although data are not usually so unambiguous, Figure 9.7 gives a clear example of a tomography plot in which multiple modes seem almost certain.

Although considering these possibilities for alternative distributions on the basis of a detailed contextual knowledge of a problem prior to any data analysis is generally best, a tomography plot like that in Figure 9.7 (or Figure 9.3) would strongly suggest that the assumption of a single mode is incorrect. In this situation, it would be best to find the source of the problem and correct or model it, as described below, prior to using the basic statistical method.

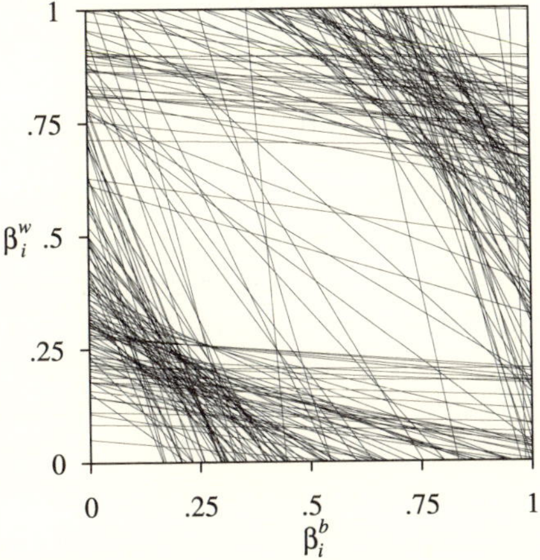

Figure 9.7 A Tomography Plot with Evidence of Multiple Modes. The data for this plot were generated from independent truncated bivariate normal distributions with the same variances and correlation but different means. The two areas of this plot at the lower left and upper right, where many lines cross (and thus "emissions" seem to be coming from), are where the evidence seems to indicate that multiple modes are located.

In many real situations, multiple modes will not do much damage to inferences from the ecological inference model, so long as aggregation bias is not also present. For example, applying the basic model to the data from Figure 9.7 produces 80% confidence intervals that cover 91% of the true points for β_i^b and 88% for β_i^w. Although these intervals are wider than they should be, they are still reasonably accurate. This is especially good news given how seriously the model's truncated bivariate normality assumption is violated in this example. Indeed, in some cases, fixing a problem with multiple modes will rid the data of bias but in many data sets the bias from multiple modes will be small even if ignored. Thus, much of the reason to pay attention to multiple modes is not to reduce bias but as an opportunity to generate more precise inferences. For example, instead of fitting one very wide set of contours to the entire tomography plot in Figure 9.7, we could fit contours with much smaller variances to each mode. The result would be inferences with much narrower confidence intervals and correspondingly higher levels of certainty.

A straightforward parametric solution to the problem of multiple modes is to find covariates Z_i and use the model described in Section 9.2.1. This will allow for separate contours to fit each mode. A more detailed study of the differences among the precincts that appear to be in each mode would probably reveal what covariate would need to be included. If, on the other hand, evidence of multiple modes appear but no plausible covariate can be identified (that is, without merely coding on the basis of the results), then the truncated bivariate normal assumption could be substituted with a truncated mixture of bivariate normal distributions. I have not pursued this possibility because I have not found data with multiple modes like this, and because the nonparametric version of the model in Section 9.3.2 can easily handle multiple modes. But a truncated mixture of bivariate normals (probably using Gibbs sampling to aid in computation) would seem to be a good approach, both for this problem and as the basis for a potential formal test of multi-modality, since the single truncated bivariate normal distribution assumption would be a limiting special case.

More generally, one could replace the truncated bivariate normal with some version of a bivariate beta distribution, or one of a variety of other possibilities, but the differences from the more mathematically tractable truncated normal do not seem great enough to make a sufficiently large difference. Another possibility is to reparameterize β_i^b and β_i^w so they are unbounded (such as with a logit transformation) and use an untruncated bivariate normal distribution, or generalizations thereof. The problem with this approach is that the quantities of interest often cluster near and exactly on the boundaries of the unit square, meaning that a truncated distribution will fit patterns in real data much better. Moreover, in my experience, because the reparameterizations stretch small and substantively trivial regions of the unit square over most of the real number line for estimation, this procedure is numerically instable in many practical instances. Additionally, of course, the absence of truncation would result in a model that is not identified when the covariates include X_i.

A third possible violation from truncated bivariate normality is for the β_i^b and β_i^w values to follow a related distribution, such as one with wide tails. For example, Table 9.2 reports Monte Carlo evidence on the consequences of distributional misspecification using a t distribution with 3 degrees of freedom, as is commonly used to evaluate the robustness of normal distribution-based models.

Each pair of rows in Table 9.2 compares estimation errors when using the model with data drawn from it (a truncated normal distribution, TN) to data drawn from a truncated t distribution with three degrees of freedom (tt). In all cases, the estimation errors are near zero and the errors in confidence interval coverage are small and without systematic pattern. In addition, the standard deviation across estimates of the aggregate quantities of interest are about the

			Aggregate Level			*Precinct Level*	
Dist.	*p*	*Truncation*	*Error*	*(S.D.)*	*Avg.S.E.*	*Error*	*(S.D.)*
TN	100	Low	.001	(.020)	.020	.02	(.07)
tt	100	Low	.002	(.020)	.021	.01	(.06)
TN	100	High	.001	(.011)	.012	.00	(.05)
tt	100	High	.001	(.019)	.018	−.02	(.04)
TN	25	Low	.003	(.038)	.038	.02	(.10)
tt	25	Low	.001	(.038)	.038	−.01	(.11)
TN	25	High	.001	(.024)	.021	−.06	(.12)
tt	25	High	.000	(.036)	.029	−.06	(.10)

Table 9.2 Consequences of Distributional Misspecification: Monte Carlo Evidence. Each row summarizes 250 simulations drawn from a distribution that is truncated normal (TN) or truncated t with 3 degrees of freedom (tt). For parameter values that imply different levels of truncation, and different numbers of observations, the aggregate-level columns report the average absolute difference between the truth and estimates from the model. The precinct-level columns give the deviation from 80% in coverage of the 80% confidence intervals (in both cases with standard deviations across simulations in parentheses).

same size as the true standard deviation across the Monte Carlo experiments. The analyses in this table make comparisons between TN and tt for low and high levels of truncation (using the same parameter values as in Figure 9.6), and also for 100 and then 25 observations (p). The smaller number of observations is used because distributional assumptions in some models require larger samples to take affect. Fortunately, although ecological data sets typically have far more than 100 observations, even as few as 25 does not appear to cause much problem. The one possible exception is the underestimation of uncertainty levels for $p = 25$ and high truncation, although the narrow bounds in the high truncation case is when the confidence intervals matter least.

Possible distributional violations can also be revealed by comparing the data to other observable implications of the model (and of course the more the better). Probably the best approach is to evaluate the conditional distributions of $T_i|X_i$ implied by the model, which can be easily compared with the data on a graph of X_i horizontally and T_i vertically, as was done in Figure 6.1 (page 100) with hypothetical data. In this figure, the estimated conditional distributions are summarized on the graph with a solid straight line representing the conditional expectation function, $E(T_i|X_i)$ from Equation 6.8 (page 97), and two dashed curved lines, on either side of the expected value, for 80% confidence intervals computed from the conditional variance, $V(T_i|X_i)$ in Equation 6.9 (page 98). (Computing the confidence intervals is described in Section 8.5.) For each fixed value of X_i, the vertical scatter of real data points on this graph should be centered at the expected value line, and roughly 80% of the points should fall between the two dashed lines. If this pattern is true for some values of X_i but not others in a systematic pattern, the model's distributional assumption is probably violated. For an example of a real data set that violates the truncated bivariate normal distributional assumption, and can be clearly detected in this type of graph from aggregate data, see the left graph in Figure 13.5 (page 242).

Finally, an empirical problem that occurs on occasion, and often implies a distributional violation, is values of ρ very close to one. This corresponds to an X_i by T_i scatter plot with confidence intervals or standard deviations around the expected value line that have no dip in the middle (see, for example, Figure 6.1 graph (B), page 100).[9] The problem is that it implies that the correlation between β_i^b and β_i^w is very high, which seems implausible for most substantive examples. To put it another way, because all nontrivial examples predicting one observed social science variable from another do not yield perfect correlations, we should probably not think it reasonable for unobserved (but observable) variables to behave much differently. For the cases where β_i^b and β_i^w are observed, extreme correlations do not appear. In addition to being unrealistic, a large value of $\breve{\rho}$ is sometimes indicative of unusually narrow uncertainty estimates of the precinct-level quantities of interest. When $\breve{\rho}$ is near 1 or -1, the maximum likelihood ellipses are extremely thin, meaning that the posterior distribution of each precinct parameter cut out of the distribution by each tomography line will have an unusually small variance. In these situations, the confidence intervals may be too small. Of course, this is not certain, since $\breve{\rho}$ could in fact be high and the confidence intervals appropriately small; indeed, we could generate data from such a model. The point, therefore, is a substantive one: that large absolute values of $\breve{\rho}$ are empirically suspect and should be evaluated carefully.

In some cases, unrealistic values of $\breve{\rho}$ are remedied by including covariates. In some other cases, one may need to modify the model by allowing $\breve{\sigma}_b$, $\breve{\sigma}_w$, or $\breve{\rho}$ to vary over precincts as a function of measured covariates, just as I have already done for $\breve{\mathfrak{B}}^b$ and $\breve{\mathfrak{B}}^w$. Another

[9] A large bulge in middle of a scatter plot of X_i by T_i would be even more indicative of distributional difficulties, since this outcome is very unlikely to occur under the assumption of a single truncated bivariate normal distribution.

possibility, which is also an option for multiple modes where the variances or correlation seem to differ between the modes, is to let all elements of $\breve{\psi}$ vary. This can be done quite easily by dividing the sample of precincts into mutually exclusive groups and running separate analyses.

9.3.2 A Nonparametric Approach

In this section, I introduce a fully nonparametric version of the model, one that does not require the assumption of truncated bivariate normality. This alternative ecological inference model provides nonparametric inferences about all quantities of interest as in the parametric model. It also provides a diagnostic for truncated bivariate normality, which can be useful in deciding whether to make use of the basic parametric version of the model. Technical details appear in Appendix E.

Begin by considering what information exists in the data about the bivariate distribution without making any assumptions. The known information is represented by a tomography plot and its set of negatively sloping (and some flat) lines. Without additional information (that is, assumptions), all we know about the bivariate distribution of β_i^b and β_i^w is that it must have some positive density over at least one point on each and every tomography line. One way to portray this minimal knowledge is by characterizing the range of bivariate distributions that cannot be rejected by the data. To do this, imagine drawing *any* curve that connects the bottom left corner of a tomography plot ($\beta_i^b = 0$ and $\beta_i^w = 0$) to the top right corner ($\beta_i^b = 1$ and $\beta_i^w = 1$). For example, a straight 45° diagonal line is one such curve, which corresponds to Freedman et al.'s (1991) neighborhood model assumption that $\beta_i^b = \beta_i^w$ (see Equation 3.6, page 43). Because no tomography line can be positively sloping, any of these possible curves will cross every line at least once, and thus any distribution that includes positive density over such a curve cannot be rejected by the data. Of course many other distributions can be effectively ruled out by the specific pattern of tomography lines.

To get farther than this, some assumptions are required. The truncated bivariate normal distribution assumption is an example of a *global* assumption that characterizes the likely position of all the β_i^b, β_i^w points in a tomography plot simultaneously. This assumption is a formalization of the idea that, at least after taking into account X_i, all the precincts in the data set share something in common. Since most areal units were created for administrative convenience and aggregate individuals with roughly similar patterns, ecological observations from the same data sets usually do have a lot in common. Even though Goodman's assumption that β_i^b and β_i^w are constant over i is usually false, the assumption that they vary but have a single mode usually fits aggregate data. Parametric generalizations of this global assumption appear in Section 9.3.1. Continuing along that logical path, by expanding the number of components of mixtures of truncated bivariate normal distributions, can lead to arbitrarily flexible distributions. Parametric models like these are generally to be preferred, the only problem being that the models which result can become increasingly difficult computationally (cf. Escobar and West, 1995).

An alternative approach to making a global assumption about how strength will be borrowed is to make a set of *local* assumptions for different parts of the tomography plot. I do this in this section nonparametrically via "kernel density estimation." Kernel density estimation is generally not admissible from a Bayesian standpoint (West, 1991: 424–425), but it is relatively intuitive and easy and quick to compute. I use it here primarily to provide a different look at the data in the form of a useful visual diagnostic. The fully nonparametric procedure, also described here, provides a useful "local smoothing" complement to the "global" assumptions of the parametric model; it can be used on its own, but in most cases I prefer it as a diagnostic for suggesting covariates and other parametric generalizations.

The basic idea behind this approach is to replace the truncated bivariate normality distributional assumption with an assumption of local smoothing. In other words, the distribution of β_i^b and β_i^w is assumed not to have any discrete jumps in it within the unit square. Since β_i^b and β_i^w are both continuous variables, this is not a demanding requirement, but it is an assumption. As I demonstrate below, the amount of local smoothing assumed is equivalent to the amount of strength to be borrowed from other precincts in estimating the quantities of interest in each one. The goal here, as in the parametric procedure, is to come up with a posterior distribution for the precinct parameters, or in other words to find a distribution over each tomography line. In words, kernel density estimation gives higher probability to those points on each tomography line that pass closest to portions of the other lines.

The procedure begins with a tomography plot and replaces each line with a bivariate distribution, known in this context as a "kernel." The nonparametric kernel density estimate of the full bivariate distribution of β_i^b and β_i^w then comes from adding together all the kernels, and dividing each by a scale factor to make the total volume integrate to one.

The specific kernel chosen is a density, and it should be uniform in the direction of the line so that the prior distribution within the bounds on both β_i^b and β_i^w is "uninformative" (i.e., flat). Then there should be some spread in the direction *perpendicular* to the line in order to represent borrowed strength.[10] To construct this *bivariate* kernel we can use any scaled *univariate* distribution oriented, for every point on the line, perpendicular to the line. A univariate normal is an easy and obvious choice, but my experiments indicate that the particular choice of univariate distribution in constructing this bivariate kernel does not have much effect on the ultimate estimates (a common result in the literature; see Silverman, 1986). The standard deviation of the kernel is the smoothing parameter and is chosen prior to the procedure by the analyst in interaction with the data. For example, the standard deviation might be set at 0.08 to start and then adjusted up or down if more or less smoothing seems desirable. (Automatic methods for choosing kernel standard deviations do exist, but there is little advantage and much cost to not studying the sensitivity of the final estimates to the smoothing decision.) Finally, each kernel is truncated within the unit square and scaled so that its area sums to one. (On the behavior of kernel estimators near boundaries, see Müller, 1991).

Figure 9.8 gives an example of the procedure based on two hypothetical precincts (with data $T_1 = 0.5$, $T_2 = 0.6$, $X_1 = 0.3$ and $X_2 = 0.8$). Real applications will almost always involve more data, but this example helps show more clearly how the method works. Data from the two precincts are represented on the left graph in tomography format as dashed lines. The resulting nonparametric density estimate is given as a contour plot on the left, and surface plot on the right. Because there are only two lines, the individual kernel around each is easily identified. In addition, the area where the lines cross, and the kernels interfere, is a region of higher density. Thus, this nonparametric estimate indicates that the true β_i^b, β_i^w point is more likely to lie near where the two lines cross. Just as with the parametric model, the posterior distribution of each quantity of interest is the univariate distribution that the tomography line cuts out of the contours,

[10] An alternative approach might be to use a circular kernel centered at each point where every pair of tomography lines cross, if they do. For example, the truncated bivariate normal distribution, with zero correlation and equal standard deviations, could serve as a kernel. The mode of this distribution would be placed at each tomography line crossing, whether each is inside or outside the unit square. This method might reduce bias but would also be less computationally feasible for large data sets as it requires $p(p-1)/2$ kernel evaluations for each β_i^b, β_i^w point in the nonparametric density.

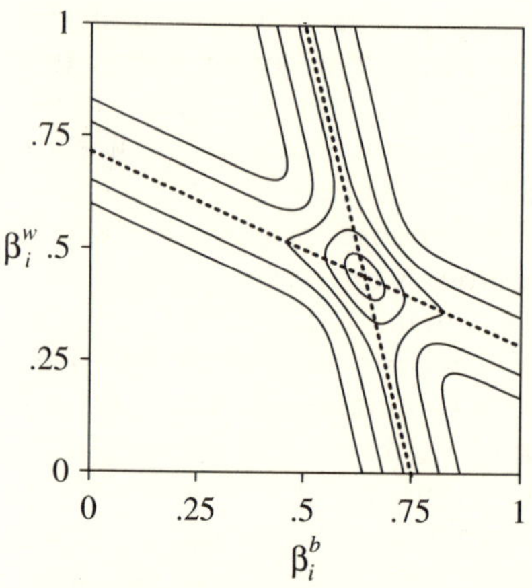

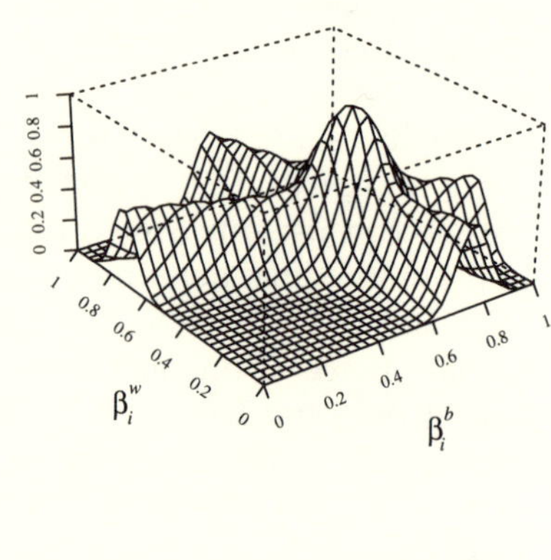

Figure 9.8 Building a Nonparametric Density Estimate. This example demonstrates how the kernel density estimation works. The contour plot (on the left) and the surface plot (on the right) are different representations of the same estimated density. The data for this example appear in the contour plot as the two (dashed) tomography lines.

which in this case is unimodal with a mode occurring where the lines cross.

Figure 9.8 also makes clear how strength is borrowed from other precincts to estimate the probable position of the quantities of interest in estimating each one. When the standard deviation of the kernel is set near zero, little strength is borrowed. This can be seen since most of the original uniform distribution over each tomography line is unchanged by the distributions over other precincts. In fact, for very small kernel standard deviations, lines that do not cross contribute essentially no strength to the estimation of each other's parameters. For larger standard deviations, more strength is borrowed and thus more of the distribution over the line is changed from its original uniform shape.

An example of nonparametric density estimation with a more realistic number of precincts is given in Figure 9.9. This is the density estimate, in contour and surface plot representations, of the same difficult multi-mode data created for the tomography plot from Figure 9.7 (page 187). As can be seen, the nonparametric estimate easily picks up the modes in the top right and bottom left corners. (The contour labels refer to the fraction of distance from the mode of the estimated distribution.) This could not have been the case with the parametric version of the model unless specific steps had been taken, such as those suggested in Section 9.3.1.

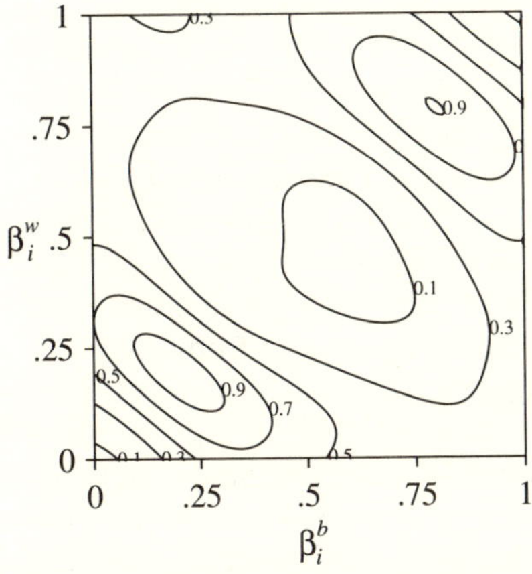

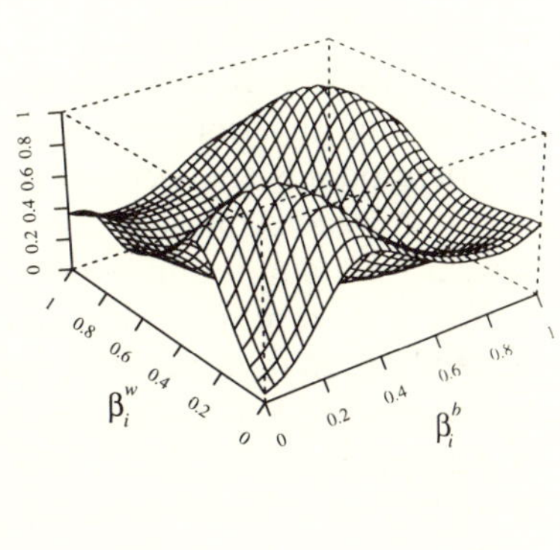

Figure 9.9 Nonparametric Density Estimate for a Difficult Case. This figure gives contour and surface representations of a nonparametric density estimate for the multi-mode data represented in the tomography plot in Figure 9.7 (page 187). As the labeled contours and the surface plot indicate, the area in the middle of the graph is a valley, and those at the ends are hills.

The same procedure can be used with real data sets as a test for multimodality or other distributional problems (see, for example, Figure 12.2, page 229). In addition, to define the nonparametric estimates of the quantities of interest, we only need to draw simulations of β_i^b and β_i^w. This is done by using the univariate distribution defined by the portion of the bivariate nonparametric density that falls over each line.

Every statistical technique requires assumptions, even one that falls into categories with names like "nonparametric" or "distribution-free." In the present case, the advantage of the nonparametric model is that it can pick up multiple modes and other non-normal features. These problems occur most frequently if the precincts in the data set do not have much in common, or different groups of observations do not have roughly the same things in common. But there are also advantages of choosing the parametric model, such as more powerful estimators and (often but not always) narrower confidence intervals. If the precincts have a lot in common, so that the β_i^b and β_i^w coordinates cluster around a single mode, then the parametric model will be superior. The parametric model can also be modified more easily. For example, although covariates could in theory be included in the nonparametric version of the model, the ultimate estimates of the quantities of interest would depend much more heavily on the smoothing assumptions, and other prior distributions would probably be needed too.[11]

In summary, nonparametric density estimation will be especially useful in applications where the distributional assumption of the parametric model is suspect. For example, if it is not reasonable to assume that the precincts in the data set have enough in common to be represented by a single unimodal distribution, displaying the contours or surface plot representation can be very informative. These graphs can be studied qualitatively and compared to the contours from the parametric model. The parametric and nonparametric versions can even be compared formally and a test statistic computed, although studying the graphics will often be more informative than any single statistic. If the nonparametric contours clearly have a single mode, so that the data can be fit by a truncated bivariate normal distribution, then the parametric version can be more confidently used to compute estimates of the quantities of interest. If, on the other hand, multiple modes or outliers appear likely, then some of suggestions in Section 9.3.1 might be used to expand the parametric model. If these suggestions appear unworkable, or the researcher has insufficient information about the data at hand, then the full nonparametric estimates of the quantities of interest can be used.

[11] Some topics for future research include bias reduction that might occur if the problem were rescaled so that symmetric densities could be used. In addition, because the tomography lines cannot be positively sloping, detecting a positive correlation between β_i^b and β_i^w is difficult with this nonparametric method.

PART IV

Verification

In this part, I compare thousands of ecological inferences from the model with individual level truths that are observed in the real data sets analyzed here. Chapter 10 analyzes a fairly typical ecological data set, a study of Southern voter registration by race. This analysis validates the model by comparing its estimates to the individual level truth, and helps work through all the intermediate steps of computing estimates in order to explain the workings of the method in detail. Chapter 11 demonstrates, through a study of poverty status by sex, that the model generates accurate inferences even in the presence of aggregation bias and a highly restricted variance across aggregate units. Chapter 12 makes inferences about black registration in a Kentucky data set with very little information about blacks and with even more serious versions of aggregation bias and restricted variance. Finally, Chapter 13 verifies the model in some classic contexts, including studies of voter transitions and Robinson's example of literacy by race.

CHAPTER 10

A Typical Application Described in Detail: Voter Registration by Race

IN THIS CHAPTER, the method developed in Part III is used to analyze one fairly typical ecological data set in detail. This example portrays the model from several perspectives, highlights the information it can extract from the data, and evaluates its ability to make valid ecological inferences. This chapter alone provides more than ten times as many comparisons between the individual-level truth and inferences from aggregate data as in the entire history of research on the ecological inference problem, albeit all from one data set. Subsequent chapters provide many additional comparisons.

This chapter also displays a large variety of intermediate results computed along the way to making inferences about the quantities of interest. Many of these intermediate results need not normally be examined during ordinary empirical applications of the method, but they are useful here in order to understand the model and the various numerical calculations required. Subsequent chapters in this part will continue with the task of checking the validity of the inferences but will suspend the detailed presentation of intermediate results except where relevant to the analysis at hand. Finally, all chapters in this part emphasize the value of the basic model by not making use of the model extensions and procedures introduced in Chapter 9. In any real application where the substantive answer matters, a prudent data analyst should always consider these as well (see Chapter 16).

10.1 THE DATA

The data analyzed in this chapter include voter registration and racial background of people from 275 counties in four Southern U.S. States: Florida, Louisiana, North Carolina, and South Carolina. The data from each county in these states include the total voting age population (N_i) and the proportions of this population who are black (X_i), white ($1 - X_i$), and registered (T_i) in 1968. Applying the ecological inference model to these data yields estimates of the fraction of blacks registered, and the fraction of whites registered, in each county.[1]

This collection of data is especially valuable because it also includes the *true* fraction of blacks (β_i^b) and of whites (β_i^w) registered. That is, these Southern states record the race of each registrant and make the data available to the public. Thus, these data can be used to verify the inferences based on the model.

In a few counties, public records indicate that the number of people registered of a certain race is larger than the census count of voting-age people of that race. This problem may be due in part to a census undercount, but it probably occurs more often because some counties purge their registration rolls with insufficient frequency: when voters die or move out of town, they remain on the rolls for a time. In these cases, I changed the reported registration figure to equal the number of voting-age people of that race. The implied 100% registration figure is almost certainly an overestimate, but because of the relatively few such cases with this problem this procedure does not materially affect these ecological inferences.

Figure 10.1 plots the proportion of each county's voting-age population who are African American (horizontally) by the fraction of the voting-age population who are registered (vertically). The 275 Southern counties that appear in the graph are labeled with the first letter of the state from which they come.

This scattercross graph also includes the ⊠ pattern so we can assess the information about each county-level quantity of interest available from the deterministic bounds (see Section 5.3). Since the triangle on the right is nearly empty, and fairly distant from most of the data points, we can see that the data contain considerable deterministic information about the fraction of whites who are registered (β_i^w). This is reasonably good news, since, as is common in many applications, these aggregate data are very informative about this quantity of interest. However, since many of the points lie in and near the triangle on the left, much less deterministic information exists in the data about the fraction of blacks who are registered (β_i^b).

10.2 Likelihood Estimation

Maximizing the log of the likelihood function in Equation 7.1 (page 134) with respect to the parameters, conditional on these data (also

[1] The data for this example come from the Civil Rights Commission reports, collected by Philip Wood, and first analyzed by James Alt (1993).

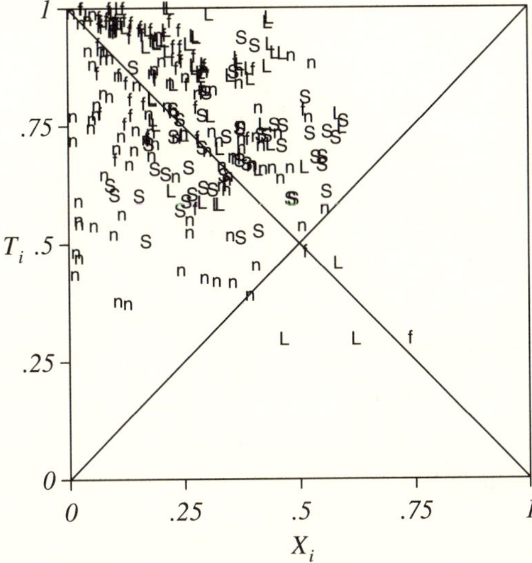

Figure 10.1 A Scattercross Graph for Southern Counties, 1968. Proportion registered by proportion black. Counties are plotted with a symbol representing the first letter of the state name (florida, Louisiana, north Carolina, and South Carolina), with lower case used to improve visual clarity.

using the prior distribution described in Section 7.4) took 11 iterations for a total of 1 minute and 18 seconds. Most of this time was consumed with calculating the truncation portion of the likelihood at each iteration, without which the procedure takes only about 5 seconds (see Appendix F for details). This maximization yields point estimates and a variance matrix for ϕ. One summary of these results appears in Table 10.1. The first column of numbers are elements of $\hat{\phi}$, which are the values of ϕ that maximize the likelihood function.

Since estimates of ϕ are reparameterized, they are not in the most easy-to-understand format. Thus, first reparameterize its elements into the parameters of the truncated bivariate normal distribution, on the untruncated scale. To do this, invert Equations 7.4 (page 136) and substitute in the values from Table 10.1:

$$\hat{\breve{\psi}} = \begin{pmatrix} \hat{\breve{\mathfrak{B}}}^b \\ \hat{\breve{\mathfrak{B}}}^w \\ \hat{\breve{\sigma}}_b \\ \hat{\breve{\sigma}}_w \\ \hat{\breve{\rho}} \end{pmatrix} = \begin{pmatrix} \phi_1(0.25 + \breve{\sigma}_b^2) + 0.5 \\ \phi_2(0.25 + \breve{\sigma}_w^2) + 0.5 \\ e^{\phi_3} \\ e^{\phi_4} \\ \frac{e^{2\phi_5} - 1}{e^{2\phi_5} + 1} \end{pmatrix}$$

Parameters	*Estimates*	*Standard Error*
ϕ_1	1.28	.34
ϕ_2	1.94	.36
ϕ_3	−1.11	.16
ϕ_4	−1.32	.20
ϕ_5	1.61	.36

Table 10.1 Maximum Likelihood Estimates.

$$= \begin{pmatrix} 1.28\left(0.25 + e^{-1.11^2}\right) + 0.5 \\ 1.94\left(0.25 + e^{-1.32^2}\right) + 0.5 \\ e^{-1.11} \\ e^{-1.32} \\ \frac{e^{2(1.61)}-1}{e^{2(1.61)}+1} \end{pmatrix} = \begin{pmatrix} .96 \\ 1.12 \\ .33 \\ .27 \\ .92 \end{pmatrix} \tag{10.1}$$

For comparison, these numbers are reproduced in Table 10.2, along with recomputed standard errors. Standard errors of the reparameterized coefficients were computed via simulation.[2]

In order to understand the maximum likelihood estimates and their fit to the data, Figure 10.2 gives a tomography plot with lines representing the data and 50% and 95% contours drawn from the parameters $\breve{\psi}$ from Table 10.2. This figure has a variety of features worthy of note. First, the highest density of lines occurs in the upper right corner of the graph, with a decline in line density at coordinates farther from that point. Thus, it is appropriate that the maximum likelihood procedure found the mode near that corner. In fact, it located the mode on the untruncated scale just outside the square at 0.96,1.12 (whether the mode is outside the square depends on how fast the density of lines falls off at different distances from the mode). The lines cutting off the upper right corner are the most informative about β_i^b and β_i^w as their bounds for these counties have very narrow widths (which can be seen by projecting the lines onto each axis).

The figure also has roughly three distinct patterns of tomography lines. As noted, those that cut off the top right corner of the graph

[2] The standard errors cannot be computed by inserting them into Equation 10.1 directly as with the coefficients. They can be computed analytically via Taylor series approximation, or more easily via simulation. The latter required taking 10,000 random draws from their posterior distribution using a normal distribution with mean $\hat{\phi}$ and variance $\hat{V}(\hat{\phi})$ as the first approximation and importance sampling to improve the simulation. Calculating $\breve{\psi}$ for each simulation requires applying Equation 10.1, and computing the standard deviations over the 10,000 simulations gives the standard errors.

Parameters (elements of $\breve{\psi}$)	*Estimates*	*Standard Error*
$\breve{\mathfrak{B}}^b$	.96	.15
$\breve{\mathfrak{B}}^w$	1.12	.18
$\breve{\sigma}_b$	.33	.05
$\breve{\sigma}_w$	.27	.06
$\breve{\rho}$	.92	.07

Table 10.2 Reparameterized Maximum Likelihood Estimates, on the scale of the untruncated bivariate normal distribution.

have tight bounds and high values on both β_i^b and β_i^w. Second, the figure includes a large number of nearly flat lines, which come from predominately white counties (because the slope of these lines is $-X_i/(1 - X_i) \approx 0$). These lines are extremely informative about β_i^w, because projecting them onto the left vertical axis implies a very narrow possible range. However these flat lines also provide no narrowing of the [0,1] bounds for β_i^b. A third pattern is of diagonal lines that go from top left to bottom right (resembling a driving rain). Most of these lines, which come from counties that are nearly half African American, imply parameter bounds that are not especially informative about either quantity of interest, although those farther from the 0,1–1,0 diagonal do provide more information about each. Both the flat and diagonal lines are somewhat more dense closer to the upper right corner; in fact, no line crosses the 45° diagonal at less than about $\beta_i^b = \beta_i^w = 0.3$. Since the level of registration (T_i) in any county can be read off where its tomography line crosses this diagonal, registration rates are higher than 0.3 in all counties. Note also the absence of very steep lines that would be indicative of very narrow bounds on β_i^b. Substantively, a maximum of only 17 of 275 counties could have fewer than 25% white registration (although it could be as few as zero), which can be seen by counting the number of lines that descend below $\beta_i^w = 0.25$. The upper bound on the number of counties with fewer than 25% registered blacks is much higher.

Finally, transform these parameters a second time to the ultimate truncated scale:

$$\hat{\psi} = \begin{pmatrix} \hat{\mathfrak{B}}^b \\ \hat{\mathfrak{B}}^w \\ \hat{\sigma}_b \\ \hat{\sigma}_w \\ \hat{\rho} \end{pmatrix} = \begin{pmatrix} .62 \\ .83 \\ .19 \\ .14 \\ .77 \end{pmatrix}$$

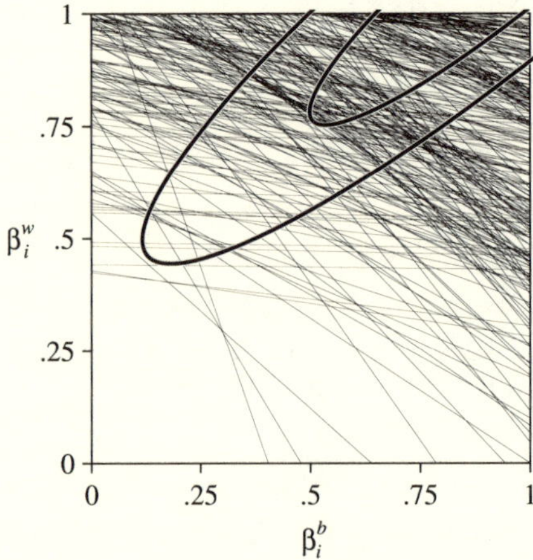

Figure 10.2 Tomography Plot of Southern Race Data with 50% and 95% Maximum Likelihood Contours Ellipses. Each line maps all *possible* values of β_i^b and β_i^w for one precinct. The contours identify the portions of the lines with the highest *probability* of containing the true coordinate.

As described in Section 6.2.2, this final transformation from the untruncated to the truncated scale requires drawing a large number of values from the truncated bivariate normal distribution, using the untruncated normal parameters, and then taking the means, variances, and correlation to produce the numbers above.

For example, the parameter $\hat{\mathfrak{B}}^b = .62$ is an intermediate estimate of the fraction of blacks who are registered, but it is a simple (unweighted) average over all counties in the sample. This makes it a lot less interesting because some counties are many times larger than others. For example, Dade County, Florida, includes the city of Miami and, in 1968, 613,000 voting-age residents. At the other end of the population continuum is Glades County, Florida; on the western shore of Lake Okeechobee, its 1,800 voting-age residents were mostly members of the Seminole Indian reservation. Thus, this parameter is not of much direct interest. It is also a partial statistical estimate, as it includes only some information from the known deterministic bounds on each of the county-level parameters. Yet it indicates that the "average county" has about two-thirds of its African Americans of voting age on the registration rolls. The corresponding intermediate, preliminary parameter for whites is $\hat{\mathfrak{B}}^w = .83$, which indicates that the average county has 83 percent of its white voting-age population registered. The large racial difference in registration for the 1968 South is consistent with much knowledge of the region, but the estimate will be improved on in several ways.

The point estimates also indicate that the variance across counties in the fraction of blacks who are registered ($\hat{\sigma}_b = .19$) is much larger than for the fraction of whites who are registered ($\hat{\sigma}_w = .14$). In part this reflects greater uncertainty in black than in white registration. This pattern is easy to see in Figure 10.2, since the many relatively flat lines are clustered in the top half of the figure, hence narrowing the bounds and variance in possible values of β_i^w, but very few lines narrow the bounds on β_i^b; those that do narrow these bounds tend to cluster less than for β_i^w.

Figure 10.3 portrays these results by plotting the black fraction of the voting-age population by the fraction of the voting-age population registered. Instead of labeling each county with the state from which it comes, a circle represents each county with the circle's area proportional to its voting-age population. This helps emphasize the vast differences in county sizes. Also on this graph are lines to represent the likelihood estimates. For example, the dark, solid line on the graph represents the basic accounting identity. This line intersects the left vertical axis at $\hat{\mathfrak{B}}^w = .83$ which, according to the horizontal axis, corresponds to counties with all whites ($X_i = 0$). It intersects the right vertical axis at $\hat{\mathfrak{B}}^b = .62$, corresponding to where the horizontal axis indicates homogeneously black counties ($X_i = 1$). The curved dashed lines are plots of 80% confidence intervals around the regression line, computed using the procedure described at Equation 8.2 (page 157). The larger uncertainty in black registration is easy to see from the absence of points on the right side of the graph and wider dashed lines, which also corresponds to the larger standard errors on $\mathfrak{B}^b$ and σ_b than on $\mathfrak{B}^w$ and σ_w. The model clearly fits these data.[3]

Finally, we can evaluate these parameter estimates based on the likelihood model by comparing them to the moments computed directly from the true parameter values (calculated by taking the means, standard deviations, and correlation of the true fractions of blacks and whites registered). Because each tomography line is known with certainty, the likelihood contours only need be approximately placed to pick out the correct area where the true β_i^b, β_i^w point probably lies; as a result, accurate estimates of these intermediate parameters (that is, those which determine the placement of the contours) is helpful, but not always essential for accurate inferences about the quantities of interest. Table 10.3 shows that the parameters track reasonably well. $\mathfrak{B}^w$,

[3] The slight vertical asymmetry in this graph, with more points falling below the lower dashed line than above the upper dashed line, is due to the truncation from above at one. Because the expected value line is high especially for large values of X_i, much of the conditional distribution of $T_i|X_i$ is clustered not far below $T_i = 1$, and has a skewed shape and longer tail for smaller values of T_i.

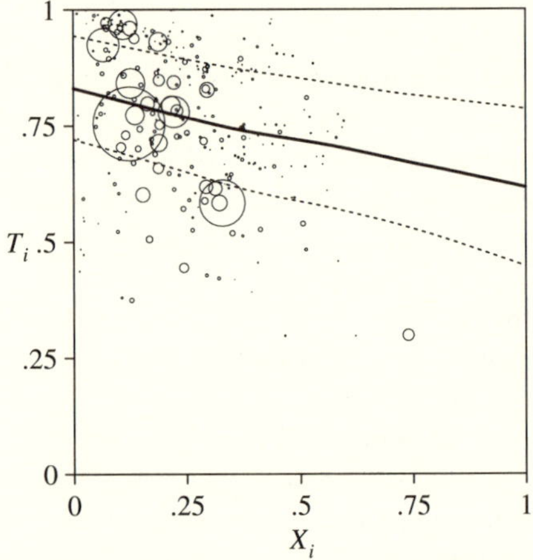

Figure 10.3 Scatter Plot with Maximum Likelihood Results Superimposed. The size of each circle is proportional to county population. The solid line is the expected value of T_i given X_i, and dashed lines are 80% confidence intervals around the expected value.

σ_b, and σ_w are essentially right on the mark. The point estimates for $\mathfrak{B}^b$ and ρ are somewhat further off, although all the parameters are within a standard error or two of the true value. The estimate of ρ, as usual, is more uncertain (as indicated by its large standard error), but it too is within two standard errors of the true value. Even though the ultimate estimates of the quantities of interest do not depend heavily on ρ, our uncertainty in its estimate will be well reflected in the final results.

10.3 Computing Quantities of Interest

The most convenient way to compute the quantities of interest is to draw K samples for each county from its posterior distribution, as described in Section 8.2. Then this store of simulations can be used in a variety of ways for whatever purposes are desired.

First draw 100 samples of β_i^b and of β_i^w for each of the 275 counties from their posterior distribution. This involved drawing simulations via importance sampling of $\breve{\psi}$, inserting them into the precinct-level posterior distribution, and drawing β_i^b and computing β_i^w. These simulations took 4 minutes and 45 seconds (for a total run time, including likelihood maximization, of 6 minutes and 3 seconds). Most of this time was taken by importance sampling (the normal approximation

	Truth	*Estimate*	*Standard Error*
$\mathfrak{B}^b$	.56	.62	.04
$\mathfrak{B}^w$	.85	.83	.01
σ_b	.21	.19	.02
σ_w	.15	.14	.01
ρ	.52	.77	.16

Table 10.3 Verifying Estimates of $\breve{\psi}$. This table shows the correspondence between the true values of these intermediate parameters and estimates from aggregate data. Good estimates are helpful, but not always essential in producing accurate estimates of the quantities of interest.

reduces the total run time to well under 2 minutes). The simulation procedure gave no indication of any specification difficulties (see Appendix F for these computational details). All other computations from these data were completed from these 27,500 numbers for β_i^b and the same number for β_i^w.

10.3.1 *Aggregate*

I first explore the simulations by comparing them with the true levels of black and white registration they were intended to estimate. To study the aggregate-level results, compute a simulated aggregate parameter by taking the weighted average of the first simulation from each of the 275 counties. This procedure is repeated for each of the 100 county-level simulations, yielding a set of 100 simulations of the aggregate-level parameters (see Section 8.3).

Figure 10.4 summarizes these aggregate parameter simulations with density estimates of the simulations of B^b and B^w. These density estimates are summaries of the posterior distributions of these parameters. Density estimates are smooth versions of histograms (not smoothed histograms; see Silverman, 1986), and can be interpreted as histograms. It is perhaps easiest to think of each of these as representing a pile of simulations. The more the pile is centered within a range on the horizontal axis, the more confidence we have that that range includes the value of the aggregate parameter. For example, the density estimate for blacks, at the left, has a larger variance than the one for whites, on the right. This indicates that the model contains more information about the value of B^w than B^b. The model encourages us to think of the (usually unobserved) true values as a random draw from this distribution. Indeed, the idea of a posterior

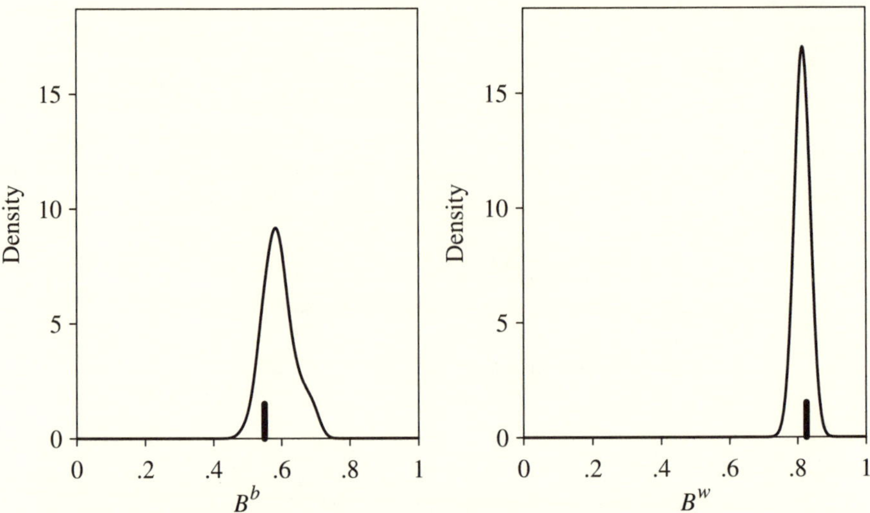

Figure 10.4 Posterior Distribution of the Aggregate Quantities of Interest. The true values (the small vertical bars) are estimated accurately by these distributions.

distribution is intended to be a model of the process by which the true values are generated. Thus, the probability that the fraction of whites registered is less than 0.5 is zero. More generally, the probability of the true value falling in a range of values is given by the area under the curve falling over that range.

The true fractions of blacks and whites registered are indicated in each panel of Figure 10.4 as small vertical bars. Each density estimate has a large fraction of its area near the true value, thus confirming the validity of the model's estimates. Note how the final result accurately and closely estimates the true value, even though the intermediate parameters in Table 10.3 did not fit their true values as closely. This improvement is due to including the more appropriate weighted averages of the precinct parameters and the very informative precinct-level bounds.

The true value need not be exactly at the center of the distribution to be considered confirming information about the model. Indeed, the model implies that the true value is only somewhere in the distribution estimated. Sometimes the true value should appear in ranges with smaller areas above them. In fact, a model for which the true value always falls at the center of the posterior distribution would be flawed, since its uncertainty estimates are wrong. For example, about

5% of the time, the true estimate should fall in the leftmost extreme 5% of the area of the distribution, etc. Fortunately, the distribution of each quantity of interest is very narrow, and the true value falls only a small fraction of a standard deviation from the mean of its respective distribution (which can serve as a point estimate). In each of these graphs, we only observe one test of the model and so, by itself, it cannot be used to verify all aspects of the posterior distribution.

Of course, because of the distributions' relative location along the horizontal axes, the results also indicate that white voter registration is considerably higher than black registration in these southern states in the late 1960s.

10.3.2 County Level

The model provides considerably more information about racial registration than merely the posterior distributions of the aggregate quantities of interest. They also provide separate posterior distributions of β_i^b and β_i^w for each of the 275 counties. However, instead of printing 550 density estimates analogous to Figure 10.4, consider the following four summaries of these results.

One method of presentation is to use a point estimate for each of the 550 county-level parameters by separately computing the mean of its 100 simulations (as per Equation 8.1, page 148). The result of this computation is a point estimate of β_i^b and β_i^w for each county. The first panel in Figure 10.5 plots the estimated fraction of blacks registered by the true fraction of blacks registered for each county that they were meant to estimate. The size of each circle is proportional to the number of voting-age blacks in the county, so that large circles represent counties with more blacks. The same information is provided for white registrants in the second panel.

If each of the 275 county estimates were equal to the true values, with no uncertainty, the center of all circles in Figure 10.5 would fall exactly on the 45° line. In fact, the estimated values track the true values fairly closely, and are spread roughly randomly around the 45° line. By the standards evident in the social science literature, if either scatter plot in Figure 10.5 were merely a dependent variable plotted by the fitted values of the same dependent variable, the fit would be considered very good. But, unlike fitting y to $\hat{y}$ (where $\hat{y}$ is calculated based on y), the "true proportion registered" in this figure was not used during the estimation process.

In fact, in the few cases in the social sciences for which out-of-sample predictions are made, scholars use past realizations of the process to forecast future values. For example, in forecasting presi-

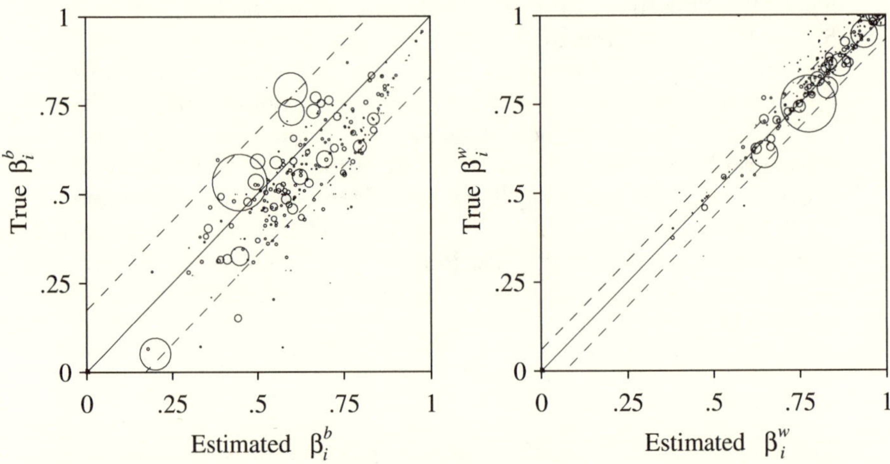

Figure 10.5 Comparing Estimates to the Truth at the County Level. Each circle represents one county's black (for the left graph) or white (for the right graph) voting-age population. That the center of most circles fall near the solid diagonal line indicates that the estimated values are very close to the true values. The 80% confidence intervals, represented by the dashed lines, accurately predict the differing levels of fit for blacks and whites. The area of each circle is proportional to the number of blacks or whites.

dential approval, past values of approval are a major predictive factor. This is extremely useful, but it also makes empirical evaluations of those models more hazardous: researchers have to worry about being fooled into seeing a series that closely fits the predicted values as one that would forecast well. Indeed, in practice, it is often the case that models which fit observed realizations of the process within a sample "too well" also forecast poorly (because the model maps idiosyncrasies unique to one year rather than any underlying structure that persists). Furthermore, very few social science forecasting studies exist for which numerous out-of-sample comparisons can be made between forecasts and the true values. More commonly, forecasts are made for a single observation every few years (such as an election) or months (such as presidential popularity). This situation is generally inadequate for model evaluation, except in the long run. The result is often that forecasting models proliferate more quickly than data to evaluate them. Fortunately, these problems do not occur here, since the ecological analyses include no information about the internal cell values; "out-of-sample" comparisons of the estimated to true fractions registered will never become "in-sample" values; and 550 new comparisons are available here.

In Figure 10.5, estimates for white registrants are closer to the true values than for black registrants, as is to be expected. Indeed, this pattern was predicted as an integral part of the estimation procedure. For example, as a rough estimate of the uncertainty associated with each precinct parameter, the figure also includes the average 80% confidence interval as dashed lines.[4] Because of the different statistical and deterministic information from each county, individual confidence intervals vary considerably across the counties in these data (and thus in these points in the graph), so these averages are quite rough. Nevertheless, one can see that the model predicts that the black estimates will be more variable than the white estimates, as indeed they are. That the confidence intervals appear roughly right is an important feature of the model, since, when the true values are not available for comparison, researchers using the method will not be mislead by data that are less informative about ecological inferences. Finally, the two graphs in this figure also do not appear to reveal any notable patterns not picked up by the model.

A second way of understanding the model is through Figure 10.6. This is a close-up look at all 27,500 simulations drawn for the fraction of whites registered, β_i^w. This figure plots simulations of β_i^w by the true fraction registered. It is the same as Figure 10.5 except that each circle is replaced by a smear of all 100 simulations that were previously averaged to produce each of the 275 circles. The figure helps emphasize the many simulations drawn. It also gives a sense of the uncertainty about each estimate, since each of the 275 horizontal sets of 100 dots on the graph represents a posterior distribution of β_i^w for one county. All the distributions at least touch the 45° line, which indicate that the true value is always within the range of simulations.

The graph also creates one unfortunate optical illusion: it overemphasizes posterior distributions with larger variances. For example, at roughly the 0.6,0.6 point, two sets of 100 simulations on the graph happen to have a tiny range of variation. Cases such as these are "good" in that they make relatively certain ecological inferences, but they are unfortunately very difficult to see in the graph. In contrast, the posteriors with larger variances and thus more uncertain inferences, such as the one closest to the bottom of the graph, take up

[4] The 80% confidence interval was computed for each county by sorting the 100 simulations in numerical order and taking the 10th and 90th values (see Section 8.2). The average confidence interval was computed by taking the average of the individual intervals over the 275 counties.

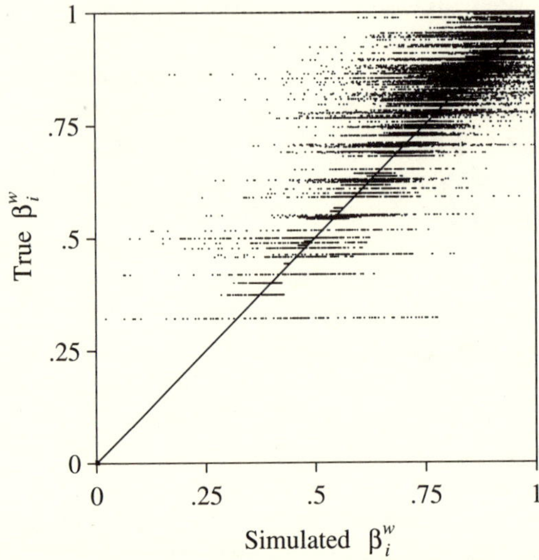

Figure 10.6 27,500 Simulations of β_i^w. This figure plots 100 simulations representing the posterior distribution for each of 275 counties. The horizontal variation in simulations for each true β_i^w represents the model's uncertainty estimate about this parameter. That all the distributions appear to cross the 45° line indicates the success of the model's ecological inferences.

a disproportionate share of the figure. (Because of its larger average variances, this illusion is exacerbated in the analogous plot for β_i^b, which I do not present.)

Third, the uncertainty estimates can be evaluated more completely in the following way. For each county, compute the percentile of the posterior distribution at which the true value is found. If the uncertainty estimates are correct, these percentiles should be spread roughly evenly over the [0,1] interval. That is, 95% of the true values should fall within the 95% confidence intervals; 25% should fall higher than the 25th percentile of the distribution; etc. If too many values are focused around the 50th percentile, indicating that the true value is very close to the estimated value, then the method would be producing reliable results but reporting that they were not to be trusted. If, in contrast, values were too far from the 50% mark, then inferences made would be overconfident. (An asymmetric pattern would reflect a systematic bias.)

This is also not a perfect means of assessing uncertainty estimates, given the wide variation in types of distributions for the county-level results. For example, homogeneous precincts, which are perfectly predicted, are not even considered in this scheme, and posterior distribu-

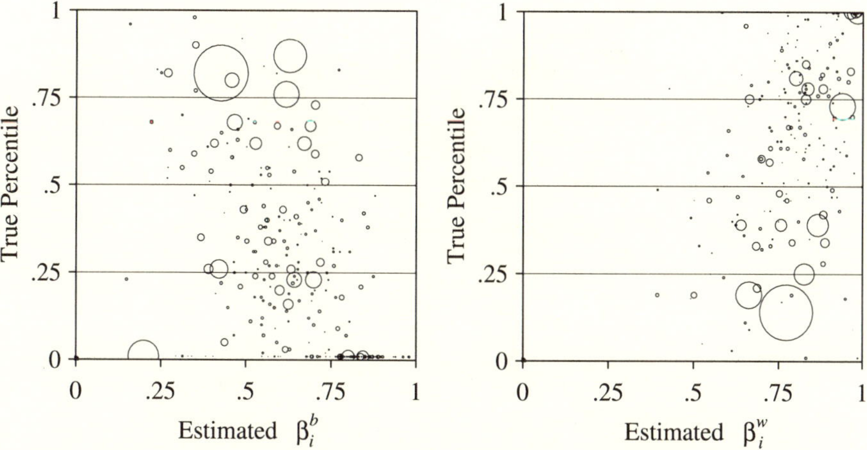

Figure 10.7 Verifying Uncertainty Estimates. The validity of the uncertainty estimates is indicated by the roughly even spread of people in these precincts across the vertical dimension of each graph. The size of each circle is proportional to the black or white voting-age population, respectively.

tions with very small variances that include the true value might be close to it substantively (on the scale of β_i^b and β_i^w) but far from it on this percentile scale. Asymmetric distributions will also be problematic, as they would require disproportionately more simulations to get accurate assessments of their uncertainty.

With these qualifications in mind, Figure 10.7 plots the percentile of each distribution at which the true value falls (vertically) by the mean of each distribution (horizontally). Each graph is divided into four areas in order to judge the evenness of the spread of points more easily. As can be seen, the points are not spread exactly evenly over the vertical [0,1] percentile range, but given the statistical variation in estimating these percentiles, the result is quite good, with similar numbers of points (and even more similar numbers of people) in each of the four panels of the figures. The uncertainty estimates are thus reasonably accurate.[5]

A related evaluation of the uncertainty estimates from the model is the coverage of the confidence intervals. For example, half of the true values ought to fall within the corresponding estimated 50% confi-

[5] The cluster of points at the bottom of the graph on the left and the top of the graph on the right is largely an artifact of the counties recoded as 100% registered and discussed in Section 10.1.

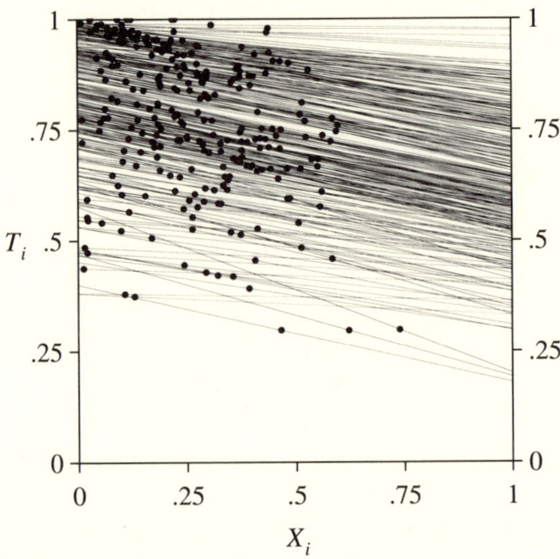

Figure 10.8 275 Lines Fit to 275 Points. The black dots form a scatterplot of X_i by T_i (just as in Figure 10.1 but without the state designated, and Figure 10.3 without the size of county indicated). Each line crosses the left vertical axis at the estimated (mean posterior) value of β_i^w and the right vertical axis at the estimated β_i^b for each county i. It is possible to estimate $2p$ parameters from only p observations by "borrowing strength" statistically from all precincts to help estimate the parameters in each one.

dence interval. In fact, 51% do for the fraction of blacks registered and 47% for the fraction of whites. In addition, 78% of the true fraction of blacks registered, and 77% for whites, fall within the 80% confidence interval. These values are very close to the theoretically correct values, which is especially impressive since the data were not simulated from the model but instead are from a real application.

Finally, this section provides a different way of conceptualizing the results. This is done by presenting an X_i by T_i plot, but instead of fitting one line to all these points as in Goodman's regression, or one expected value line as in Figure 10.3, Figure 10.8 gives one line fit to each data point. The purpose of this graph is to help understand the method, not as a way to pick out individual county results. Each line intersects the left vertical axis ($X_i = 0$) at $\hat{\beta}_i^w$ and the right vertical axis ($X_i = 1$) at $\hat{\beta}_i^b$. The overall pattern of lines is diagonally downward from left to right, indicating that in most counties white registration is higher than black registration ($\hat{\beta}_i^w > \hat{\beta}_i^b$). Also apparent is the smaller variance among whites (at the left intercept) than among blacks (at the right intercept). The positive correlation between β_i^b and β_i^w can be seen by the relatively few lines that cross: high values of β_i^b usually imply high values of β_i^w. The line for any county in this figure can also be used to generate the fraction of the total voting-age population who are registered: begin with the black fraction of the voting-age population in the county (X_i), go up to the line for that county and over at a right angle to the vertical axis (T_i).

Figure 10.8 also emphasizes a fact about this model that may take some getting use to. Instead of Goodman's model, which fits a single line to all the observations, this model fits 275 lines to 275 points. The reason that fitting as many lines as points is possible here, and the reason it is desirable, is that the lines are not being estimated independently. Although the model gives estimates of 275 lines, and 550 separate quantities of interest, the equivalent of only five (partly) independent parameters (the elements of ϕ) need be estimated from the 275 observations. The model is able to accomplish this by *borrowing strength* from the data in all the counties to estimate the parameters of interest in each one.

Analogously, in an ordinary regression model, the best forecast of the dependent variable for given values of the explanatory variables is the fitted value. The best forecast is not the value of the dependent variable in the row of the data matrix that happens to have the desired values of the explanatory variables. The latter method is inferior because it does not borrow strength from the entire set of observations, whereas the fitted value does borrow strength. A very similar result occurs here, except that without borrowing strength each line could not even be uniquely drawn since it would be based on only a single data point.

10.3.3 Other Quantities of Interest

Finally, numerous other quantities of interest may be calculated from these simulations. For example, of the four states in the data set, a researcher might for part of a project only be interested in North Carolina. In this situation, just the North Carolina county simulations could be pulled out, and some quantity of interest computed.

To complicate the example further, imagine if the researcher were only interested in racially polarized registration in North Carolina, the degree to which white registration levels was higher than for blacks. To study this question, take the difference between the black and white simulations in each North Carolina county:

$$\tilde{\beta}_i = \tilde{\beta}_i^w - \tilde{\beta}_i^b$$

Then take the weighted average of $\tilde{\beta}_i$ over counties for each simulation. The result is a set of 100 simulations of racially polarized voting in the state. From these simulations, a researcher could compute a mean for a point estimate or plot a histogram or density estimate to summarize the full posterior distribution.

Using similar procedures, researchers could compute estimates of the average differences in black registration between Florida and South Carolina; the ratio of white registration rates in Dade County to Glades County, Florida; or any of an infinite variety of other quantities.

CHAPTER 11

Robustness to Aggregation Bias: Poverty Status by Sex

THIS CHAPTER analyzes a data set with very high levels of aggregation bias. Existing methods applied to these data give extremely misleading results for the statewide aggregates, and no other information. In contrast, the method offered in this book gives accurate inferences at the level of the statewide aggregate and for the more than 3,000 precinct-sized geographic units. Moreover, the model used in this chapter includes no special features to deal explicitly with aggregation bias (such as those in Chapter 9). The empirical example is a very difficult one: estimating the fraction of males and females in poverty in South Carolina in 1990. This is an especially difficult application because of high levels of aggregation bias in the data and also because the fraction of the population who are male varies only very slightly over the geographic units.

11.1 Data and Notation

The data for this analysis come from the 1990 U.S. Census in South Carolina. The census designation of "block groups" serve as the geographic units which, for South Carolina, are slightly larger than electoral precincts. The 3,187 block groups in this state have an average of 1,057 voters each (with a standard deviation of 747).

The cross-tabulation in each block group, at the individual level, is the 2×2 table of poverty status by sex. The goal is to estimate the cells from the marginals. The first marginal is the outcome variable (T_i), in this case the fraction of individuals in each block group falling below the official federal government poverty level. The government defines the poverty status of individuals according to whether their family's monetary income is above the official poverty level for families. The family poverty level is adjusted for family size and persons under 18 years old. The average poverty level for a family of four at the time of the census was $12,674. The government does not correct for regional differences in cost of living, nonmonetary income, money earned from the sale of property, in-kind government benefits, or payment of taxes (U.S. Bureau of the Census, 1989).

According to this definition, about 0.15 (that is 15%) of the state's population was living in poverty (T_i), with a standard deviation across block groups of 0.14. The fraction male (X_i) varies considerably less across the state. About 0.48 of South Carolinians are male with a standard deviation over block groups of only 0.05.

These data are especially useful for evaluating ecological inferences because the Census Bureau provides not only the marginals X_i and T_i and the population total N_i in each block group, but also the cells of the cross-tabulation of poverty status by sex. Thus, X_i, T_i, and N_i are used to *estimate* the fraction of males in poverty (β_i^b) and the fraction of females in poverty (β_i^w). (If you like mnemonics, think of the superscript b as standing for "boys and men" and the superscript w as referring to "women and girls.") I then compare these estimates to the *true* levels of poverty for each sex in order to verify the model. (The true levels of poverty were not consulted until after running the analysis.)

11.2 Verifying the Existence of Aggregation Bias

Chapter 3 proved that all versions of aggregation bias reduce to a single problem. One of the equivalent ways to express aggregation bias is via the indeterminacy problem. And one way to portray the indeterminacy problem is to observe what happens to inferences if the true values of β_i^b and β_i^w are correlated with X_i. Substantial evidence exists to show that this kind of relationship destroys the properties of estimates from Goodman's model. Fortunately, this same problem does not always affect inferences from the model introduced in this book. That is, because the model fixes all the statistical problems discussed in Chapter 4, biased estimates of ψ do not necessarily generate biased estimates of the quantities of interest. (Recall the terminology introduced in Section 3.5: "aggregation bias" exists when Goodman-type models produce biased inferences because of non-zero discrepancies. Under the model introduced here, "aggregation bias" in the data does not necessarily generate biased estimates of the quantities of interest.)

More specifically, the indeterminacy problem was introduced in Section 3.2. Beginning with the basic accounting identity (Equation 3.1, page 38), that section analyzed what would happen to existing methods if the aggregation process generating the data induced a correlation between β_i^b and X_i or between β_i^w and X_i. The way the correlation was induced was by letting β_i^b and β_i^w vary as separate linear functions of X_i (Equation 3.3, page 42). The reason the model was seen to be indeterminate in that section is because substituting these two linear functions into the accounting identity produced an equation with

Dependent Variable		Coefficient	Standard Error
β_i^b	Constant	.35	.02
	X_i	−.44	.05
β_i^w	Constant	.56	.03
	X_i	−.78	.05

Table 11.1 Evidence of Aggregation Bias in South Carolina. Regressions of β_i^b and β_i^w (fractions of males and females in poverty, which are known in these data) on a constant term and X_i. The large coefficient (and small standard error) on X_i reveals high levels of aggregation bias in these data.

T_i as a quadratic function of X_i, but with one too many parameters than can be estimated under the Goodman framework (see Equation 3.5, page 42).

Thus, in any real empirical example, we would not normally be able to estimate all the necessary parameters using only versions of Goodman's approach. However, because β_i^b and β_i^w are both known in the South Carolina data, we have the opportunity to peek behind the curtain and see what kind of data we are analyzing. Although this information is not used in the estimation procedure, it is worthwhile to look at here in order to gauge how difficult the example is.

Thus, first run the regressions of β_i^b on X_i and β_i^w on X_i, as implied by Equation 3.3 (page 42), for the present data set. The results appear in Table 11.1. If there were no aggregation bias, the coefficient on X_i in each regression would be zero, or at least not statistically distinguishable from zero. In fact, the table indicates that both β_i^b and β_i^w are very strongly related to X_i, which is precisely the condition identified in Chapter 3 for generating aggregation bias.

Substantively, the results in Table 11.1 indicate that the fraction of males in poverty is higher in areas with disproportately large numbers of females. The fraction of females in poverty is even higher in these areas. More specifically, block groups with 10% more females than average have about 4.4% more males in poverty and about 7.8% more females in poverty than the average area. These relationships are undoubtedly real, as the standard errors on both of these coefficients are very small. (Note that these are descriptive relationships and not causal effects.)

Thus, these data constitute a prototypical example of high levels of aggregation bias. Because of this bias, and also because of the very narrow variance over which X_i is observed, the example constitutes an especially difficult ecological inference and thus a useful test case.

Fraction in Poverty	*Estimate*	*Standard Error*
Males	−.20	.03
Females	.50	.02

Table 11.2 Goodman Model Estimates: Poverty by Sex. According to this model, South Carolina has zero males living in poverty (in fact 20% fewer males in poverty than there are males), whereas fully half of all females have family incomes below the poverty level.

Applying Goodman's model, as in Table 11.2, demonstrates the severity of aggregation bias in these data. This table shows some particularly "creative" estimates. In particular, Goodman's model estimates the fraction of males in poverty at *negative* 20%. The model also indicates that half of all females have incomes that fall below the poverty level. South Carolina may be a relatively poor state, but this estimate is surely wrong. Indeed, the method of bounds proves that it is impossible: by applying Equation 5.1 (page 79), the upper bound on the fraction of females in poverty is only 0.29.

Point estimates that are off the mark are not a problem as long as the uncertainty estimates are sufficiently wide. However, as is common in applications of Goodman's model, the uncertainty estimates indicate wild overconfidence. The *true* values of the statewide fraction of males and females in poverty are $B^b = 0.129$ and $B^w = 0.177$, respectively. The estimate for males is more than 6 standard deviations from the smallest value that is even possible, and 11 standard deviations from the true value. Goodman's estimate of the fraction of females in poverty is more than 16 standard deviations from the truth. According to this regression, the odds of observing the result in table 11.2 for females, if Goodman's model is an appropriate model of the world (i.e., if there is no aggregation bias), is 5.68×10^{-59}, or in other words approximately the same odds of tossing one molecule into the Mediterranean sea and, with a single random draw, selecting out the same molecule. It seems safe to conclude that these data contain aggregation bias.

11.3 Fitting the Data

Figure 11.1 gives a tomography plot for the South Carolina poverty by sex data. It also plots contour lines estimated with the ecological inference model. Note that the straight lines all have a slope of roughly −1 since, by Equation 6.27 (page 113) and because $X_i \approx 0.5$, the slope

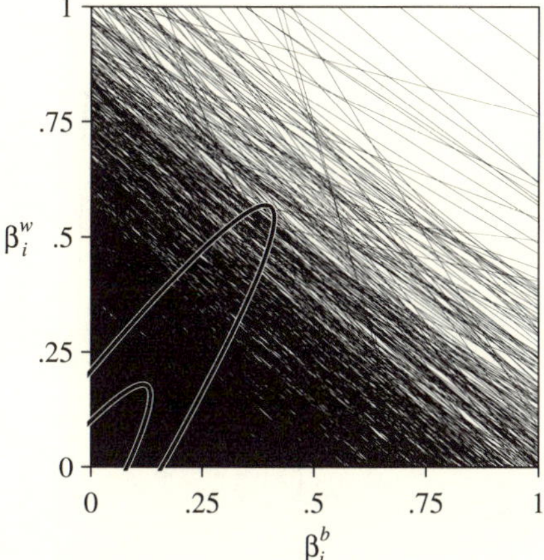

Figure 11.1 South Carolina Tomography Plot, with 50% and 95% Maximum Posterior Contour Ellipses.

of most of these lines is computed as

$$-\frac{X_i}{1-X_i} \approx -\frac{0.5}{1-0.5} = -1$$

The restricted variance for which X_i is observed thus translates into a small range of slopes in this figure. This will cause difficulties because, from a tomography perspective, the data provide little more than one "camera angle" with which to locate the truncated bivariate normal distribution. It seems clear that the mode of the distribution is near the origin (0,0), since the largest collection of lines congregate near there and, because the farther within the unit square we are from that point, the less dense the lines are. In addition, the lines near the origin have somewhat tighter bounds for both parameters, so the mode of the distribution can be readily located.

The tomography problem is ascertaining where on these lines the contours should be drawn. Having a mode in the corner helps in identifying the contours since, despite the camera angle coming from the top left corner (or, equivalently, the bottom right), the entire distribution cannot slide anywhere along the lines with the same posterior probability. For example, imagine taking the contours pictured and, without changing their shape, sliding them along the lines one-half inch toward the top left of the figure. This configuration would have a lower likelihood because the high density of lines near the origin

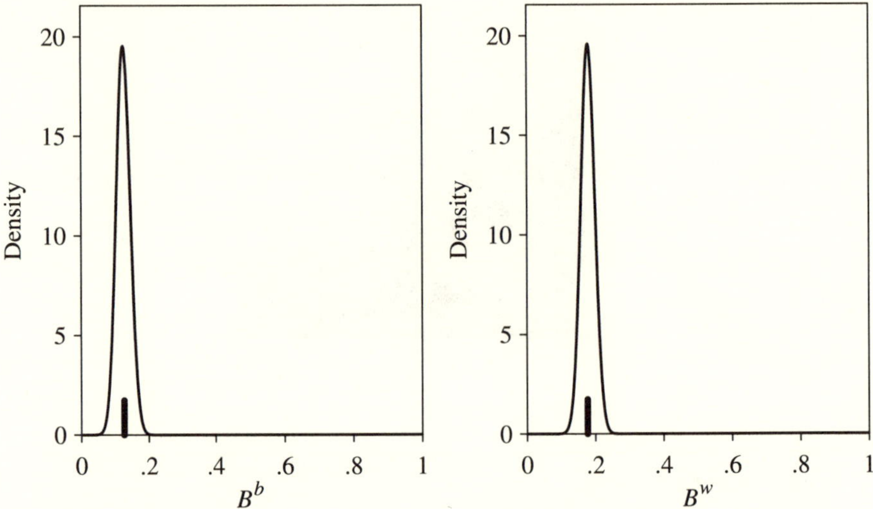

Figure 11.2 Posterior Distributions of the State-Wide Fraction in Poverty by Sex in South Carolina. The graph for Males is on the left and that for females is on the right. The true fractions in poverty, indicated by short vertical lines, are accurately estimated by the posterior distributions.

would be excluded from the contours, or at least not properly centered. Alternatively, if the contours are left centered near the origin, then the only question is whether the distribution, which now implies a high correlation, falling as it does near the 45° line on figure 11.1, could be tilted upward or downward, pivoting on the origin. This is the source of the remaining uncertainty in locating the contour lines, and the result is higher estimation variances for ϕ, despite having over 3,000 observations. Nevertheless, as is apparent, the truncated bivariate normal distribution does appear to fit reasonably well.[1]

11.4 Empirical Results

This section evaluates how the model performs with these data in three ways: by comparing state-wide and block group-level estimates to the true values, and by assessing the accuracy of the uncertainty statements implied by the model.

[1] Indeed, the maximum posterior point estimates of $\hat{\psi} = \{.13, .16, .10, .15, .62\}$ correspond reasonably well to the true values, $\psi = \{.14, .19, .13, .15, .87\}$.

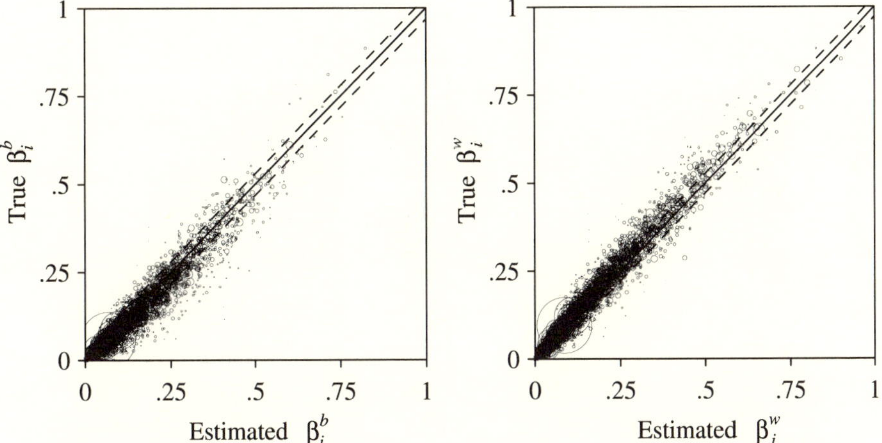

Figure 11.3 Fractions in Poverty for 3,187 South Carolina Block Groups. That the estimated values are very close to the true values (as evidenced by almost all the circles falling on or near the 45° line) is strong confirmation of the model. Note also the narrow predictive confidence intervals, indicated by the dashed lines.

First is a comparison of the true and estimated state-wide results. This provides the most straightforward comparison with Goodman's model. Figure 11.2 portrays the posterior distribution of the state-wide fraction of males in poverty and females in poverty. These distributions are fairly narrow because of the large number of block groups. The true fractions in poverty are portrayed in the graph with short vertical lines. Obviously, the posterior distribution in each case is very narrowly focused around the true values. This is in remarkable contrast to the results from Goodman's model (in Table 11.2).

For the second evaluation of the model, we compute estimates of the fractions of males and females in poverty at the block group level, and compare these to the true levels. No useful information is available from the Goodman model about block group-level quantities of interest except for its (inaccurate) state-wide aggregate assumed constant over the observations.

Figure 11.3 plots the estimated fractions of males and females in poverty by the true poverty levels in each block group. The size of each block group's circle in the graph is proportional to the number of males or females, respectively. Remember that the true values used in this figure were not part of the estimation procedure, and the figure is not a dependent variable being plotted against its fitted values. Each

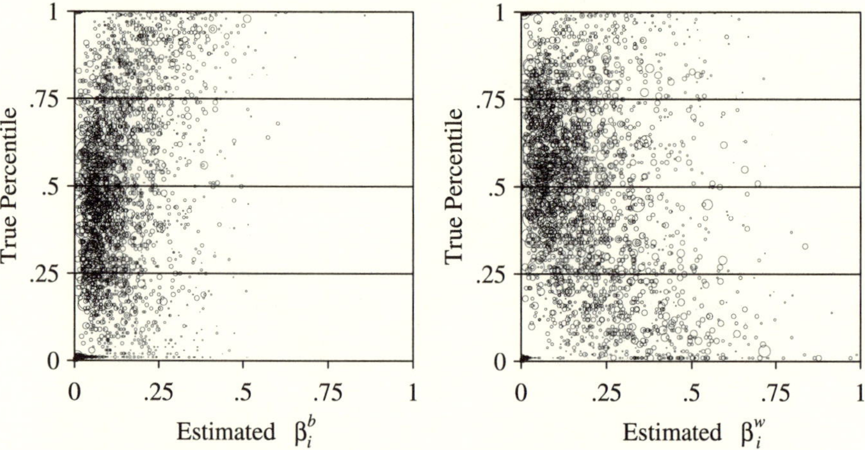

Figure 11.4 Percentiles at Which True Values Fall. The validity of the uncertainty estimates is indicated by the roughly even spread of people in these precincts across the vertical dimension of each graph.

panel in Figure 11.3 includes 3,187 separate out-of-sample evaluations of the model.

If the estimates were all exactly equal to the true values being estimated, all points would fall on the 45° line. In fact, the points all fall very close to the diagonal, indicating remarkably good ecological inferences. For the most part, the deviations from the diagonal line are random. If there is any hint of another pattern it is that the fraction of males in poverty may be slightly underestimated for very high estimated fractions in poverty; the opposite pattern may exist for females. But these are minor patterns relative to the strikingly good fit between the estimated and true values.

Finally, I use the numerous individual block-group analyses to evaluate the uncertainty estimates from the model. This is done in a manner parallel to Figure 10.7. Thus, Figure 11.4 plots the actual percentile of the simulations for each block group at which the true value falls by the estimated mean fraction in poverty for each sex.

The way to understand the figure is to see if roughly the same fraction of circles falls in each of the four areas of the figure. Overall, the pattern supports the reliability of the confidence intervals. There is some tendency for points on the graph for males to be clustered near the bottom and females to cluster near the top. This is another manifestation of the same pattern that was also seen in Figure 11.3, but it again does not appear to be a serious problem. For example, the

50% confidence intervals cover 62% of the true values in block groups for both males and females. Similarly, the true fraction in poverty falls within the 80% confidence interval for 85% of the observations for males and 84% for females. These figures indicate that the confidence intervals are slightly too conservative, but they indicate that even in this data set, chosen for its difficulty in making ecological inferences, the inferences are accurate.

CHAPTER 12

Estimation without Information: Black Registration in Kentucky

THE DATA on poverty status by sex analyzed in Chapter 11 were chosen to illustrate the robustness of the model to the problems of aggregation bias and a restricted range of X_i. This chapter includes an analysis of voter registration by race in Kentucky, a data set with even more serious versions of both problems, and one additional. Because so few blacks live in Kentucky, the range of X_i is restricted near one extreme, making inferences about blacks very hazardous. Indeed, this problem is exacerbated because most blacks are concentrated in a small number of very large counties with even larger numbers of whites. Extrapolating well beyond the range of available data is required in situations such as this with an essential lack of useful information at the aggregate level. These data are useful for demonstrating how the model performs in situations where ecological inferences are nearly impossible.

12.1 THE DATA

Kentucky is a Southern state with only about 8% African Americans of voting age. Moreover, this black population is concentrated in a relatively small fraction of the 118 counties. For example, only 9 counties have over 10% African American populations. The average county is only 3.7% black, even though 6.7% of the population in the state is black. In addition, about 75% of Kentucky's voting-age population was registered in 1988, the year from which these data were collected.

The goal of this analysis is substantively similar to that in Chapter 10. Given the proportion of each county that is black (X_i), the fraction registered (T_i), and the total population (N_i) the goal is to estimate the proportion of blacks who are registered (β_i^b) and the proportion of whites who are registered (β_i^w). Kentucky reports registration by race, so after running the analysis we can evaluate the model by comparing the estimates to the true values.

Because so few blacks are submerged in a sea of white votes—both in the state as a whole and in a few huge counties—it should be difficult for any method of ecological inference to learn much about

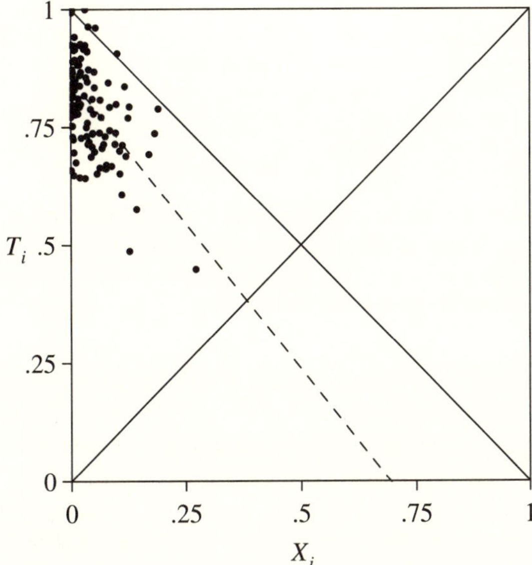

Figure 12.1 A Scattercross Graph of Fraction Black by Fraction Registered. Goodman's regression appears as a dashed line; if extended, it would intersect the right vertical axis at −.38, which is the Goodman estimate of the fraction of blacks registered.

black registration from only aggregate data. In contrast, learning about white registration in Kentucky should be trivially easy: even ignoring the black population should not throw off an estimate of the proportion of whites who are registered by very much.

12.2 Data Problems

Figure 12.1 presents a scattercross graph of X_i by T_i for the Kentucky data. Since the points fall in or near the left triangle, the width of the bounds for almost all the counties is [0,1] for β_i^b, and extremely narrow for β_i^w. (See Figure 5.4, page 88.) Indeed, the average county-level width of the β_i^b bounds is 0.998, whereas for β_i^w it is only 0.071.

Learning the rate at which African Americans register in Kentucky from these aggregate data requires extrapolating from the observed data at the left end of this figure to the far right extreme. Since this is a long distance to traverse, indeed nearly the longest one would have to extrapolate for any ecological inference problem, and because X_i does not vary much even where it is observed, this should generate a very uncertain inference.

Dependent Variable		*Coefficient*	*Standard Error*
β_i^b	Constant	.77	.03
	X_i	−1.47	.52
β_i^w	Constant	.85	.01
	X_i	−1.18	.21

Table 12.1 Evidence of Aggregation Bias in Kentucky. Regressions of β_i^b and β_i^w (proportions of blacks and whites who are registered, which are known in these data) on a constant term and X_i.

Also appearing on Figure 12.1, as a dashed line, is Goodman's regression. The line intersects the right vertical axis (beneath the figure) at −0.38, which is its obviously ridiculous estimate for the fraction of blacks who are registered. The Goodman estimate for the fraction of whites who are registered, 0.85, appears on the graph where the dashed line intersects the left vertical axis. This estimate, although numerically closer to the corresponding true fraction of whites registered, 0.76, is still outside the possible bounds [0.71,0.80]. (The standard errors for Goodman's model are better in this example than in Chapter 11, but they are still unreasonable.)

One of the reasons why Goodman's estimate goes so far off in this example is a high degree of aggregation bias, as reflected in the strong relationship between X_i and both β_i^b and β_i^w. Table 12.1 presents the evidence. A powerful relationship between each parameter and X_i is evident in this regression (even stronger than in the poverty status by sex example in Table 11.1, for example).

12.3 Fitting the Data

The left graph in Figure 12.2 presents a tomography graph for the Kentucky data. Note first that almost all of the lines in the graph are nearly flat, which reflects the large collection of almost homogeneously white counties in this state. As is obvious, the nearly single "camera angle" that this restricted range of X_i produces, devastates our ability to locate where on the lines the β_i^b, β_i^w points are likely to fall. If we had another set of counties (or precincts) with camera angles coming nearly straight down (or up), we would be more easily able to triangulate to an answer.

Locating the mode from the lines, especially in the horizontal direction, of the truncated bivariate normal distribution is difficult. There exists no obvious mode, and no gradation in the density of lines. The

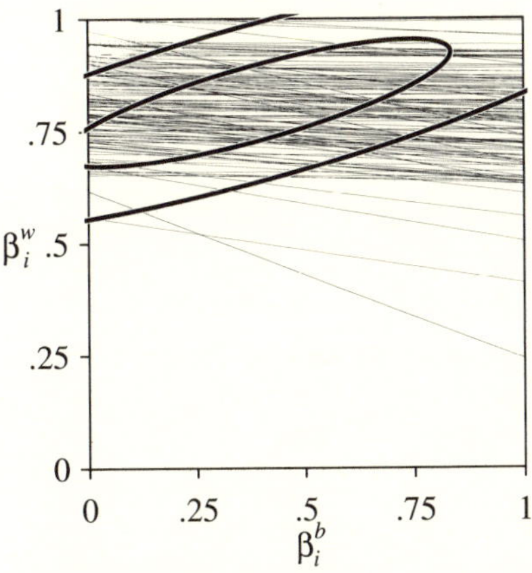

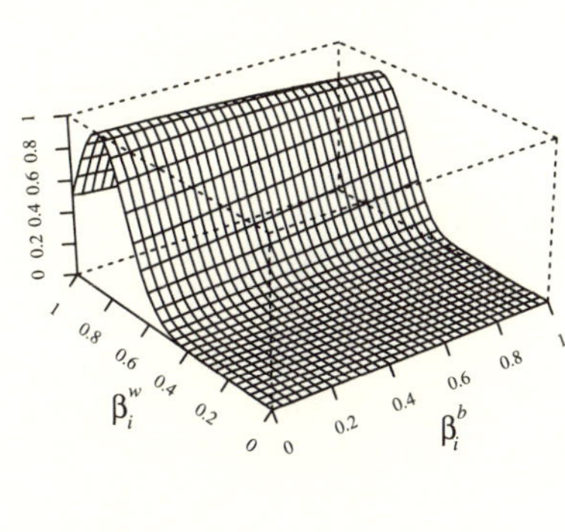

Figure 12.2 Tomography Plot with Parametric Contours and a Nonparametric Surface Plot. The absence of more than approximately one camera angle in the tomography plot (which corresponds to a restricted range of X_i) generates contours with a very large variance in β_i^b and a narrow variance in β_i^w. This pattern is confirmed by the nonparametric surface plot on the right.

β_i^w coordinate of the mode is well determined in these data, but the β_i^b coordinate is not at all well identified. Thus, inferences about any distribution fit to these data should be highly uncertain. Indeed, if the estimated contours implied much certainty in the β_i^b dimension, we should be suspicious that the model is not being fit properly or that it is being heavily influenced by a few outliers, in which case steps should be taken that result in wider contours. Furthermore, because all inferences are conditional on X_i, the limited camera angle only introduces uncertainty; it does not indicate a lack of fit. The nonparametric surface plot on the right in this figure also indicates the absence of a clear mode in the horizontal direction.

The left graph in Figure 12.2 also plots the contour lines representing the posterior mode of the parameters of the truncated bivariate normal distribution. These contours seem to fit the data in that they focus the area of the joint distribution over the observed lines. They also clearly indicate the lack of information about β_i^b and nearly deterministic information about β_i^w through a much larger variance horizontally than vertically. However, when there is no clear mode in the lines, as in this case, and the distribution is fitting merely by not providing much information, we need to verify that this uncertainty is adequately represented in all inferences based on these data. Indeed, there is additional uncertainty owing to the fact that the contours

	Untruncated			*Truncated*	
	Lower	*Upper*		*Lower*	*Upper*
$\breve{\mathfrak{B}}^b$	−.25	.77	$\mathfrak{B}^b$	.32	.55
$\breve{\mathfrak{B}}^w$	.75	.87	$\mathfrak{B}^w$	.74	.82
$\breve{\sigma}_b$	.34	.82	σ_b	.23	.28
$\breve{\sigma}_w$	.11	.18	σ_w	.10	.14
$\breve{\rho}$	.34	.87	ρ	.15	.70

Table 12.2 80% Confidence Intervals for $\breve{\psi}$ and ψ. Contours in Figure 12.2 are drawn based on the center of the intervals for the untruncated parameters.

represent merely the posterior mode of the parameters of the joint distribution, and, given the problems with this data set, the posterior distribution is widely dispersed around this mode. Adding to this uncertainty is the fact that the Kentucky population has been divided in this data set into only 118 geographic units (fewer than half the number used in Chapter 10 and just 4% of the number in the South Carolina data set in Chapter 11). Fortunately, the method incorporates the uncertainty and information both in the posterior distribution of the parameters and in the truncated bivariate normal, conditional on the parameters from this posterior. Understanding these two sources of uncertainty is important in seeing exactly what is being fit to the data and in interpreting the tomography plot with very uncertain contour lines fit to it.

One way to represent the uncertainty in the contour lines would be to draw (say) 100 simulations from the posterior distribution for ψ and to present 100 tomography graphs so it is possible to see how the contour lines vary across the graphs. This is a very good procedure, but not a particularly exciting method of presentation. As an alternative, Table 12.2 gives the 80% posterior confidence interval for each of the five parameters. These confidence intervals were computed by drawing 100 values of the vector ϕ from its posterior distribution (as is required while estimating the model), reparameterizing each into the untruncated scale, and then the truncated scale, sorting the values, and, for each element, taking the 10th and 90th values. For ease of interpretation, these intervals are presented for both the untruncated scale, with which the parameters of the contours are drawn, and the truncated scale, which is of more substantive interest.

Table 12.2 gives a sense of the degree of uncertainty for each of the parameters governing where the contour lines are (the untruncated scale), and how this translates into the somewhat more substantively meaningful values (on the truncated scale). The posterior uncertainty

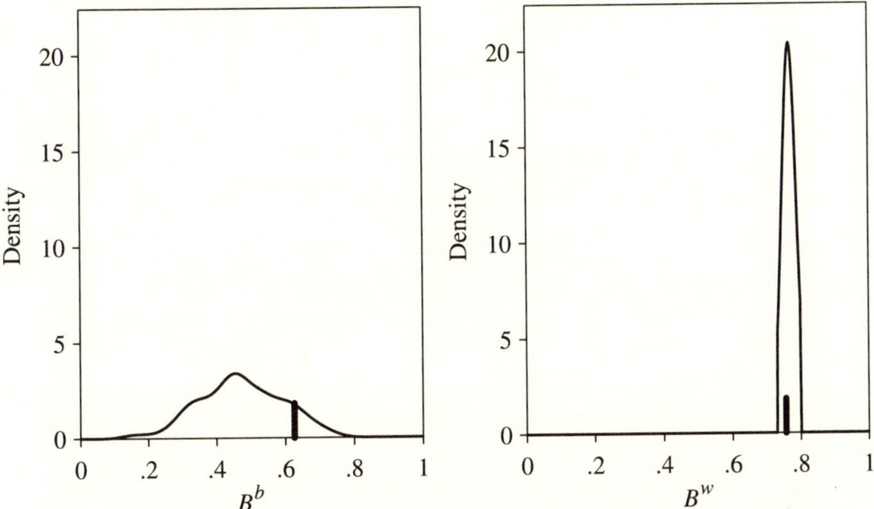

Figure 12.3 Posterior Distributions of the State-wide Fraction of Blacks and Whites Registered. The true fraction registered is represented by short vertical lines.

is very large for $\mathfrak{B}^b$ and ρ, as little information exists in the data with which to estimate these parameters. σ_b also has a fairly wide interval on the untruncated scale, but in this case, this translates into a reasonably narrow range on the ultimate truncated scale.

The results in Table 12.2 can be used to interpret the contours in Figure 12.2. The wide confidence intervals for $\mathfrak{B}^b$ means that the contour lines can be slid horizontally a fair distance with equal likelihood. This means that the ultimate distribution being fit to the data is nearly flat in the horizontal direction. Similarly, the data support a large range of values for the estimated correlation between β_i^b and β_i^w, so the variation in the shape of the distribution also tends to make the ultimate distribution being sampled fairly flat. A lot of information does exist about $\mathfrak{B}^w$, so the mean of contours on the vertical axis will remain near 0.8.

It is easy to see from this exercise that the likelihood function is very uncertain in some of the parameters. There is little evidence that the distribution does not fit, because all inferences are conditional on X_i. However, the absence of much more than one camera angle prevents extracting more certain information from the data. Fortunately, inferences based on these data and these intermediate results, do appear to reflect an appropriately high degree of uncertainty in the data. Since

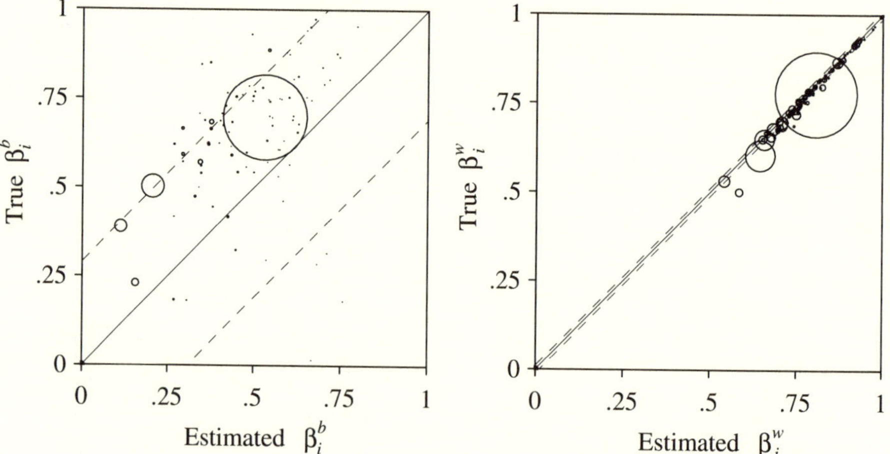

Figure 12.4 Fractions Registered at the County Level. Circles are proportional to the (widely varying) number of blacks or whites in each county. Note how much better the predictions for whites fit than for blacks, and how this was anticipated by the relative widths of the two average confidence intervals (indicated by dashed lines).

the ultimate inferences about the quantities of interest in this problem depend on the entire posterior distribution of $\breve{\psi}$, they should include accurate levels of uncertainty. Nevertheless, in a real application, this type of data set should always elicit great care in drawing ecological inferences.

12.4 Empirical Results

The posterior distributions of the state-wide fraction of blacks and whites registered appear in Figure 12.3. The posterior for whites has a very small variance concentrated around the true value. In contrast, the inference about the state-wide fraction of blacks registered is highly uncertain. The true value falls to the side of the posterior distribution for blacks, but it is satisfactory in the sense that the true value could easily have been generated by this distribution.

How much information does the model give at the more difficult county level? Figure 12.4 provides a first view of the evidence by plotting the posterior mean of the estimated fraction registered by the true fraction registered. The size of the circles is proportional to the number of voting-age blacks, or whites, living in each county. The fit between the estimated and true fractions in the figure for whites is extremely

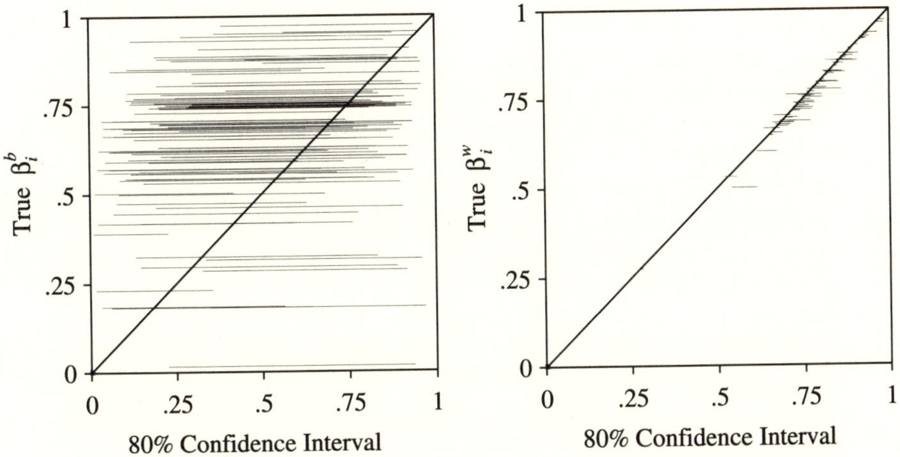

Figure 12.5 80% Posterior Confidence Intervals by True Values. The diagonal line, indicating where the true value lies, is crossed by 73% of the lines (weighted by population) in the figure for blacks (on the left) and 74% for whites (on the right).

tight. For blacks, the distribution is much more uncertain. Most of the circles fall above the 45° line, reflecting again the same pattern as in Figure 12.3, but there does remain a strong correlation between the estimated and true fractions registered. But, more importantly, the test of a model is not its point estimates considered in isolation, especially when the analysis indicates high levels of uncertainty. In the present data, for example, the average 80% confidence intervals (printed as dashed lines in the figure) indicate that inferences based on the model are quite accurate. That is, a researcher would not be mislead by overconfident inferences even in this difficult data set.

To give a better sense of the model's uncertainty estimates, Figure 12.5 presents the 80% confidence interval for the black and white posterior of every county. Each horizontal line in this plot represents one posterior confidence interval for a single county. The vertical position of the line is determined by the true value of the parameter being estimated. When a confidence interval crosses the 45° line, it means that the true value falls within this interval. Obviously, the black posteriors are far more uncertain, as evidenced by the longer lines. More importantly, most of the true values (represented by the diagonal line) fall well within the intervals. More formally, 73% of the people in these observations fall within these 80% confidence intervals for β_i^b and 74%

fall within the same intervals for β_i^w, both which are reasonably close to the theoretically correct 80% mark.

A method that would give the exact individual-level answer from aggregate data every time regardless of the problems in the data would be preferable, but that seems impossible in these data, at least without considering the generalized version of the model. This data set has massive levels of aggregation bias, extreme restrictions in the variation of X_i, most blacks submerged in large counties with even more whites, a relatively small number of geographic units, and a problem that requires nearly the largest possible extrapolation, from observed data at one extreme of X_i to the required inferences at the other extreme, than can exist for an ecological inference problem. Existing methods give impossible results in these data. Yet, in spite of all this, the method is able to generate trustworthy inferences about the quantities of interest.

CHAPTER 13

Classic Ecological Inferences

THIS CHAPTER evaluates the model as applied to classic problems in the field of ecological inference. Section 13.1 analyzes a voter transition study, and Section 13.2 analyzes literacy by race as in Robinson's (1950) original study.

13.1 VOTER TRANSITIONS

Verifying ecological inferences about voter transitions at the subnational level is not usually possible. Surveys are available at the national level, but almost never for every individual areal unit of analysis, such as precincts or districts. We know from national surveys that voters are creatures of habit and tend to stick loyally to their political party in successive elections rather than defecting to the opposition. However, even the most cursory study of changes in election results reveals enormous regional variations. As such, we have every reason to suspect that these national averages do not apply consistently across the entire political system.

Although the secret ballot means that individual votes are unavailable, attendance at the polls is sometimes known and can thus be used to verify ecological inference methods. This is an especially important issue in American politics, where scholars have long sought to explain the pattern in and consequences of the massive differences in voter turnout from presidential election years to off-year congressional contests, including possibly the predictable loss of seats in the House of Representatives by members of the president's party.

13.1.1 Data

Fulton County in Georgia provides a uniquely valuable data set to study voter transitions. This county includes the city of Atlanta and, in 1994, 295,120 registered people in 289 precincts. The county keeps a remarkable data set with every currently registered voter, along with information about whether they voted in each of the last 20 elections. (The data set also includes every registered person's race, sex, age, which party's primary they voted in, along with their name, full address, and social security number.)

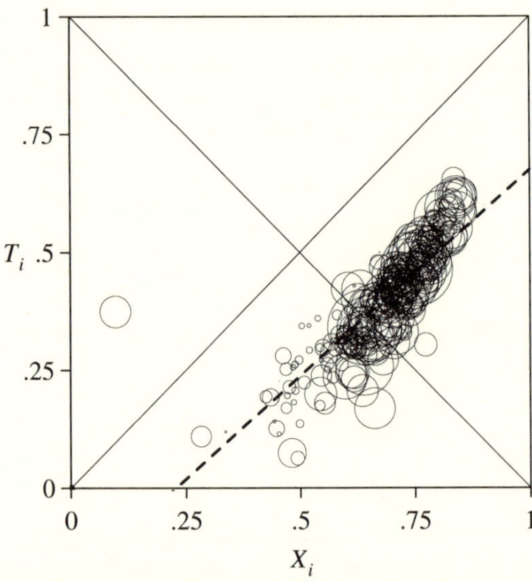

Figure 13.1 Fulton County Voter Transitions. This scattercross graph plots voter turnout among those registered in 1992 (X_i) by turnout in 1994 (T_i) for 289 precincts, with circle size proportional to the number of registered voters. The dashed line represents Goodman's regression; if extended, it would cross the left vertical axis at -0.2, which gives an impossible estimate for the fraction of 1992 nonvoters who show up at the polls in 1994.

This section includes a study of voter turnout transitions from presidential year 1992 to congressional year 1994 in Fulton county's precincts. The aggregate data include the fraction voting in 1992 (X_i), the fraction voting in 1994 (T_i), and the number of people in each precinct (N_i). With these aggregate data, it is possible to *estimate* the proportion of voters in 1992 who vote in 1994 (β_i^b) and the proportion of nonvoters in 1992 who vote in 1994 (β_i^w). Of course, the advantage of these data is that they include the true fractions of voter-voters and nonvoter-voters to validate to these estimates.[1]

The basic data are presented in a scattercross graph in Figure 13.1. This figure plots X_i by T_i, with each circle representing one precinct with size proportional to the precinct's population. As expected, voter turnout in 1994 is closely related to turnout in 1992: precincts with high turnout in one election year are the same precincts with high turnout in the next election. In addition, all but one of the precincts have lower turnout in the congressional election year than in the pre-

[1] The fraction of 1992 voters who do not vote in 1994 is $1 - \beta_i^b$, and the fraction of 1992 nonvoters who stay away from the polls in 1994 is $1 - \beta_i^w$.

ceding presidential election. Because a large fraction of points fall in the right triangle, the β_i^b quantities of interest, the fraction of 1992 voters who vote again, will have relatively narrow bounds, whereas most values of β_i^w will have very wide bounds.

Goodman's regression line is superimposed on this graph as a dashed line fit to the circles. Although this regression fits the data very well, it does not produce accurate estimates of the quantities of interest. Indeed, neither estimate is even logically possible. The Goodman estimate of B^b, the county-wide fraction of voters who vote again, can be read off the figure where the dashed line intersects the right vertical axes. This figure, 0.67, is larger than the upper bound on the aggregate parameter of 0.59. The Goodman estimate of B^w, -0.2, is where the dashed line would intersect the left vertical axis if extended. These results suggest impossible conclusions.

To provide a sense of the nature of aggregation bias in these data—both the true levels and those that can be ascertained from the aggregate data—Figure 13.2 plots X_i by the true β_i^b and, separately, by the true β_i^w. The dots are the true coordinates and the dashed line is a regression fit to these coordinates. Any nonzero slope denotes aggregation bias. The slope of the dashed lines, and hence the degree of aggregation bias in these data, is steeper for β_i^b but unambiguously strong for both quantities of interest.

Figure 13.2 also plots X_i by the bounds on the parameters, calculated from the aggregate data. For each precinct, a vertical line represents these bounds in the format of all the *possible* values of β_i^b, for the left graph, and β_i^w for the right graph, based on X_i and T_i (and Equations 5.1, page 79). That is, even if we did not know the true values of β_i^b and β_i^w for these data, we would still be able to plot these vertical lines to get a sense of the degree of aggregation bias. This is another way of expressing the fact that by including the precinct-level bounds, the model is able to control for some of the information about these relationships.

Even by ignoring the points (and the dashed line fit to them), the vertical lines make relatively clear that X_i and both parameters are positively related: *aggregation bias is confirmed on the basis of aggregate data alone.* In particular, a straight flat line cannot be drawn through all the parameter bounds in the left graph. But the position of the true points within the bounds should be a warning about using only the bounds, or the naive first instinct many have of using the middle of the bounds as an estimate: The true points in both figures fall near the extreme ends of their respective bounds. This is not something that we would have any idea about from looking at individual precincts in isolation. Only by borrowing strength via the statistical model will

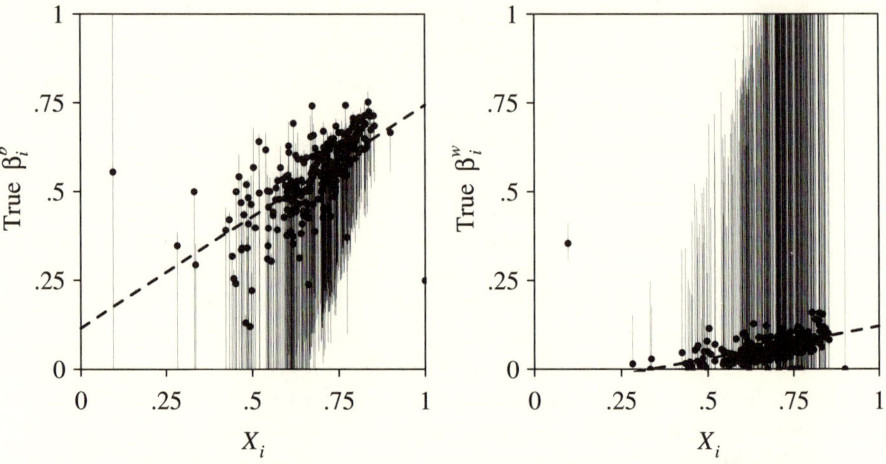

Figure 13.2 Aggregation Bias in Fulton County Data. The strong relationship between β_i^b (the fraction of voters who vote in the next election) and X_i (turnout in 1992) and between β_i^w (the fraction of nonvoters who vote again) and X_i, as indicated by the points, demonstrates the severe aggregation bias in these data. The bounds on the parameters (indicated by the vertical lines) demonstrate that some of the relationship between the β_i's and X_i can be ascertained from the aggregate data alone. However, because the true points fall near one extreme, the figure demonstrates that the bounds should not be used in isolation to make inferences.

it be possible to locate the position of the true points appropriately within the bounds.

13.1.2 Estimates

Figure 13.3 gives a tomography plot with maximum posterior contours computed from these aggregate data. The limited range into which most values of X_i fall in these data (as seen in Figure 13.1) translates into a small range of "camera angles" for this plot. The lines are not all parallel, but instead appear to be "emanating" in a fan shape from the same general vicinity beneath the unit square. This area was identified by the estimation procedure as the mode of the truncated bivariate normal distribution. The fit therefore appears to be excellent, with most of the coordinates of β_i^b, β_i^w indicating that about half of 1992 voters but only a tiny fraction of nonvoters turned out again in 1994. This overall pattern is consistent with our knowledge of national level trends, and it therefore gives us confidence in moving on to interpret the precinct-level results.

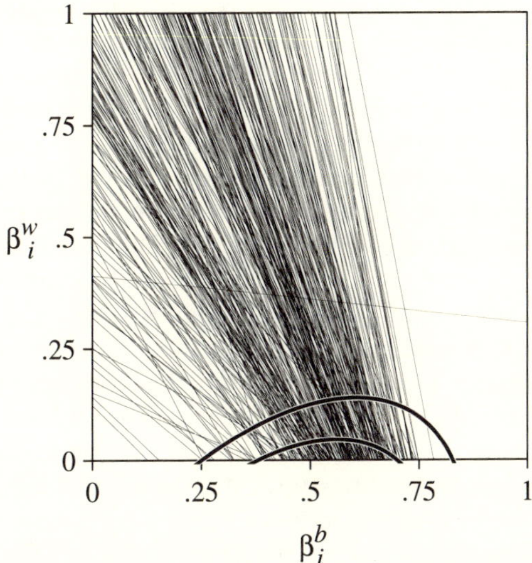

Figure 13.3 Fulton County Tomography Plot with Maximum Posterior Contours. The tomography lines all appear to be "emanating" from near a point beneath the plot, where the likelihood procedure found the mode of the truncated bivariate normal.

Data sets like these with such a narrow range of X_i values should always be treated with caution, since it is possible that the true points could lie near the other end of each of the tomography lines, and thus render inferences invalid.

The best approach to any statistical problem is always to get better data, as complicated statistical models are almost always dominated by data solutions. (For example, if we knew the individual-level data with certainty, ecological inference would not be a problem.) In the present situation, if no survey data were available, it would be best to collect ecological data from additional precincts, presumably from neighboring counties, so that we could expand the range in which X_i is observed. Precincts with less than half of the registered population turning out to vote for president in 1992 would be especially helpful, so we should probably first collect data from poor or uneducated counties near Fulton. These additional data would appear in the tomography plot as relatively flat lines (like the one, isolated, and probably outlier precinct observed). If these flat lines were mostly near the bottom of the graph, we would gain considerable confidence in the location of the mode of the truncated bivariate normal.

Collecting new data is almost always an option, especially if you care about the substantive conclusions of the research, but suppose this were a historical study and there were no other data. It thus pays to consider what we would need to assume about the world in order for the tomography plot in Figure 13.3 to mislead us. For example, if the true coordinates were near the top of the lines, there would no longer be a single mode, because the tomography lines fan out in somewhat different directions. This also means that the parameters' placements would be very strongly correlated with X_i, since steeper lines would have larger values of β_i^b. The latter is not only plausible; it is true, as Figure 13.2 demonstrates (of course, we would not normally be so certain about this correlation with access to only aggregate data). It would be considerably less plausible to claim that the true distribution would map the odd shape indicated by the intersection of the lines with the upper and left edges of the tomography plot. Instead, decades of survey research should give us moderately strong priors that the mode would be roughly where it is.[2] In addition, if the data have this type of bias, we would still get fairly good estimates of many values of β_i^b because of their relatively narrow bounds (which can be seen in the tomography plot by projecting the lines downward onto the horizontal axis). Although most values of β_i^w would be more uncertain, those for which we do have narrow bounds all indicate small values, consistent with the mode identified. Thus, from the aggregate data, and additional substantive knowledge, it seems quite reasonable to conclude that the fit of this first stage of the model is quite good.

The true county-wide aggregates are $B^b = 0.56$ and $B^w = 0.063$. The estimates from the model closely parallel these true values at $\hat{B}^b = 0.57$ and $\hat{B}^w = 0.044$, each with standard errors of about 0.01.

The more detailed comparisons between the estimated and true precinct-level values of β_i^b and β_i^w appear in Figure 13.4. The fit is obviously extremely tight for both sets of quantities of interest. The average 80% confidence intervals in each graph, represented as dashed lines, are also narrow, which indicates that we would have some sense of how good the fit would be from aggregate data alone. The actual confidence intervals for each are slightly larger than they need to be, as the 80% confidence intervals cover 93% of the true points for β_i^b and 90% of the true points for β_i^w.

[2] These priors should probably be included in the estimation by changing the distributions specified in Section 7.4, as described in Section 14.2. I have not taken this step here.

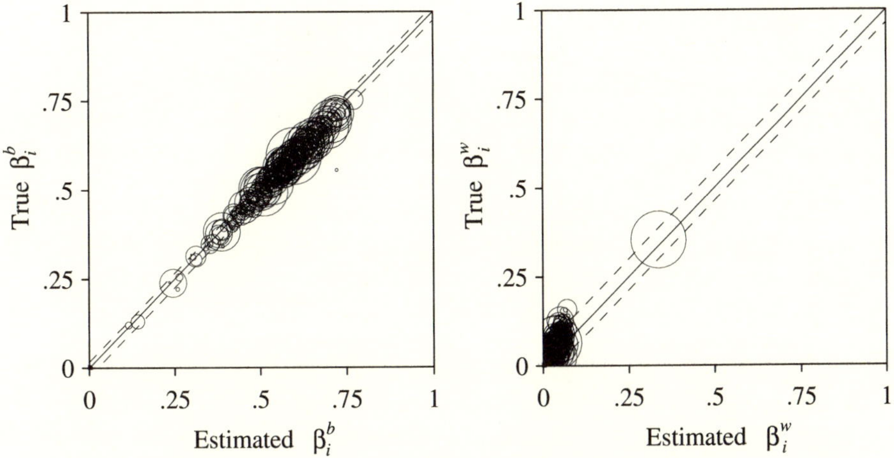

Figure 13.4 Comparing Voter Transition Rate Estimates with the Truth in Fulton County. This figure shows the fraction of 1992 voters who vote again in 1994 (for the graph on the left) and the fraction of 1992 nonvoters who vote in 1994 (for the right graph). Each precinct is represented by a circle with size proportional to population. Dashed lines represent 80% confidence intervals.

13.2 Black Literacy in 1910

William Robinson (1950) first introduced the idea of using census data to verify models of ecological inference, and he did so with a study of black literacy. Robinson's empirical demonstration was based on 9 observations of literacy rates from U.S. regions, and the 49 cases representing states. Because these data are aggregated to an unnecessarily high degree and since very little information remains at the aggregate level, he also made clear that any serious analysis of the substantive questions he raised would require more detailed data, such as at the county or precinct level (Robinson, 1950: 353). Thus, to study this question, I coded county-level data from the paper records of the 1910 census. This included the proportion of each county's residents over 10 years of age who are black (X_i), the proportion of those who can read (T_i), and the population over 10 (N_i). These aggregate data are then used to estimate the proportions of blacks (β_i^b) and whites (β_i^w) who are literate.[3]

[3] My brief analysis of some of Robinson's smaller original data sets clearly indicates the lack of available information with which to make ecological inferences. Because all the methodological issues relevant to this analysis have already arisen in previous chapters (primarily Chapter 12), I focus on the county-level results for the remainder of this section.

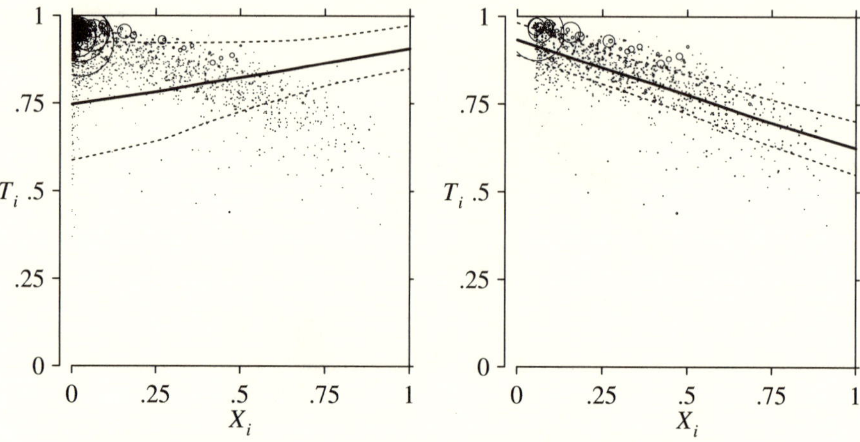

Figure 13.5 Alternative Fits to Literacy by Race Data. The graph on the left includes expected values and 80% confidence intervals that do not fit the 2,933 counties. The graph on the right clearly does fit its data due to the exclusion of counties with less than 5% black population.

The X_i by T_i graph on the left of Figure 13.5 provides the maximum likelihood fit to the 2,933 counties in this data set. The (solid) expected value line is surrounded by (dashed) 80% confidence intervals. The model clearly does not fit these data, as the errors around the expected value portray unambiguous nonrandom patterns for different values of X_i. That is, just as in least squares regression, only the vertical deviations from the expected value line for given values of X_i are relevant for assessing fit. The nonrandom patterns can be seen especially in the massively differing conditional distributions of points: for small values of X_i, many of the points are above the expected value line, whereas for large values of X_i almost all the points are below the line.

The graph as a whole conveys two general patterns, and almost certainly two different data generation processes. Over most of the graph is a downwardly sloping linear trend of points. The other pattern is at the left of the graph, for counties whose populations are less than about 5% black, where the points are spread vertically from below half to 100% literate. The model produces an uncomfortable average of these two patterns of data points. Overall, the expected value line is increasing, even though in most of the graph the conditional averages of the points are clearly dropping. In addition, the confidence intervals at the left vertical axis open up to fit the wide spread of T_i, even

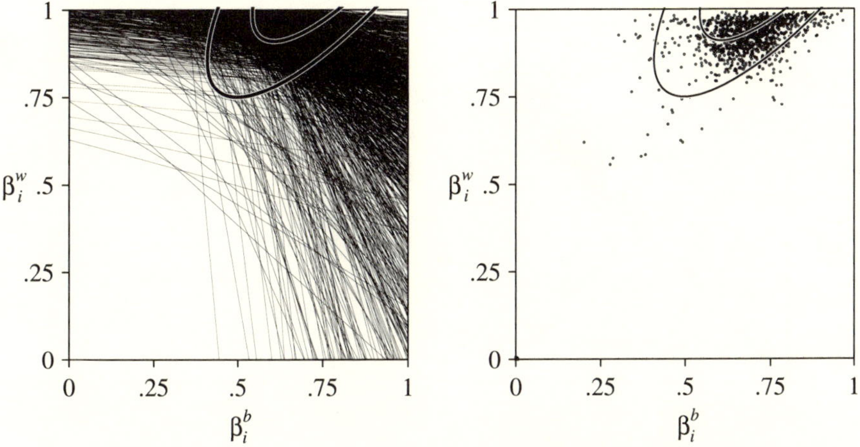

Figure 13.6 Black Literacy Tomography Plot and True Points. The left graph is the tomography plot with maximum likelihood contours for the 1910 literacy by race data set. The right graph gives the true β_i^b, β_i^w points, and reproduces the same contours (fit using only aggregate data). Note how most of the distribution of true points is captured by the contour lines.

though for all other values of X_i a much narrower confidence interval is clearly called for. Substantively, the problem appears to be that different processes generate literacy rates in overwhelmingly white counties than in other areas of the country.

There are several ways of remedying this lack of fit. One possibility is to include a covariate for Z_i^w that is 0 if $X_i < 0.05$ and 1 otherwise. Although this would take care of the problem with differing means, σ_w also appears to differ dramatically between the two parts of the graph. Thus, instead of expanding the model to also let σ_w vary as a function of covariates, I opt for the conservative approach of dropping those observations with fewer than 5% blacks. This eliminates about two-thirds of the counties, but only about 10% of blacks nationwide. In addition, white literacy in these counties can be estimated very easily, if desired, given the tight bounds on β_i^w for the excluded observations.

Because the model is conditional on X_i, deleting observations as a function of X_i does not introduce selection bias, but it does dramatically improve the fit of the model to the data. The graph on the right of Figure 13.5 demonstrates this by displaying the expected values and confidence intervals fit to this sample of counties. For any value of X_i, the distribution of points around the expected value line

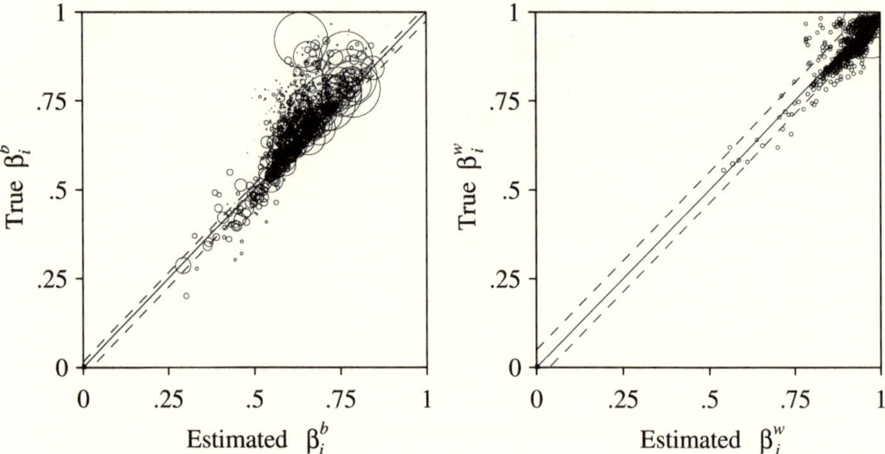

Figure 13.7 Comparing Estimates to the County-Level Truth in Literacy by Race Data. This figure shows the good fit between the county estimates and true values of the proportion of blacks (on the left) and whites (on the right) who are literate. Circles within each figure are proportional to county population, with the exception of a lower bound for the circle size so that all counties are visible.

is approximately the same, and the pattern is picked up well by the model.[4]

The graph on the left of Figure 13.6 portrays the tomography plot for the selected sample of counties. This portrayal of the data also appears to indicate a reasonably good fit. The mode of the truncated bivariate normal is located where the tomography lines are crossing (and thus appear to be "emanating" from). The other way to think about tomography graphs is first to consider the slopes of the lines (since the model is conditional on X_i) and then to see where lines with specific slopes cross the 45° line. For example, the lines with relatively flat slopes (counties with small fractions of blacks) are all near the top of the graph, indicating high values of β_i^w, most crossing where the contours were estimated. The steeper lines are also consistent with a

[4] The full data set in Figure 13.5 is not fit well by the model, but the ultimate estimates from this poor fit are still close to the true values. In some ways, the results are even better than for the selected sample. (Goodman's estimates are about 10 percentage points off for the aggregate fraction of blacks who are literate in the full sample and 6 percentage points off in the selected sample.) Because a researcher would not have access to this information in the usual case in which only aggregate data were known, the selected sample is used for the remainder of this section.

good fit, as they too are much more likely to pass through where the contours were estimated.

One way to evaluate these results is by comparing this tomography plot with the bivariate scatter plot of the true values of β_i^b by β_i^w. Figure 13.6 also gives this scatter plot, at the right, along with the contour lines estimated using only the aggregate data. (Each line in the tomography plot is associated with one true point in the scatter plot.) The contours are intended to capture most of the true points in the scatter plot, and a comparison of the two graphs indicates that the method does a reasonably good job. There is some evidence that the contours are too wide on the left and perhaps slightly too small on the right, but overall the actual fit is quite good.

Finally, the results can be evaluated with the same procedure as for all the other examples by plotting the county-level estimates by their true values. Figure 13.7 gives these results. The fit between the estimated and true values are not as tight as in some examples, and there is some tendency to overestimate the true values of β_i^w. There is also a group of counties with the highest true values of β_i^b that are underestimated by this procedure. Nevertheless, the overall fit between the estimates and the truth is quite good.

PART V

Generalizations and Concluding Suggestions

Chapter 14 generalizes the model to nonecological aggregation problems, such as when the object of inference is a rate or causal effect rather than the cell of a cross-tabulation, as is common in economics, or when aggregate and survey data are used together to make inferences, a common concern in statistics. This chapter also provides a solution to the geographer's "modifiable aggregate unit problem." Chapter 15 discusses generalizations of the basic model to large tables with many categories and multidimensional designs.

Chapter 16 concludes with a checklist of items to consider when applying the methods described in this book to real data sets.

CHAPTER 14

Non-Ecological Aggregation Problems

IN THIS CHAPTER, I analyze problems of aggregation and information loss that are not properly classified as ecological inferences. The ecological inference problem arises when a researcher tries to infer from the marginals of a set of cross-tabulations from aggregate units such as precincts to the cell entries for each. Thus, the individual-level variables making up the cross-tabulations are first, organized into a set of fixed aggregate units, second, unobserved, and third, discrete. The three primary sections in this chapter discuss deviations from each of the three parts of this traditional definition of ecological inference.

Section 14.1 studies the geographer's "modifiable areal unit problem," which is the problem that occurs if inferences change when the aggregate units, such as precinct boundary lines, change. Section 14.2 contributes to the related problem analyzed in statistics of how to improve ecological inferences if limited survey data are used to compliment available aggregate information. And Section 14.3 discusses the corresponding aggregation problem more commonly analyzed in econometrics by generalizing the basic model in order to allow inferences about relationships among individual-level variables that are continuous, such as rates and causal effects.

14.1 THE GEOGRAPHER'S MODIFIABLE AREAL UNIT PROBLEM

The "modifiable areal unit problem" (or MAUP) has been considered a serious problem in geography and related fields for about four and a half decades, since Yule and Kendall (1950) described it in their popular text. Openshaw (1984: 4) gives a modern definition of the MAUP as follows:

> Whereas census data are collected for essentially non-modifiable entities (people, households) they are reported for arbitrary and modifiable areal units (enumeration districts, wards, local authorities). The principal criteria used in the definition of these units are the operational requirements of the census, local political considerations, and government administration. As a result none of these census areas have any intrinsic geographical meaning. Yet it is possible, indeed very likely, that the results of any subsequent analyses depend on these definitions. If the areal units or zones are arbitrary and modifiable, then the value of any work based upon them must be

in some doubt and may not possess any validity independent of the units which are being studied.

14.1.1 *The Problem with the Problem*

Despite the clarity with which the MAUP seems to be stated, most statements have propagated a fundamental confusion between the definition of theoretical quantities of interest and the estimates that result in practice. Geographers and statisticians have studied the MAUP by computing a statistic on areal data aggregated to different levels, or in different ways, and watching the results vary wildly in sign and magnitude (e.g., see Openshaw, 1979, 1984; Steinnes, 1980; Fotheringham and Wong, 1991). This basic research design has been applied to many different areal distributions, some with real data and some artificially generated, and for a variety of statistics such as correlations or regression coefficients. The conclusions of these studies are almost always extreme pessimism that lead the authors to question the veracity of all empirical analyses based on aggregated geographic data. From this perspective, it certainly does seem that there is a serious problem. After all, there is nothing special about most precinct boundary lines. In many cases they are set up for administrative convenience, which does not give researchers any reason to choose the value of the correlation that results from the aggregation we observe rather than that from any of the possible reaggregations. Moreover, the very concept of areal units with "intrinsic geographical meaning," occasionally proposed in geography, is not at all obvious or necessarily useful (cf. Hatt, 1946; Isard, 1956; Duncan et al., 1961: 98ff). Indeed, the more meaningful boundary lines that represent the outcomes of formal redistricting struggles can induce far worse biases (see also Section 6.2.5).

The search for a solution to the MAUP problem has always been empirical: scholars have tried to identify a data set, or type of substantive problem, for which modifiable areal units do not dramatically affect calculated statistics. The hope has been that, through a detailed understanding of local context and the nature of zoning schemes, researchers might be able to identify types of geographical distributions or configurations of areal units for which we need not worry about the problem. Findings such as these would enable methodologists to provide some guidance to applied researchers, or at least some indications as to when the MAUP is a serious problem. The empirical goal has been to find a problem for which reaggregations do not wreak havoc on standard descriptive statistics.

The problem with this approach in the literature is that *the modifiable areal unit problem is not an empirical problem; it is a theoretical problem.* Moreover, as a theoretical problem, it is usually not difficult to solve. Unfortunately, the statistics used to study these issues have not been *aggregation-invariant* (or "scale-invariant"). If a researcher wishes to have statistics that are invariant to the areal units chosen, then there is no reason to choose correlation coefficients, which depend heavily on the definition of available areal units (Tobler, 1990; King, 1996). Solving the MAUP only requires identifying or developing statistics that are invariant to the level of aggregation.

To take an extremely simple example, suppose we wished to know the number of people in a district, but data were available only at the level of precincts within the district. To compute this quantity of interest, we could use the following procedure: first, count the number of people in each of the precincts and, second, add the numbers. This statistic is aggregation invariant: even if the precinct boundary lines were changed, or the number of precincts were increased or decreased, the total number of people counted would not change. The units are modifiable, but this aggregation-invariant statistic does not budge even when they are modified.

Before discussing this problem in the context of ecological inference, consider two other statistics that are more politically meaningful than the simple example of district population, but still relatively straightforward: The (unweighted) Democratic proportion of the vote averaged over districts in U.S. House elections,

$$\mathcal{V} = \frac{1}{p}\sum_{i=1}^{p} V_i$$

and the nation-wide vote for the Democrats for the House, which is a weighted average:

$$\bar{V} = \frac{\sum_{i=1}^{p} N_i V_i}{N}$$

Thus, we obtain $\mathcal{V}$ by computing the Democratic proportion of the two-party vote in each House district and averaging them. To compute $\bar{V}$, we either take the weighted average or merely add up the number of people who vote for the Democratic candidate in all the states and divide by the number of votes cast in all House elections that year. Note that $\mathcal{V} \neq \bar{V}$.

If we imagine for a moment that people do not change their votes as a function of where the district lines are drawn (a false assumption, incidentally; see Gelman and King, 1994a, b), then $\bar{V}$ is invariant to aggregation but $\bar{\mathcal{V}}$ is not. This means that $\bar{V}$ is not subject to the modifiable areal unit problem, but $\bar{\mathcal{V}}$ is. Does this mean that we should always use $\bar{V}$? Certainly not. $\bar{V}$ ignores the effects of the district lines in which elections really take place. If we wish to know the effects of these districts, then we should not be looking for statistics that are invariant to precisely the phenomenon we wish to study. (Similarly, having a bathroom scale that is invariant to weight is useful for some purposes, but accuracy is not one of them.) In fact, the difference between $\bar{\mathcal{V}}$ and $\bar{V}$ is one measure of the consequences of districting (or redistricting) on the allocation of legislative seats to political parties.

Thus, the modifiable areal unit problem is not an empirical problem. Rather, it is a theoretical requirement of statistics that is appropriate in some, but not all, circumstances. Deriving statistics invariant to aggregation for the relationships between variables, corresponding to correlation or regression coefficients, may be more difficult, but it is a theoretical difficulty.

14.1.2 *Ecological Inference as a Solution to the Modifiable Areal Unit Problem*

At the extreme, if ecological inferences are wholly successful, then the ecological inference problem is resolved and all individual-level data are known with certainty. In this situation, estimates can be invariant to aggregation if desired, just as available survey data aggregated by the analyst can be invariant to aggregation or not invariant, depending on the theoretical quantity of interest. For example, if β_i^b and β_i^w were known, then the district-wide quantities of interest B^b and B^w would be invariant to the precinct boundaries. In contrast, $\mathfrak{B}^b$ and $\mathfrak{B}^w$, the unweighted averages estimated by techniques such as Goodman's regression, depend heavily on the definitions of the areal units.

In the more usual case, when estimates of B^b and B^w are unknown, inferences will depend on the precinct boundary lines, but only in individual samples, not in expectation or in asymptotic comparisons. Thus, for all practical purposes, good estimates of the quantities of interest—anchored as they are to the nonmodifiable individual-level units—will not be affected by the modifiable areal unit problem. As such, a solution to the ecological inference problem, in combination with an aggregation-invariant theoretical quantity of interest, is a solution to the MAUP.

To explain these points more specifically, I now demonstrate that the model proposed here is almost, although not completely, invariant to the modification of the areal units analyzed, so long as this modification does not induce new aggregation biases. (If modifying the areal units does induce aggregation bias, in the same way that the original precinct boundaries could induce bias, then either the procedure will be robust to this violation or the technique may need to be modified as per the extensions in Chapter 9.) The basic story is that, according to the model, four of the five features that lead to estimates of the precinct-level parameters are aggregation-invariant. Only the correlation between β_i^b and β_i^w changes as units are modified.

The way to study the effect of the MAUP on the proposed model is to focus on the conditional distribution, $P(T_i|X_i)$. An important idea behind conditional distributions is exchangeability, which means in this case that any two random variables T_i and $T_{i'}$ have the same distribution (given the parameters) if $X_i = X_{i'}$ and thus the indices i and i' can be exchanged without any loss of information. That is, for a given set of parameters, all probabilistic differences between two distributions can be traced to X_i. Because the basic distributions are all built from the normal in this model, two conditional probability distributions are identical if their conditional expected values and conditional variances are each identical. In the model proposed here, modifying areal units (without inducing aggregation bias) causes no changes in the conditional expected value, and a small change in the conditional variance.

To explain this result intuitively, consider a hypothetical example with three precincts. In order to avoid complications caused by the Manhattan Effect (see page 32), suppose that Precincts 1 and 2 each has the same number of voting-age people and Precinct 3 has twice that number: $N_1 = N_2 = N_3/2$. Suppose further that Precinct 1 is all white ($X_1 = 0$), Precinct 2 is all black ($X_2 = 1$), and the racial composition of Precinct 3 is evenly divided ($X_3 = 0.5$). Thus, for there to be no MAUP, the distribution of $T_i|X_i$ in Precinct 3 must have the identical distribution to the aggregation of the first two.

Now consider what happens if we aggregate Precincts 1 and 2, and compare this aggregate to Precinct 3, first for the conditional means, and then for the conditional variances. Under the model, the two expected values are as follows:

$$E(T_3|X_3 = 0.5) = \frac{\mathfrak{B}^b + \mathfrak{B}^w}{2}$$

$$E\left(\frac{T_1 + T_2}{2}\,\middle|\,\frac{X_1 + X_2}{2} = 0.5\right) = \frac{\mathfrak{B}^b + \mathfrak{B}^w}{2}$$

Because these conditional expected values are identical, the modifiable areal unit problem causes no difficulties with this main feature of the model.

Following a parallel procedure, the conditional variances for Precinct 3 and the aggregation of Precincts 1 and 2 are:

$$V(T_3|X_3 = 0.5) = \frac{\sigma_b^2 + \sigma_w^2}{4} + \frac{\rho\sigma_b\sigma_w}{2} \tag{14.1}$$

$$V\left(\frac{T_1 + T_2}{2}\middle|\frac{X_1 + X_2}{2} = 0.5\right) = \frac{\sigma_b^2 + \sigma_w^2}{4} \tag{14.2}$$

Thus, these two conditional variances differ, despite the fact that the racial populations (X_i) are identical. This is evidence that the definitions of the quantities of interest are not entirely invariant to the aggregation of the areal units.

Consider now the causes and consequences of this non-aggregation-invariant feature of the model from three perspectives. First, because Equation 14.2 and the first term in Equation 14.1 are identical, the difference between the two expressions is $\rho\sigma_b\sigma_w/2$. Because this difference is composed of three parameters, each less than one ($0 < \sigma_b < 1$, $0 < \sigma_w < 1$, and $-1 < \rho < 1$), half of their product will be reasonably small in most situations. This implies that inferences from the model will not be very sensitive to areal units that are modified.

Second, the model offered here is precisely invariant to aggregation if $\rho = 0$. Although we cannot expect this to occur regularly, we do know that inferences about the quantities of interest do not depend heavily on the value of ρ (see Section 6.2.3), and that spatial autocorrelation does not have much negative effect on inferences from the model (see Section 9.1.3). This insensitivity of model estimates to correlations both *within* and *between* observations, and the near aggregation-invariance of the conditional variance functions, give sufficient reason to conclude that the model is, in practice, nearly invariant to aggregation.

Finally, the model could be altered so that it is fully invariant to aggregation even without restricting $\rho = 0$. The basic problem indicated by this dependence is that the model allows the correlation of β_i^b and β_i^w within each precinct to be ρ but restricts correlations across precincts to be zero. This discrepancy would be perfectly appropriate if the areal units were coherent and relatively isolated local communities, so that whites and blacks in one neighborhood knew each other but not those in other neighborhoods. Indeed, we should expect the intraprecinct correlation to exceed in absolute value the cross-precinct correlation in most applications. However, since most areal units used in practice are constructed from arbitrarily imposed boundary lines, we would not always expect correlations among neighboring precincts to be exactly zero.

A model that was wholly invariant to aggregation would thus need to allow the cross-observation dependence of β_i^b and β_i^w to differ from zero. Such a revised model would build on insights from the spatial autocorrelation literature (Anselin, 1988). However, a key practical problem would need to be resolved first. In the spatial autocorrelation literature, spatial information is usually summarized in a $p \times p$ "spatial contiguity" matrix, which quantifies the relationships among the areal units, usually up to a scalar parameter. The problem is that this representation is neither unique nor usually close to complete. For example, the spatial contiguity matrix could include 0/1 indicators for whether precincts are contiguous, for measures of the distance between precincts, the degree of contact between people in each pair of precincts—such as transportation systems, commuting practices, telephone traffic, etc.—or the extent to which precinct pairs have any of a large set of external variables in common. The difficulty is that no one representation is likely to be adequate for this problem, and no scheme is likely to apply equally well to the entire set of precincts. The result is that although one can easily construct a method of extracting information about ρ from the cross-observation dependence, the estimates may be heavily dependent upon the particular specification chosen. Since the ecological inference problem is due to a lack of information, finding ways of extracting even more information from existing aggregate data in this way may well be worth additional research. However, because the benefits are not likely to be very substantial, I do not pursue these possibilities here (see also Section 9.1.3).

14.2 The Statistical Problem of Combining Survey and Aggregate Data

Coincident with the widespread recognition of the ecological inference problem in the 1950s, research based on public opinion polls was vastly expanded. The (appropriate) suspicions about aggregate data held by most researchers were especially prevalent among survey researchers since Robinson (1950). Indeed, many of the best survey researchers entered their field because of the roadblock in the form of the ecological inference problem.

Likewise, the intrepid researchers who persisted in using ecological data have been similarly suspicious of the value of survey research.

They have often legitimate concerns about whether respondents honestly report their opinions on controversial matters, such as racial politics or sexual behavior, or the outcomes of complicated decision processes where sincere answers are elicited but strategic responses are more likely. Economists have long preferred measures of "revealed preferences," based as they are on aggregate observed behavior in real economic transactions, rather than answers to the questions posed by academics in artificial situations. Survey researchers have made enormous progress over the years, but they must be always wary of the numerous pitfalls of their art, including the inadvertent consequences of interviewer effects, question wordings, question order, interpersonally incomparable responses, Hawthorne effects, and, in recent years, massive increases in survey nonresponse (e.g., Schuman and Presser, 1981).

Much of this mutual suspicion between ecological and survey researchers is appropriate, but it is also unproductive (Doogan and Rokkan, 1969: vii–viii; Scarbrough, 1991). For it is possible to combine both sources, when available, to improve our inferences. Moreover, inferences are almost always improved by using data from both survey and ecological data together (see Deming and Stephan, 1940; Good, 1963; Johnston and Hay, 1982; Little and Wu, 1991; Ansolabehere and Rivers, 1992).

If a census of all the normally unobserved individual-level data is observed for an application, then the cells of the cross-tabulations can be filled in with certainty, and ecological inference is unnecessary. Alternatively, if we had a large probability sample of individuals in each precinct, we could *estimate* the quantities of interest directly with the proportions in each precinct. These survey estimates would resolve the ecological inference problem if sufficient observations were available in each precinct, answers to the survey questions were sufficiently reliable, and survey nonresponse did not cause other problems.

Unfortunately, in most applications for which some survey data exist, neither a census nor a large sample is available for every aggregate unit. Instead, surveys are almost always designed to make inferences about national, state, or more rarely district-level quantities of interest. Thus, continuing with our running example, a survey might be able to provide good estimates of the district-wide aggregate quantities of interest, but only in extraordinary circumstances will it provide enough information at the precinct level.

The model of ecological inference proposed here is designed to provide information about the precinct-level quantities of interest; aggregate quantities, if desired, may be computed from them. Fortunately, we can reverse the process to a degree if information about the aggregate quantities is available. Thus, if survey data are available in sufficient numbers to get a reasonable handle on the aggregate quantity of interest, this information can be directly incorporated in the model. The procedure is to modify the prior distributions in Section 7.4 to reflect this knowledge. Even a few dozen observations district-wide can provide useful informative priors on $\breve{\mathfrak{B}}^b$ and $\breve{\mathfrak{B}}^w$. Such priors will often be enough to avoid some of the worst problems of aggregation bias or incorrect distributional assumptions, such as those created from artificial data in Chapter 9 (see Figures 9.1 and 9.2, pages 160 and 163). Informative priors such as these have the effect of increasing the probability that the truncated bivariate normal contours are properly centered over most of the true β_i^b, β_i^w points, even if the precinct quantities of interest are correlated with X_i. If, in addition, several observations are available in each precinct, and it is known in which precincts they are located, then priors on $\breve{\sigma}_b$, $\breve{\sigma}_w$, and $\breve{\rho}$ can also be provided.

The formal method of formulating priors on the five parameters of the truncated bivariate normal distribution is to choose a distribution to represent $P(\phi)$. For example, estimates from a survey of the mean and variance-covariance matrix of ϕ could be used as the hyper-parameters in a multivariate normal distribution.

The one complication here is the parameterization. The temptation is to skip directly to estimates of the aggregate quantities of interest, B^b and B^w, but these are inappropriate for direct use for several reasons. First, these are weighted averages, which may be the district-level quantities of interest, but for the priors we need the unweighted averages. Second, we require these estimates on the untruncated instead of truncated scale, and finally, we ultimately need the distribution of ϕ, which is on the scale of estimation, instead of ψ or $\breve{\psi}$.

These complications may be resolved in several ways. The easiest is to ignore the first two difficulties (effectively ignoring the differences between $\mathfrak{B}$, $\breve{\mathfrak{B}}$, and B), compute a prior estimate of B^b and B^w, and translate to ϕ. Computing the point estimates of B^b and B^w would only involve tabulating the proportion of blacks who vote and whites who vote; computing ϕ requires feeding them into the reparameterizations in Equations 7.4 (page 136). If the precinct-level quantities of interest are not highly correlated with the precinct populations, and if the true mode of the truncated bivariate normal is within the unit square, this is a very reasonable procedure. Even if the true mode is outside the unit square, this simple procedure will often be helpful.

If more detailed geographic information is included in the data set, this simple procedure can be improved upon. The best procedure in this instance is to compute direct estimates of β_i^b and β_i^w

based on however many survey observations are available in each precinct. Then apply the model in Section 9.2.4 without covariates, and with one additional change. That is, let the survey estimates of these precinct quantities be the outcome variables in a direct estimation of the parameters of the truncated bivariate normal. The one change required is that we need to model the additional variability due to the very small number of observations that will usually be available in most precincts for the typical survey. To do this, we merely add a binomial component to the model in Section 9.2.4, making sure to *add* this source of variability in such a way that if we had a large number of observations in a precinct the total variability would not vanish (see also note 2, page 94).

If a significant number of observations exist in each precinct, we can improve on even this procedure. That is, priors at the level of the precincts can be included. Because this would take us even farther from ecological inference, I do not pursue this possibility here.

14.3 The Econometric Problem of Aggregating Continuous Variables

The ecological inference problem involves individual-level variables that are all *discrete*, but an important and closely related aggregation problem begins with unobserved individual-level variables that are *continuous* (or discrete interval-level). In economics, this problem is known to be quite severe, as scholars have shown that biases that result from aggregating continuous variables are of the same order of magnitude as biases caused by the most well-known empirical problems in this discipline, such as the Lucas (1976) Critique (Geweke, 1985). In this section, the same model and identical estimation procedures as discussed in the rest of this book are used to make inferences about relationships among several types of mixed (that is, continuous and discrete) and purely continuous individual-level variables, given information from their aggregates. At its most general, the models discussed in this section translate the ecological inference problem into the harder econometric problem of "aggregation over individuals" (Theil, 1954; Stoker, 1993, and the citations therein).

Begin by summarizing the relationship between the unobserved individual-level dichotomous variables ($\mathbb{T}_{ij}$ and $\mathbb{X}_{ij}$) and observed aggregate-level proportions (T_i and X_i):

$$T_i = \frac{\sum_{j=1}^{N_i} \mathbb{T}_{ij}}{N_i}, \qquad X_i = \frac{\sum_{j=1}^{N_i} \mathbb{X}_{ij}}{N_i} \tag{14.3}$$

Also relevant is the relationship between the same unobserved individual-level variables and the unobserved precinct-level quantities of interest:

$$\beta_i^b = \frac{\sum_{j=1}^{N_i} \mathbb{T}_{ij}\mathbb{X}_{ij}}{\sum_{j=1}^{N_i} \mathbb{X}_{ij}}, \qquad \beta_i^w = \frac{\sum_{j=1}^{N_i} \mathbb{T}_{ij}(1-\mathbb{X}_{ij})}{\sum_{j=1}^{N_i}(1-\mathbb{X}_{ij})} \tag{14.4}$$

In the basic ecological inference model, $\mathbb{T}_{ij}$ and $\mathbb{X}_{ij}$ are dichotomous variables, and T_i, X_i, β_i^b, and β_i^w are fractions of individuals in precinct i falling in specific categories. The remainder of this section includes generalizations of this setup by gradually allowing the individual-level variables to be continuous and then unbounded in four steps.

First, suppose $\mathbb{T}_{ij}$ is a continuous variable that ranges between zero and one. For example, it could represent the fraction of time employed, proportion of income that is disposable, the proportion correct on a test, or the fraction of elections in which a person voted. The variable $\mathbb{T}_{ij}$ could also represent a continuous variable with a different range, or a discrete interval-level variable, so long as it is scaled to the [0,1] interval. Applying Equation 14.3 to this new definition of $\mathbb{T}_{ij}$ means that the aggregate variable T_i is now an average, such as an average proportion.

By applying Equations 14.4 to the new continuous variable $\mathbb{T}_{ij}$, the precinct-level quantities of interest turn into *conditional averages*. For example, suppose $\mathbb{T}_{ij}$ is the proportion correct on a standardized test for an elementary school student, $\mathbb{X}_{ij}$ is a dichotomous variable representing boys and girls, and the aggregate units are defined by the class so that T_i is the average standardized test score of children in class i, and X_i is the fraction of boys in the class. Suppose the school provides statistics on T_i and X_i but, due to confidentiality laws, not on $\mathbb{T}_{ij}$ or $\mathbb{X}_{ij}$. Given this setup, the quantities of interest are β_i^b, the average standardized test score for boys (i.e., given $\mathbb{X}_{ij} = 1$), and β_i^w, the average standardized test score for girls (for $\mathbb{X}_{ij} = 0$).

Even with this modification, the accounting identity $T_i = \beta_i^b X_i + \beta_i^w(1 - X_i)$ still holds. Thus, if we are still willing to assume that β_i^b and β_i^w are truncated bivariate normal, mean independent of X_i (or the bounds or truncation is sufficient to correct for this aggregation bias), and spatially independent, then the basic model still applies. All the estimation procedures, methods of calculating quantities of interest, diagnostic routines, benefits of the observation-level bounds, and graphical aids still apply exactly as before. The only real difference is that the resulting estimates of the quantities of interest are now *average proportions*, for boys and girls separately.

Second, we can now modify this alternative model so that $\mathbb{X}_{ij}$ is also a continuous variable ranging between zero and one, or scaled to the [0,1] interval. In this situation, both X_i and T_i are averages (such as average proportions), and the parameters β_i^b and β_i^w are *weighted averages*. Thus, β_i^b is the district-wide average of $\mathbb{T}_{ij}$ weighted by $\mathbb{X}_{ij}$, and β_i^w is the average of $\mathbb{T}_{ij}$ weighted by $1 - \mathbb{X}_{ij}$. The accounting identity, the model, and all the statistical procedures defined in this book still apply as indicated.

These first two generalizations of the basic model do not require any changes in statistical procedures: even the same computer code, described in the preface, that is applied to solve the ecological inference model can be used to make inferences about relationships among continuous individual-level variables. Generalizations beyond this point require modifications of the model. Thus, a third generalization of the model could include situations where $\mathbb{T}_{ij}$, and therefore β_i^b and β_i^w, are permitted to be continuous variables bounded only from below. For example, we might wish to make inferences about categories of the demand or supply of some good, each of which can take on only non-negative values. The model in this book could be generalized to this situation by letting β_i^b and β_i^w be truncated bivariate normal, but with only lower truncation bounds. If this assumption were plausible for an application, the remainder of the model, the estimation procedure, the diagnostics, and the graphics would remain essentially unchanged.

Because of the presence of the lower bound, this third nonecological generalization of the model in this section would in some cases be as robust as the basic model offered here. However, when β_i^b and β_i^w are both large, the model would not differ much from ordinary (untruncated) random effects models. In this case, most of the robustness of the model to aggregation bias would be lost.

A final modification of the model in this direction would let the individual-level relationship be stochastic, so that the quantities of interest would need to be estimated even if the individual-level data were available. The result of this is equivalent to adding an error term onto the accounting identity at the aggregate level, making it essentially a linear regression with no truncation bounds. The existence of the error term means that one precinct-level parameter cannot be identified, unless strong additional assumptions are made (see Griffiths, Drynan, and Prakash, 1979; Hildrith and Houck, 1968). Thus, for example, the quantity $(\beta_i^b - \beta_i^w)$ can be estimated but its individual components usually cannot.

This last version of the model is equivalent to the econometric problem of aggregation over individuals, which is easier to see via an economic interpretation of our notation, using the running example given by Stoker (1993: 1832). That is, let i represent time periods, $i = 1, \ldots, p$, and j denote individual households, $j = 1, \ldots, N_i$. Let $\mathbb{T}_{ij}$ denote the demand for a commodity by household j at time i, and $\mathbb{X}_{ij}$ be the total expenditure budget (or "income") for household j at time i. The aggregate version of these variables, which results from applying Equations 14.3, are average demand T_i and average income X_i. Also known is the price of the commodity at time i. The fact that price varies over time is a substantively important issue, but one that is easier to deal with statistically than aggregation; for simplicity I largely ignore it here.

The economic problem of aggregation of continuous individual-level variables involves determining how aggregate demand T_i depends on aggregate income X_i (and price). This generally requires understanding how individual household demand depends upon income (and price) from solely aggregate-level data. The problems in making these inferences involve all the difficulties inherent in making ecological inferences, but without the benefits of the individual-level bounds. Moreover, there are other problems in making inferences about continuous, individual-level variables that make this an even more difficult problem.

Perhaps most important is that more information is lost in aggregating continuous than dichotomous individual-level variables. For the ecological inference problem, where $\mathbb{X}_{ij}$ and $\mathbb{T}_{ij}$ are dichotomous variables, aggregation into X_i and T_i, respectively, by Equation 14.3, produces aggregate variables with no loss of marginal information. In fact, in the ecological inference problem, the only information lost in aggregation is contained in the cells of the contingency tables (assuming no information is available even at the individual level to avoid exchangeability assumptions). The reason is that the entire distribution of a dichotomous individual-level variable can be reproduced from only one number, the fraction of individuals in a category, which is precisely X_i or T_i. All other marginal moments can be calculated from these means.

For continuous variables, Equation 14.3 also produces means, but these means are no longer sufficient to represent the entire distribution. Information not represented by the mean includes the variance, skewness, and all other moments of the distribution. And of course, aggregation of continuous variables also obliterates much information about the joint distribution, which is the analogous information to the cells of the cross-tabulation in the ecological inference problem. In fact, the missing joint information for continuous variables is much more detailed and also not uniquely summarized by a single parameter. Thus, β_i^b and β_i^w, as defined in Equations 14.4 do not uniquely determine the joint distribution of $\mathbb{X}_{ij}$ and $\mathbb{T}_{ij}$ if these individual-level variables are continuous.

14.4 Concluding Remarks on Related Aggregation Research

This chapter has provided connections between the ecological inference model proposed here and the related aggregation problems raised in geography, statistics, and economics. The geographer's modifiable areal unit problem turned out to be a useful perspective on the model, and the model, in turn, provided a path around the MAUP for this particular class of problems. Insights from the research in statistics that seeks to combine aggregate data and individual-level survey responses were useful in modifying the model to achieve this goal if some survey data are available. Finally, the chapter provided connections to the more diverse and difficult aggregation problems in econometrics, and several procedures were noted for using the model when the individual-level variables are a combination of discrete and continuous, or solely continuous.

Much further research could profitably be conducted in the connections between this model and the aggregation problems in each of these three fields. In addition, the model, or new variants of it, might be relevant to other related aggregation problems that have been studied somewhat less. For example, survey researchers are frequently in the position of having data collected from independent crosssections. They can observe whether the fraction of Democrats from the Southern U.S. supporting the Democratic presidential candidate has increased or decreased, but the lack of a panel study prevents them from knowing what happens to individuals in this region between the two periods. Has individual support eroded? Has, instead or in addition, a new politically distinct cohort moved into the South while others stopped participating? If data from a good panel study are unavailable, researchers cannot track individuals with certainty, and a type of ecological inference problem remains.

Many other areas of statistics exist for which we do not have models to estimate the same parameters at different levels of analysis, even if we were willing to assume the absence of aggregation bias. These models need to be developed prior to, or at least concomitant with, solutions to these related aggregation issues (see Alt et al., 1996).

CHAPTER 15

Ecological Inference in Larger Tables

IN THIS CHAPTER, I generalize the model to tables of any size and complexity.

To get a sense of the diverse set of larger tables that might be of interest in applied research, consider the extensive literature developed to analyze contingency tables when the interior cells are observed, as is common in survey research. Techniques such as log-linear models have been developed to extract information from these arbitrarily complex contingency tables (see Bishop, Fienberg, and Holland, 1975; Kritzer, 1978a, b). Tables with arbitrarily large numbers of outcome categories ($2 \times C$), are introduced in Section 8.4. This chapter considers fully general $R \times C$ tables.

The most straightforward generalization of the race and voting running example would allow larger numbers of racial groups and candidates. Other examples include voter transition studies, which can include tables with many candidates (or parties) at time one horizontally, and the same candidates at time two vertically. Occupational mobility tables are logically similar to voter transition studies, except a list of occupations for parents and (grown) children are listed on each axis. Scholars are also interested in multidimensional tables, such as race by sex by turnout, or education by poverty status by voter choice. Ecological inferences in the context of multidimensional tables have not previously been studied, although when the complete cross-tabulation of all the explanatory variables is available, as is usually the case with census data, then multidimensional tables can be analyzed as a series of separate smaller tables.

A key to understanding how to generalize the model to larger tables is to recognize that arbitrarily complicated tables can usually be rearranged as $R \times C$ rectangles. Thus, the model in the following sections of this chapter will treat the general $R \times C$ case, since with it we will be able to make ecological inferences in its many special cases. Nonrectangular tables are also possible, such as sex by pregnancy by employment, where the impossible cells with "pregnant males" are referred to as "structural zeros." These can also be modeled with minor modifications of $R \times C$ tables.

Most of the generalizations below require more detailed notation but no new substantive assumptions. Except when new assumptions are required, the intuitions provided in the more basic version of the model discussed in Part III are not duplicated. As a result, the presentation here is more terse. In addition, unlike the work in the rest of this book on 2×2 and $2 \times C$ tables, I do not yet have an extensive range of experience with these larger tables. As a result, parts of this chapter are more conjectural.

Multidimensional and larger two-dimensional tables provide difficult challenges. Although writing down generalized versions of the model presented in Part III is relatively straightforward, the procedures are harder to evaluate. The primary problem is visualization, since many of the graphs presented in earlier chapters would need to be presented in three, four, or higher dimensions. The tomography plot, for example, would turn into hyper-planes intersecting a hyper-cube, which would be difficult to summarize in a static, two-dimensional, black-and-white format that is suitable for traditional publication formats. Thus, before presenting the most direct generalizations of the model, Section 15.1 gives a more intuitive and practical, albeit less elegant, approach to making ecological inferences in larger tables. The remaining sections of this chapter develop the more general approach.

15.1 An Intuitive Approach

This section presents an easy, practical approach to making inferences from larger tables that parallels the first approach to $2 \times C$ tables introduced in Section 8.4. The strategy is to decompose the larger table into a series of 2×2 (or $2 \times C$) tables that we already know how to analyze from previous chapters (cf. Thomsen, 1987). This procedure makes it possible to use the model, estimation procedures, and diagnostic graphics already developed.

Table 15.1 expands our running example by adding an extra row for Hispanics (and where white is now defined as non-black, non-Hispanic). The table has one additional precinct-level quantity of interest, β_i^h, the proportion of Hispanics who vote. In addition, what was X_i now represents three categories, the proportions of the voting-age population who are black X_i^b, white X_i^w, and Hispanic $(1 - X_i^b - X_i^w)$. Although the procedure described below encompasses tables of any size, this simplest possible generalization of the basic 2×2 setup is easier to follow and contains all the logical features of the larger tables.

As a result of the expansion to an extra row in this larger table, the accounting identity now has an extra term:

$$T_i = \beta_i^b X_i^b + \beta_i^w X_i^w + \beta_i^h (1 - X_i^b - X_i^w) \tag{15.1}$$

Race of Voting-Age Person	Voting Decision		
	Vote	No Vote	
black	β_i^b	$1-\beta_i^b$	X_i^b
white	β_i^w	$1-\beta_i^w$	X_i^w
hispanic	β_i^h	$1-\beta_i^h$	$1-X_i^b-X_i^w$
	T_i	$1-T_i$	

Table 15.1 Example of a Larger Table. The goal is to infer the quantities of interest, the proportions of blacks (β_i^b), whites (β_i^w), and Hispanics (β_i^h) who vote, from the aggregate variables, the proportions of the voting-age population who are black (X_i^b), white (X_i^w), and Hispanic ($1-X_i^b-X_i^w$), and the fraction of people who vote (T_i), along with the number of voting-age people in the precinct (N_i).

The most straightforward way to generalize this model is by letting the three quantities of interest, β_i^b, β_i^w, and β_i^h, be modeled as if they follow a truncated *tri*variate normal distribution across districts, and are independent of X_i^b and X_i^w, and over precincts. This is the direct extension to the model presented in Section 6.1. This approach is described in the remaining sections of this chapter.

This section shows how to make inferences by reformulating Table 15.1 as two 2×2 subtables. The analysis using these subtables requires three steps. First, form the 2×2 subtable that combines whites and Hispanics into one group, so that it is voter turnout by blacks versus nonblacks. This effectively collapses the last two rows of Table 15.1. The two precinct-level parameters for this subtable are then β_i^b and

$$\beta_i^{wh} = \left(\frac{X_i^w}{1-X_i^b}\right)\beta_i^w + \left(\frac{X_i^h}{1-X_i^b}\right)\beta_i^h \tag{15.2}$$

where the weights are the relative fractions of whites and Hispanics. By applying the methods of Part III, we could make all the usual inferences about these two parameters, only the first (β_i^b) of which is a quantity of interest.

Second, collapse the white and black categories (the first two rows) of Table 15.1 into one group, leaving a 2×2 subtable of voter turnout by non-Hispanics versus Hispanics that overlaps the subtable from stage one. The two parameters for each precinct in this subtable are β_i^h and

$$\beta_i^{bw} = \left(\frac{X_i^b}{X_i^b + X_i^w}\right)\beta_i^b + \left(\frac{X_i^w}{X_i^b + X_i^w}\right)\beta_i^w \tag{15.3}$$

Only β_i^h is a quantity of interest. The usual methods can be applied to this subtable to evaluate all inferences.

Finally, combine the results of the two first stages of analysis to compute all three quantities of interest. Stage one gives fine estimates of β_i^b, including simulations, posterior distributions, etc. Stage two gives good estimates of β_i^h, which could also include any of the specific calculations already demonstrated. The final quantity of interest, β_i^w, can be computed deterministically by solving the accounting identity in Equation 15.1 for β_i^w:

$$\beta_i^w = \frac{T_i - \beta_i^b X_i^b - \beta_i^h(1 - X_i^b - X_i^w)}{X_i^w} \tag{15.4}$$

Because all of the computational techniques, diagnostic procedures, and graphical displays are available for verifying the inferences made from stages one and two, we can be reasonably confident of the application of each stage of this approach. Of course, like any method, we should verify that the observable implications of this model are consistent with the data. In the case of this procedure, we need to also check one feature not already analyzed in the separate stages. That is, because the procedure works in two separate stages, it can sometimes give internally inconsistent results, which would be evidence that the model may need to be extended, as per the next section. Fortunately, it is easy to verify the existence of this potential problem. The key is that the method allows for two (additional) methods of computing simulations for β_i^w from the combined parameters. That is, we can solve either Equation 15.2 to yield

$$\beta_i^w = \frac{\beta_i^{wh}(1 - X_i^b) - \beta_i^h X_i^h}{X_i^w}$$

or Equation 15.3 as follows:

$$\beta_i^w = \frac{\beta_i^{bw}(X_i^b + X_i^w) - \beta_i^b X_i^b}{X_i^w}$$

If these two computations give results for a data set similar to that in Equation 15.4, then the internal consistency problem vanishes and, if each of the individual stages were applied correctly, the method should give reasonable results. (The specific numerical estimates used should probably be those computed from Equation 15.4.) However, if the different methods of computing β_i^w give substantively different answers, then it may be that another model should be applied. In some cases, one of these computations will be clearly correct and the other wrong, in which case this approach might be salvaged.

Unlike the basic and extended models presented in this book for 2×2 and $2 \times C$ tables, the internally inconsistent results this method can yield will disqualify it for some applications. However, because of the ease with which this procedure can be implemented and both its parts and the whole two-stage procedure evaluated, a reasonable approach is to use it first, and of course to verify its internal consistency. The method will be accurate at times even if the different methods of computing β_i^w give different answers, but researchers should proceed much more cautiously in these circumstances, seeking out the reasons for the inconsistency and trying to resolve them before drawing substantive conclusions. Finally, even if the internal inconsistency problem remains, and this model is rejected, researchers should probably use this approach anyway, in order to understand better the data and potential alternatives, prior to considering the more complicated model discussed in the rest of this chapter.

15.2 Notation for a General Approach

Let the notation N_i^{rc} represent the raw counts for a cell in an arbitrarily large table applied to precinct i. The superscripts refer to the row and column position in the table, where $r = 1, \ldots, R$ and $c = 1, \ldots, C$. If you prefer to think of this in terms of our running example, the superscripts can also stand for the race of the voting-age person (black, white, Hispanic, etc.) and the candidate (Democratic, Republican, Liberal, Independent, etc.) who receives this person's vote. For many applications, the last unobserved column or set of columns (number C) of the table has a special "residual" status. For our running example, this column would refer to nonvoters. It could also indicate a residual category or categories for other types of choice situations.

Table 15.2 summarizes this basic notation. The last column and row of this table are the observed marginals. The cell entries are unobserved and are the object of the ecological inference problem. Each element in the last column is a sum of cell entries in its corresponding

N_i^{11}	N_i^{12}	$\ldots$	N_i^{1C}	N_i^{1+}
N_i^{21}	N_i^{22}	$\ldots$	N_i^{2C}	N_i^{2+}
$\vdots$	$\vdots$	$\ddots$	$\vdots$	$\vdots$
N_i^{R1}	N_i^{R2}	$\ldots$	N_i^{RC}	N_i^{R+}
N_i^{+1}	N_i^{+2}	$\ldots$	N_i^{+C}	N_i

Table 15.2 Notation for a Large Table. When there is no ambiguity in subsequent discussion, I drop the "+" in the superscripts.

row (so that for each column c, $N_i^c = \sum_{r=1}^{R} N_i^{rc}$), and elements of the last row are sums of their corresponding columns ($N_i^r = \sum_{c=1}^{C} N_i^{rc}$).

We summarize the margins of the table with three sets of variables. The rows are summarized by X_i^r (the fraction of the voting-age population who are members of race r) for each row r. The columns are summarized by D_i^c (the fraction of the voting-age population casting ballots for candidate c) and T_i (as before, the fraction of the voting-age population turning out to vote). The formal definitions of these variables are as follows:

$$X_i^r = \frac{N_i^r}{N_i}$$

$$D_i^c = \frac{N_i^c}{N_i}$$

$$T_i = \frac{N_i - N_i^C}{N_i} = \frac{N_i^T}{N_i}$$

where $N_i^T = \sum_{c=1}^{C-1} N_i^c = N_i - N_i^C$. Note the analogies between these definitions and the corresponding definitions in Chapter 2.

Summarize the internal cell entries of the table with two types of parameters of interest: β_i^r (the fraction of race r who vote) and λ_i^{rc} (the proportion of voters of race r who cast ballots for candidate c). These are defined as follows:

$$\beta_i^r = \frac{\sum_{c=1}^{C-1} N_i^{rc}}{N_i^r} = \frac{N_i^{rT}}{N_i^r}$$

$$\lambda_i^{rc} = \frac{N_i^{rc}}{N_i^{rT}}$$

where $N_i^{rT} = \sum_{c=1}^{C-1} N_i^{rc} = N_i^r - N_i^{rC}$ and for $r = 1, \ldots, R$ and $c = 1, \ldots, C$. For convenience, I also define the intermediate parameter $\theta_i^{rc} = N_i^{rc}/N_i^r$ (which is of no direct substantive interest) so that

$$\lambda_i^{rc} = \frac{\theta_i^{rc}}{\beta_i^r}$$

Note that λ_i^{rc} is calculated as a function of voters only and therefore excludes the residual category C. This category could include multiple columns via a straightforward extension of the expressions below.

This notation implies accounting identities that are generalizations of the basic Goodman identities:

$$T_i = \sum_{r=1}^{R} \beta_i^r X_i^r$$

$$D_i^c = \sum_{r=1}^{R} \theta_i^{rc} X_i^r \tag{15.5}$$

These expressions will serve as the basis for the model generalization.

15.3 Generalized Bounds

This section derives bounds on the parameters of the larger table. Algebraic bounds, such as these, have not appeared in the literature. The derivation proceeds in parallel to that in Chapter 5. Begin with the bounds on β_i^r, the unknown component of which is N_i^{rT}, and define the set of all rows (or races) as $\mathbf{R}$ and the set of all rows except r as $\mathbf{R} \setminus r$. First the maximum:

$$\max(N_i^{rT}) = \min(N_i^T, N_i^r)$$

Dividing through by the (known) marginal N_i^r gives an expression for the maximum of the parameter of interest:

$$\begin{aligned}\max(\beta_i^r) &= \max\left(\frac{N_i^{rT}}{N_i^r}\right)\\ &= \frac{\max(N_i^{rT})}{N_i^r}\\ &= \frac{\min(N_i^T, N_i^r)}{N_i^r}\end{aligned}$$

and dividing numerator and denominator by N_i,

$$= \min\left(1, \frac{T_i}{X_i^r}\right)$$

Then, because

$$N_i^{rT} = N_i^T - \sum_{k \in \mathbf{R} \setminus r} N_i^{kT}$$
$$= N_i^T - N_i^{\bar{r}T}$$

where $N_i^{\bar{r}T} = \sum_{k \in \mathbf{R} \setminus r} N_i^{kT}$, we can calculate the minimum in similar fashion. First, compute

$$\min(N_i^{rT}) = N_i^T - \max(N_i^{\bar{r}T})$$
$$= N_i^T - \min(N_i^T, N_i^{\bar{r}})$$

and then divide through by N_i^r:

$$\min(\beta_i^r) = \frac{\min(N_i^{rT})}{N_i^r}$$
$$= \frac{N_i^T - \min(N_i^T, N_i^{\bar{r}})}{N_i^r}$$

and dividing numerator and denominator by N_i,

$$= \frac{T_i - \min(T_i, \sum_{k \in \mathbf{R} \setminus r} X_i^k)}{X_i^r}$$
$$= \max\left(0, \frac{T_i - (1 - X_i^r)}{X_i^r}\right)$$

where $1 - X_i^r = \sum_{k \in \mathbf{R} \setminus r} X_i^k$.

Collecting these results and, by analogous derivations for θ_i^{rc}, the bounds for these parameters are:

$$\max\left(0, \frac{T_i - (1 - X_i^r)}{X_i^r}\right) \leq \beta_i^r \leq \min\left(1, \frac{T_i}{X_i^r}\right)$$
$$\max\left(0, \frac{D_i^c - (1 - X_i^r)}{X_i^r}\right) \leq \theta_i^{rc} \leq \min\left(1, \frac{D_i^c}{X_i^r}\right) \qquad (15.6)$$

Finally, to compute bounds on λ_i^{rc}, first define $\mathbf{C}$ as the set of all columns (or candidates) excluding the residual category C and $\mathbf{C} \setminus c$ as the set of all columns except C and c. Then expand the definition in terms of the raw cell counts.

$$\lambda_i^{rc} = \frac{N_i^{rc}}{N_i^{rT}}$$

$$= \frac{N_i^{rc}}{N_i^{rc} + \sum_{k \in \mathbf{C} \setminus c} N_i^{rk}}$$

$$= \frac{N_i^{rc}}{N_i^{rc} + N_i^{r\bar{c}}}$$

where $N_i^{r\bar{c}} = \sum_{k \in \mathbf{C} \setminus c} N_i^{rk}$.

Then the maximum is

$$\max(\lambda_i^{rc}) = \frac{\max(N_i^{rc})}{\max(N_i^{rc}) + \min(N_i^{r\bar{c}})}$$

$$= \frac{\min(N_i^c, N_i^r)}{\min(N_i^c, N_i^r) + N_i^c - \min(N_i^c, N_i^{\bar{r}})}$$

$$= \frac{\min(D_i^c, X_i^r)}{\min(D_i^c, X_i^r) + D_i^c - \min[D_i^c, (1 - X_i^r)]}$$

and the minimum is

$$\min(\lambda_i^{rc}) = \frac{\min(N_i^{rc})}{\min(N_i^{rc}) + \max(N_i^{r\bar{c}})}$$

$$= \frac{N_i^c - \min(N_i^c, N_i^{\bar{r}})}{N_i^c - \min(N_i^c, N_i^{\bar{r}}) + \min(N_i^{\bar{c}}, N_i^r)}$$

$$= \frac{\min[D_i^c, (1 - X_i^r)] - D_i^c}{-\min(D_i^{\bar{c}}, X_i^r) - D_i^c + \min[D_i^c, (1 - X_i^r)]}$$

15.4 The Statistical Model

For simplicity, the focus in this section is on θ_i^{rc}. The notation can be easily extended to include β_i^r if desired.

Begin with the basic accounting identity for the larger table:

$$D_i^c = \sum_{r=1}^{R} \theta_i^{rc} X_i^r$$

The most straightforward generalization of the model in Chapter 6 then requires θ_i^{rc} to be generated by a truncated multivariate normal distribution.

Denote the expected values of this distribution as

$$E(\theta_i^{rc}) = \mathfrak{T}^{rc}$$

and separate error terms as

$$\theta_i^{rc} = \mathfrak{T}_i^{rc} + \xi_i^{rc} \tag{15.7}$$

where the error terms ξ_i^{rc} are distributed as the multivariate truncated normal with mean $E(\xi_i^{rc}) = 0$. In addition, the variances require slightly more notation because cross-equation covariances are possible:

$$C(\xi_i^{rc}, \xi_i^{sd}) = \tau_{rc}^{sd}$$

$$C(\xi_i^{rc}, \xi_i^{rc}) = V(\xi_i^{rc}) = \tau_{rc}^{rc} = \tau_{rc}^2 \tag{15.8}$$

Before the D_i^c are observed, the truncation limits on each are [0,1]; afterwards, they are given in Equation 15.6.

The key complicating assumption of generalizing the model to more than three columns is this truncated multivariate normal distribution, and, at least in principle, roughly the same issues apply as in "seemingly unrelated" regression models or other multi-equation systems. Separate equation-by-equation estimates are equivalent to assuming that the cross-equation covariances are zero. This restriction may be more robust than many forms of joint estimation, but it will also be less efficient and may be biased. Separate estimation will surely be easier computationally. A Bayesian prior on the large number of covariance terms would probably be especially helpful in estimation.

The one difficult issue with this generalized model is computation. The implied likelihood function on T_i requires a variety of calculation-intensive numerical calculations, primarily multivariate normal cumulative distribution functions. There are several approaches to this problem. For one, recent advances in Bayesian simulation for multinomial probit make about eight dimensions feasible through direct computation (see Geweke, Keane, and Runkle, 1994; Breslaw, 1994). A second possibility, as an approximation, is to drop the truncation portion of the likelihood model. We would still be able to take advantage of the information in the precinct bounds, but only at the second stage. This procedure would sacrifice the advantages the bounds give in improving the likelihood estimates in the first stage of the model. In addition, without truncation in the likelihood function, the model would be internally inconsistent. In my experience, dropping truncation does not always affect empirical estimates for the simpler 2×2 and 2×3 tables in many empirical applications. Whether the effects are larger for this general case is a task I leave to future research. Finally, it may be most efficient to estimate the parameters of the truncated multivariate normal simultaneously with the precinct-level quantities of interest. An EM approach would likely make this approach feasible.

Another possibility for larger tables is to generalize the model in other ways. For example, we could estimate a mean function on the truncated scale. This would require restricting the parameters to the unit interval, such as via a logit transformation, and dropping the truncation. Then the second stage could be implemented by randomly drawing the unrestricted parameters in the logistic function from a multivariate normal distribution subject to the accounting identity, and hence the implied parameter bounds. Ad hoc procedures would need to be followed in order to estimate the variance parameters, and the variance matrix of the parameters. This procedure would not be as statistically efficient, it is unlikely to fit the data as well, and numerical instabilities seem likely at the extremes, but it would be far more computationally efficient.

15.5 Distributional Implications

The likelihood function depends on the joint distribution of D_i^c for all c. To form it, substitute Equations 15.7 into the accounting identities in Equations 15.5:

$$\begin{aligned} D_i^c &= \sum_{r=1}^{R} \theta_i^{rc} X_i^r \\ &= \sum_{r=1}^{R} (\mathfrak{T}_i^{rc} + \xi_i^{rc}) X_i^r \\ &= \sum_{r=1}^{R} \mathfrak{T}_i^{rc} X_i^r + \xi_i \end{aligned} \tag{15.9}$$

where $\xi_i = \sum_{r=1}^{R} \xi_i^r X_i^r$ is the composite error for the variable D_i^c. Only $C-1$ of these equations need to be estimated; the final one is repetitive since $\sum_{c=1}^{C} D_i^c = 1$.

Dropping the truncation term means that D_i^c is the equivalent of a normally distributed variable (for any c). In addition, the set of variables D_i^c for all c's is jointly normal with expected values

$$\mathrm{E}(D_i^c) = \sum_{r=1}^{R} \mathfrak{T}_i^{rc} X_i^r$$

with variances,

$$\mathrm{V}(D_i^c) = \sum_{r=1}^{R} \sum_{s=1}^{r} \tau_{rc}^{sc} X_i^r X_i^s$$

and cross-equation covariances

$$\mathrm{C}(D_i^c, D_i^d) = \sum_{r=1}^{R} \sum_{s=1}^{R} \tau_{rc}^{sd} X_i^r X_i^s$$

The intermediate parameters to be estimated are:

$$\psi = (\mathfrak{T}_i^c, \tau_{rc}^{sd}; r, s = 1, \ldots, R; c, d = 1, \ldots, C)$$

As before, these are of no particular interest in and of themselves, but they provide valuable information with which to compute the quantities of interest.

Let D_i represent a vector of the $C-1$ values of $\{D_i^c\}$. The likelihood function without the truncation portion is then

$$L(\psi | D_i) = \prod_{i=1}^{p} \mathrm{N}(D_i | \mu_i, \Sigma_i) \tag{15.10}$$

with mean μ_i, a $(C-1) \times 1$ vector with representative element μ_i^c and where

$$\mu_i^c = \sum_{r=1}^{R} \mathfrak{T}_i^{rc} X_i^r$$

and variance matrix

$$\Sigma_i = \{\sigma_{cd}\} = \begin{pmatrix} \sigma_1^2 & \sigma_{21} & \cdots \\ \sigma_{12} & \sigma_2^2 & \cdots \\ \vdots & \vdots & \ddots \end{pmatrix}$$

where

$$\sigma_c^2 = \text{V}(D_i^c) = \sum_{r=1}^{R}\sum_{s=1}^{r} \tau_{rc}^{sc} X_i^r X_i^s$$

$$\sigma_{cd} = \text{C}(D_i^c, D_i^d) = \sum_{r=1}^{R}\sum_{s=1}^{R} \tau_{rc}^{sd} X_i^r X_i^s$$

Our knowledge of ψ is summarized with the multivariate normal posterior,

$$\psi \sim \text{N}[\psi|\hat{\psi}, \text{V}(\hat{\psi})] \tag{15.11}$$

or with this distribution as an approximation to the correct posterior via importance sampling.

Via a derivation parallel to Appendix C, the conditional posterior distribution of the precinct-level parameters is truncated normal:

$$\text{P}(\theta_i^{rc}|D_i^c, \psi) \propto \text{TN}[\theta_i^{rc}|\text{E}(\theta_i^{rc}|D_i^c, \psi),\ \text{V}(\theta_i^{rc}|D_i^c, \psi)] \tag{15.12}$$

with truncation bounds given in Equation 15.6. The expected value is

$$\text{E}(\theta_i^{rc}|D_i^c, \psi) = \mathfrak{T}_i^{rc} + \frac{\omega_i^{rc}}{\sigma_c^2}\xi_i$$

and variance

$$\text{V}(\theta_i^{rc}|D_i^c, \psi) = \tau_{rc}^2 - \frac{\omega_i^{rc2}}{\sigma_c^2}$$

where

$$\begin{aligned} \omega_i^r &\equiv \text{C}(\theta_i^{rc}, D_i^c) \\ &= \sum_{s=1}^{R} X_i^r \text{C}(\theta_i^{rc}, \theta_i^{sc}) \\ &= \sum_{s=1}^{R} \tau_{rc}^{sc} X_i^r \end{aligned}$$

15.6 Calculating the Quantities of Interest

To draw simulations of the precinct parameter θ_i^{rc},

1. Maximize the log of the likelihood function (Equation 15.10), or a reparameterized version, plus the log of the prior if used;
2. Draw $\tilde{\psi}$ from its multivariate normal posterior distribution (Equation 15.11), or use importance sampling via importance ratios to draw from the correct posterior;
3. Insert $\tilde{\psi}$ into the conditional posterior distribution of the precinct parameter (Equation 15.12); and
4. Draw $\tilde{\theta}_i^{rc}$ from its posterior.

As with the simpler case in Chapter 8, this posterior can be summarized as a point estimate with the mean of the simulations, and a measure of uncertainty, such as confidence intervals based on percentiles of the simulations. Of course, the entire posterior distribution can easily be plotted as well.

Simulations of the aggregate district-wide parameters can be computed by taking the appropriate weighted averages of these precinct parameters, with weights based on fraction of the population in each racial group.

15.7 Concluding Suggestions

Multicategory and multidimensional tables is a topic that deserves much future methodological research. Some of the interesting issues that need exploration include graphic visualization in hyperspace of data and diagnostics, efficient computation of multidimensional probability integrals, and appropriate prior distributions for the proliferating variances and covariances in large tables. For researchers who wish to make inferences in large tables now, without waiting for this future research, the approach in Sections 8.4 and 15.1 is a good place to start. With these approaches, all the methods introduced in this book are immediately applicable, and tests are given to verify whether this intuitive approach is consistent with the evidence in the data. Researchers studying large tables should also routinely compute the multivariate bounds given in Section 15.3. If these approaches prove to be insufficient for an application, then the more complete generalization of the model given in the rest of this chapter should be tried.

CHAPTER 16

A Concluding Checklist

SECTION 1.1 gives a sense of the vast array of empirical projects that a valid method of ecological inference would make possible. This chapter provides a checklist of items for researchers applying the method offered here to these and other problems.

The following checklist highlights many of the steps that would be productive for researchers who use these methods to follow. It is presented in roughly the order that would be followed by a researcher with real data, conducting a substantively oriented project. However, like any such advice, it should not always be followed exactly. Indeed, scholars in almost any field who implement their research proposals precisely and accomplish exactly what they set out to the first time through probably do not learn very much. In almost all research, it is usually best to go back several times, try things different ways, explore new hypotheses, seek out unexpected questions to answer, collect diverse sets of data, and track down all available observable implications of each idea. This takes time and creativity, and no standardized list can encompass all these tasks (which is perhaps why it is called *re*search, rather than merely search).

The following checklist uses our running example of voter turnout by race. As throughout the book, this example is only meant to stand in for any of the numerous other applications possible.

1. Begin by deciding what you would do with the ecological inferences once they were made. Imagine you knew the true values of the quantities of interest, and decide what you would do with them. (The actual inferences will be more uncertain than this, and should thus be accompanied by confidence intervals or posterior distributions.) Some possibilities follow.
   a. Present a list of β_i^b and β_i^w for each precinct, or B^b and B^w for each district. This basic descriptive information can be enormously important for a variety of uses. Some examples of these uses follow:
      i. Current methods used to apply the Voting Rights Act are a fairly blunt instrument, even when they are taken at face value (that is, as if they were accurate), since they only provide a single measure for the entire district or other area under study. With precinct-level estimates, the Voting

Rights Act can be applied to only those geographic areas for which the remedy is appropriate. Policymakers will no longer wind up "fixing" districting schemes that aren't broken, or missing areas of application of the Act that would not be detected by less powerful methods.[1]

ii. Precinct-level estimates provide essential information for redistricters who need to understand how to recombine specific precincts into new districts, for the Voting Rights Act or other purposes.

iii. Even if the purpose of the analysis is to produce a single number for the entire state, or only one district, using observation-level estimates enables scholars to bring more information to bear on this estimate. They can borrow strength statistically from data in numerous similar (and presumably neighboring) geographic areas in order better to accomplish their original goal.

iv. Apparently "uninteresting" precincts or districts can be enormously helpful, not only in improving estimation of the original quantity of interest, but also as additional observable implications of whatever theory one is studying. For example, suppose the goal of the analysis is to determine the extent to which voting in District 4 is racially polarized, and the estimate for that district indicates a high level. In this case, finding highly polarized voting in numerous surrounding districts (with similar types of people and similar election contests) would lend plausibility to the conclusion one might draw from the single estimate in District 4.

b. A second use of precinct-level estimates is for geographic mapping (see Figure 1.2, page 25). For example, precincts (or districts) could be colored or shaded according to the values of racially polarized

[1] Statisticians often debate about whether judges (or policy makers) will understand sophisticated statistical methods sufficiently to allow them as evidence in trials. In my limited experience, judges vary considerably in their knowledge of statistics (and even in their ability to stay awake during trials!), but they are usually interested in learning the right answer. I know of no judge who, when confronted with the inaccurate results produced by Goodman's regression in Table 1.3 (page 16) and the accurate results generated by the method offered here in Figure 1.1 (page 23), would choose the old, inaccurate method. Even judges who attempt to engineer a partisan outcome would choose the better method and search for some other way to decide the case as they deemed appropriate or desirable. Of course, whether judges judge correctly, whether the goal of the judicial system has anything to do with generating truth, or policymakers make good policy, is not the concern here.

turnout, $\beta_i = \beta_i^b - \beta_i^w$, or perhaps β_i^b and β_i^w on separate maps. Portraying this information or other quantities of interest on a map, using darker shades (or different colors) to represent larger values, is a powerful way to present information. Most people find geographic presentations easy to understand, perhaps because they seem to carry around in their head rough measures of the values of many variables with the attached geographic codes. (For example, think of all the ways you know that the South differs from the North.) Because survey research usually does not include such geographic codes, there is much opportunity in the field of political geography which precinct-level estimates could further.

c. Another very creative use of precinct-level estimates is as dependent variables in subsequent analyses. For example, we might be interested in the extent to which black turnout (β_i^b) is higher in integrated than segregated neighborhoods. In this situation, we could produce estimates of β_i^b with the method offered here, and then try to explain them statistically, via a regression or similar procedure (about which more later in the checklist), with a precinct-level measure of residential segregation obtained from U.S. Census data. This procedure has enormous potential for uncovering new information. It is an interesting combination of ecological inference and appropriate aggregate data analysis: estimating β_i^b is a straightforward ecological inference, but the second-stage regression is only relevant at the aggregate level.[2]

   Second-stage analyses such as this should be carefully distinguished from a bad version of Goodman's ecological regression. If the explanatory variable at the second stage is really an aggregated individual-level variable and the goal is to break down the contingency table even further, then one of the methods offered in Section 8.4 or Chapter 15 should be used instead of a second-stage analysis. This second-stage analysis should instead be reserved for variables that are characteristics of a community, such as measures of residential segregation, candidate characteristics, or political culture. Of course, the same quantitative variable could represent an individual characteristic or an attribute of the community, depend-

[2] This two-stage procedure follows the logic of "hierarchical linear modeling," which is popular among education researchers (see Bryk and Raudenbush, 1992). These models include a component to explain individual-level variation (as for example within precincts or schools) and a second stage level to explain contextual differences among the different aggregate units. This second stage is closely related to the second-stage analysis suggested in the text, the additional difficulty in ecological inference being that the individual-level data (β_i^b and β_i^w) need to be estimated before the second stage analysis can commence.

ing on the interests of the researcher. For example, if the goal were to estimate the degree of racially polarized voting among college graduates and those who did not have college degrees, then this sociological question is merely a case of an ecological inference from a larger table. Alternatively, if the goal were the policy issue of whether racially polarized voting was reduced in communities that have large compositions of college-educated people (such as college towns), then this two-stage procedure would be appropriate.[3]

2. After deciding what to do with the ecological inferences to be obtained, it is usually a good idea to see what data are available, and collect more if possible. Obviously, the equivalent of T_i and X_i will be required, and they should be checked for errors and obvious outliers. But all other available information should be organized as well. Additional precincts from neighboring areas should be included as additional observations if possible and if they represent reasonably similar political areas. Collect data on covariates Z_i, for possible use with the extended model, if that proves necessary (Section 9.2.1). Other information, too, can be very valuable. For example, for turnout by race, some survey data are available to give a general sense of the levels of black and white turnout rates. These data may not be available for the local area of interest, and are almost certainly not known for any one district or almost any precinct, but even state-wide or nation-wide survey data can give one a good general sense of what to expect from a specific ecological inference. If the survey data are good enough to justify a formal approach, then the procedures for combining survey and aggregate data discussed in Section 14.2 should be used. If they are only good enough to give one a general sense of the mode of the truncated bivariate normal, and a formal Bayesian analysis does not seem desirable, the survey data can at least be used as an after-the-fact check on the results of the ecological inference.

   Other information can also be very useful to check the results of the ecological inference, and everything available and sufficiently easy to gather should be mined. Researchers can use results from prior research, such as a very limited survey in only one part of one precinct, or news-

[3] This two-stage procedure should also be distinguished from the fix for aggregation bias or distributional problems that involves including external variables Z_i in the model (as described in Sections 9.2.1 and 9.2.3). These two models should be built separately. A covariate should only be used as part of the extended model to avoid aggregation bias. Once the first stage produces valid estimates of β_i^b and β_i^w, with or without the extended model, the second-stage analysis can proceed. But variables that are candidates for the second stage should only be included as covariates in the original model if they help avoid aggregation bias and do not create other problems.

paper accounts of differences among people in various neighborhoods. If it is possible to go to the area, spending even one day conducting interviews can be extremely valuable, even if it is not possible to administer a probability sample and formal questionnaire. Just walking around some of these neighborhoods, or standing by polling places, or reading the local press, or going to the supermarkets in the area can produce rich amounts of qualitative information. Data beat statistics every time.

3. Beginning the data analysis with a scattercross plot (e.g., Figure 5.5, page 89) is often helpful. This gives a sense of how much information exists in the deterministic bounds about each of the quantities of interest (by comparing it to Figures 5.2, 5.3, and especially 5.4). Recall that the data points that fall in or near the left triangle have narrow bounds for β_i^w and wide bounds for β_i^b, whereas points that fall in the right triangle have narrow bounds for β_i^b and wide bounds for β_i^w. Labeling the data points in this plot in some way is often helpful for identifying the categories of precincts and types of questions that will be produce the most certain answers. For example, Figure 10.1 (page 201) plots Southern U.S. counties with letters corresponding to each state name.
4. This is a good time to begin making some inferences based on precincts that have narrow bounds. Almost all data sets contain at least a few such precincts, and many have a substantial number. Although the values of β_i^b and β_i^w for these precincts may not be fully representative of those with wider bounds, they are known with a very high level of certainty. These precincts can therefore serve as highly reliable observable implications of the theory to be evaluated. They should be exploited to their maximum potential, and this might as well be done prior to using the statistical model to extract inherently less certain information from the remaining precincts.

   For example, if your goal is to list values of the quantities of interest by precinct, you can start a list, since the answer is known for these precincts. If the goal is to draw maps, then some geographic areas can be filled in; in some cases, these partially completed maps may be very informative or may suggest further hypotheses to test. If the goal is to use the precinct-level quantities of interest as dependent variables, then these precincts provide an excellent first test of these relationships. For all these purposes and others, we should be aware that precincts with wide bounds may generate different substantive conclusions, but even in that unfortunate situation these observations will provide useful tests for some observations.
5. If the purpose of your analysis is to explain variations in β_i^b and β_i^w over precincts, then an excellent procedure is to draw a plot with one of these parameters on the vertical axis and a selected explanatory variable on the horizontal axis. If the true values of the parameters were known,

they would be points on this scatterplot. Since they are not known, we can put in their place a vertical line, based on the bounds, that covers all possible values of the quantity of interest. Figure 13.2 (page 238) gives an example with X_i as the explanatory variable and the true points drawn in (which, obviously will not be part of the one you would draw). In some cases, such as the left graph in this figure, these bounds are sufficiently narrow to identify a relationship between the parameter and the explanatory variable, even without any statistical procedures to ascertain where, within the bounds, the true parameters lie.

6. One diagnostic for the presence of aggregation bias is to note where Goodman's regression line would be fit to the points of an X_i by T_i graph. This can be easily done visually, or, if it is helpful, the line could even be added to the graph (such as in the scattercross graph in Figure 13.1 on page 236). If Goodman's regression line does not cross both the left and the right vertical axes within the [0,1] interval, there is a high probability of aggregation bias. If the line does cross both axes within this interval, we have less evidence of whether aggregation bias exists. Note that the steepness of the slope of this line (what might be interpreted as the strength of the relationship between the aggregate variables) is not relevant to the quality or certainty of the resulting ecological inferences.
7. A second useful summary of the data is a tomography plot with only the lines (such as Figure 5.1, page 81). This reexpresses the data in terms of what we know about β_i^b and β_i^w, which are the two axes in this graph. Tomography plots portray all deterministic information available about these quantities of interest, with each precinct considered in isolation: Each line traces out all possible values of the β_i^b, β_i^w coordinates.

   The bounds on the quantities of interest can be seen in the graph by the positions of the lines. Relatively flat lines give narrow bounds on β_i^w and wide bounds for β_i^b. Similarly, steep lines indicate narrow bounds for β_i^b but wide bounds for β_i^w. Lines that cut off the upper right or lower left corner of the figure have narrow bounds for both β_i^b and β_i^w. The only lines with [0,1] bounds for both parameters go from the upper left corner to the bottom right corner of the figure. All tomography lines must be negatively sloped, which indicates that when the true value of one parameter falls near the upper end of its bounds, the other must fall near the lower end of its bounds. This deterministic inverse relationship between β_i^b and β_i^w can be useful if some external information is available about one but not the other.

   At this point, you should try to identify where the mode of the truncated bivariate normal distribution should be located. Try to see where the true β_i^b, β_i^w points appear to be "emanating" from, and where the likelihood contours will be drawn.

8. As a check on your intuition about where the mode will be, it is useful also to consider an X_i by T_i graph (such as a scattercross plot). Roughly speaking, the average of the points near the left ($X_i \approx 0$) and right ($X_i \approx 1$) of the graph gives the vicinity of where the mode of the truncated bivariate normal will be for β_i^w and β_i^b, respectively. (If no data points can be found near one end of the graph, you can extrapolate from a regression line fit to all the points.) This is only the rough vicinity because the mode needs to be identified on the untruncated scale (and so, for example, it could even be outside the unit interval), and of course because the likelihood model will use information from all the data points to locate the mode more efficiently.
9. The tomography plot does not represent unanimous precincts (although they could be represented by putting a number at the 0,0 and 1,1 corners of the plot), and their presence should be checked. Unanimous precincts for which $T_i = 0$ would be represented as points at the extreme lower left corner of the graph (indicating that $\beta_i^b = \beta_i^w = 0$), and those for which $T_i = 1$ would be at the extreme upper right (so that $\beta_i^b = \beta_i^w = 1$). These points are often the result of arbitrary data corrections, such as if official statistics indicate that turnout exceeds 100% and is arbitrarily truncated. The result is that the process generating these data may be different from the process generating the uncorrected data. Thus, it always pays to evaluate whether unanimous precincts are sufficiently far from the likely mode of the truncated bivariate normal distribution to be considered outliers, which would inappropriately and disproportionately influence the estimation procedure. If this seems likely, a good procedure would be to remove these points from the likelihood stage of the analysis, so that the contours would be based solely on the remaining points. If $T_i = 1$ and $T_i = 0$ are reasonable values for these points, they could be added in for subsequent calculations. (Running the analysis both ways is the easiest way to judge the effects of these points.) Be aware, however, that because substantial statistical strength can be borrowed from these observations, leaving unanimous precincts in the analysis is best if it is likely that they were generated by approximately the same process as the rest of the data.
10. The degree of aggregation bias (defined in Section 3.5) present in the data can be checked further than the initial cut suggested in step 6. This can be done by a careful consideration of the tomography plot, as the extreme case in Figure 9.3 (page 176) demonstrates. One of the best checks can be done by plotting X_i horizontally, β_i^b and β_i^w vertically (in separate graphs), and plotting a vertical line that represents the deterministic bounds for each precinct (see Figure 13.2, page 238). When evaluating this graph, it is important to not be drawn into the misleading inference that the true parameter values are always at the middle of

each of the bounds. Nevertheless, the bounds in this type of display can be used to ascertain the relationship between X_i and these parameters, which indicates the degree of aggregation bias. Other useful checks on aggregation bias are discussed at length in Section 9.2.

11. If there is minimal aggregation bias in the data, then running the basic model is called for. Even if there is a large amount of aggregation bias in the data, the basic model can still be run if the bounds are sufficiently narrow or the truncated bivariate normal looks as if it will be heavily truncated. Since determining the degree of truncation is easier after running the model, it is often easiest to run the basic model first as a diagnostic.
12. After running the basic model, the position of the contours should be located and drawn on a tomography plot (for example, see the left graph of Figure 13.6, page 243). These contours are an estimate of the position of most of the true β_i^b, β_i^w points. Since the likelihood maximization step is iterative and requires searching over a five-dimensional surface, the final estimates, like the result of any iterative procedure, should be checked carefully. Some of the important questions to ask yourself about this fit follow:
    a. Did the procedure identify a plausible mode, compared to your judgment of the set of tomography lines? Do the contours identify the vicinity from where the lines seem to be "emanating"? Do the lines seem to cross more at this mode?
    b. Is there evidence of an additional mode in the data not picked up by the contours? An example of this problem would arise if only one of the modes from Figure 9.7 (page 187) were captured by the contours. It would be less of a problem if this graph were fit by very wide contours that captured both modes, but the model should probably be modified to fit this feature of the data anyway. Thus, if there appears to be a second mode, try to identify what the precincts that belong to this mode have in common, such as a regional effect or other external variable. To fix the problem, if one exists, the best approach is either to find a covariate to control for the difference in modes (as per the extended model in Section 9.2.1), or separate the data into disjoint sets and run two separate analyses (see Section 9.3.1). If this parametric approach proves unsatisfactory, or too difficult computationally, the nonparametric procedures may be called for (see Section 9.3.2).
    c. Are there outliers? Figure 7.1 (page 126) gives an example of checking for outliers with a tomography plot, although this can also be checked with a plot of X_i by T_i with expected value and confidence intervals drawn in (see Figure 13.1, page 236). Data from precincts that appear to be outliers should probably first be checked for cod-

ing errors. If that is not the problem, it is worth trying to determine whether these observations have something in common that could be picked up by some covariate that should probably have been included from the start. As a last resort, they could be dropped from the statistical analysis altogether and only studied in terms of their deterministic bounds. An alternative possibility, in situations without many outliers, is to see what their effect is on the result: if they only serve to make inferences somewhat more conservative by widening the contours and thus opening the confidence intervals, then it may be safe to leave them in the analysis. If, however, they appear to disrupt the inferences about the precincts that are not outliers, then they might best be removed. A compromise approach is to delete the outliers from the likelihood maximization and importance sampling stage; this procedure prevents the outliers from affecting the placement of the contours or estimation of the posterior distributions for the remaining observations.

d. Is the mode in a place that is substantively reasonable? That is, do the results of this likelihood maximization correspond with what you know about the substance of your problem from other sources, such as those raised in step 2? If not, then you might consider adjusting the contours (physically moving them) after the analysis. An equivalent step would be to include this information by modifying the prior distribution and rerunning the procedure.

13. If the precincts in the data set do not have much in common, then it is worth considering nonparametric estimation. At a minimum, researchers should always at least consider using a nonparametric density estimate as a diagnostic, as in Section 9.3.2 (see also the example in Figure 12.2, page 229). As a specification test for truncated bivariate normality, this plot can be compared directly to the parametric contours. One should be careful in making this comparison, because the methods are intended to pick up different features of the data. In particular, positive correlations between β_i^b and β_i^w will be more easily found by the parametric than nonparametric method.

    If this graphic indicates problems, then it is best to consider first whether steps can be taken within the context of the parametric framework, such as including additional covariates. But if this proves insufficient, the fully nonparametric estimates of the quantities of interest could be used instead.

14. Always evaluate the tomography plot for how much information exists in the data to make the ecological inference you seek. This involves not only the bounds, which are crucial, but also the degree of variation in X_i. In general, the less variation in X_i, the more uncertainty you should associate with the results from the model. If X_i takes on a small range of

values, then all the lines in the tomography plot will be nearly parallel (as in Figure 12.2, page 229). This limited range of "camera angles" will make the mode especially difficult to identify. Data sets like these should be treated with great care. Since the model is conditional on X_i, this uncertainty is not all indicated by the estimates unless you are careful during the likelihood estimation to ensure that the contours have a wide enough variance to reflect the uncertainty you would attach to them. If they are not wide enough, according to your qualitative judgment, you should consider increasing the variance, adjusting the priors, including or excluding the unanimous precincts, or (always the best option) getting more data.

Parallel lines are less of a concern if they cut off the top right or bottom left corners of the tomography graph, since these would indicate very narrow bounds on each of the precinct quantities of interest. See, for example, Figure 11.1 (page 221) which has both features, and thus suggests that the model will be successful in extracting significant information from the data.

15. The fit of the model is sufficiently important that it is also worth checking the conditional distributions, $T_i|X_i$, which are relevant since X_i is taken as fixed in the model. That is, the five parameters of the truncated bivariate normal distribution can also be represented on an X_i by T_i plot since they form the parameters of the conditional expected value and variance functions (Equations 6.8 and 6.10, page 97), which are the only two quantities that determine the conditional distributions. Figure 6.1 (page 100) gives examples of this type of plot. Most such examples in this book include the conditional expected value plotted as a solid line, and the conditional variance represented by 80% confidence intervals portrayed as dashed lines around the expected value. Of course, other confidence levels can be checked too, as they are all observable implications of the model.

    If the model fits, the expected value line should be drawn through the middle of most of the points, much like a regression line. However, this line (and all of the conditional distributions) are constrained to pass through the [0,1] interval at the left and right vertical axes. This is one of the fixes the model imposes for aggregation bias. If the expected value line is pinned near zero or one at either of the vertical axes, then aggregation bias may be a serious possibility, although it is less likely to cause difficulties due to the heavy truncation.

    If the model fits, the distribution of T_i for given values of X_i (that is, vertical slices of the graph) should each be well represented by the expected value and variance lines. That is, the expected value line should pass through the middle of each of these conditional distributions (the vertical scatter of points for each value of X_i), and the confidence intervals should capture roughly 80% of the points for each conditional distribution. A clear example of a problem with this distributional assumption in real data is revealed in the left graph of Figure 13.5 (page 242). This problem can be fixed by dropping a subset of observations during the likelihood stage of analysis, as was done in the right graph of the same figure. For real applications, observations excluded from the likelihood stage should still be exploited for the information they can provide through their deterministic bounds. The other remedies discussed above for distributional assumptions can all also be used here.

16. If aggregation bias is severe, then you should check to see whether the distribution is sufficiently truncated to ensure that the results are robust. One way to do this is to look again at the tomography plot with the truncated bivariate normal contours included. All estimated distributions are truncated to some degree, but we are looking for distributions that have at least part of their 95% contours lopped off by the edge of the tomography plot, and preferably some of the 50% contours as well. If this kind of heavy truncation is present, then it is sometimes best to ignore aggregation bias and use the results from the basic ecological inference model. Figure 13.3 (page 239) gives an example of this kind of truncation. Even better is when the bounds are also very narrow on both parameters and heavy truncation is present, such as in Figure 11.1 (page 221).
17. If aggregation bias is a possibility, and the truncation effects or the bounds are not sufficient to ensure the robustness of the basic model, then the tomography plot should be studied for a different purpose. Recall that all possible values of β_i^b, β_i^w are traced out by a tomography line, with the probable values identified by where the line passes near the center of the contours. If the contours are incorrect, due to aggregation bias, the tomography lines are nevertheless still accurate and information in them still exploited. One useful way to do this is to imagine where the true values might be if aggregation bias of various types exist. Thus, if X_i and β_i^b were positively correlated, the true coordinates of the parameters would be slid down the lines away from the contours in a specific direction. In most cases, this would spread out the true values in different directions. Ask yourself whether your qualitative knowledge of the problem is sufficient to rule out some of the more extreme possibilities. For example, if you only saw the lines in the tomography plot in the the top left graph of Figure 9.2 (page 163), where along the lines would you expect the true values to fall? Is it plausible for the true points to fall in a circle like that in the bottom left graph? Or see Figure 13.3 (page 239), and ask yourself whether in this application it is plausible for the true points to be much farther up along the tomography lines, and hence spread out. Even a very limited qualitative

knowledge of a problem can be enough to rule out many possibilities such as these.

18. If none of these options works and your ultimate goal is to use ecological inferences as dependent variables in a second-stage analysis, then the basic procedure may still be appropriate. That is, aggregation bias often will leave the relative positions of the estimates the same but will bias their absolute positions. The result is that aggregation bias will often produce an arbitrary, nearly uniform shift applied to all precinct estimates. (For example, all values of β_i^b could be too small by say 0.05, except for those already at their lower bound.) This common result can be exploited in a second-stage analysis by using some sort of linear model, such as a version of regression analysis, and ignoring the constant term. That is, aggregation bias in many cases will only bias the constant term in the second stage, but the regression coefficients would still be estimated appropriately.
19. Finally, it is important to consider the extended model procedures in Section 9.2. These involve, in different versions, letting $\breve{\mathfrak{B}}^b$ and $\breve{\mathfrak{B}}^w$ vary over the observations as a specific function of some chosen covariates or even X_i. This means that we are substituting the assumption of no aggregation bias (or robustness to aggregation bias) with an alternative assumption about how the truncated bivariate normal means depend on external covariates. In order to lessen the demands of this alternative assumption, it is sometimes best to choose covariates that are dichotomous (or several dichotomous variables to represent multiple categories of a continuous variable). This way we do not need to worry about the linearity assumption when extrapolating to portions of the parameter space for which few observations exist. Whatever functional form and covariates are chosen, it is best to evaluate this model as described above for the basic model. The only difference is that there is now a different set of contours for each precinct (or group of precincts). Thus, alternative versions of tomography plots like that in Figure 9.5 (page 179) can be used.

    Including external covariates Z_i, or letting Z_i include X_i, can substantially improve model estimates when applied to data with aggregation bias or distributional problems. However, this extended model can degrade the quality of the estimates if the data did not suffer from the problems in the first place. Figure 9.6 (page 180) makes this point and suggests ways of evaluating the tradeoff involved in making the decision to include external covariates. For the vast majority of applications of the extended model, researchers should include a prior distribution on the α^b and α^w parameters (probably with a mean of zero and a positive standard deviation), as a compromise between the extremes of unrestricted inclusion and zero-restriction exclusion of external covariates (see Section 9.2.3). If aggregation bias seems like it will have an important effect on the results, it may be worth including X_i in Z_i and estimating the model several times for a range of prior standard deviations, or at least determining how large α^b and α^w must be to alter your substantive conclusions.

20. Once the model is chosen and the ecological inferences are computed, they should be checked in various ways. Some examples follow:
    a. Most importantly, compare the results with what is known from survey or qualitative evidence. If you have visited one precinct and interviewed some people, how do the results from the quantitative estimates compare to your qualitative evidence? Do not forget to include the uncertainty estimates from the model.
    b. If survey data are not available from the same area you are studying, collect survey data from other regions or the entire country. Even simple analyses such as these can help you ascertain whether the contours are appropriately placed.
    c. An after-the-fact evaluation of aggregation bias can be conducted, as per the procedures in Section 9.2.4, such as most simply by plotting estimates of β_i^b by X_i and β_i^w by X_i.
    d. This same plot used to study aggregation bias also serves as a very informative observable implication of your model and data. The relationships between β_i^b and X_i and between β_i^w and X_i indicated in the plot should be studied to see whether they are consistent with your substantive understanding of the problem.
    e. Second-stage analyses can be used solely for the purpose of checking the results. For example, it would be surprising if black turnout is not higher in stable communities than in areas with very high residential mobility.
    f. Even if the goal of the analysis is not to draw a map, mapping can be extremely useful for evaluating the results, comparing them with what we know about various geographic areas, and identifying outliers.
21. If a second-stage analysis is conducted, least squares regression should probably not be used in most cases, even though it may not be particularly misleading. The best first approach is usually to display a scatter plot of the explanatory variable (or variables) horizontally and (say) an estimate of β_i^b or β_i^w vertically. In many cases, this plot will be sufficient evidence to complete the second-stage analysis.

    If it proves useful to have more of a formal statistical approach, and many of the actual values of β_i^b fall near zero or one, then some method should be used that takes this into account. The data could be transformed, via a logit or probit transformation, or a model like the one in Section 9.2.2 could be applied by replacing X_i with the explanatory variables. Whatever method is chosen, the researcher should be careful to include the fact that some estimates of β_i^b are more uncertain than others.

In practice, a weighted least squares linear regression may be sufficient in many applications, with weights based on the standard error of β_i^b (or other quantity of interest). Researchers should be careful in applying this simplified method here, and should verify its assumptions with scatter plots. The problem is that, according to the model, the variance of β_i^b over i is the sum of two quantities: its estimation variance, which varies over the observations (and is an output of the basic ecological inference model described in this book), and its fundamental variability not explained by the aggregate explanatory variables. That is, even if β_i^b were known with certainty in every precinct, we would not expect the variability in it from precinct to precinct to be perfectly explained by any set of measured explanatory variables. A reasonable approach can be kludged by first running a (homoskedastic) least squares regression and computing the variance of the residuals, which is a rough measure of the total variability of β_i^b over precincts. Then, for each observation, compute the variance, from which the weight will be determined, by subtracting the estimation variance from the total variance. Finally, run a weighted least squares regression. This is not as theoretically elegant a procedure as the more formal setup in Section 9.2.2, but it is simple, relatively robust, and probably complete enough to be of use in many applications.

22. Consider going to Step 1, changing some of your decision rules, and trying everything again.
23. Do you have information from the marginals that breaks the outcome variable into a larger number of categories, such as the 2×3 in Table 2.2 (page 30)? If so, you should use the first procedure developed in Section 8.4 to break the variable into a sequence of dichotomous outcomes. For example, suppose you have the aggregate marginals from a 2×4 table with black/white and outcome categories Democrat/Republican/minor party/no vote. In this case, you can analyze vote/no vote by following steps 1–22 above and then reapply these same steps to study the major/minor party dichotomy, among those who voted, and the Democrat/Republican vote, among those who voted for major party candidates. Section 8.4 explains how to incorporate the additional uncertainty created by having to estimate the outcome marginals from items farther down the list of dichotomous decisions. That section also explains how covariates can be used to improve estimation if the quantities of interest in one item in the sequence are related to those in another.
24. Do you have additional information from the marginals that breaks the classifying variable into additional categories? For example, Table 15.1

(page 265) is black/white/Hispanic by vote/no vote. Data of this type should first be analyzed by breaking the table into a series of 2×2 tables or $2 \times C$ tables, and first analyzed as described in Section 15.1. It may also be desirable to use the methods described in the remainder of Chapter 15.

PART VI

Appendices

APPENDIX A

Proof That All Discrepancies Are Equivalent

THIS APPENDIX proves Equations 3.15–3.19 (page 53). Equations 3.17 and 3.18 were shown to be equal in Section 3.3, and Equation 3.15 is definitional. What remains is to prove the equivalence of Equations 3.16 and 3.18 explicitly.[1] That is,

$$\mathbf{D}(\check{B})_1 = \mathbf{D}(\check{B})_2$$

(Equation 3.19 will also become clear in the course of the proof.)

To begin, define the following expected value, variance, and covariance operators. They can be interpreted as unweighted computations on individuals or weighted calculations on precinct-level averages:

$$\mathbf{E}(a_i) = \frac{1}{N}\sum_{i=1}^{p} N_i a_i \equiv \bar{a},$$

$$\mathbf{V}(a_i) = \frac{1}{N}\sum_{i=1}^{p} N_i (a_i - \bar{a})^2 \equiv \sigma_a^2$$

$$\mathbf{C}(a_i, b_i) = \frac{1}{N}\sum_{i=1}^{p} N_i (a_i - \bar{a})(b_i - \bar{b})$$

for any variables a_i and b_i. In this appendix, these are purely algebraic concepts with no necessarily statistical content. The unweighted averages are for the analogous functions when operating on individual-level data, $\mathrm{E}(a_{ij})$, $\mathrm{V}(a_{ij})$ and $\mathrm{C}(a_{ij}, b_{ij})$.

Factor F out of Equation 3.9:

$$\mathbf{D}(\check{B})_1 = F\left[\frac{\sigma_x^2}{\bar{X}} b_{bx} + \frac{\sigma_x^2}{1-\bar{X}} b_{wx} - \frac{\sigma_h^2}{F\sigma_x^2} b_{rh}\right] \tag{A.1}$$

[1] Because of the way they were each derived in Chapter 3, the equivalence of these expressions has already been proven implicitly. This appendix provides a more direct proof.

where the last term is

$$\frac{\sigma_h^2}{F\sigma_x^2}b_{rh} = \frac{\sigma_h^2}{F\sigma_x^2}\frac{\mathbf{C}(\beta_i, h_i)}{\sigma_h^2}$$

$$= \frac{\mathbf{C}(\beta_i, h_i)}{\bar{X}(1-\bar{X}) - \sigma_x^2}$$

$$= \frac{\mathbf{C}(\beta_i, h_i)}{F\sigma_x^2}$$

and where, using $\beta_i = \beta_i^b - \beta_i^w$ and $h_i = X_i(1 - X_i)$,

$$\begin{aligned}\mathbf{C}(\beta_i, h_i) &= \mathbf{E}(\beta_i h_i) - \mathfrak{B}\mathbf{E}(h_i)\\ &= \mathbf{E}(\beta_i^b h_i) - \mathbf{E}(\beta_i^w h_i) - \mathfrak{B}^b\mathbf{E}(h_i) + \mathfrak{B}^w\mathbf{E}(h_i)\\ &= \mathbf{E}(\beta_i^b X_i) - \mathbf{E}(\beta_i^b X_i^2) - \mathbf{E}(\beta_i^w X_i) + \mathbf{E}(\beta_i^w X_i^2)\\ &\quad - \mathfrak{B}^b\bar{X} + \mathfrak{B}^b\mathbf{E}(X_i^2) + \mathfrak{B}^w\bar{X} - \mathfrak{B}\mathbf{E}(X_i^2) \qquad \text{(A.2)}\end{aligned}$$

To continue with Equation A.2, first note that $\mathbf{E}(X_i^2) = \sigma_x^2 + \bar{X}$, and the parameters to be estimated,

$$B^b = \frac{\sum_{i=1}^p N_i^b \beta_i^b}{N^b} = \frac{\sum_{i=1}^p N_i X_i \beta_i^b}{\sum_{i=1}^p N_i X_i} = \frac{\mathbf{E}(X_i\beta_i^b)}{\bar{X}}$$

and

$$B^w = \frac{\sum_{i=1}^p N_i^w \beta_i^w}{N^w} = \frac{\sum_{i=1}^p N_i(1 - X_i)\beta_i^w}{\sum_{i=1}^p N_i(1 - X_i)} = \frac{\mathfrak{B}^w - \mathbf{E}(X_i\beta_i^w)}{1 - \bar{X}}$$

where

$$\mathfrak{B}^b = \frac{1}{N}\sum_{i=1}^p N_i\beta_i^b, \quad \mathfrak{B}^w = \frac{1}{N}\sum_{i=1}^p N_i\beta_i^w, \quad \mathfrak{B} = \mathfrak{B}^b - \mathfrak{B}^w$$

This gives a solution for

$$\mathbf{E}(X_i\beta_i^b) = B^b\bar{X}$$

$$\mathbf{E}(X_i\beta_i^w) = \mathfrak{B}^w - B^w(1 - \bar{X})$$

I then substitute these into Equation A.2:

$$\begin{aligned}\mathbf{C}(\beta_i, h_i) &= B^b\bar{X} - \mathbf{E}(\beta_i^b X_i^2) - \mathfrak{B}^w + B^w(1-\bar{X}) + \mathbf{E}(\beta_i^w X_i^2)\\ &\quad - \mathfrak{B}^b\bar{X} + \mathfrak{B}\sigma_x^2 + \mathfrak{B}^b\bar{X}^2 + \mathfrak{B}^w\bar{X} - \mathfrak{B}^w\sigma_x^2 - \mathfrak{B}^w\bar{X}^2\\ &= B^b\bar{X} + \mathfrak{B}^b\sigma_x^2 - \mathfrak{B}^w\sigma_x^2 - \mathfrak{B} + B^w(1-\bar{X})\\ &\quad - \mathbf{E}(\beta_i^b X_i^2) + \mathbf{E}(\beta_i^w X_i^2) - \mathfrak{B}^b\bar{X}(1-\bar{X}) + \mathfrak{B}^w\bar{X}(1-\bar{X})\\ &= B\bar{X} + B^w - \mathfrak{B}^w + \mathfrak{B}\sigma_x^2 - \mathbf{E}(\beta_i X_i^2) - B\bar{X}(1-\bar{X}) \qquad \text{(A.3)}\end{aligned}$$

Now expand the expression in Equation 3.18 in order to compare to these results:

$$\mathbf{D}(\breve{B})_2 = F(B - b_{tx\cdot z}) = F(B^b - B^w - b_{tx\cdot z})$$

But, since

$$b_{bx} = \frac{\mathbf{C}(X_i, D_i)}{\mathbf{V}(X_i)} = \frac{\mathbf{E}(X_i\beta_i^b) - \mathfrak{B}_i^b\bar{X}}{\sigma_x^2} \qquad \text{(A.4)}$$

we can solve for B^b:

$$B^b = \frac{\sigma_x^2}{\bar{X}} b_{bx} + \mathfrak{B}^b \qquad \text{(A.5)}$$

Similarly,

$$\begin{aligned}B^w &= \frac{\mathfrak{B} - \mathbf{E}(X_i\beta_i^w)}{1-\bar{X}}\\ &= \frac{\mathfrak{B}^w - b_{wx}\sigma_x^2 - \mathfrak{B}^w\bar{X}}{1-\bar{X}}\\ &= \frac{-\sigma_x^2}{1-\bar{X}} b_{wx} + \mathfrak{B}^w \qquad \text{(A.6)}\end{aligned}$$

Note the similarity of the right side of Equations A.5 and A.6 to Equation A.1.

Completing the proof requires decomposing $b_{tx\cdot z}$, which involves moving to the individual level. To do this, let a variable with a dot on top indicate that the precinct average was subtracted from each individual in the precinct (e.g., $\dot{\mathbb{X}}_{ij} = \mathbb{X}_{ij} - X_i$). In addition, let $\bar{\mathbb{X}} = \mathbb{H}\mathbb{X}$

be a $(N \times 1)$ vector resembling $\mathbb{X}$ except that each element is replaced by the precinct average. Then,

$$b_{tx\cdot z} = (\mathbb{X}'\mathbb{M}\mathbb{X})^{-1}\mathbb{X}'\mathbb{M}\dot{\mathbb{T}}$$

$$= \frac{C(\dot{\mathbb{X}}_{ij}, \dot{\mathbb{T}}_{ij})}{V(\dot{\mathbb{X}}_{ij})} \tag{A.7}$$

Now derive a simpler expression by decomposing each factor in the last line of this equation beginning with the denominator:

$$V(\dot{\mathbb{X}}_{ij}) = E[(\mathbb{X}_{ij} - \bar{\mathbb{X}}_{ij})^2] - 0$$

$$= E(\mathbb{X}_{ij}^2) - 2E(\mathbb{X}_{ij}\bar{\mathbb{X}}_{ij}) - E(\bar{\mathbb{X}}_{ij}^2)$$

$$= \bar{X} - 2E(\mathbb{X}_{ij}\bar{\mathbb{X}}_{ij}) - E(\bar{\mathbb{X}}_{ij}^2)$$

The last two terms in this equation are further reducible as follows:

$$E(\mathbb{X}_{ij}\bar{\mathbb{X}}_{ij}) = \frac{1}{N_i}\sum_{i=1}^{p}\sum_{j=1}^{N_i}\mathbb{X}_{ij}\bar{\mathbb{X}}_{ij}$$

$$= \frac{1}{N_i}\sum_{i=1}^{p}X_i\sum_{j=1}^{N_i}\mathbb{X}_{ij}$$

$$= \frac{1}{N}\sum_{i=1}^{p}N_iX_i^2$$

$$= \mathbf{E}(X_i^2)$$

and similarly for

$$E(\bar{\mathbb{X}}_{ij}^2) = \frac{1}{N_i}\sum_{i=1}^{p}\sum_{j=1}^{N_i}\bar{\mathbb{X}}_{ij}^2$$

$$= \frac{1}{N}\sum_{i=1}^{p}N_iX_i^2$$

$$= \mathbf{E}(X_i^2)$$

Then, noting that $\mathbf{E}(X_i^2) = \sigma_x^2 + \bar{X}^2$, collect terms to produce the final form for the denominator of Equation A.7:

$$\begin{aligned} \mathrm{V}(\dot{\mathbb{X}}_{ij}) &= \bar{X} - 2\mathbf{E}(X_i^2) + \mathbf{E}(X_i^2) \\ &= \bar{X} - \mathbf{E}(X_i^2) \\ &= \bar{X}(1-\bar{X}) - \sigma_x^2 \\ &= F\sigma_x^2 \end{aligned}$$

the penultimate line of which is the individual-level variance minus the aggregate (cross-precinct) variance.

The numerator of Equation A.7 is then

$$\begin{aligned} \mathrm{C}(\dot{\mathbb{X}}_{ij}, \dot{\mathbb{T}}_{ij}) &= \mathrm{E}(\dot{\mathbb{X}}_{ij}\dot{\mathbb{T}}_{ij}) - 0 \\ &= \mathrm{E}(\mathbb{X}_{ij}\mathbb{T}_{ij}) - \mathrm{E}(X_i T_i) \\ &= B^b\bar{X} - \mathbf{E}\left[X_i\left(\beta_i^b X_i + \beta_i^w(1-X_i)\right)\right] \\ &= B^b\bar{X} - B^w + B^b(1-\bar{X}) - \mathbf{E}(\beta_i^b X_i^2) - \mathbf{E}(\beta_i^w X_i^2) \end{aligned}$$

Combining results, this now yields:

$$b_{tx\cdot z} = \frac{1}{F\sigma_x^2}\left[B^b\bar{X} - B^w + B^b(1-\bar{X}) - \mathbf{E}(B_i^b X_i^2) - \mathbf{E}(B_i^w X_i^2)\right]$$

Now use these expressions to prove the final result. First note that

$$\mathbf{D}(\breve{B})_2 = F\left[\frac{\sigma_x^2}{\bar{X}}b_{bx} + \frac{\sigma_x^2}{1-\bar{X}}b_{tx} + C_2\right]$$

where

$$\begin{aligned} C_2 = {} & \mathfrak{B}^b - \mathfrak{B}^w \\ & + \frac{1}{F\sigma_x^2}\left[B^b\bar{X} - B^w + B^b(1-\bar{X}) - \mathbf{E}(\beta_i^b X_i^2) - \mathbf{E}(\beta_i^w X_i^2)\right] \end{aligned}$$

If $C_2 = \mathbf{C}(\beta_i, h_i)/F\sigma_x^2$ (from Equation A.3), then we will have proven that $\mathbf{D}(\check{B})_1 = \mathbf{D}(\check{B})_2$. Thus, factoring out the common denominator, gives

$$C_2 = \frac{1}{F\sigma_x^2}\Big[\mathfrak{B}^b\bar{X}(1-\bar{X}) - \mathfrak{B}^b\sigma_x^2 - \mathfrak{B}^w\bar{X}(1-\bar{X}) + \mathfrak{B}^w\sigma_x^2$$

$$+ B^b\bar{X} - B^w + B^b(1-\bar{X}) - \mathbf{E}(\beta_i^b X_i^2) - \mathbf{E}(\beta_i^w X_i^2)\Big]$$

$$= \frac{1}{F\sigma_x^2}\left[B\bar{X} + B^w - \mathfrak{B}^w + \mathfrak{B}\sigma_x^2 - \mathbf{E}(\beta_i X_i^2) - B\bar{X}(1-\bar{X})\right]$$

$$= \frac{\mathbf{C}(\beta_i, h_i)}{F\sigma_x^2} \qquad \text{QED.}$$

APPENDIX B

Parameter Bounds

THIS APPENDIX provides proofs of the expressions for the bounds on the quantities of interest given in Chapter 5. To follow these proofs, it is helpful to refer to the notation in Tables 2.1 and 2.2 (pages 29 and 30).

B.1 Homogeneous Precincts

Proving the result for homogeneous precincts requires writing down the formulas for each of the parameters in terms of the cell frequencies, substituting in known values in the margins, and finally substituting in for the summary variables, D_i, X_i, and T_i. For example, for $X_i = 1$,

$$\beta_i^b = \frac{N_i^{bT}}{N_i^b} = \frac{N_i^T}{N_i^b} = \frac{T_i}{X_i} = T_i$$

$$\theta_i^b = \frac{N_i^{bD}}{N_i^b} = \frac{N_i^D}{N_i^b} = \frac{D_i}{X_i} = D_i$$

$$\lambda_i^b = \frac{N_i^{bD}}{N_i^{bT}} = \frac{N_i^D}{N_i^T} = \frac{D_i}{T_i} = V_i \qquad \text{(B.1)}$$

In the absence of white voters, β_i^w, θ_i^w, and λ_i^w are undefined.

The same logic provides similar results for homogeneously white precincts, that is where $X_i = 0$:

$$\beta_i^w = \frac{N_i^{wT}}{N_i^w} = \frac{N_i^T}{N_i^w} = \frac{T_i}{(1 - X_i)} = T_i$$

$$\theta_i^w = \frac{N_i^{wD}}{N_i^w} = \frac{N_i^D}{N_i^w} = \frac{D_i}{(1 - X_i)} = D_i$$

$$\lambda_i^w = \frac{N_i^{wD}}{N_i^{wT}} = \frac{N_i^D}{N_i^T} = \frac{D_i}{T_i} = V_i \qquad \text{(B.2)}$$

and in the absence of black voters β_i^b, θ_i^b, and λ_i^b are undefined.

B.2 Heterogeneous Precincts: β's and θ's

Begin by deriving the formal algebraic expressions for the upper bound on $\beta_i^b = N_i^{bT}/N_i^b$. Since N_i^b is known, the only unknown component of β_i^b is N_i^{bT}. Moreover, N_i^{bT} cannot be larger than the total number of people represented in the first column of Table 2.3 (N_i^T) since the column total includes N_i^{bT} ($N_i^T = N_i^{bT} + N_i^{wT}$). Similarly, N_i^{bT} cannot exceed the total number in its row (N_i^b). Thus:

$$\max(N_i^{bT}) = \min(N_i^T, N_i^b) \tag{B.3}$$

where $\min(a, b)$ equals a if $a \leq b$ and b otherwise, and where both a and b are known (i.e., they are in the last column or row of Table 2.3); and where $\max(a)$ is the largest possible value of a given the known values from the last column and row of Table 2.2. Dividing both sides of this equation by N_i^b, gives an upper bound on β_i^b:

$$\begin{aligned}\max(\beta_i^b) &= \max\left(\frac{N_i^{bT}}{N_i^b}\right) = \min\left(\frac{N_i^T}{N_i^b}, \frac{N_i^b}{N_i^b}\right)\\ &= \min\left(\frac{T_i}{X_i}, 1\right)\end{aligned}$$

By a parallel derivation, the largest possible value of β_i^w is:

$$\begin{aligned}\max(\beta_i^w) &= \max\left(\frac{N_i^{wT}}{N_i^w}\right) = \min\left(\frac{N_i^T}{N_i^w}, \frac{N_i^w}{N_i^w}\right)\\ &= \min\left(\frac{T_i}{1 - X_i}, 1\right)\end{aligned}$$

A slightly different procedure will generate the minimum values of these parameters. For β_i^w, use $N_i^{wT} = N_i^T - N_i^{bT}$ and compute:

$$\begin{aligned}\min(N_i^{wT}) &= N_i^T - \max(N_i^{bT})\\ &= N_i^T - \min(N_i^T, N_i^b)\end{aligned}$$

where the last line holds due to Equation B.3. Then divide through by N_i^w to yield the minimum bound for β_i^w:

$$\min(\beta_i^w) = \min\left(\frac{N_i^{wT}}{N_i^w}\right) = \frac{N_i^T}{N_i^w} - \min\left(\frac{N_i^T}{N_i^w}, \frac{N_i^b}{N_i^w}\right)$$

dividing all numerators and denominators by N_i,

$$= \frac{T_i - \min(T_i, X_i)}{1 - X_i}$$

$$= \max\left(0, \frac{T_i - X_i}{1 - X_i}\right)$$

Finally, by collecting the results above, and via parallel derivations for the other parameters, the formal algebraic bounds on the β's and θ's are given in Equations 5.1 (page 79).

B.3 Heterogeneous Precincts: λ_i's

The most straightforward way to find the bounds on λ_i^b is to use the relation

$$\lambda_i^b = \frac{N_i^{bD}}{N_i^{bT}} = \frac{N_i^{bD}}{N_i^{bD} + N_i^{bR}}$$

and, by the procedures followed above, $\min(N_i^{bR}) = N_i^R - \min(N_i^R, N_i^w)$. Now derive the upper bound as follows:

$$\max(\lambda_i^b) = \frac{\max(N_i^{bD})}{\max(N_i^{bD}) + \min(N_i^{bR})}$$

$$= \frac{\min(N_i^D, N_i^b)}{\min(N_i^D, N_i^b) + N_i^R - \min(N_i^R, N_i^w)}$$

$$= \frac{\min(D_i, X_i)}{\min(D_i, X_i) + (T_i - D_i) - \min(T_i - D_i, 1 - X_i)}$$

$$= \frac{\min(D_i, X_i)}{\min(D_i, X_i) + \max(0, (T_i - D_i) - (1 - X_i))}$$

Following parallel procedures for the lower bound on λ_i^b, and both bounds on λ_i^w, yields the results given in Equations 5.4 (page 83).

Conditional Posterior Distribution

THIS APPENDIX proves the result in Equation 6.19 (page 108), which is repeated here:

$$\mathrm{P}(\beta_i^b|T_i, \breve{\psi}) = \mathrm{TN}\left(\beta_i^b \;\middle|\; \breve{\mathfrak{B}}^b + \frac{\omega_i}{\sigma_i^2}\epsilon_i,\; \breve{\sigma}_b^2 - \frac{\omega_i^2}{\sigma_i^2}\right) \tag{C.1}$$

where

$$\omega_i = \breve{\sigma}_b^2 X_i + \breve{\sigma}_{bw}(1 - X_i)$$

$$\epsilon_i = T_i - \mu_i$$

$$\mu_i = \breve{\mathfrak{B}}^b X_i + \breve{\mathfrak{B}}^w(1 - X_i)$$

and

$$\sigma_i^2 = \breve{\sigma}_b^2 X_i^2 + \breve{\sigma}_{bw} 2X_i(1 - X_i) + \breve{\sigma}_w^2(1 - X_i)^2$$

This result is proven in two ways in order to help communicate the logic more clearly. The first is based on Bayes theorem and completing the square. The other approach is based on the properties of normal distributions. Both proofs begin with the corresponding untruncated distributions and then truncate at the end of the proof within the bounds specified in Equations B.1 (page 301) and 5.1 (page 79). This essential algebraic trick makes the mathematics easier and produces a result equivalent to truncating at the start for this problem. For convenience, the mean and variance are parameterized as from the underlying untruncated normal distribution. Note that after truncating, $\breve{\mathfrak{B}}^b + (\omega_i/\sigma_i^2)\epsilon_i$ and $\breve{\sigma}_b^2 - (\omega_i^2/\sigma_i^2)$ are still exactly the two parameters of this distribution, even though they are no longer its expected value and variance.

C.1 Using Bayes Theorem

The first method of proving this result is by applying Bayes Theorem and factoring the resulting joint untruncated distribution (see Griffiths, Drynan, and Prakash, 1979):

$$\begin{aligned}
P(\beta_i^b|T_i, \breve{\psi}) &= \frac{P(\beta_i^b, T_i|\breve{\psi})}{P(T_i|\breve{\psi})} \\
&= \frac{P(\beta_i^b|\breve{\psi})P(T_i|\beta_i^b, \breve{\psi})}{P(T_i|\breve{\psi})} \\
&\propto P(\beta_i^b|\breve{\psi})P(T_i|\beta_i^b, \breve{\psi}) \qquad \text{(C.2)}
\end{aligned}$$

The first factor in the last line of Equation C.2 is given as part of the model (Section 6.1):

$$P(\beta_i^b|\breve{\psi}) = N(\beta_i^b|\breve{\mathfrak{B}}^b, \breve{\sigma}_b^2)$$

The second factor is a normal distribution, similar to the likelihood function in Equation 7.1 (page 134), for one observation and without truncation. The difference is that it is now conditional on $\breve{\psi}$ and so the expected value and variance change. In particular,

$$P(T_i|\beta_i^b, \breve{\psi}) = N(T_i|\dot{\mu}_i, \dot{\sigma}_i^2)$$

where, because β_i^b is constant after conditioning on it, and using the properties of conditional normal distributions,

$$\begin{aligned}
\dot{\mu}_i &\equiv E(T_i|X_i, \beta_i^b) \\
&= \beta_i^b X_i + E(\beta_i^w|\beta_i^b)(1 - X_i) \\
&= \beta_i^b X_i + \left[\breve{\mathfrak{B}}^w + \frac{\breve{\sigma}_{bw}}{\breve{\sigma}_b^2}(\beta_i^b - \breve{\mathfrak{B}}^b)\right](1 - X_i)
\end{aligned}$$

and

$$\begin{aligned}
\dot{\sigma}_i &= V(T_i|X_i, \beta_i^b) \\
&= V(\beta_i^w|\beta_i^b)(1 - X_i)^2 \\
&= \breve{\sigma}_w^2\left(1 - \frac{\breve{\sigma}_{bw}^2}{\breve{\sigma}_b\breve{\sigma}_w}\right)(1 - X_i)^2
\end{aligned}$$

To derive the final untruncated distribution, substitute in the normal distributions from the equations above:

$$P(\beta_i^b|T_i, \breve{\psi}) \propto N(\beta_i^b|\breve{\mathfrak{B}}^b, \breve{\sigma}_b^2)N\left(T_i|\dot{\mu}_i, \dot{\sigma}_i^2\right)$$

Then, by substituting in the algebraic formulas for these expressions and completing the square, this gives the untruncated normal distribution. Truncating this distribution at the bounds in Equation 5.1 (page 79) gives the final result in Equation C.1.

C.2 Using Properties of Normal Distributions

The second method of proving this result involves using the known properties of normal distributions.[1] By putting off truncation until the end, β_i^b and β_i^w are bivariate normal, and T_i is a linear combination of β_i^b and β_i^w ($T_i = \beta_i^b X_i + \beta_i^w(1 - X_i)$); thus, T_i and β_i^b are also bivariate normal. The marginal mean and variance of β_i^b is $\breve{\mathfrak{B}}_i^b$ and σ_b^2. The marginal mean and variance of T_i are $E(T_i) = \mu_i = \breve{\mathfrak{B}}_i^b X_i + \breve{\mathfrak{B}}_i^w(1 - X_i)$ and $\breve{\sigma}_i^2$, respectively. The covariance is $C(\beta_i^b, T_i) = \omega_i$.

Then, using the well-known property from probability theory on how to compute conditional distributions from a bivariate normal distribution, $\beta_i^b|T_i$ is normally distributed. The expected value of this conditional distribution is

$$E(\beta_i^b|T_i) = E(\beta_i^b) + \frac{C(\beta_i^b, T_i)}{V(T_i)}[T_i - E(T_i)] = \breve{\mathfrak{B}}^b + \frac{\omega_i}{\sigma_i^2}\epsilon_i$$

and variance is

$$V(\beta_i^b|T_i) = V(\beta_i^b) - \frac{C(\beta_i^b, T_i)^2}{V(T_i)} = \breve{\sigma}_b^2 - \frac{\omega_i^2}{\sigma_i^2}$$

By truncating this normal distribution of β_i^b at its bounds, we are left with Equation C.1.

[1] My thanks to Andrew Gelman for pointing out this alternative to me.

The Likelihood Function

THE GOAL of this appendix is to derive the likelihood function, $L(\breve{\psi}|T) \propto \prod_{i=1}^{p} P(T_i|\breve{\psi})$, for observations containing heterogeneous precincts ($0 < X_i < 1$), homogenous precincts ($X_i = 0$ or $X_i = 1$), and unanimous precincts ($T_i = 1$ or $T_i = 0$, for $0 < X_i < 1$).[1]

For heterogeneous precincts, begin with the bivariate distribution $P(\beta_i^b, \beta_i^w|\breve{\psi})$, which is joint normal, truncated at $[0,1] \times [0,1]$ (as in Equation 6.14, page 103). Since $\beta_i^w = (T_i - \beta_i^b X_i)/(1 - X_i)$, we can easily transform from $P(\beta_i^b, \beta_i^w|\breve{\psi})$ to $P(\beta_i^b, T_i|\breve{\psi})$ (see DeGroot, 1986: 161ff). The result is also a truncated bivariate normal distribution:

$$P(\beta_i^b, T_i|\breve{\psi}) = \frac{\mathbf{1}(T_i)\mathbf{1}(\beta_i^b)}{R(\breve{\mathfrak{B}}, \breve{\Sigma})} N\left(\beta_i^b, T_i|\breve{\mathfrak{B}}^b, \mu_i, \breve{\sigma}_b^2, \sigma_i^2, \omega_i/(\breve{\sigma}_b\sigma_i)\right)$$

where $\mathbf{1}(T_i)$ equals one if $T_i \in [0,1]$ and zero otherwise, and where $\mathbf{1}(\beta_i^b)$ is one if it falls within its bounds

$$\beta_i^b \in \left[\max\left(0, \frac{T_i - (1 - X_i)}{X_i}\right), \ \min\left(1, \frac{T_i}{X_i}\right)\right]$$

and zero otherwise (see Appendix B or Equation 6.22, page 108), so that together $\mathbf{1}(T_i)$ and $\mathbf{1}(\beta_i^b)$ imply that the support of (β_i^b, T_i) under the distribution is a parallelogram. In addition, $R(\breve{\mathfrak{B}}, \breve{\Sigma})$ is defined in Equation 7.2 (page 134), μ_i is given in Equation 6.16 (page 106), σ_i^2 is in Equation 6.17 (page 106), and ω_i appears in Equation 6.20 (page 108).

Factor this joint distribution into the product of the marginal and conditional distributions, which gives

$$P(\beta_i^b, T_i|\breve{\psi}) \propto \frac{\mathbf{1}(T_i)}{R(\breve{\mathfrak{B}}, \breve{\Sigma})} N(T_i|\mu_i, \sigma_i^2)$$
$$\times N\left(\beta_i^b \,\middle|\, \breve{\mathfrak{B}}^b + \frac{\omega_i}{\sigma_i}\epsilon_i, \breve{\sigma}_b^2 - \frac{\omega_i^2}{\sigma_i^2}\right)\mathbf{1}(\beta_i^b)$$

[1] My thanks to Doug Rivers and Wendy Tam for correcting an error in the derivation for homogeneous precincts and for other suggestions.

Finally, integrate out β_i^b to yield the likelihood function for heterogeneous precincts:

$$P(T_i|\breve{\psi}, 0 \le X_i \le 1) \propto \int_{\max\left(0, \frac{T_i-(1-X_i)}{X_i}\right)}^{\min\left(1, \frac{T_i}{X_i}\right)} P(\beta^b, T_i|\breve{\psi}) d\beta^b$$

$$\propto \frac{\mathbf{1}(T_i)}{R(\breve{\mathfrak{B}}, \breve{\Sigma})} N(T_i|\mu_i, \sigma_i^2) S(\breve{\mathfrak{B}}, \breve{\Sigma})$$

where $S(\breve{\mathfrak{B}}, \breve{\Sigma})$ is defined in Equation 6.23 (page 109).

For homogeneous precincts, we need the marginal distribution of the truncated bivariate normal since if $X_i = 1$ then $T_i = \beta_i^b$, and if $X_i = 0$, then $T_i = \beta_i^w$. Thus, if $X_i = 1$,

$$P(T_i|\breve{\psi}, X_i = 1) = \int_0^1 TN(T_i, \beta^w|\breve{\psi}) d\beta^w$$

$$= \frac{\mathbf{1}(T_i)}{R(\breve{\mathfrak{B}}, \breve{\Sigma})} N(T_i|\breve{\mathfrak{B}}^b, \breve{\sigma}_b^2)$$

$$\times \int_0^1 N\left(\beta^w|\breve{\mathfrak{B}}^w + \breve{\rho}\frac{\breve{\sigma}_w}{\breve{\sigma}_b}(T_i - \breve{\mathfrak{B}}^b), \sigma_w^2(1-\breve{\rho}^2)\right) d\beta^w$$

Analogously, if $X_i = 0$,

$$P(T_i|\breve{\psi}, X_i = 0) = \int_0^1 TN(\beta^b, T_i|\breve{\psi}) d\beta^b$$

$$= \frac{\mathbf{1}(T_i)}{R(\breve{\mathfrak{B}}, \breve{\Sigma})} N(T_i|\breve{\mathfrak{B}}^w, \breve{\sigma}_w^2)$$

$$\times \int_0^1 N\left(\beta^b|\breve{\mathfrak{B}}^b + \breve{\rho}\frac{\breve{\sigma}_b}{\breve{\sigma}_w}(T_i - \breve{\mathfrak{B}}^w), \sigma_b^2(1-\breve{\rho}^2)\right) d\beta^b$$

where for both equations, the last term, which is the difference between two univariate normal cumulative distribution functions, is the only change from the heterogeneous case given the different restrictions on X_i.

Finally, unanimous precincts reveal both β_i^b and β_i^w. When $T_i = 1$, the data become $\beta_i^b = 1$ and $\beta_i^w = 1$, and the likelihood function is a truncated bivariate normal distribution, $TN(1, 1|\breve{\psi})$. Similarly, when $T_i = 0$, the likelihood function is $TN(0, 0|\breve{\psi})$.

The Details of Nonparametric Estimation

THIS APPENDIX summarizes the technical details of the nonparametric model given in Section 9.3.2. To determine the value of the nonparametric density estimate at any point β^b_*, β^w_* in the unit square, compute the following expression:

$$\hat{P}(\beta^b_*, \beta^w_*) = \frac{1}{\sqrt{2\pi p}} \sum_i^p \exp\left(-\frac{1}{2hc_i} d_i^2\right) \tag{E.1}$$

where h is the smoothing parameter, d_i is the perpendicular distance between the coordinates of the point being evaluated (β^b_*, β^w_*) and the tomography line representing the data (T_i and X_i) in precinct i, and c_i is the area under the untruncated bivariate distribution used to make the resulting distribution integrate to one (see Silverman, 1986: 76).

I compute c_i numerically. First determine the coordinates for a set of points equally spaced along the tomography line from precinct i (11 points is sufficient for most applications). For each point, compute the area under a univariate normal distribution, with standard deviation h, that falls perpendicular to the tomography line and between the bounds implied by its intersection with the unit square. The average of these values for the set of points gives a numerical approximation of the area of the constructed distribution.

To sample from the nonparametric posterior distribution for a precinct-level quantity of interest, first evaluate the density for a set of points equally spaced along the line. Then construct a density by piecewise linear approximation (or, in other words, connect the dots). To draw a single value of β^b_i, first decide which category it falls in by assigning probabilities to each interval based on the trapezoidal areas under the new approximate piecewise linear density. Determine the interval into which the drawn value falls by taking a number randomly from the discrete probability distribution given by the cumulative probabilities corresponding to the areas of the trapezoids. Then use the inverse CDF method to draw a random value from the trapezoidal density defined within the chosen interval. Increasing the number of points being evaluated produces simulations arbitrarily close to the correct nonparametric distribution, but in practice most distributions are sufficiently smooth to be well approximated by a dozen or so points.

Once β_i^b is drawn randomly, β_i^w can be computed deterministically by Equation 6.27 (page 113). Any other quantities of interest, such as those at the district level, can be computed from these precinct-level simulations, following the same procedures as in Chapter 8 for parametric estimates.

APPENDIX F

Computational Issues

THE STATISTICAL PROCEDURES introduced in this book were programmed in Gauss (Aptech Systems). (See the Preface, page xix, for information about obtaining these Gauss programs or a stand-alone version that does not require Gauss.) Figure 8.2 was drawn with xfig, and Figure 1.2 was produced with ArcView. The remaining figures were first produced in Gauss, for data analyses, and then redrawn in S+ (StatSci) for inclusion in this manuscript. All software was run on a Hewlett-Packard 715/80 Unix-based workstation. Timing runs on Unix systems is not so obvious because these systems do so many different things at the same time, and different things at different times. Nevertheless, one run of the method on a 2×2 table with about 300 precincts usually took 5–7 minutes.

The log-posterior function was maximized with the help of Aptech System's constrained maximum likelihood module, written by Ronald J. Schoenberg (because of the reparameterizations, the constraints in this algorithm are unnecessary in theory but helpful in practice). I approximated the double integral $R(\breve{\mathfrak{B}}, \breve{\Sigma})$ defined in Equation 7.2 (page 134) using Gauss's bivariate cumulative distribution function CDFBVN (which is from Daley, 1974), as well as with Martin van der Ende's more accurate version, which extends work by Divgi (1979). I verified these and other procedures by direct numerical integration on the unit square. I also experimented with an approximation to the log of this function, and the more general GHK simulation technique (Geweke, Keane, and Runkle, 1994). Relatively infrequently, the chosen function will fail, which is easy to verify by comparing the estimated contours with a plot of the simulated $\tilde{\beta}_i^b$s by $\tilde{\beta}_i^w$s. For certain combinations of the parameter values, an imprecise cumulative bivariate normal function can also give the profile likelihood (Figure 9.4, page 178) an artificial plateau, which is roughly speaking a numerically-induced version of set-valued consistency (Brady, 1985).

There is usually little uncertainty about convergence, which in my experience occurs almost every time. The main exceptions I find are artificially generated data sets that the model does not remotely fit. Problems can be evaluated via tomography plots of T_i by X_i with conditional expected values and confidence intervals included. Extensive explorations of contour plots lead me to believe that the log-posterior probably has no local minima, although I have no mathematical proof. Of course, because the exact posterior distribution is used via importance sampling, the procedure would in principle work the same even if the optimization program converged at a point other than the global maximum.

Simulating from a truncated normal distribution is fastest via the *sample rejection method* in most cases. That is, I drew random numbers from the corresponding untruncated normal distribution and discarded and redrew them for any values that fell outside the allowable bounds (from Chapter 5). If the model is correctly specified, this is almost always the fastest procedure. In some cases when the model is not well specified, sample rejection will take inordinately long. For example, if the model includes an explanatory variable Z_i that leaves the mean ten standard deviations outside the bounds, sampling all week on a fast computer would probably not yield even one admissible value. Warning messages are printed for these cases, since they may suggest a problem with the model specification. For intermediate cases where speed is being sacrificed, but model specification does not appear to be an issue, five attempts were made with the sample rejection method. For the remaining values, I used the *inverse CDF method* to draw directly from the truncated normal distribution. I sampled from the truncated bivariate normal distribution by factoring it into the product of a marginal and conditional normal using the result given in Appendix C. The same rejection sampling and inverse CDF methods were then applied. This is all programmed to operate automatically in the software that accompanies this book.

I used 100 simulations for all estimates presented in this book except where indicated otherwise. Importance sampling generally required about ten draws for each accepted sample; this meant drawing about 1,000 simulations to achieve the required 100 acceptable ones. Experiments with much larger numbers of simulations had only minor consequences, none of substantive interest.

Glossary of Symbols

THIS GLOSSARY includes mathematical symbols used in more than one section or chapter to represent the same concept. (Parenthetical notes provide references back to the text for further information.)[1]

α^b, α^w — Linear effect of the covariates Z_i^b on the precinct means $\breve{\mathfrak{B}}_i^b$, and of Z_i^w on $\breve{\mathfrak{B}}_i^w$, used for the extended model (Equation 9.2, page 170).

B^b, B^w — District-wide fractions of blacks and whites who vote, respectively; district-level quantities of interest, weighted averages of β_i^b and β_i^w (Equation 2.1, page 33).

β_i^b, β_i^w — Proportion of voting age blacks who vote, N_i^{bT}/N_i^b, and whites who vote, N_i^{wT}/N_i^w, respectively, precinct-level quantities of interests (Table 2.3, page 31); $\tilde{\beta}_i^b$ and $\tilde{\beta}_i^w$ are values of β_i^b and β_i^w drawn randomly drawn from their posterior distributions (Section 8.2).

$\mathfrak{B}^b$, $\mathfrak{B}^w$ — Unweighted average of the precinct fractions of blacks and whites who vote respectively (Equation 2.2, page 33); $\mathfrak{B}$ is a vector of $\mathfrak{B}^b$ and $\mathfrak{B}^w$; $\breve{\mathfrak{B}}^b$, $\breve{\mathfrak{B}}^w$, and $\breve{\mathfrak{B}}$ are on the untruncated scale (Section 6.2.2).

D_i — Proportion of voting age population choosing the Democratic candidate, N_i^D/N_i (Table 2.2, page 30).

$\mathbf{D}(\cdot)$ — The Discrepancy, defined as the difference between a given ecological regression estimate and the true value (Equation 3.8, page 45).

$\breve{\mathrm{E}}(\cdot|\cdot)$ — The conditional "expected value" on the untruncated scale, defined for interpretative purposes because when the truncation bounds have little effect it is approximately equal to the actual conditional expected value, $\mathrm{E}(\cdot|\cdot)$ (Equation 6.16, page 106).

ϵ_i — Difference between T_i and its conditional "expected value" μ_i (Equation 6.21, page 108; also Equation 6.25, page 110).

i — Index number for aggregate observations (i.e., precincts), $i = 1, \ldots, p$ (Table 2.1, page 29).

[1] A trend in statistical notation seems to have developed whereby authors occasionally drop subscripts, the limits of summation signs, or other symbols so that their equations look uncluttered or even "pretty." My alternative strategy is to maximize clarity of the concepts these symbols represent, which rarely involves dropping anything.

j — Index number for individuals, $j = 1, \ldots, N_i$ (Section 3.3).

λ_i^b, λ_i^w — Proportion of black voters, N_i^{bD}/N_i^{bT}, and white voters, N_i^{wD}/N_i^{wT}, choosing the Democratic candidate, precinct-level quantities of interest (Table 2.2, page 30).

Λ^b, Λ^w — District-wide fraction of blacks and whites who vote for the Democrats, respectively; district-level quantities of interest (Equation 2.1, page 33).

μ_i — Conditional "expected value" of T_i given X_i on the untruncated scale (Equation 6.16, page 106).

$N(\cdot|\cdot,\cdot)$ — The univariate or multivariate normal distribution, depending on context.

N_i^{gP} — Number of members of ethnic group g who vote for the candidate of party P in precinct i, where ethnic groups include b for blacks and w for whites, and where parties include D for Democrats, R for Republicans (which together is T for voter Turnout), and superscript N for Nonvoters (Table 2.1, page 29). For example, N_i^{bD} is the number of blacks of voting age who cast their ballots for the Democratic candidate in precinct i.

N_i^g — Number of voting-age members of ethnic group g in precinct i, where ethnic groups include b for blacks and w for whites, (Table 2.1, page 29); N^g is the number in this group in the entire district (page 33).

N_i^P — Number of votes for the candidate of party P, where parties include D for Democrats, R for Republicans, (which together is T for voter Turnout), and N for Nonvoters (Table 2.1, page 29); N^P is the number voting for party P in the entire district.

N_i — Number of voting-age people in precinct i (Table 2.1, page 29); N is number of voting-age people in the entire district.

ω_i — The "covariance" (i.e., on the untruncated scale) of β_i^b and T_i (Equation 6.20, page 108; also Section C.2).

p — Number of aggregate observations (i.e., precincts), (Table 2.1, page 29).

ϕ — Vector of five parameters of the truncated bivariate normal on the scale most convenient for estimation (Section 7.3); $\tilde{\phi}$ is a value of ϕ randomly drawn from its posterior distribution (Section 8.2).

ψ — Vector of five parameters of the truncated bivariate normal on the ultimate truncated scale; $\breve{\psi}$ is on the untruncated scale (Section 6.2.2).

$R(\breve{\mathfrak{B}}, \breve{\Sigma})$ Volume under the untruncated normal above the unit square, a normalizing constant (Equation 6.15, page 104; also Equation 7.2, page 134).

ρ Correlation of β_i^b and β_i^w across precincts (Equation 6.4, page 96); $\breve{\rho}$ is on the untruncated scale (Section 6.2.2).

$S(\breve{\mathfrak{B}}, \breve{\Sigma})$ The area of the bivariate normal distribution above the tomography line segment that crosses the unit square divided by the area of the bivariate normal above the untruncated line, a normalizing constant for the likelihood function (Equation 7.3, page 135; also Equation 7.1, page 134).

$\mathrm{TN}(\cdot|\cdot,\cdot)$ The truncated univariate or truncated multivariate normal distribution, depending on context.

σ_i^2 Conditional "variance" of T_i given X_i on the untruncated scale (Equation 6.17, page 106).

σ_b, σ_w, σ_{bw} Standard deviations of β_i^b and β_i^w, and their covariance, across precincts (Equation 6.4, page 96); $\breve{\sigma}_b$, $\breve{\sigma}_w$, and $\breve{\sigma}_{bw}$ are on the untruncated scale (Section 6.2.2).

Σ Variance matrix of the truncated bivariate normal distribution on the ultimate truncated scale; $\breve{\Sigma}$ is on the untruncated scale (Section 6.2.2).

T_i The outcome variable, the proportion of voting age population Turning out to vote, observed at the precinct level, N_i^T/N_i (Table 2.3, page 31); $\bar{T}$ is the district-wide weighted average of T_i, (Equation 3.11, page 47)

$\mathbb{T}_{ij}$ Equals one if voting-age person j in precinct i Turns out to vote and zero if he or she does not (Section 3.3); $\mathbb{T}$ is a stacked vector with elements $\mathbb{T}_{ij}$.

θ_i^b, θ_i^w black vote for the Democratic candidate as a proportion of the black voting-age population in precinct i, N_i^{bD}/N_i^b, and white vote for the Democrat as a fraction of the white voting-age population, N_i^{wD}/N_i^w, (Equation 2.3, page 34).

Θ_i^b, Θ_i^w District-wide black vote for the Democratic candidate as a proportion of the black voting-age population, and white vote as proportion of white voting-age population (Equation 2.4, page 34).

V_i Democratic proportion of the two-party Vote, N_i^D/N_i^T (Section 4.2).

$\breve{\mathrm{V}}(\cdot|\cdot)$ The conditional "variance" on the untruncated scale, defined for interpretative purposes, since because when the truncation bounds have little effect it is approximately equal to the actual conditional variance, $V(\cdot|\cdot)$ (Equation 6.17, page 106).

X_i — Proportion of voting-age people who are black, N_i^b/N_i (Table 2.3, page 31); $\bar{X}$ is the district-wide weighted average of the precinct proportions of voting-age people who are black (note 5, page 45); x_i is the usually unobserved proportion of voters who are black N_i^{bT}/N_i^T (Section 4.2).

$\mathbb{X}_{ij}$ — Equals one if voting-age person j in precinct i is black and zero if white (Section 3.3); $\mathbb{X}$ is a stacked vector with elements $\mathbb{X}_{ij}$.

Z_i^b, Z_i^w — Vectors of covariates used to model variation in $\breve{\mathfrak{B}}_i^b$ and $\breve{\mathfrak{B}}_i^w$, respectively, in the extended model (Section 9.2.1).

References

Achen, Christopher H. 1986. "Necessary and Sufficient Conditions for Unbiased Aggregation of Cross-Sectional Regressions." Paper presented at the annual meetings of the American Political Science Association, Washington D.C., 28–31 August.

Achen, Christopher H. 1993. "MLE, Aggregate Data, and the Montana Test." Paper prepared for delivery at the annual meetings of the American Political Science Association, Washington, D.C., 1–5 September.

Achen, Christopher H., and W. Phillips Shively. 1995. *Cross-Level Inference*. Chicago: University of Chicago Press.

Agnew, John. 1996. "Mapping Politics: How Context Counts in Electoral Geography." *Political Geography* 15: 129–146.

Aigner, Dennis J., and Stephen M. Goldfeld. 1974. "Estimation and Prediction from Aggregate Data when Aggregates are Measured More Accurately Than Their Components." *Econometrica* 42: 113–134.

Akdeniz, Fikri, and George A. Milliken. 1975. "The Relationship between Macro and Micro Parameters." *International Economic Review* 16: 511–515.

Alba, Richard D., and John R. Logan. 1992. "Analyzing Locational Attainments: Constructing Individual-Level Regression Models Using Aggregate Data." *Sociological Methods and Research* 20: 367–397.

Alker, Hayward R., Jr. 1969. "A Typology of Ecological Fallacies," pp. 69–86 in Dogan and Rokkan (1969).

Allardt, Erik. 1969. "Aggregate Analysis: The Problem of Its Informative Value," pp. 41–52 in Dogan and Rokkan (1969).

Allenby, Greg M., and Peter E. Rossi. 1991. "There Is No Aggregation Bias: Why Macro Logit Models Work." *Journal of Business and Economic Statistics* 9: 1–14.

Allport, Floyd H. 1924. "The Group Fallacy in Relation to Social Science." *American Journal of Sociology* 29: 688–703.

Alt, James E. 1993. "Persistence and Change in Southern Voter Registration Patterns, 1972–1990." Paper prepared for the workshop on Race, Ethnicity, Representation, and Governance, Harvard University, 21–22 January.

Alt, James E., Gary King, and Curtis Signorino. 1996. "Estimating the Same Quantities from Different Levels of Data: Time Dependence and Aggregation in Event Process Models." Paper presented at the annual meeting of the Midwest Political Science Association, Chicago, Illinois.

Amemiya, Takeshi. 1973. "Regression Analysis When Variance of Dependent Variable is Proportional to the Square of its Expectation," *Journal of the American Statistical Association* 68: 928–934.

Anselin, Luc. 1988. *Spatial Econometrics: Methods and Models*. Boston: Kluwer Academic Publishers.

Ansolabehere, Stephen, and Douglas Rivers. 1992. "Using Aggregate Data to Correct for Nonresponse and Misreporting in Surveys." Paper presented to the annual meeting of the Political Methodology Group, Harvard University.

Ansolabehere, Stephen, and Douglas Rivers. 1994. "Bias in Ecological Regression Estimates." Unpublished paper, Stanford University.

Attanasio, Orazio P., and Guglielmo Weber. 1993. "Consumption Growth, the Interest Rate and Aggregation." *Review of Economic Studies* 60: 631–649.

Bacharach, Michael. 1971. *Biproportional Matrices and Input-Output Change*. Cambridge, Cambridge University Press.

Barker, Terry S., and M. Hashem Pesaran, eds. 1990. *Disaggregation in Econometric Modeling*. London: Routledge.

Beck, Nathaniel. 1983. "Time Varying Parameter Regression Models." *American Journal of Political Science* 27: 557–600.

Ben-Akiva, Moshe, and Steven R. Lerman. 1989. *Discrete Choice Analysis: Theory and Application to Travel Demand*. Cambridge: MIT Press.

Beran, Rudolf, Andrey Feuerverger, and Peter Hall. 1996. "On Nonparametric Estimation of Intercept and Slope Distributions in Random Coefficient Regression." Unpublished paper, Department of Statistics, University of California, Berkeley.

Berelson, Bernard R., Paul F. Lazarsfeld, and William N. McPhee. 1954. *Voting*. Chicago: University of Chicago Press.

Berg, S. 1988. "Spatial Influence on Voter Transitions in Swedish Elections: An Application of Johnston's Maximum Entropy Method." *Electoral Studies* 7: 233–250.

Berglund, Sten, and Søren Risbjerg Thomsen. 1990. *Modern Political Ecological Analysis*. Abo: Abo Akademis Forlang.

Bergström, R., and P.-A. Edin. 1992. "Time Aggregation and the Distributional Shape of Unemployment Duration." *Journal of Applied Econometrics* 7: 5–30.

Bernstein, F. 1932. "Über eine Methode, die Soziologische und Bevölkerungsstatistische Gliederung von Abstimmungen bei Geheimem Wahlverfahren Statistisch zu Ermitteln." *Allgemeines Statistisches Archiv* 22: 253–56. ["A Method to Determine Statistically the Sociological and Demographic Structure of Voting in Secret Elections," translated by W. Phillips Shively and reprinted in pp. 25–28 of Achen and Shively (1995).]

Bidwell, Charles E., and John D. Karsarda. 1975. "Specification of Models for Organizational Effectiveness." *American Sociological Review* 40: 55–70.

Birdsall, Nancy, and Jere R. Behrman. 1984. "Does Geographical Aggregation Cause Overestimates of the Returns to Schooling?" *Oxford Bulletin of Economics and Statistics* 46: 55–72.

Bishop, Y. M. M., S. E. Fienberg, and P. W. Holland. 1975. *Discrete Multivariate Analysis*. Cambridge: MIT Press.

Blalock, Hubert M., 1964. *Causal Inferences in Nonexperimental Research*. Chapel Hill: University of North Carolina Press.

Blau, Judith, and Peter Blau. 1982. "The Cost of Inequality: Metropolitan Structure and Violent Crime." *American Sociological Review* 47: 114–29.

Blau, Peter M., 1960. "Structural Effects." *American Sociological Review* 25: 178–193.

Blundell, Richard, Panos Pashardes, and Guglielmo Weber. 1993. "What Do We Learn about Consumer Demand Patterns from Micro Data?" *American Economic Review* 83: 570–597.

Bogue, Donald J., and Elizabeth J. Bogue. 1982. "Ecological Correlation Reexamined: A Refutation of the Ecological Fallacy," pp. 88–103 in George A. Theodorson ed., *Urban Patterns: Studies in Human Ecology*. University Park: Pennsylvania State University Press.

Booth, David E., and Stephane E. Booth. 1988. "An Introduction to the Use of Ecological and Robust Regression in Historical Research." *Historical Methods* 21: 35–44.

Borgatta, Edgar F., and David J. Jackson, eds. 1980. *Aggregate Data: Analysis and Interpretation*. Beverly Hills: Sage Publications.

Boudman, A. R. 1983. "The Neighbourhood Effect: A Test of the Butler-Stokes Model." *British Journal of Political Science* 13: 243–249.

Boudon, Raymond. 1963. "Propriétés individuelles et propriétés collectives: Un problème d'analyse écologique." *Revue Française de Sociologie* 4: 275–299.

Boyd, Lawrence H., and Gudmund R. Iversen. 1979. *Contextual Analysis: Concepts and Statistical Techniques*. Belmont, Cal.: Wadsworth.

Brady, Henry E. 1985. "Statistical Consistency and Hypothesis Testing for Nonmetric Multidimensional Scaling," *Psychometrika* 50: 509–537.

Brenner, H., D. A. Savitz, K. H. Jöckel, S. Greenland. 1992. "Effects of Nondifferential Exposure Misclassification in Ecologic Studies." *American Journal of Epidemiology* 135: 85–95.

Breslaw, Jon A. 1994. "Evaluation of Multivariate Normal Probability Integrals Using a Low Variance Simulator." *Review of Economics and Statistics* 76: 673–682.

Breslow, Norman. 1990. "Biostatistics and Bayes" (with discussion). *Statistical Science* 5: 269–298.

Brown, Philip J., and Clive D. Payne. 1986. "Aggregate Data, Ecological Regression, and Voting Transitions." *Journal of the American Statistical Association* 81: 452–460.

Bruner, Jere. 1976. "What's the Question to that Answer? Measures and Marginals in Crosstabulation." *American Journal of Political Science* 20: 781–804.

Brunner, Ronald D., and Klaus Liepelt. 1972. "Data Analysis, Process Analysis, and System Change." *Midwest Journal of Political Science* 16: 538–569.

Bryk, Anthony S., and Stephen W. Raudenbush. 1992. *Hierarchical Linear Models: Data Analysis Methods*. Newbury Park, Cal: Sage Publications.

Bullock, Charles S., III. 1991. "Misinformation and Misperceptions: A Little Knowledge Can Be Dangerous." *Social Science Quarterly* 72: 834–839.

Bulmer, Martin. 1984. *The Chicago School of Sociology: Institutionalization, Diversity, and the Rise of Sociological Research*. Chicago: University of Chicago Press.

Buse, Adolph. 1992. "Aggregation, Distribution and Dynamics in the Linear and Quadratic Expenditure Systems." *Review of Economic Statistics* 74: 45–53.

Butler, David, and Donald Stokes. 1969. *Political Change in Britain: Forces Shaping Electoral Choice*. New York: St. Martin's Press.

Byrne, James, and Robert J. Sampson, eds. 1986. *The Social Ecology of Crime*. New York: Springer-Verlag.

Carlin, Bradley. 1989. "Counteracting the Ecological Fallacy: Improved Estimation of Individual Correlation from Aggregate Data." *American Statistical Association, Proceedings of the Social Statistics Section*, pp. 234–239.

Cartright, Phillip A., and Cheng F. Lee. 1987. "Time Aggregation and the Estimation of the Market Model: Empirical Evidence." *Journal of Business and Economic Statistics* 5: 131–143.

Chambers, Robert G., and Rulon D. Pope. 1991. "Testing for Consistent Aggregation." *American Journal of Agricultural Economics* 73: 808–818.

Childers, Thomas. 1983. *The Nazi Voter: The Social Foundations of Fascism in Germany, 1919–1933*. Chapel Hill: University of North Carolina Press.

Choi, In. 1992. "Effects of Data Aggregation on the Power of Tests for a Unit Root." *Economics Letters* 40: 397–401.

Claggett, William, and John Van Wingen. 1993. "An Application of Linear Programming to Ecological Inference: An Extension of an Old Procedure." *American Journal of Political Science* 37: 633–661.

Clark, William A. V., and K. L. Avery. 1976. "The Effects of Data Aggregation in Statistical Analysis." *Geographic Analysis* 8: 428–433.

Clark, William A. V., and Peter A. Morrison. "Demographic Paradoxes in the Los Angeles Voting Rights Case." *Evaluation Review* 15: 712–726.

Cleave, Nancy. 1992. *Ecological Inference*. Ph.d. dissertation, University of Liverpool.

Cleave, Nancy, P. J. Brown, and C. D. Payne. 1995. "Evaluation of Methods for Ecological Inference. Unpublished paper, University of Liverpool.

Cohen, Bernard L. 1990. "Ecological versus Case-Control Studies for Testing a Linear-No Threshold Dose Response Relationship." *International Journal of Epidemiology* 19: 680–684.

Cohen, Bernard L. 1994. "Invited Commentary: In Defense of Ecologic Studies for Testing a Linear-No Threshold Theory." *American Journal of Epidemiology* 139: 765–768.

Connor, Michael J., Dennis B. Gillings, Sandra B. Greene. 1981. "The Ecological Fallacy: Assessing the Effects of Changing Units of Analysis." *Proceedings of the American Statistical Association, Social Statistics Section*, pp. 183–188.

Converse, Philip E. 1969. "Survey Research and the Decoding of Patterns in Ecological Data," pp. 459–486 in Dogan and Rokkan (1969).

Cox, David R. 1957. "Note on Grouping." *Journal of the American Statistical Association* 52: 543–547.

Cox, Lawrence H. 1995. "Network Models for Complementary Cell Suppression." *Journal of the American Statistical Association* 90: 1,453–1,462.

Cramer, J. S. 1964. "Efficient Grouping, Regression, and Correlation in the Engle Curve Analysis." *Journal of the American Statistical Association* 59: 233–250.

Cramer, J. S. 1986. *Economic Applications of Maximum Likelihood Methods*. New York: Cambridge University Press.

Cressie, Noel A. C. 1993. *Statistics for Spatial Data*. Revised ed. New York: Wiley.

Crewe, Ivor, and Clive Payne. 1976. "Another Game with Nature: An Ecological Regression Model of the British Two-Party Vote Ratio in 1970." *British Journal of Political Science* 6: 43–81.

Daley, D. J. 1974. "Computation of Bi- and Tri-variate Normal Integrals." *Applied Statistics* 23: 435–438.

Davis, James A., Joe L. Spaeth, and Carolyn Huson. 1961. "A Technique for Analyzing the Effects of Group Composition." *American Sociological Review* 26: 215–225.

Debreu, Gerard. 1974. "Excess Demand Functions." *Journal of Mathematical Economics* 1: 15–23.

Deming, W. E., and F. F. Stephan. 1940. "On a Least Squares Adjustment of a Sampled Frequency Table when Expected Marginal Totals are Known." *Annals of Mathemtical Statistics* 11: 427–444.

Deutsch, Karl W., 1969. "On Methodological Problems of Quantitative Research," pp. 19–40 in Dogan and Rokkan (1969).

De Wolff, Pieter. 1941. "Income Elasticity of Demand, a Micro-Economic and a Macro-Economic Interpretation." *Economics Journal* 51: 140–145.

DeGroot, Morris. 1986. *Probability and Statistics*. Second ed. Reading, MA: Addison-Wesley.

Divgi, D. R. 1979. "Calculation of the Univariate and Bivariate Normal Integral." *Annals of Statistics* 7: 903–910.

Dogan, Mattei, and Stein Rokkan. 1969. *Quantitative Ecological Analysis in the Social Sciences*. Cambridge: MIT Press.

Drost, Feike C., and Theo E. Nijman. 1993. "Temporal Aggregation of Garch Processes." *Econometrica* 61: 909–927.

Duncan, Otis Dudley, and Beverly Davis. 1953. "An Alternative to Ecological Correlation." *American Sociological Review* 18: 665–666.

Duncan, Otis Dudley, Ray P. Cuzzort, and Beverly Duncan. 1961. *Statistical Geography: Problems in Analyzing Areal Data*. Westport, Conn.: Greenwood Press.

Dunn, D. M., W. H. Williams, and T. L. DeChaine. 1976. "Aggregate versus Subaggregate Models in Local Area Forecasting." *Journal of the American Statistical Association* 71: 68–71.

Dykstra, Robert R. 1986. "Ecological Regression Estimates: Alchemist's Gold?" *Social Science History* 10: 85–90.

Efron, Bradley, and Carl Morris. 1973. "Combining Possibly Related Estimation Problems" (with discussion). *Journal of the Royal Statistical Society*, Series B, 35: 379–421.

Elklit, Jorgen. 1985. "Nominal Record Linkage and the Study of Non-Secret Voting: A Danish Case." *Journal of Interdisciplinary History* 15: 419–443.

Engstrom, Richard L. 1990. "Getting the Numbers Right: A Response to Wildgen." *The Urban Lawyer* 22: 495–502.

Epstein, Seymour. 1986. "Does Aggregation Produce Spuriously High Estimates of Behavior Stability?" *Journal of Personality and Social Psychology* 50: 1,199–1,210.

Erbring, Lutz. 1989. "Individuals Writ Large: An Epilogue on the 'Ecological Fallacy'." *Political Analysis* 1: 235–269.

Ersson, Svante, and Ingemar Wörlund. 1990. "Level of Aggregation and Ecological Inference: A Study of the Swedish Elections in 1944 and 1979," pp. 131–147 in Berglund and Thomsen (1990).

Escobar, Michael D., and Mike West. 1995. "Bayesian Density Estimation and Inference Using Mixtures." *Journal of the American Statistical Association* 90: 577–588.

Ezzati, A. 1974. "Forecasting Market Shares of Alternative Home-Heating Units by Markov Process Using Transition Probabilities Estimated from Aggregate Time Series Data." *Management Science* 21: 462–473.

Fairfield Smith, H. 1938. [untitled article]. *Journal of Agricultural Science* 28: 1–23.

Falter, Jürgen W. 1991. *Hitlers Wähler*. Münich: Beck.

Farebrother, R. W. 1979. "Estimation with Aggregated Data." *Journal of Econometrics* 10: 43–55.

Farkas, George. 1974. "Specification, Residuals and Contextual Effects." *Sociological Methods and Research* 2: 333–363.

Feige, Edgar L., and Harold W. Watts. 1972. "An Investigation of the Consequences of Partial Aggregation of Micro-Economic Data." *Econometrica* 40: 343–360.

Firebaugh, Glenn. 1978. "A Rule for Inferring Individual-Level Relationships from Aggregate Data." *American Sociological Review* 43: 557–572.

Firebaugh, Glenn. 1993. "Are Bad Estimates Good Enough for the Courts?" *Social Science Quarterly* 74: 488–496.

Fisher, Ronald A. 1915. "Frequency Distribution of the Values of the Correlation Coefficient in Samples from an Indefinitely Large Population." *Biometrika* 10: 507–521.

Fisher, Walter D. 1969. *Clustering and Aggregation in Economics*. Baltimore: Johns Hopkins University Press.

Fisher, Walter D. 1979. "A Note on Aggregation and Disaggregation." *Econometrica* 47: 739–746.

Flanigan, William H., and Nancy Zingale. 1985. "Alchemist's Gold: Inferring Individual Relationships from Aggregate Data." *Social Science History* 9: 71–92.

Forcina, A., and G. M. Marchetti. 1989. "Modelling Transition Probabilities in the Analysis of Aggregated Data," pp. 157–164 in A. Decarli, B. J. Francis, R. Gilchrist, and G. U. H. Seber, eds., *Statistical Modeling (Proceedings, Trento 1989)*. Berlin: Springer-Verlag.

Forcina, A., and G. M. Marchetti. 1991. "Effects of Misspecification in the Brown and Payne Model." Paper presented at the European Consortium for Political Research Workshop, Essex, England, 22–26 March.

Fotheringham, A. S., and D. W. S. Wong. 1991. "The Modifiable Areal Unit Problem in Multivariate Statistical Analysis." *Environment and Planning, A,* 23: 1,025–1,045.

Freedman, David A., Stephen P. Klein, Jerome Sacks, Charles A. Smyth, and Charles G. Everett. 1991. "Ecological Regression and Voting Rights." *Evaluation Review* 15: 673–711, with introduction by David L. Rubinfeld, comments by William V. Clark, Peter A. Morrison, William O'Hare, Bernard Grofman, and Allan J. Lichtman, and rejoinder.

Fromm, Gary, and George R. Schink. 1973. "Aggregation and Econometric Models." *International Economic Review* 14: 1–32.

Gardner, R. J. 1995a. *Geometric Tomography*. New York: Cambridge University Press.

Gardner, R. J. 1995b. "Geometric Tomography." *Notices of the American Mathematical Society*, 42: 422–429.

Gehlke, C. E., and Katherine Biehl. 1934. "Certain Effects of Grouping upon Size of the Correlation Coefficient in Census Tract Material." *Journal of the American Statistical Association Supplement* 29: 663–664.

Gelman, Andrew, John B. Carlin, Hal S. Stern, and Donald B. Rubin. 1995. *Bayesian Data Analysis*. London: Chapman and Hall.

Gelman, Andrew, and Gary King. 1990. "Estimating the Electoral Consequences of Legislative Redistricting." *Journal of the American Statistical Association* 85: 274–282.

Gelman, Andrew, and Gary King. 1994a. "Enhancing Democracy through Legislative Redistricting." *American Political Science Review* 88: 541–559.

Gelman, Andrew, and Gary King. 1994b. "A Unified Method of Evaluating Electoral Systems and Redistricting Plans." *American Journal of Political Science* 38: 514–554.

Geweke, John. 1978. "Temporal Aggregation in the Multiple Regression Model" (with comments). *Econometrica*, 46: 643–661.

Geweke, John. 1985. "Macroeconomic Modeling and the Theory of the Representative Agent." *American Economic Review (papers and proceedings)* 75: 206–210.

Geweke, John, Michael Keane, and David Runkle. 1994. "Alternative Computational Approaches to Inference in the Multinomial Probit Model." *Review of Economics and Statistics* 76: 609–631.

Giles, Michael W., and Kaenan Hertz. 1994. "Racial Threat and Partisan Identification." *American Political Science Review* 88: 317–326.

Goldberger, Arthur. 1991. *A Course in Econometrics*. Cambridge: Harvard University Press.

Good, I. J. 1963. "Maximum Entropy for Hypothesis Formulation, Especially for Multidimensional Contingency Tables." *Annals of Mathematical Statistics* 64: 911–934.

Goodfriend, Marvin. 1992. "Information-Aggregation Bias." *American Economic Review* 82: 508–519.

Goodman, Leo. 1953a. "Ecological Regressions and the Behavior of Individuals." *American Sociological Review* 18: 663–666.

Goodman, Leo. 1953b. "A Further Note on Miller's 'Finite Markov Processes in Psychology'." *Psychometrika* 18: 245–248.

Goodman, Leo. 1959. "Some Alternatives to Ecological Correlation." *American Journal of Sociology* 64: 610–624.

Gordon, Stephen. 1992. "Costs of Adjustment, the Aggregation Problem and Investment." *Review of Economics and Statistics* 74: 422–429.

Gorman, William M. 1953. "Community Preference Fields." *Econometrica* 21: 63–80.

Gow, David John. 1985. "Quantification and Statistics in the Early Years of American Political Science, 1880–1922." *Political Methodology* 11: 1–18.

Granger, Clive W. J. 1980. "Long Memory Relationships and the Aggregation of Dynamic Models." *Journal of Econometrics* 14: 227–238.

Granger, Clive W. J. 1987. "Implications of Aggregation with Common Factors." *Econometric Theory* 3: 208–222.

Graunt, John. 1662. *Natural and Political Observations Mentioned in a Following Index, and Made upon the Bills of Mortality*. London: John Martyn and James Allestry.

Green, H. A. John. 1964. *Aggregation in Economic Analysis*. Princeton: Princeton University Press.

Greenland, Sander. 1992. "Divergent Biases in Ecologic and Individual-level Studies." *Statistics in Medicine* 11: 1,209–1,223.

Greenland, Sander, and H. Brenner. 1993. "Correcting for Nondifferential Misclassification in Ecologic Analyses." *Applied Statistics* 42: 117–126.

Greenland, Sander, and H. Morgenstern. 1989. "Ecological Bias, Confounding, and Effect Modification." *International Journal of Epidemiology* 18: 269–274.

Greenland, Sander, and James Robins. 1994a. "Invited Commentary: Ecologic Studies—Biases, Misconceptions, and Counterexamples." *American Journal of Epidemiology* 139: 747–760.

Greenland, Sander, and James Robins. 1994b. "Accepting the Limits of Ecologic Studies: Drs. Greenland and Robins Reply to Drs. Piantadosi and Cohen." *American Journal of Epidemiology* 8: 769–771.

Griffiths, William E., Ross G. Drynan, and Surekha Prakash. 1979. "Bayesian Estimation of a Random Coefficient Model." *Journal of Econometrics* 10: 201–220.

Grofman, Bernard. 1991a. "Straw Men and Stray Bullets: A Reply to Bullock." *Social Science Quarterly* 72: 840–843.

Grofman, Bernard. 1991b. "Statistics without Substance: A Critique of Freedman et al. and Clark and Morrison." *Evaluation Review* 15: 746–769.

Grofman, Bernard, Lisa Handley, and Richard G. Niemi. 1992. *Minority Representation and the Quest for Voting Equality*. New York: Cambridge University Press.

Grofman, Bernard, Michael Migalski, and Nicholas Noviello. 1985. "The 'Totality of Circumstances' Test in Section 2 of the 1982 Extension of the Voting Rights Act: A Social Science Perspective." *Law and Policy* 7: 209–223.

Grunfeld, Yehuda, and Zvi Griliches. 1960. "Is Aggregation Necessarily Bad?" *Review of Econometrics and Statistics*, 42: 1–13.

Gupta, Kanhya L., 1969. *Aggregation in Economics*. Rotterdam: Rotterdam University Press.

Gupta, Kanhya L. 1971. "Aggregation Bias in Linear Economic Models." *International Economic Review* 12: 293–305.

Haitovsky, Yoel. 1966. "Unbiased Multiple Regression Coefficients Estimated from One-Way Classification Tables When the Cross-classifications are Unknown." *Journal of the American Statistical Association* 61: 720–728.

Hamilton, Richard F. 1982. *Who Voted for Hitler?* Princeton: Princeton University Press.

Hammond, John L. 1973. "Two Sources of Error in Ecological Correlations." *American Sociological Review* 38: 764–777.

Hand, Carol A., and James E. Prather. 1986. "The Impact of Aggregation Bias upon the Interpretation of Test Scores across Schools." *American Statistical Association, Proceedings of the Social Statistics Section*, pp. 80–82.

Hannan, Michael T. 1971. "Problems of Aggregation," pp. 403–440 in H. M. Blalock, ed., *Causal Models in the Social Sciences*, Chicago: Aldine-Atherton.

Hannan, Michael T. 1974. "Estimation from Grouped Observations." *American Sociological Review* 39: 374–392.

Hannan, Michael T. 1991. *Aggregation and Disaggregation in the Social Sciences*. Revised ed., Lexington, Mass. Lexington Books.

Hannan, Michael T., and Leigh Burstein. 1974. "Estimation from Grouped Observations." *American Sociological Review* 39: 374–392.

Hanushek, Erik A., John E. Jackson, and John F. Kain. 1974. "Model Specification, Use of Aggregate Data, and the Ecological Correlation Fallacy." *Political Methodology* 1: 89–107.

Hanushek, Eric A., Steven G. Rivkin, and Lori L. Taylor. 1995. "Aggregation and the Estimated Effects of School Resources." Rochester Center for Economic Research, Working Paper no. 397. Rochester, N.Y.

Hatt, P. K. 1946. "The Concept of Natural Area." *American Sociological Review* 11: 423–428.

Hauser, Robert M. 1974. "Contextual Analysis Revisited." *Sociological Methods and Research* 2: 365–375.

Hawkes, A. G. 1969. "An Approach to the Analysis of Electoral Swing." *Journal of the Royal Statistical Society* 31: 68–79.

Heckman, James J., and Guilherme Sedlacek. 1985. "Heterogeneity, Aggregation and Market Wage Functions: An Empirical Model of Self-Selection in the Labor Market." *Journal of Political Economy* 93: 1,077–1,125.

Heineke, John M., and Herschel M. Shefrin. 1990. "Aggregation and Identification in Consumer Demand Systems." *Journal of Econometrics* 44: 377–390.

Heitjan, Daniel F. 1989. "Inference from Grouped Continuous Data: A Review." *Statistical Science* 4: 164–183.

Heitjan, Daniel F., and Donald B. Rubin. 1990. "Inference from Coarse Data via Multiple Imputation with Application to Age Heaping." *Journal of the American Statistical Association* 85: 304–314.

Hildreth, C., and J. P. Houck. 1968. "Some Estimates for a Linear Model with Random Coefficients." *Journal of the American Statistical Association* 63: 584–595.

Hsiao, Cheng. 1975. "Some Estimation Methods for a Random Coefficient Model." *Econometrica* 43: 305–325.

Huckfeldt, Robert, and John Sprague. 1987. "Networks in Context: The Social Flow of Political Information." *American Political Science Review* 81: 1,197–1,116.

Huston, James L. 1991. "Weighting, Confidence Intervals, and Ecological Inference." *Journal of Interdisciplinary History* 21: 631–654.

Ijiri, Yuji. 1965. "The Linear Aggregation Coefficient as the Dual of the Linear Correlation Coefficient." *Econometrica* 36: 252–259.

Ijiri, Yuji. 1971. "Fundamental Queries in Aggregation Theory." *Journal of the American Statistical Association* 66: 766–782.

Irwin, Galen A. 1967. "Two Methods for Estimating Voter Transition Probabilities." Ph.D. dissertation, Florida State University.

Irwin, Galen A., and Duane A. Meeter. 1969. "Building Voter Transition Models from Aggregate Data." *Midwest Journal of Political Science* 13: 545–566.

Irwin, Laura, and Allan J. Lichtman. 1976. "Across the Great Divide: Inferring Individual Level Behavior from Aggregate Data." *Political Methodology* 2: 411–439.

Isard, Walter. 1956. "Regional Science, the Concept of Region, and Regional Structure." *Papers and Proceedings of the Regional Science Association* 2: 13–26.

Ivansson, S. 1987. "Crosshole Transmission Tomography," chapter 7 in Guust Nolet, ed., *Seismic Tomography*. Boston: D. Reidel.

Iversen, Gudmund R. 1969. "Estimation of Cell Entries in Contingency Tables when Only Margins Are Observed." Ph.D. dissertation, Harvard University.

Iversen, Gudmund R. 1973. "Recovering Individual Data in the Presence of Group and Individual Effects." *American Journal of Sociology* 79: 420–434.

Jackman, Simon. 1996. "Bayesian Tools for Social Scientists." Paper presented at the Annual Meetings of the American Political Science Association, San Francisco.

Jackson, John E. 1991. "Estimation of Models with Variable Coefficients." *Political Analysis* 3: 27–49.

Janson, Carl-Gunnar. 1969. "Some Problems of Ecological Factor Analysis," pp. 301–342 in Dogan and Rokkan (1969).

Johnston, R. J., and A. M. Hay. 1982. "On the Parameters of the Uniform Swing in Single-Member Constituency Electoral Systems." *Environment and Planning, A* 14: 61–74.

Johnston, R. J., A. M. Hay, and P. J. Taylor. 1982. "Estimating the Sources of Spatial Change in Election Results: A Multiproportional Matrix Approach." *Environment and Planning, A* 14: 951–961.

Johnston, R. J., and C. J. Pattie. 1990. "Estimating and Analyzing the Unknown: Entropy-Maximising Procedures, Flow-of-the-Vote Matrices, and Tactile Voting in Great Britain." Unpublished paper, Department of Geography, University of Sheffield.

Johnstone, Iain M., and Bernard W. Silverman. 1990. "Speed of Estimation in Positron Emission Tomography and Related Inverse Problems." *Annals of Statistics* 18: 251–280.

Jorgenson, Dale W., Lawrence J. Lau, and Thomas M. Stoker. 1980. "Welfare Comparisons under Exact Aggregation." *American Economic Review* 70: 268–272.

Jorgenson, Dale W., Lawrence J. Lau, and Thomas M. Stoker. 1982. "The Transcendental Logarithmic Model of Aggregate Consumer Behavior," pp. 97–238 in Robert L. Basemann and Georges Rhodes, eds., *Advances in Econometrics*, vol. 1. Greenwich, Conn.: JAI Press.

Kalbfleisch, J. D., and J. F. Lawless. 1984. "Least-Squares Estimation of Transition Probabilities from Aggregate Data." *Canadian Journal of Statistics* 12: 169–182.

Kalbfleisch, J. D., J. F. Lawless, and V. M. Vollmer. 1983. "Estimation in Markov Models from Aggregate Data." *Biometrics* 39: 907–919.

Kanoh, Satoru, and Takamitsu Sawa. 1976. "What Can We Infer from a Single Aggregated Proportion?" *International Economic Review* 17: 763–768.

Kao, Richard C. W. 1953. "Note on Miller's 'Finite Markov Processes in Psychology'." *Psychometrica* 18: 241–243.

Keane, Michael P. 1994. "A Computationally Practical Simulation Estimator for Panel Data." *Econometrica* 62: 95–116.

Key, V. O. 1949. *Southern Politics in State and Nation.* New York: Alfred A. Knopf.

King, Gary. 1989a. *Unifying Political Methodology: The Likelihood Theory of Statistical Inference.* New York: Cambridge University Press.

King, Gary. 1989b. "Representation through Legislative Redistricting: A Stochastic Model." *American Journal of Political Science* 33: 787–824.

King, Gary. 1990. "Electoral Responsiveness and Partisan Bias in Multiparty Democracies." *Legislative Studies Quarterly* 15: 159–181.

King, Gary. 1991. "On Political Methodology." *Political Analysis* 2: 1–30.

King, Gary. 1995. "Replication, Replication," *PS: Political Science and Politics,* with comments and a response, 27: 443–499.

King, Gary. 1996. "Why Context Should Not Count." *Political Geography,* forthcoming.

King, Gary, James Alt, Nancy Burns, and Michael Laver. 1990. "A Unified Model of Cabinet Dissolution in Parliamentary Democracies." *American Journal of Political Science* 34: 846–871.

King, Gary, and Robert X Browning. 1987. "Democratic Representation and Partisan Bias in Congressional Elections." *American Political Science Review* 81: 1,251–1,273.

King, Gary, John Bruce, and Andrew Gelman. 1995. "Standards of Racial Fairness in Legislative Redistricting," pp. 85–110 in Paul E. Peterson, ed., *Classifying by Race.* Princeton: Princeton University Press.

King, Gary, Robert O. Keohane, and Sidney Verba. 1994. *Designing Social Inquiry: Scientific Inference in Qualitative Research.* Princeton: Princeton University Press.

Kirman, Alan P. 1992. "Whom or What Does the Representative Individual Represent?" *Journal of Economic Perspectives* 6: 117–136.

Klein, Lawrence R. 1946. "Remarks on the Theory of Aggregation." *Econometrica* 14: 303–312.

Klein, S. P., J. Sacks, and David A. Freedman. 1991. "Ecological Regressions versus the Secret Ballot." *Jurimetrics Journal* 31: 393–413.

Kleppner, Paul. 1985. *Chicago Divided: The Making of a Black Mayor.* De Kalb: Northern Illinois University Press.

Kodell, R. L., and J. H. Matis. 1976. "Estimating the Rate Constants in a Two-Compartment Stochastic Model." *Biometrics* 32: 377–400.

Koopman, James S., and Ira M. Longini, Jr. 1994. "The Ecological Effects of Individual Exposures and Nonlinear Disease Dynamics in Populations." *American Journal of Public Health* 84: 836–842.

Kousser, J. Morgan. 1973. "Ecological Regression and Analysis of Past Politics." *Journal of Interdisciplinary History* 4: 237–262.

Kousser, J. Morgan. 1974. *The Shaping of Southern Politics: Suffrage Restriction and the Establishment of the One-Party South, 1880–1910*. New Haven: Yale University Press.

Kousser, J. Morgan. 1986a. "Must Historians Regress? An Answer to Lee Benson." *Historical Methods* 19.2: 62–81.

Kousser, J. Morgan. 1986b. "Speculation or Specification? A Note on Flanigan and Zingale." *Social Science History* 10: 71–84.

Kousser, J. Morgan. 1993. "A Generation of Ecological Regression: A Survey and Synthesis." Unpublished paper, California Institute of Technology.

Kousser, J. Morgan. 1995. "*Shaw v. Reno* and the Real World of Redistricting and Representation." Unpublished paper, California Institute of Technology.

Kousser, J. Morgan, and Allan J. Lichtman. 1983. "'New Political History' Some Statistical Questions Answered." *Social Science History* 7: 321–344.

Kraemer, Helena Chmura. 1978. "Individual and Ecological Correlation in a General Context." *Behavioral Science* 23: 67–72.

Kramer, Gerald H. 1983. "The Ecological Fallacy Revisited: Aggregate- versus Individual-Level Findings on Economics and Elections and Sociotropic Voting." *American Political Science Review* 77: 92–111.

Kritzer, Herbert M. 1978a. "An Introduction to Multivariate Contingency Table Analysis." *American Journal of Political Science* 21: 187–226.

Kritzer, Herbert M. 1978b. "Analyzing Contingency Tables by Weighted Least Squares: An Alternative to the Goodman Approach." *Political Methodology* 5: 277–326.

Krivo, Lauren J., and Robert L. Kaufman. 1990. "Estimating Macro-Relationships Using Micro-Data." *Sociological Methods and Research* 19: 196–202.

Lau, Lawrence J. 1982. "A Note on the Fundamental Theorem of Exact Aggregation." *Economic Letters* 9: 119–126.

Leamer, Edward E. 1990. "Optional Aggregation of Linear Net Export Systems," pp. 150–170 in Barker and Pesaran (1990).

Lee, T. C., G. G. Judge, and T. Takayama. 1965. "On Estimating the Transition Probabilities of a Markov Process." *Journal of Farm Economics* 47: 742–762.

Lee, T. C., G. G. Judge, and A. Zellner. 1968. "Maximum Likelihood and Bayesian Estimation of Transition Probabilities." *Journal of the American Statistical Association* 63: 1,162–1,179.

Lee, T. C., G. G. Judge, and A. Zellner. 1970. *Estimating the Parameters of the Markov Probability Model from Aggregate Time Series Data*. Amsterdam: North-Holland.

Lewbel, Arthur. 1994. "Aggregation and Simple Dynamics." *American Economic Review* 84: 905–918.

Lewbel, Arthur. 1992. "Aggregation with Log-Linear Models." *Review of Economic Studies* 59: 635–642.

Lewbel, Arthur. 1989. "Exact Aggregation and a Representative Consumer." *Quarterly Journal of Economics* 104: 622–633.

Lichtman, Allan J. 1974. "Correlation, Regression, and the Ecological Fallacy: A Critique." *Journal of Interdisciplinary History* 4: 417–433.

Lichtman, Allan J. 1991. "Passing the Test: Ecological Regression Analysis in the Los Angeles County Case and Beyond." *Evaluation Review* 15: 770–799.

Linz, Juan J. 1969. "Ecological Analysis and Survey Research," pp. 91–132 in Dogan and Rokkan (1969).

Little, Roderick J. A., and Mei-Miau Wu. 1991. "Models for Contingency Tables with Known Margins When Target and Sampled Populations Differ." *Journal of the American Statistical Association* 86: 87–95.

Loewen, James. 1982. *Social Science in the Courtroom: Statistical Techniques and Research Methods for Winning Class-Action Suits*. Lexington, Mass.: Lexington Books.

Loewen, James W. and Bernard Grofman. 1989. "Recent Developments in Methods Used in Vote Dilution Litigation." *The Urban Lawyer* 21: 589–604.

Lubin, Jay H. 1994. "Invited Commentary: Lung Cancer and Exposure to Residential Radon." *American Journal of Epidemiology* 140: 323–332.

Lucas, Robert E. 1976. "Econometric Policy Evaluation: A Critique," pp. 19–46 in K. Brunner and A. H. Meltzer, eds. *The Phillips Curve and Labor Markets*, Carnegie-Rochester Conferences on Public Policy, Vol. 1 of *Journal of Monetary Economics*.

Lupia, Arthur, and Kenneth McCue. 1990. "Why the 1980s Measures of Racially Polarized Voting are Inadequate for the 1990s." *Law and Policy* 12: 353–387.

MacRae, Duncan, Jr., and James A. Meldrum. 1969. "Factor Analysis of Aggregate Voting Statistics," pp. 487–506 in Dogan and Rokkan (1969).

MacRae, Elizabeth Chase. 1977. "Estimation of Time-Varying Markov Processes with Aggregate Data." *Econometrica* 45: 183–198.

Malinvaud, Edmond. 1955. "Aggregation Problems in Input-Output Models," pp. 187–202 in Tibor Barna, ed., *Structrual Interdependence of the Economy*. New York: John Wiley and Sons.

Manski, Charles F. 1995. *Identification Problems in the Social Sciences*. Cambridge: Harvard University Press.

Manski, Charles F., and Daniel McFadden. 1981. *Structural Analysis of Discrete Data with Econometric Applications*. Cambridge: MIT Press.

Marksjö, Bertil. 1984. "Simple Aggregation and Disaggregation Subject to Minimal Information Loss and Other Criteria." *Regional Science and Urban Economics* 14: 465–478.

Marshak, Jacob. 1939. "Personal and Collective Budget Functions." *Review of Economics and Statistics* 21: 161–170.

Mason, William M., George Y. Wong, and Barbara Entwisle. 1983. "Contextual Analysis through the Multilevel Linear Model." pp. 72–103 in Samuel Leinhardt, eds., *Sociological Methodology, 1983–84*. Washington, D.C.: Jossey-Bass.

Matis, J. H., and H. O. Hartley. 1971. "Stochastic Compartmental Analysis: Model and Least Squares Estimation from Time Series Data." *Biometrics*, 27: 71–102.

Matsusaka, John G., and Filip Palda. 1993. "The Downsian Voter Meets the Ecological Fallacy." *Public Choice* 77: 855–878.

Matthews, Donald R., and James W. Prothro. 1966. *Negroes and Southern Politics*. New York: Harcourt, Brace & World.

May, Kenneth. 1946. "The Aggregation Problem for a One-Industry Model." *Econometrica* 14: 285–312.

McCarthy, Colm, and Terence M. Ryan. 1977. "Estimates of Voter Transition Probabilities from the British General Elections of 1974." *Journal of the Royal Statistical Society, A* 140: 78–85.

McCarthy, John L., and John W. Tukey. 1978. "Exploratory Analysis of Aggregate Voting Behavior: Presidential Elections in New Hampshire, 1896–1972." *Social Science History* 2: 292–331.

McCue, Kenneth F. 1995. "The Ecological Fallacy Redux." Unpublished paper, California Institute of Technology.

Meckstroth, Theodore W. 1974. "Some Problems in Cross-Level Inference." *American Journal of Political Science* 28: 45–66.

Meckstroth, Theodore W. 1975. "'Ecological Inference' and the Disaggregation of Individual Decisions." *Political Science Annual* 6: 113–174.

Menzel, Herbert. 1960. "A Comment on Robinson's 'Ecological Correlations,'" *American Sociological Review* 18: 674.

Messner, Steven. 1982. "Inequality and the Urban Homicide Rate." *Criminology* 20: 103–114.

Miller, George A. 1952. "Finite Markov Processes in Psychology." *Psychometrica* 17: 149–167.

Miller, W. L. 1972. "Measures of Electoral Change Using Aggregate Data." *Journal of the Royal Statistical Society, A* 135: 122–142.

Miller, W. L., Gillian Raab, and K. Britto. 1974. "Voting Research and the Population Census 1918–71: Surrogate Data for Constituency Analyses." *Journal of the Royal Statistical Society, A* 137: 384–427.

Morgenstern, H. 1982. "Uses of Ecologic Analysis in Epidemiologic Research." *American Journal of Public Health* 72: 1,336–1,344.

Müller, Hans-Georg. 1991. "Smooth Optimum Kernel Estimators Near Endpoints." *Biometrika* 78: 521–530.

Natterer, Frank. 1986. *The Mathematics of Computerized Tomography*. New York: Wiley.

Norberg, Ragnar. 1977. "Inference in Random Coefficient Regression Models with One-Way and Nested Classifications." *Scandinavian Journal of Statistics* 4: 71–80.

Norström, Thor. 1988a. "Deriving Relative Risks from Aggregate Data. I. Theory." *Journal of Epidemiology and Community Health* 42: 333–335.

Norström, Thor. 1988b. "Deriving Relative Risks from Aggregate Data. II. An Application to the Relationship between Unemployment and Suicide." *Journal of Epidemiology and Community Health* 42: 336–340.

O'Hare, William. 1991. "The Use of Demographic Data in Voting Rights Litigation." *Evaluation Review* 15: 729–745.

Ogburn, William F., and Inez Goltra. 1919. "How Women Vote: A Study of an Election in Portland, Oregon." *Political Science Quarterly* 34: 413–433.

Openshaw, Stan. 1979. "A Million or So Correlation Coefficients: Three Experiments on the Modifiable Areal Unit Problem," pp. 127–144 in N. Wrigley, ed., in *Statistical Methods in the Spatial Sciences*. London: Pion.

Openshaw, Stan. 1984. "The Modifiable Areal Unit Problem." *Concepts and Techniques in Modern Geography, No. 38*. Norwich, England: Geo Books.

Orcutt, Guy H., Harold W. Watts, and John B. Edwards. 1968. "Data Aggregation and Information Loss." *American Economic Review* 58: 773–787.

Owen, Guillermo, and Bernard Grofman. 1994. "Estimating the Likelihood of Fallacious Ecological Inference: Linear Ecological Regression in the Presence of Context Effects." Unpublished paper, University of California, Irvine.

Pagan, Adrian. 1980. "Some Identification and Estimation Results for Regression Models with Stochastically Varying Coefficients." *Journal of Econometrics* 13: 341–363.

Palmquist, Bradley Lowell. 1993. "Ecological Inference, Aggregate Data Analysis of U.S. Elections, and the Socialist Party of America." Ph.D. dissertation, University of California, Berkeley.

Palmquist, Bradley Lowell. 1994. "Respecification Approaches to Ecological Inference: A Comparison of Control Variables and the Quadratic Model." Paper prepared for delivery at the annual meetings of the American Political Science Association, New York, 1–4 September.

Park, Wayne I., and Philip Garcia. 1994. "Aggregate versus Disaggregate Analysis: Corn and Soybean Acreage Response in Illinois." *Review of Agricultural Economics* 16: 17–26.

Parsons, George R., and Michael S. Needleman. 1992. "Site Aggregation in a Random Utility Model of Recreation." *Land Economics* 68: 418–433.

Pesaran, M. H., R. G. Pierse, and M. S. Kumar. 1989. "Econometric Analysis of Aggregation in the Context of Linear Prediction Models." *Econometrica* 57: 861–888.

Pesaran, M. H., R. G. Pierse and K. C. Lee. 1993. "Persistence, Cointegration, and Aggregation." *Journal of Econometrics* 56: 57-88.

Pesaran, M. H., R. G. Pierse and K. C. Lee. 1994. "Choice between Disaggregate and Aggregate Specifications Estimated by Instrumental Variables Methods." *Journal of Business and Economic Statistics* 12: 11–21.

Peston, M. H. 1959/60. "A View of the Aggregation Problem." *Review of Economic Studies* 27: 58–64.

Petty, Sir William. 1690. *Political Arithmetick*. London: Robert Clavel and Hen. Mortlock.

Petty, Sir William. 1691. *The Political Anatomy of Ireland*. London: D. Brown and W. Rogers.

Piantadosi, Steven. 1994. "Invited Commentary: Ecologic Biases." *American Journal of Epidemiology* 139: 761–764.

Piantadosi, S., D. P. Byar, and S. B. Green. 1988. "The Ecological Fallacy." *American Journal of Epidemiology* 127: 893–904.

Powell, James L., and Thomas M. Stoker. 1985. "The Estimation of Complete Aggregation Structures." *Journal of Econometrics* 30: 317–344.

Prais, S. J. and J. Aitchison. 1954. "The Grouping of Observations in Regression Analysis." *Review of the International Institute of Statistics* 22: 1–22.

Press, William H., et al. 1987. *Numerical Recipes*. Cambridge: Cambridge University Press.

Price, Hugh D. 1968. "Micro- and Macro-Politics: Notes on a Research Strategy," pp. 102–140 in Oliver Garceau, ed., *Political Research and Political Theory*. Cambridge: Cambridge University Press.

Prsby, Charles L. 1976. "Community Partisanship and Individual Voting Behavior: Methodological Problems of Contextual Analysis." *Political Methodology* 3: 183–198.

Przeworski, Adam. 1974. "Contextual Models of Political Behavior." *Political Methodology* 1: 27–60.

Pu, Shou Shan. 1946. "A Note on Macroeconomics." *Econometrica* 14: 299–302.

Putnam, Robert D. 1966. "Political Attitudes and the Local Community." *American Political Science Review* 60: 640–654.

Raj, Baldev. 1975. "Linear Regression With Random Coefficients: The Finite Sample and Convergence Properties," *Journal of the American Statistical Association* 70: 127–137.

Raj, Baldev, Virender Kumar Srivastava, and Sushama Upadhyaya. 1980. "The Efficiency of Estimating a Random Coefficient Model." *Journal of Econometrics* 12: 285–299.

Ranney, Austin. 1962. "The Utility and Limitations of Aggregate Data in the Study of Electoral Behavior," pp. 91–102 in Ranney, ed., *Essays on the Behavioral Study of Politics*. Urbana: University of Illinois Press.

Rao, J. N. K. 1989. "Ratio Estimators," in Samuel Kotz, Normal L. Johnson, and Campbell B. Read, eds., *Encyclopedia of Statistical Sciences*, vol. 7. New York: Wiley.

Richardson, S., I. Stücker, and D. Hemon. 1987. "Comparison of Relative Risks Obtained in Ecological and Individual Studies: Some Methodological Considerations." *International Journal of Epidemiology* 16: 111–120.

Richmond, J. 1976. "Aggregation and Identification." *International Economic Review* 17: 47–56.

Ripley, B. D. 1987. *Stochastic Simulation*. New York: Wiley.

Rivers, Douglas, and Wendy Tam. 1996. "Estimation of Random Coefficient Models," Unpublished paper, Stanford University.

Robinson, William S. 1950. "Ecological Correlation and the Behavior of Individuals." *American Sociological Review* 15: 351–357.

Rosenbaum, Paul R., and Donald B. Rubin. 1984. "Difficulties with Regression Analyses of Age-Adjusted Rates." *Biometrics* 40: 437–443.

Rosenthal, Howard. 1973. "Aggregate Data," pp. 915–927 in Ithiel de Sola Pool et al., eds., *Handbook of Communications*. Chicago: Rand McNally.

Roth, Randolph A. 1986. "Ecological Regression and the Analysis of Voter Behavior." *Historical Methods* 19: 103–117.

Rubin, Donald B. 1980. "Using Empirical Bayes Techniques in the Law School Validity Studies" (with discussion). *Journal of the American Statistical Association* 75: 801–827.

Rubin, Donald B. 1987. *Multiple Imputation for Nonresponse in Surveys*. New York: Wiley.

Rubinfeld, Daniel L. 1991. "Statistical and Demographic Issues Underlying Voting Rights Cases." *Evaluation Review* 15: 659–672.

Sampson, Robert J. 1987. "Urban Black Violence: The Effect of Male Joblessness and Family Disruption." *American Journal of Sociology* 93: 348–382.

Scarbrough, Elinor. 1991. "Micro and Macro Analysis of Elections," *European Journal of Political Research* 19: 361–374.

Schlicht, Ekkehart. 1985. *Isolation and Aggregation in Economics.* New York: Springer-Verlag.

Schuman, Howard, and Stanley Presser. 1981. *Questions and Answers in Attitude Surveys: Experiments on Question Form, Wording, and Context.* New York: Academic Press.

Schwallie, Daniel P. 1982. "Unconstrained Maximum Likelihood Estimation of Contemporaneous Covariances." *Economics Letters* 9: 359–364.

Schwartz, Sharon. 1994. "The Fallacy of the Ecological Fallacy: The Potential Misuse of a Concept and the Consequences." *American Journal of Public Health* 84: 819–824.

Selvin, Hanan C. 1965. "Durkheim's *Suicide*: Further Thoughts on a Methodological Classic," pp. 113–136 in Robert A. Nisbet, ed., *Emile Durkheim*, Englewood Cliffs, N.J.: Prentice-Hall.

Shin, Jeong-Shik. 1987. "Aggregation and the Endogeneity Problem." *International Economic Journal* 1: 57–65.

Shively, W. Phillips. 1974. "Utilizing External Evidence in Cross-Level Inference." *Political Methodology* 1: 61–73.

Shively, W. Phillips. 1977. " 'Ecological' Inference: The Use of Aggregate Data to Study Individuals." *American Political Science Review* 63: 1,183–1,196.

Shively, W. Phillips. 1985. "A Strategy for Cross-Level Inference under an Assumption of Breakage Effects." *Political Methodology* 11: 167–179.

Shively, W. Phillips. 1991. "A General Extension of the Method of Bounds, with Special Application to Studies of Electoral Transition." *Historical Methods* 24: 81–94.

Shively, W. Phillips. 1992. "From Differential Absention to Conversion: A Change in Electoral Change, 1864–1988." *American Journal of Political Science*, 36: 309–330.

Sigelman, Lee. 1991. "Turning Cross Sections into a Panel: A Simple Procedure for Ecological Inference." *Social Science Research* 20: 150–170.

Silverman, B. W. 1986. *Density Estimation for Statistics and Data Analysis.* London: Chapman and Hall.

Singer, J. David. 1961. "The Level-of-Analysis Problem in International Relations," pp. 77–92 in Klaus Knorr and Sidney Verba, eds., *The International System.* Princeton: Princton University Press.

Singh, Balvir, A. L. Nagar, N. K. Choudhry, and Baldev Raj. 1976. "On the Estimation of Structural Change: A Generalization of the Random Coefficients Regression Model." *International Economic Review* 17: 340–361.

Smith, Kent W. 1977. "Another Look at the Clustering Perspective on Aggregation Problems." *Sociological Methods and Research* 5: 289–315.

Sonnenschein, Hugo. 1972. "Market Excess Demand Functions." *Econometrica* 40: 549–563.

Sprague, John. 1976. "Estimating a Boudon Type Contextual Model: Some Practical and Theoretical Problems of Measurement." *Political Methodology* 3: 333–353.

Sprague, John. 1982. "Is there a Micro Theory Consistent with Contextual Analysis?" pp. 99–121 in Elinor Ostrom, ed., *Strategies of Political Inquiry*. Beverly Hills: Sage Publications.

Spurrier, John D., and Sandra J. Kohta. 1993. "Estimation of Proportions of White and Non-White Voters Voting for a Candidate with Applications to Possible Violations of Section 2 of the Voting Rights Act." *Communications in Statistics—Simulation* 22: 845–862.

Srivastava, V. K., G. D. Mishra, and A. Chaturveda. 1981. "Estimation of Linear Regression Model with Random Coefficients Ensuring Almost Non-Negativity of Variance Estimators." *Biometrical Journal* 23: 3–8.

Steel, D. G., and D. Holt. 1996. "Analyzing and Adjusting Aggregation Effects: The Ecological Fallacy Revisited." *International Statistical Review* 64: 39–60.

Steinnes, Donald N. 1980. "Aggregation, Gerrymandering, and Spatial Econometrics." *Regional Science and Urban Economics* 10: 561–569.

Stidley, C. A. and J. M. Samet. 1993. "A Review of Ecologic Studies of Lung Cancer and Indoor Radon." *Health Physiology* 65: 234–251.

Stoker, Thomas. 1984. "Completeness, Distribution Restrictions, and the Form of Aggregate Functions." *Econometrica* 52: 887–907.

Stoker, Thomas M. 1985. "Aggregation, Structural Change, and Cross-section Estimation." *Journal of the American Statistical Association* 80: 720–729.

Stoker, Thomas M. 1986. "Aggregation, Efficiency and Cross-Section Regression." *Econometrica* 54: 171–188.

Stoker, Thomas M. 1993. "Empirical Approaches to the Problem of Aggregation over Individuals." *Journal of Economic Literature* 33: 1,827–1,874.

Stokes, Donald E. 1969. "Cross-Level Inference as a Game against Nature," in James L. Bernd, ed., *Mathematical Applications in Politcial Science*, 4: 62–83. Charlottesville: University Press of Virginia.

Susser, Mervyn. 1994a. "The Logic in Ecological: I. The Logic of Analysis." *American Journal of Public Health* 84: 825–829.

Susser, Mervyn. 1994b. "The Logic in Ecological: II. The Logic of Design." *American Journal of Public Health* 84: 830–835.

Swamy, P. A. V. B. 1971. *Statistical Inference in Random Coefficient Regression Models*. Berlin: Springer-Verlag.

Swamy, P. A. V. B., and J. S. Mehta. 1975. "Bayesian and Non-Bayesian Analysis of Switching Regressions and of Random Coefficient Regression Models." *Journal of the American Statistical Association* 70: 593–602.

Swamy, P. A. V. B., and J. N. K. Rao. 1972. "Maximum Likelihood Estimation of Distributed Lag Model with Autocorrelated Errors." *Journal of the Indian Statistical Association* 10, 87–99.

Tannenbaum, Arnold S., and Jerald G. Bachman. 1964. "Structural versus Individual Effects." *American Journal of Sociology* 69: 85–95.

Tanner, Martin A. 1996. *Tools for Statistical Inference: Methods for the Exploration of Posterior Distributions and Likelihood Functions*. Third ed., New York: Springer-Verlag.

Telser, Lester G. 1963. "Least-Squares Estimates of Transition Probabilities," pp. 270–293 in Charl F. Christ et al., eds., *Measurement in Economics*. Stanford: Stanford University Press.

Theil, Henri. 1954. *Linear Aggregation of Economic Relations*. Amsterdam: North-Holland.

Theil, Henri. 1957. "Linear Aggregation in Input-Output Analysis." *Econometrica* 25: 111–122.

Thompson, Gary D. 1991. "A Test for Spatial and Temporal Aggregation." *Economics Letters* 36: 391–396.

Thompson, Gary D., and Charles C. Lyon. 1992. "A Generalized Test for Perfect Aggregation." *Economics Letters* 40: 389–396.

Thomsen, Søren Risbjerg. 1987. *Danish Elections, 1920–79: A Logit Approach to Ecological Analysis and Inference*. Arhus: Politica.

Thomsen, Søren Risbjerg, and Hyun-woo Kim. 1993. "Electoral Dynamics in South Korea since 1981." *Korean Studies* 17: 39–66.

Thomsen, Søren Risbjerg, Sten Berglund, and Ingemar Worlund. 1991. "Assessing the Validity of the Logit Method for Ecological Inference." *European Journal of Political Science* 19: 441–477.

Thornburg v. Gingles, 478 U.S. 30 (1986).

Thorndike, E. L. 1939. "On the Fallacy of Imputing the Correlations Found for Groups to the Individuals or Smaller Groups Composing Them." *American Journal of Psychology* 52: 122–124.

Tiao, George, C., and W. Y. Tan. 1965. "Bayesian Analysis of Random-Effect Models in the Analysis of Variance, I." *Biometrika* 52: 37–53.

Tobler, Waldo. 1990. "Frame Independent Spatial Analysis," pp. 115–122 in M. Goodchild, ed., *Accuracy of Spatial Data Bases*. London: Taylor and Frances.

United States. Bureau of the Census. 1989. *Poverty in the United States: 1988 and 1989*. Current Population Reports, P-60, no. 171. Washington, D.C.: U.S. Government Printing Office.

United States. Department of Health, Education, and Welfare. 1976. *The Measure of Poverty*. Washington, D.C.: U.S. Government Printing Office.

Upton, Graham J. G. 1978. "A Note on the Estimation of Voter Transition Probabilities." *Journal of the Royal Statistical Society, A* 141: 507–512.

Valkonen, Tapani. 1969. "Individual and Structural Effects in Ecological Research," pp. 53–68 in Dogan and Rokkan (1969).

van Daal, Jan, and Arnold H. Q. M. Merkies. *Aggregation in Economic Research*. Dordrecht: D. Reidel.

Vangrevelinghe, G. 1961. "Étude composée des résultats des Referendums de 1958 et 1961." *Revue de Statistique Appliqué* 9: 83–100.

Vardi, Y., L. A. Shepp, and L. Kaufman. 1985. "A Statistical Model for Positron Emission Tomography," with discussion and rejoinder. *Journal of the American Statistical Association* 80: 8–37.

Venezia, Itzhak. 1978. "A Decision-Theoretic Approach to the Aggregation Problem at the Pre-Data-Collection Stage." *Journal of the American Statistical Association* 73: 552–558.

Von Korff, M., T. Koepsell, S. Curry, and P. Diehr. 1993. "Multi-Level Analysis in Epidemiologic Research on Health Behaviors and Outcomes." *American Journal of Epidemiology* 135: 1,077–1,082.

Wanat, John. 1979. "The Application of a Non-Analytic, Most Possible Estimation Technique: The Relative Impact of Mobilization and Conversion of Votes in the New Deal." *Political Methodology* 6: 357–374.

Wanat, John. 1982. "Most Possible Estimates and Maximum Likelihood Estimates." *Sociological Methods and Research* 10: 453–462.

Waterhouse, David. 1983. "The Estimation of Voter Behavior from Aggregated Data: A Test." *Journal of Social History* 16: 35–54.

Webb, Steve. 1990. *From the Watching of Shadows: The Origins of Radiological Tomography*. New York: Adam Hillger.

Wei, William W. S. 1982. "The Effects of Systematic Sampling and Temporal Aggregation on Causality—A Cautionary Note." *Journal of the American Statistical Association* 77: 316–322.

Wellhofer, E. Spencer. 1991. "Confounding Sources of Variance in the Macro-Analysis of Electoral Data." *European Journal of Political Research* 19: 425–439.

West, Mike. 1991. "Kernel Density Estimation and Marginalization Consistency." *Biometrika* 78: 421–425.

Whittle, P. 1956. "On the Variation of Yield Variance with Plot Size." *Biometrika* 43: 337–343.

Wildgen, John K. 1988. "Adding *Thornburg* to the Thicket: The Ecological Fallacy and Parameter Control in Vote Dilution Cases." *The Urban Lawyer* 20: 155–173.

Wildgen, John K. 1990. "Vote Dilution Litigation and Cold Fusion Technology." *The Urban Lawyer* 22: 487–493.

Worsley, K. J., A. C. Evans, S. C. Strother, and J. L. Tyler. 1991. "A Linear Spatial Correlation Model, with Applications to Positron Emission Tomography." *Journal of the American Statistical Association* 86: 55–67.

Yule, G. Udny. 1911. *An Introduction to the Theory of Statistics*. London: Griffin.

Yule, G. Udny, and M. G. Kendall. 1950. *An Introduction to the Theory of Statistics*. London: Griffin.

Zellner, Arnold. 1969. "On the Aggregation Problem: A New Approach to a Troublesome Problem," pp. 365–374 in K. A. Fox et al., eds., *Economic Models: Estimation and Risk Programming: Essays in Honor of Gerhard Tintner*. New York: Springer-Verlag.

Index

About the Author

GARY KING is Professor of Government in the Faculty of Arts and Sciences at Harvard University. Among his publications are *Designing Social Inquiry: Scientific Inference in Qualitative Research* (Princeton University Press) and *Unifying Political Methodology: The Likelihood Theory of Statistical Inference* (Cambridge University Press). His homepage on the World Wide Web can be found at `http://GKing.Harvard.Edu`.